PENGUIN BOOKS

A SOCIAL HISTORY OF ENGLAND

Asa Briggs was born in 1921 at Keighley, Yorkshire. From 1955 to 1961 he was Professor of Modern History at Leeds University, and in 1961 was the first academic to be appointed to the then new University of Sussex. Six years later he was appointed Vice-Chancellor. From 1976 to 1991 he was Provost of Worcester College, Oxford. He was Chancellor of the Open University from 1978 to 1994. In 1976 he was made a life peer. He is married with four children.

His main field of historical research has been in nineteenth- and twentieth-century social and cultural history. His trilogy, *Victorian Things, Victorian Cities* and *Victorian People*, is also published in Penguin. He is currently President of the British Social History Society and of the Victorian Society.

D0241085

ASA BRIGGS

A SOCIAL HISTORY
OF ENGLAND

Third Edition

PENGUIN BOOKS

ACKNOWLEDGEMENTS

I am deeply grateful to the people who have helped me with the preparation of this new edition, particularly, Susan Hard, Pat Spencer, Joanne King, Ronald Clark, and above all Coralie Hepburn, my editor, and Helen Williams, my copy-editor. I repeat my thanks to those who helped me with earlier editions.

PENGUIN BOOKS

Published by the Penguin Group
Penguin Books Ltd, 27 Wrights Lane, London w8 5tz, England
Penguin Putnam Inc., 375 Hudson Street, New York, New York 10014, USA
Penguin Books Australia Ltd, Ringwood, Victoria, Australia
Penguin Books Canada Ltd, 10 Alcorn Avenue, Toronto, Ontario, Canada m4v 3b2
Penguin Books (NZ) Ltd, Private Bag 102902, NSMC, Auckland, New Zealand

Penguin Books Ltd, Registered Offices: Harmondsworth, Middlesex, England

First published in Great Britain by Weidenfeld & Nicolson 1983
First published in the United States of America by the Viking Press 1984
Published in Penguin Books 1985
Second paperback edition published in Pelican Books (without illustrations) 1987
Reprinted in Penguin Books with minor corrections 1991
Second hardback edition published by Weidenfeld & Nicolson 1994
Third edition published by Penguin Books (without illustrations) 1999
    3 5 7 9 10 8 6 4

Set in 10/12pt Monotype Bembo
Typeset by Rowland Phototypesetting Ltd, Bury St Edmunds, Suffolk
Printed in England by Clays Ltd, St Ives plc

CONTENTS

LIST OF MAPS AND FIGURES

Maps

Figures

PREFACE

No nation has carried its whole past so completely into the present. With us historical associations are not matters of rhetorical reference on great occasions . . . But they surround the Englishman in everything that he does, and affect his conception of rights and duties on which national life is built.

Mandell Creighton, *The English National Character*, 1896

A people without history
Is not redeemed from time, for history is a pattern
Of timeless moments. So, while the light falls
On a winter's afternoon, in a secluded chapel
History is now and England.

T. S. Eliot, *Four Quartets*, 1943

The English Character is not only stable and uniform, but various and heterogeneous; it is at once obvious and elusive, and every generalization must be not so much qualified as confounded.

Henry Steele Commager, *Britain through American Eyes*, 1948

Of the many kinds of history, social history was often thought of in the past as being more trivial than either constitutional, political or military history. They dealt with great events; it dealt with everyday things. And even when economic history was taken into the reckoning and social history was bracketed with it, as it usually has been, the economic was felt to come first. Ways of life were considered less 'fundamental' than standards of living.

In recent years, however, all this has changed. Social history has now become a favourite kind of history, and as its range and methods have expanded it has attracted serious study at every level, scholarly and popular. There are important monographs dealing with almost every period and every problem, some of them highly sophisticated. There are also local histories and family histories that try to tap roots. Their subject matter is life and death. Some scholarly history, however, concentrates more on abstractions than on people, and in the process it employs concepts, some of them of recent origin, which are not always fully explained. Meanwhile, some popular history takes too much for granted, lacking a sense of perspective. There remains a need for a synthesis, covering the centuries and based on the conclusions of scholarly research. So much has happened to society – and to history – since 1983, when the first edition of this history appeared, that the need is even greater than it was then.

There was excitement in the challenge in 1983, not least in deciding what to leave out as well as what to put in, and now, as our century – and with it a millennium – draws to a close, a new edition of this history is necessary. It is not merely that the last chapter has had to be rewritten. Every new social development forces a re-examination of the past as well as the present. At the same time, it is a mistake to see everything inexorably leading up – either triumphantly or depressingly – towards the present. We can usefully search for tendencies and lines of direction, but we must also be prepared to take the past on its own terms, and to note foregone options as well as realized choices.

For me social history is concerned both with structures and with processes of change, but the best way of exploring these is to focus on experience – the shared or contrasting experience of different individuals and of different groups, many of them overlapping, some of them common. And while it is part of the appeal of the subject that it illuminates the lives of people who left no name behind them and were often the victims of the power systems of their day, no social history would be comprehensive if it ignored people of power. Society is a network of relationships, not an abstract aggregate. There is much, however, that we can never know either about the powerless or the powerful.

The cultural dimension of social history was obvious before there was much talk of cultural history. As the social historian switches from kitchen to drawing room or to bedroom – or into the garden – from home to school and to university, from field to factory, from village to town and city, from hospital to hospice, from library to laboratory, from warehouse and office to the corridors of Westminster and Whitehall, he must learn to read every cultural signpost. He must take account too of what have come to be called 'public relations' and the role of the media, noting how things are perceived as well as 'what they were'. Curiosity is an indispensable quality. So too is the capacity to penetrate rhetoric. In the process the social historian often finds the detail more illuminating than the generalization, particularly when he seeks to identify what is distinctive to a society or to a period and what is common to others. Everything is grist to his mill.

Far more attention has been paid since 1983 to what is distinctively 'English', a term which, like 'British', was once taken for granted. More attention has been paid too to other countries' social and cultural histories, not least those of Scotland, Wales and Ireland, which with a degree of devolution will demand a new orientation. It is too early to say, however, whether a 'new Britain' or a new 'British Isles' are really in the making. Meanwhile, there is still too little comparative history of England and other countries, including those once governed from London. They cannot be ignored in this volume, although each has a history, including a social history of its own.

The social history of England has often been felt to be directly relevant – either as a model, or more recently, as a warning – to the people of other societies, including those with a quite different heritage. There are, in fact, no easy lessons to be derived from English social history taken by itself, and local and regional differences in the story must always be taken into the reckoning.

Within England I do not view the changing scene exclusively from London. I rely throughout on local and regional sources. Because of my approach, I am as much drawn to the study of language and literature as to the social sciences, although I attach importance to both. Words, which have their own history, are often keys to social history. Literature, along with architecture, art and music, is more than expression or communication. It is related to experience in complex ways and over time is at the heart of a 'heritage' (a now overworked word). In other editions I have been able to make use of illustrations not as decoration but as exposition, and they have included maps, prints, paintings and photographs. In this edition I have had to be content mostly with words.

My book is the product of years not only of reading and talk, but also of travel. My reading began in my undergraduate days in Cambridge, where I listened to Eileen Power, the most compelling lecturer on social history I ever heard. I also learnt much while there, tramping the fields with John Saltmarsh. Yet before Cambridge, I drew deep on my Yorkshire upbringing in an industrial town on the edge of the moors – as distinctive an environment as a great city like Liverpool or a village in the Cotswolds – and I travelled through France as well as through Scotland. In recent years, the United States has figured prominently on my own map, as has Scotland, and parts of this book were written there. Parts too were written for a Chinese audience. I have learnt how to compare nineteenth-century Manchester not only with the cities of the past but also with twentieth-century Hong Kong and São Paolo.

I owe an immense debt, of course, to many historians, English and non-English, among them Gilberto Freyre and George Duby. My own temperament, background and many of my conclusions are quite different from those of G. M. Trevelyan, whose *English Social History*, covering a shorter period than mine, appeared during wartime more than fifty years ago, and I am separated from him both by class (still a relevant word in England) and by more than a generation. Yet I share his feeling for the poetry in the story. I also share his confident affirmation that as we attempt to reconstruct 'the whole fabric of each passing age', we get to know 'more in some respects than the dweller in the past himself knew about the conditions that enveloped and controlled his life'. It is an inspiring, if a chastening, thought.

Asa Briggs
Lewes, Sussex, 1998

I am redye to revoke my sayenge, if any-thynge have passed my mouthe for want of lernynge and to submytte myselfe to correction, and my boke to reformatyon.

John Fitzherbert, Boke of Husbandry, 1534

I   UNWRITTEN HISTORY

Antiquities are history defaced, or some remnants of history which casually escaped the shipwreck of time.

Francis Bacon, *The Advancement of Learning*, 1605

The interest attaching to antiquity is of a very fascinating character. It is not limited to any locality or epoch. It may be intensified by historical associations, or localised by becoming centred upon any particular object; but speaking of it in its fullest . . . it is illimitable.

William Cudworth, *The Bradford Antiquary*, 1879

Prehistory deals with fundamentals. It makes the child think about what really are fundamental necessities of life, and shows the ancient origin of familiar things.

D. P. Dobson, *The Teaching of Prehistory in Schools*, 1928

The traditional view of prehistory is now contradicted at every point.

Colin Renfrew, *Before Civilization*, 1973

England is a small country − its area is only one-sixtieth that of the United States − yet it is the centre of an old society. When the American colonists declared their independence in 1776 they were proud of the newness of their virgin continent. For most of the English, by contrast, age is an asset, not a liability; time at its best can be immemorial.

There are as many varieties of scene in the English countryside as there are layers of history in English society. The landscape reflects the complex geology and varied weather of the island. Yet it reflects much else besides. Some of the wildest twentieth-century landscapes, like the bleak heathland of Dorset, were cultivated very early in English history.

'England's green and pleasant land', as the eighteenth-century English poet William Blake called it, is as much the product of history as its 'dark satanic mills'. The seashore has changed too, although the presence of the sea and the nearness of all English places, however remote, to it, have always been significant in English history, as significant as mountains or deserts in other parts of the world. Nature in the form of hill or valley, lake or fen, copse or forest, has often consoled or inspired the English when events have numbed or shocked, and the fear that nature may be threatened can still be strong. 'This is our own, our native land.' Local loyalties relate too to a sense of local landscape, and nature and culture – the latter a word derived from the land – are inextricably entangled in every part of England.

The fact that through empire and the reaction to it British achievements and problems, broader than those of England itself, are themselves historically entangled with those of other developing societies and cultures, some of them far across the oceans, encourages large numbers of non-English explorers, who might otherwise have stayed at home or nearer home, to visit England, part of a group of islands. For them, as indeed for Englishmen themselves, exploration without explanation is not enough. Even if there are no easy answers, the contemporary explorer will at least want to pose questions. The two most obvious are, 'Why have the English done what they have done?' and 'How and why have they become what they now are?'

To answer such questions it is often necessary to go very far back in time. It was a French rather than an English social historian, the great Marc Bloch, who wrote that 'a society that could be completely moulded by its immediate preceding period would have to have a structure so malleable as to be virtually invertebrate.' In his *English Social History* G. M. Trevelyan went back as far as 'Chaucer's England', when 'England was beginning to emerge as a distinct nation, and when the English language, which in itself reflects so much social history, was beginning to come into its own.' There are reasons, however, for going much further back. Very early history focuses attention on man and nature, bones and rocks, island and mainland, geography and geology. It deals with what a 1928 handbook for prehistory teachers in schools called 'fundamentals'. Less emphasis was placed then on the limitations of the available evidence than on the centrality of the questions. The authors also gave a different and more engaging reason why children should study prehistory: since they were 'primitive beings' themselves, 'primitive occupations' would appeal to them.

Time scales had changed dramatically by 1928, and since then have changed yet again as new schemes of dating, new discoveries of material remains and new methods of assessing available evidence have developed so fast, particularly since the 1960s, that earlier surveys have been rapidly outdated. It is through our late twentieth-century sense of time and space, so different from that of previous centuries in that it is governed by science and technology, that we now step backwards and reach out to our most remote ancestors. This does not mean that we should ignore the journeys of past explorers of history when we make our own journey through time, for the social historian learns much about social history not only from recent but from out-of-date and discarded explanations. Nor does it mean that as we journey ourselves, seeking 'a reasoned history of man', all wonder will disappear. We soon appreciate, indeed, that a journey into the past has even more mystery about it than a journey into strange continents. There remains so much that we cannot explain. Stonehenge, for example, recently re-explored and redated, is still an enigma. It casts as much of a spell on late twentieth-century 'travellers' as on eighteenth-century archaeologists.

The explorers of the eighteenth and nineteenth centuries were the first to lengthen the time span both of natural and human history and to seek to order it more systematically. Proud of their unprecedented material progress, they were willing, often through heated debate, to abandon old ways of thinking. They reflected with wonder on the fact that lumps of coal, for them a source of wealth and power, derived from great carboniferous forests which had flourished in the island millions of years before: indeed, it was an earlier member of the Trevelyan family who discovered twenty upright trees buried deep in a coalfield on the Northumbrian coast. The excavations necessary for the construction of railways and sewers led to other striking discoveries, as motorways have done late in this century.

The Victorians noted, with awe as well as with wonder, how lost animals, among them giant reptiles and elephantine mammals, had once roamed the island. Models of them were displayed in the gardens of the Crystal Palace at Sydenham and in the new Natural History Museum, opened in 1881. Some Victorians, too, spent hours collecting and classifying flints, not always sure whether or not they were products of nature or human tools. They knew nothing of such scientific method-ologies as pollen or bone analysis and radio-carbon dating, but in their absence they methodically divided prehistoric time into ordered periods, based on the objects that had survived. This was an age of amateur enthusiasm for archaeology, although there were always more excur-sionists observing what was happening, or would-be buyers searching trade catalogues, than there were diggers in the field.

Geological periodization provided a guide to the classification of human history. Britain is a natural museum for geologists, who, in this context, like historians in others, must take the whole island and not just England as their unit of study. Victorian geologists found examples of rocks laid down in each of the great periods in the history of the earth, and they gave native British names to them. Thus, there was a Cambrian period, which took its name from Cambria (Wales); it lasted about 100 million years. A shorter and earlier Devonian period, initially an age of ferns and fishes, lasted for about 60 million years. There were also Ordovician and Silurian periods: these less homely labels derived from the names of 'ancient British tribes'.

The labels tell us more about the social and intellectual history of the nineteenth century than they do about the making of the earth itself. There were two points in the mysterious story, both of them involving contrasts, which seemed particularly striking then. While the physical making of the island had been achieved only through cosmic violence and a consequent total transformation of the environment, human history had been more peaceful and continuous. The very same Victorians who revolutionized geology and biology were proud of this relative absence of revolutions in English history, little imagining that some late twentieth-century social historians would argue that England had suffered through their seldom having taken place.

The second point also contained a paradox. While it seemed to the Victorians that the personality of Britain was determined by its island status, it was now revealed that human history began at a time when Britain had been not an offshore island but part of a bigger landmass. In the most distant times, bands of hunters had followed their game across the unsubmerged areas of the continental shelf to what is now England. The final separation, indeed, less than 9,000 years ago, is not 'very old'. It seemed strange that the natural links that had once existed between England and the outside world had been even more intricate than the multiple economic, social and cultural links of the busy nineteenth century when the modes of human communication had been completely transformed.

It was not easy in the nineteenth century – nor, indeed, is it today – to pass serenely from the history of the earth to the history of men and women. Although, as one nineteenth-century writer put it, 'the only trustworthy annals of primitive humanity are written in the Book of Nature', the Book turned out to be neither easily accessible nor completely trustworthy. The so-called Piltdown skull, 'discovered' in Sussex in 1912, was claimed as a unique English proof of the infancy of man's development, but it turned out to be a fraud. Likewise, fanciful visual reconstructions of past modes of life, like those of the Glastonbury lake village in Somerset, 'discovered' in 1888, contained an obvious element of caricature. The interpretation of the Book of Nature has been transformed only by spectacular advances in recent research, some of them centred in the laboratory. Quantitative analysis has become far more sophisticated: bones are studied not only to trace origins but to reveal diseases, and the explorer of the Somerset levels near Glastonbury now collects from the peat ancient pollen as well as flints. New attempts are being made to explain the sequence of change. There are new discoveries too, like that of the neolithic man found buried in the ice of a Swiss glacier in 1992.

Before the development of scientific archaeology, the main key to the understanding of early Britain seemed to be a fuller understanding of other living peoples in other parts of the world. 'Archaeology is merely the past tense of anthropology,' wrote O. G. S. Crawford, founder in 1925 of the periodical *Antiquity* and himself a pioneer of new techniques of air photography applied to archaeology. Much of the anthropology was evolutionist and had nineteenth-century origins. There were, it was claimed, common evolutionary sequences to be traced in quite different parts of the world, beginning with hunters and progressing through food gatherers, farmers, metal workers and 'priests': their group 'mentalities' could be probed as well as their material cultures. In a well-known series of prehistory books that was used in schools when the 1928 *Handbook* was written, Peake and Fleure introduced a whole gallery of 'types', identifiable in different places and through the 'corridors of time'. Their first volume, published in 1927, was called *Apes and Men*, their second volume *Hunters and Artists*

(there were very early animal paintings of exceptional interest in prehistoric caves, though few in England), their third volume *Peasants and
Potters* (the evidence of pottery was of such crucial importance to
archaeologists that pots often mattered more than people) and their
fourth, and final, volume *Priests and Kings* (social structures, it was
maintained, required both religion and leadership, swords of the spirit
and real swords that could be put to the test).

While geologists and archaeologists were lengthening the time span,
therefore, they were contracting space, as were railways and ocean
ships. All mankind was deemed to be one in fundamentals, and the
earliest social history of England, now seen simply as a particular
example, could be worked out, at least partially, by processes of induction
and deduction. When early/middle neolithic female figures and phallic
objects were found at Grimes Graves in Norfolk, for example, they
could be, and were, related to a worldwide phenomenon, worship of
the goddess of the earth.

Nonetheless, the nineteenth-century naming of the periods of human
history, starting with the stone ages – palaeolithic, mesolithic and
neolithic – and running into written history through the bronze and
iron ages (the advent of metals was given special significance in the
story), was related more to the materials men used and fashioned than
to their values. It is no coincidence that the term prehistory was first
used in England in 1851, the year the Great Exhibition was displayed
in the Crystal Palace in London's Hyde Park before it moved to
Sydenham. If the products of all nations in the nineteenth century could
be assembled in witness of material progress, would it not be possible
to periodize progress through the collection and display of the products
of each of the different stages of man's past? Already, by 1851, stone,
bronze and iron age periodization was familiar in England and, despite
critical comments at the time that history could not be 'treated as a
physical science and its objects arranged in *genera* and species', the
classification had come to stay.

Eventually, in the course of decades of excavation, collection and
research, all kinds of refinements were introduced into the classification,
and the dangers of drawing too rigid boundaries between one period
and another were emphasized. Yet the framework persisted. Moreover,
just as the labels attached to geological periods reflected British influence,
so labels attached to geological collections reflected continental influ-

ence. The caves of Aurignac, for example, with their fascinating primitive art, gave their name to 'Aurignacian', to which British evidence from Creswell Crags in Derbyshire (one cave there bore the far later mythical name Robin Hood's Cave and another Mother Grundy's Parlour) was related. The quest for uniformities and links was relentless.

To account for English cultural affinities with Europe after the melting of the ice, archaeologists fell back on what has been called 'the invasion hypothesis'. Given that the dynamic of social change was either the movement of peoples (migration) or the transfer of arts and techniques (culture contact), and given also that Britain was an island, weight was attached to the former process. It had begun with the greatest of all early environmental transformations, the coming of agriculture, which was traced back to a centre of origin in the Near East, from which domesticated wheat and barley, along with domesticated animals, spread westward and northward. European barbarism was 'irradiated', as Gordon Childe put it, by 'Oriental civilization'; and while Britain was at the periphery of the process, it was nevertheless an inviting periphery for outsiders because of its estuaries and peninsulas. Childe, who did much to popularize the concept of prehistoric 'cultures', stressed that throughout prehistory the stage was occupied not by individual actors but by peoples, and that the drama lay in their 'differentiation, wanderings and interactions'. In this vein he was writing as a social historian, and his book *Prehistoric Communities of the British Isles* was published one year before Trevelyan's *English Social History*. Later in his life Childe maintained also that prehistorians seek to distil from archaeological remains 'a pre-literate substitute for conventional politico-military history, with cultures instead of statesmen as actors and migrations in place of battles'.

Such an approach, once exciting, now seems restricted, although the notion of a 'culture' (people, artefacts and 'mentalities') still survives – indeed, remains strong – and migration, a major theme in our own century, remains the key to the spread of iron age people, artefacts and mentalities across Europe from the 'type site' at Hallstatt in modern Austria, reaching Britain half a millennium before the Romans arrived. As more and more material from Britain has been studied systematically, site by site and region by region, emphasis has shifted, whatever the period, to local adaptation to environment. Furthermore, Childe's phrase 'in place of battles' now seems misleading: in telling the story of prehistoric times, it is no more possible to leave out the history of fighting than it is for the modern social historian to leave out politics, as Trevelyan tried to do. Hand axes, the earliest artefacts to survive, had more than one purpose, and hand axes dating back to the 'Old Stone Age' in interglacial times have been found along with skull fragments at Swanscombe in the gravel of the River Thames. The novelist John Fowles has perceptively suggested that 'if the best stone-age tools are for handling wood and stone, the best bronze-age ones are for killing or subjugating other human beings.' There can be no dispute about the existence of ancient violence. The skeleton of a grown man with a leaf-shaped flint arrowhead in his side has been found in a long burial mound south-west of Salisbury, Wiltshire, and one of the score of people interred in a long-chambered tomb at Wychwood forest on the edge of the Cotswolds was killed by an arrow that penetrated his right side from below, embedding itself in his backbone. The social history of any period has to be comprehensive as well as sensitive, taking full account of prestige and power.

The 'dating revolution' of the last twenty years has forced re-examination of space as well as of time. Thus, while the conception of a neolithic age, based on the development of agriculture, has been pushed further back in time, the outer islands of Britain, including those in the far north, now play a more important part in archaeological interpretation. In England itself familiar places like Stonehenge have taken on a new meaning: it has been shown, for example, that Stonehenge I was already old and that Stonehenge II had been built when the Abraham of the Old Testament was alive. The megaliths in western European countries, including those in western England, were not grouped together as megalithic tombs until the nineteenth century, but they are now known to be older than Mycenae in Greece. Stone circles are scattered throughout the British Isles. So too are standing stones.

Many different sciences have contributed not only to a new chronology but also to a new interpretation of unwritten history, for as dates change in the aftermath of radio-carbon redating (which won Willard Libby a Nobel Prize in 1954) new questions inevitably emerge. While much guesswork is eliminated, there is greater scope for inference. Some archaeologists have tried to set limits to the latter: archaeologists, they suggest, should ask and answer only a limited range of questions determined by the data. Nonetheless, generalization, however difficult

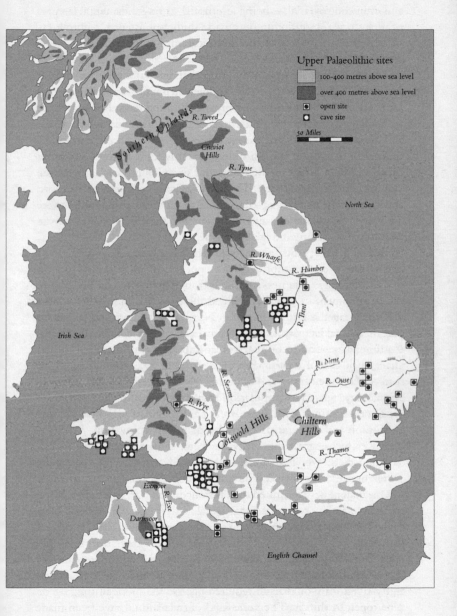

Upper Palaeolithic sites

100–400 metres above sea level

over 400 metres above sea level

⊙ open site

◻ cave site

50 Miles

Southern Uplands

R. Tweed

Cheviot Hills

R. Tyne

North Sea

R. Wharfe

R. Humber

R. Trent

Irish Sea

R. Nene

R. Ouse

R. Wye

R. Severn

Cotswold Hills

Chiltern Hills

R. Thames

Exmoor

R. Exe

Dartmoor

English Channel

and even controversial, is being attempted, as six fundamental features of prehistoric society invite systematic study: subsistence, technology, social organization, trade and communication, culture, and demography (the analysis of population).

The six features are obviously interdependent, as they are in all later societies. Thus, subsistence clearly influenced population and vice versa. Likewise, technology and social organization influenced one another: technology determined farming methods – and therefore subsistence – and social organization was clearly related both to trade and communication and to culture. It is possible to identify these features and point to relationships between them in the form of models even when empirical data is fragmentary. There is usually room for detective work, and some of the pictures of society that we can now paint are far more convincing, if still sketchy and tentative, than the old faded illustrations of palaeolithic camps and lake villages.

Subsistence is of fundamental importance in any society and archaeologists chase every scrap of evidence concerning the quest for food in prehistoric times. The neolithic shift from dependence on hunting to the development of cereal crops and the rearing of domestic animals did not mean the end of hunting. Nor did settlement, protected by fire, mean total security. It meant, however, that food had to be stored, that boundaries had to be marked, and that ancestry mattered. It also changed the social relationship between men and women. Intensive studies of the use of land and of coastal resources point to a complicated chronology, related to population movements and to the strength of social organization, with some areas passing out of use through land exhaustion and other areas being brought into cultivation. Within a narrower focus, great ingenuity has been shown recently in reconstructing diets, which included fish as well as meat and vegetables. Different sites have revealed different patterns of remains.

One major question linked to subsistence, which arises also in relation to later societies, concerns what was left over by way of food after immediate needs were met – the so-called agricultural surplus. Was it the result of 'windfalls' or was it purposefully built up? It would have been impossible to build Stonehenge without a remarkable diversion from food-gathering pursuits, since a single stone of around thirty-five tons would have required 600 or 700 men, all tugging on hide ropes, to shift it. The same kind of calculations have been made in relation to megaliths in Cumbria, a part of the country where for centuries there were to be geographic obstacles both to effective subsistence farming and to easy communications. How was the diversion achieved?

Technological processes of every kind, including stone-moving, can be deduced from a study of the tools and materials used for particular constructions. In particular, it was possible to do things with bronze that could not be done with flint, and with iron that could not be done with brass. Yet these materials could be – and were – complementary, and two other materials, wood and leather, which have not normally survived, were employed in the technology.

The links between technology and social organization always involve considerable speculation. Nonetheless, it is plausible to suggest, given the marked increase in the number of burial mounds in Wessex 4,000 years ago (mounds for single rather than communal burials) and the rich early bronze age finds there, that populations had increased and that rank had begun to count for more than it had done previously in society. And thus we begin to reconstruct the whole fabric of the past, as Colin Renfrew has done. He has noted, for example, a diminished emphasis on the mobilization of manpower for communal public works, like Silbury Hill, the largest artificial mound in Europe, and much more emphasis on the person, wealth and prestige of the chief and subchiefs. There were many signs of conspicuous consumption. An addendum is necessary. In dealing with social organization, much of the evidence relates to ways of death, or at least of burial, rather than to ways of life. So too does evidence from far later periods of history, including the Victorian.

The study of the role of culture as a set of symbols, ultimately conveyed through 'art' and 'religion', often mediated through material artefacts, has much concerned anthropologists and archaeologists. Subsistence seldom seems to have been all. Specifically English evidence is fragmentary, however, when compared with what has survived further east. There is little palaeolithic art, although an engraving of a horse's head has been found on a fragment of bone from Creswell Crags and a fish design has been traced on an ivory point from another Derbyshire cave. There are also small phallic objects of a later period which point to links between culture and fertility. The paucity of evidence has not inhibited the further generalization that there was a huge transformation in religious attitudes: looking down into the earth gave way to looking up into the sky.

Tracing the way in which material objects were moved from place to place often involves as much speculation as the diffusion of religious attitudes and rituals. Hand axes, for instance, could be used ceremonially, like the maces of medieval and modern times. The economics of production and distribution can be less speculative. Patterns of movement of pottery, for example, can be discerned and signs of trackways traced. Clearly, trade and communication had become relatively sophisticated by the time of the Roman invasion. The Romans and Greeks had known of Cornwall as a source of precious metals long before that. We also know of changes of fashion: the switch from buttons to pins for fastening garments 2,500 years ago may be compared with the switch from buckles to shoestrings two centuries ago.

Demography, one of the most challenging areas of study for the social historian – if only because demographic data was collected for its own sake so late in history (there was no national census in England until 1801) – remains a problematic subject for these distant centuries. Yet all social history must rest on demography and economics. Significantly, it was a far-reaching discussion of population growth in the eighteenth century before adequate data began to be collected that first pointed to the six fundamental features of a society and culture outlined here in relation to prehistoric society. They form not a sequence, but a circle.

As far as prehistory is concerned, until recently historians did little more than exercise ingenuity in making estimates of the number of people on particular sites and their age and sex balance, or suggest how population pressures changed from time to time and whether or not the people in question were newcomers. We can go further now, however, for our estimates of population have changed as much as our notions of time and space have done during the last twenty-five years, and our curiosity has increased accordingly. Simulation exercises have been carried out to re-enact how people actually lived on the foods available and how healthy they were. More revealing still has been the application of knowledge derived from later population and subsistence patterns to prehistoric times. Ambitious attempts have been made to construct local and British population aggregates. Thus, it has been suggested that in upper palaeolithic times there were between 250 and

5,000 people; that at the peak of the age of the hunters there were between 3,000 and 20,000 people (probably with considerable ups-and-downs of population); that in neolithic times the population numbered between 10,000 and 40,000, in the bronze age between 20,000 and 100,000 and in the iron age between 50,000 and 500,000.

Fascinating though such arguable estimates of aggregates are, it remains more rewarding to return to ways of life on specific individual sites. The present-day explorer may start at Heathrow Airport, 15 miles from London, where thousands of visitors from abroad arrive and depart every day. Archaeological evidence of ancient occupation 2,400 years ago was unearthed when work was being carried out on the airport runways during the 1950s; and it has subsequently been established that the airport is built on the site of an iron age settlement, which included a shrine. The people who lived and worshipped there were the kind of people whom the Romans encountered when they arrived in the island nearly 500 years later. There had, of course, been many other people before them, some of whom had left much behind them. 'Who the first inhabitants of Britain were,' wrote the Roman historian Tacitus, 'whether natives or immigrants, remains obscure,' adding, somewhat patronizingly, that 'one must remember that we are dealing with barbarians.'

On a different site, further from London, Kent's Cavern near Torquay, excavations opened up a hunters' base camp which was occupied until about 14,000 years ago: the rich remains found there included woolly mammoth and rhinoceros bones, as well as traces of the wolf, hyena and bear – mostly bear – and, interestingly, given its later significance in English social history, the horse. Pollen analysis has suggested that grasses and herbs, willow, juniper and occasional pine, oak and lime trees were all growing; the artefacts included spearheads, blades and bone pins.

The early hunters did not necessarily live in caves, but they did make effective use of local materials, including bone. Thus, at Star Carr, a later hunters' camp near Scarborough in Yorkshire that is no longer visible, almost all the materials found at the site could have been obtained within an hour's walk of the encampment, with the exception of iron pyrites, probably used for striking a light from flint: these are close in appearance to specimens from south Yorkshire coalfields. The importance of fire and heat in the hunters' world is obvious.

The world of neolithic man had different horizons from that of the hunters. Coming from across the sea 6,000 years ago, after the island had been formed, neolithic men and women cleared scrub and forest, made pastures for their animals, grew their own crops and lived in houses with hearths. They probably arrived in skin boats and, once settled, mined flints and baked pottery. Such activities involved a new balance between instinct and experience and put a new premium on work: archaeologists even speak of stone axe 'factories'. The neolithic people were small in stature, seldom more than 5½ feet tall, although they were capable of hard physical labour. We know little in detail of the processes whereby they settled in groups larger than individual families, nor do we know much about their families. What we do know is that they left behind them enduring monuments.

Wiltshire is rich in them. Windmill Hill, an early neolithic causewayed camp is only 1½ miles from a great stone circle at Avebury; and Stonehenge is only 11 miles away. The remains are so rich that G. M. Young, the twentieth-century cultural historian, was led to claim that the brooding sense of the distant past was stronger in this area than anywhere else in England. Young called historians 'the high priests of continuity' and a journey across the Wiltshire Downs along the Ridge-way (an ancient road crossed by the modern M4 motorway) 'a walk in the footsteps of three hundred generations'.

What makes this part of Wiltshire fascinating to the social historian is not just the sense of the very distant English past, but an equally strong sense that nature itself is a character in the story. Yet the loneliness of the scene today, except at times of solstice, should not mislead. In neolithic times, and in later phases of the iron ages, this was some of the most densely populated land in the country, as also were the Cotswolds, the Derbyshire hills and the Yorkshire wolds, all limestone areas with light soil which could be more easily farmed with the tools of the period than the deeper, richer soils to be found in the river valleys.

There are so many layers of history in Wiltshire that the works of different generations have become confused. We now know that there were at least five stages in the construction of Stonehenge, the great ruin on Salisbury Plain 60 miles from Heathrow, the final stage of which was as long after the first as we are from the misty seventh century. We know, too, that the first builders of Stonehenge began their work not less than 1,800 years before the arrival of the Romans. They seem to have been determined that their monument should last: as the American novelist Henry James observed, 'it stands as lonely in history as it does on the great plain.'

There is no doubt that interpretations of Stonehenge in different generations, including our own, reveal much about their own times and far less than the monument itself does about the work of the successive generations of builders. In the twelfth century the chronicler Geoffrey of Monmouth placed the building of Stonehenge only seven centuries earlier, which would make it contemporary to Wansdyke, a huge fortified ditch originally 50 miles long. In the seventeenth century Stonehenge came to be associated with the Druids, the 'priesthood' whom the Romans encountered, while in the twentieth century it has come to be associated not only with 'travellers' but with scientists and computers too. In between, a different perspective was offered by William Stukeley, the pioneer eighteenth-century enthusiast for archaeology, who observed that its contemplation afforded 'the highest pleasure imaginable to a regular mind'.

The continuing puzzles of Stonehenge, like those of other monuments, lie less in the vast amount of organized labour which went into its construction – eighty much prized blue stones appear to have been carried, mainly by water, a distance of 135 miles from Pembrokeshire in Wales – than in the uses to which the structure was put. Stonehenge I was built somewhere between 5,000 and 4,500 years ago; it has astronomical as well as archaeological interest. So also does Stonehenge II, as both Alexander Thom, who called the monument 'megalithic geometry in standing stones', and G. S. Hawkins, who wrote *Stonehenge Decoded*, have suggested in their detailed studies of its arrangement and orientation: the measurement of time and projection of the seasons were obviously of interest to its builders and users. Stonehenge II was the work of the so-called 'Beaker people' from the Rhine basin, the last major incursion of people to settle in England for over a millennium. They have been named after their beaker-shaped pots, but they had other outstanding characteristics: they buried their dead singly in round barrows (an innovation), although they also practised cremation. They probably mixed with, rather than subjugated, the existing population, and doubt has recently been cast on the extent to which they were innovators with a distinct culture.

Stonehenge III, the structure of which was substantially modified as sarsen (natural sandstone) stones were brought in from Marlborough, has been associated with the later so-called 'aristocratic' Wessex culture. Burials then were more rich and elaborate, and the burial barrows were often clustered together in cemeteries. Many interesting objects of copper, gold and bronze have survived from this period, as well as beads of faience, a blue vitreous paste, found in women's graves. (It has even been suggested that the richness of the women's graves might imply an improvement in their status after the Beaker period.) To what extent these relics genuinely represent the fullness of the culture has been a matter of argument. So also has the extent to which they imply dependence on improved technology (lathes) and increased trade backed by Irish gold. It has been argued instead that economic gains were based on more highly developed pastoral agriculture. A recent excavator of Stonehenge, R. J. C. Atkinson, claimed that we now have evidence 'for the concentration of political power, for a time at least, in the hands of a single man, who alone could create and maintain the conditions necessary' for an undertaking on the scale of Stonehenge.

What 'political power' meant in such a context is entirely a matter of conjecture; indeed, we might substitute for 'political' either 'coercive' or 'religious'. One point that seems clear is that in this period there was a greater specialization in society than ever before as metals were mined, mixed, fashioned and distributed. But beyond that there is more that is not clear, for there is as much mystery in the abandonment of major work on, and maintenance of, Stonehenge and other great stone circles as there used to be surrounding their construction.

The label 'late bronze age' is completely inadequate to cover the period before the iron age, or ages, which began in the millennium before the Romans came. Although the changing use of bronze itself in ornaments and weapons can be traced from plentiful bronze hoards, it is not clear how much social change was associated with bronze in its different phases – in settlement patterns, for example, or in the appearance of the landscape. That there was change has been emphasized recently. Good farm land was prized, and there were complex patterns of movement. What we know is severely limited, however, because of the accidents of survival. Archaeological exploration of the distinctive and continuous Deverel-Rimbury culture in

Dorset, which flourished 1,400 to 1,000 years ago, reveals that hoeing irregular plots had given way to ploughing square 'Celtic fields' before the iron age and that there were 'cattle ranches' and 'storage pits'. Far away in the north of England, roofed round houses were being built with central posts, and in the east there is evidence from the Fens district of hitherto marginal land being farmed. Eight centuries before the Roman invasion, trade between England and the continent seems to have been increasing, but two centuries later it had contracted again. There seems also to have been more violence in society, possibly brought about by pressure on land generated by an increasing population and by climatic change. In weaponry the double-edged heavy bronze age sword displaced the older rapier; it was designed for slashing as well as for stabbing. Not surprisingly, bronze shields were in evidence too, and horse-gear could be elaborate with bridle bits and terret rings. There were also hill forts.

Iron weapons – and implements – were being produced in England 600 years before the Roman invasion. Some were handsomely decorated. They suggest a society in which fighting was common. Iron technology, introduced from continental Europe, was at least equal in development to that of the Greeks and Romans, and although there is continuing argument about whether or not it was 'imposed' on previous inhabitants by migrants from outside the island, it seems clear that society was more fragmented. There have been important archaeological finds in the east of Yorkshire revealing direct foreign influence half a millennium before the Romans. In the north and west of England pastoral peoples seem to have favoured small, enclosed homesteads, in the Midlands and east open and undefended village settlements with scattered single farms. In the south, however, the strongly fortified hill fort was a characteristic iron age feature. There were at least 3,000 of them, of all sizes, some of which, like the most famous, Maiden Castle in Dorset, were superimposed on older structures. Many of them are still visible.

Neolithic farmers had built a causewayed camp at Maiden Castle centuries before, and in the iron age it was radically improved with an additional ditch and heightened ramparts: the height of the main sloping rampart, from the top of the walls to the bottom of the ditch, was now eighty-three feet. (This was the age of the sling as well as of the iron sword.) The interiors of some of the bigger forts, it has been suggested, now took on the appearance of towns: they were planned with roadways, round houses and pits for storing corn, and they could be very densely built up. It was during these years that horses, now shod, were beginning to stand out among the animals, and the White Horse at Uffington, on the chalk hillside close to the Ridgeway, putative ancestor of many later white horses on the hills (most of them produced during the last 200 years), may belong to this period too. Figures of horses appear on iron age buckets and coins. The real horses of the period were slender-limbed, measuring 11.2 to 12.2 hands, and were used to draw chariots which were eventually to have spoked, iron-tyred wheels. Oxen drew the plough, and there was cross-ploughing to break up the soil. Iron axes were used to clear woodland. The religion of the period and its free-flowing curvilinear art were associated with sacred places beside streams and woods, and the economy was far more complex than that of previous periods. There was an increasing production of coins.

The nearer we get in time to the Roman invasion, the more archaeological evidence we have at our disposal, although it is still patchy and incomplete. It reveals the existence of 'tribal' units bigger than the family, each with its 'kingly' leader. Among them were the Trinovantes living north-east of the Thames, the Durotriges and the Dumnonii in the south-west, and the Brigantes, who held much of the Pennines and the adjacent plain in the north of England. We can trace in several areas the distribution both of single homesteads and of nucleated settlements, and we can survey iron age agriculture in which arable farming (with wheat and barley as the main crops) and pastoral, mainly sheep, farming were closely linked in varied and efficient cultivation patterns that depended on animal breeding, manuring and careful conservation of seed corn.

In general, technology too was more varied than in previous periods. Pottery was produced by the fast-turning wheel introduced in the century before the Romans came, and there was a distinction between the coarse and better quality ware; textile spinning was assisted by bone, pottery or stone spindle whorls, as in previous periods, and weaving was now carried out on upright looms with clay weights and bone combs; iron, the metal which was to give its name to the age, was probably smelted in bowl furnaces. This was an age when the number of luxury items increased to meet the demands of a society in which consumption seems to have been socially stratified. Wines were being imported, and with them went frequently ornate drinking vessels. There were highly decorated brooches, too, and tombs might contain mirrors as well as weapons. The design of mirrors was at its finest in the century when the Romans came. The main port was at Hengistbury Head on the southern side of Christchurch harbour.

Unwritten history remains full of mystery. How many newcomers were there? Julius Caesar was to refer to the Belgae who came from across the Channel. When did they arrive? Did innovation depend on immigration? How did development in the south of England, the area best known to the Romans, relate to development further inland, in the north or in the east? Why were the first coins to be minted all gold coins, unsuitable for the ordinary purpose of exchange? Were they for tribute or for some other purpose? What part did women play in the economy? How were children brought up?

Written history begins with the 'tribal' society encountered by the Romans, which, together with the characteristic square-ploughed fields associated with that culture, was later described as Celtic. In fact, there is no ancient source to link the term 'Celtic' in any special way with England: it was only in the sixteenth and seventeenth centuries that scholars deduced that Gaelic and Welsh were derived from the language of the ancient Celts who had once inhabited England as well as Scotland, Wales and Ireland.

In one part of England, Cornwall, a Celtic language was still being spoken at that time, and then, as now, the names of many rivers and streams elsewhere in the country were Celtic: Aire, Avon, Dee and Derwent, Mersey, Severn and Thames. Leeds is the biggest modern provincial city with a Celtic name, and places like Thanet, Wight (in the Isle of Wight) and Craven, the beautiful fell country in Yorkshire, are also Celtic in origin. Nature and language moved closely together in unwritten history, and the link has survived.

What is surprising is that while we can produce a Celtic map of England, very few Celtic words from that distant period have entered the language and stayed with us through the centuries, the best known of the few being the words 'ass' and 'combe', a small valley, the latter belonging more to the map than to the dictionary. Far more Celtic words came into the language later, indirectly, through the French and Irish languages. There is, nonetheless, an old Celtic strain in the English inheritance which has been acknowledged by some writers. As the twentieth-century historian A. L. Rowse, born in Cornwall, once put it personally, 'Nineteenth-century historians were apt to regard us as Anglo-Saxon folk. In fact we are really an Anglo-Celtic people.'

2 INVASION, RESISTANCE, SETTLEMENT AND CONQUEST

> But the Romans came with a heavy hand,
> And bridged and roaded and ruled the land,
> And the Romans left and the Danes blew in –
> And that's where your history-books begin.
>
> Rudyard Kipling, *The River's Tale*, 1911

> I should like to get a clear picture of the movements of people spreading over the top of each other and getting continually mixed up, but each still keeping something that it had from the beginning. One thinks with horror of the inconceivable suffering of humanity at that time. Don't you think that an account which disregarded individuals and told of the march of peoples, a short staccato account, would paint a terrible picture but one from which much could be learnt?
>
> Alexis de Tocqueville, *Reflections on English History*, 1828

> My nose is pointed downwards; I crawl along and dig in the ground. I go as I am guided by the grey enemy of the forest, and by my lord, who walks stooping, my guardian, at my tail, pushes his way on the plain, lifts me and presses on, and sows in my track.
>
> Anglo-Saxon Riddle (Answer: The Plough)

> The Norman Conquest was a Good Thing, as from this time onwards England stopped being conquered and thus was able to become top nation.
>
> W. C. Sellars and R. J. Yeatman, *1066 and All That*, 1930

The Romans were the first invaders of Britain to document their invasion. They had long known Britain as a remote land beyond the ocean, they were aware that it was roughly triangular in shape and they knew also that there were contacts between the peoples on either side of the Channel. After Julius Caesar had conquered Gaul and received the submission of its major tribes, it was tempting for him to think of an expedition to Britain, if only for reasons of personal ambition and glory. He carried out two expeditions, neither of which led to immediate Roman settlement. Nothing was gained by the first except reconnaissance: the second was more successful, but brief. Gaul had been conquered in only two seasons of campaigning, but no Roman general was to land in Britain again for ninety-seven years. Shakespeare was to recall centuries later in *Cymbeline* that Caesar

> . . . was carried
> From off our coast, twice beaten and his shipping –
> Poor ignorant baubles! – on our terrible seas,
> Like egg-shells moved upon their surges . . .

Precise dates are less significant to social historians than the charting of longer-term social processes, but there is nevertheless a two-fold significance in the precise dates of Caesar's invasions, 55 and 54 BC. First, English history thereafter is no longer completely unwritten history. The Romans had a literature of their own, and Caesar himself was a writer as well as a general, anxious to set down an account of his exploits. From this time onwards, historians have access to a new kind of evidence about England, although for the whole Roman period it is episodic and patchy and we cannot reconstruct society on the basis of it. Second, the dates 55 and 54 BC belong to a calendar which is itself new to the story. The BC and AD chronology is important because it indicates that, through Rome, England was to be drawn into a Christian orbit, a point of major importance in subsequent social and cultural, as well as political, history. The Christian calendar itself was devised only in the sixth century, a by-product of arguments about the timing of Easter, and it took the place of genealogical dating through lists of the dates of kings only in the seventh century. Yet before there was a Christian chronology there was a Christian history. The oldest indigenous British historical text was written in Latin by a monk, Gildas, in the mid-sixth century.

What did the Celts and their island seem like to Caesar and his contemporaries? Theirs was the first recorded outsider's view, which may be compared with colonists' views of the Polynesian 'noble savage' or American 'Red Indian' centuries afterwards. The island, they noted, had many physical assets: as a later outsider from Italy was to remark in the sixteenth century, 'Nature has endowed it with beauty and great bounty.' Tacitus, who was son-in-law of an early governor of Britain, emphasized, however, that the British were disunited. The island was not one, and there were 'warring factions', even in the distinct parts of it. In the few pages which a later English historian Edward Gibbon devoted to the island in his *Decline and Fall of the Roman Empire* (1776–88) he balanced his phrases, as always, when he wrote of Celtic Britain that 'the proximity of its situation to the coast of Gaul' invited Roman armies and 'the doubtful intelligence of a pearl fishery attracted their avarice.' As for the Celts – and, like Tacitus, he used the word 'barbarians' – they showed 'valour without conduct and the love of freedom without the spirit of union'.

For Strabo, the Roman geographer and historian, who was a boy when Caesar landed, 'the greater part of the island' was 'level and wooded', but there were many 'hilly tracts'. This obvious contrast between upland and lowland was to fascinate many subsequent geographers and to point later to geographical interpretations of British history. These have subsequently been considerably qualified, but in the most general terms – and subject to local variations – the wetter upland, or highland, pastoral zone in the west was to have a different history from the drier arable lowland zone in the east, and the Fens were to have a history of their own. The island, Strabo went on, produced corn – one of the early tribal coins bore the design of an ear of barley – cattle, gold, silver, iron, tin, hides, slaves and 'dogs useful for hunting'. Tacitus, born a century after Caesar's invasion, took this inventory for granted, but added that the island's northern shores were 'beaten by a wild and open sea'. These northern shores were never to become the boundary of the Roman Empire; like Ireland, they remained beyond it to the end, a fact of cardinal importance in later British history. The Romans never conquered the whole island: there were large numbers of Celts who remained outside the bounds.

For Caesar, who knew the north of the island only by repute, 'by far the most civilized inhabitants' lived in the maritime districts of Kent, where he landed. They were certainly most like the people he had already conquered in Gaul and there were many contacts between them. The inhabitants of other areas were to retain a separate identity. 'Most of the tribes in the interior', he believed, did not grow corn, but 'lived on milk and meat' and wore skins. It was their fearful appearance in battle which most impressed him. They carried long Celtic swords and wore no body armour. 'All the Britons dye their bodies with woad,' he explained, 'which produces a blue colour . . . They wear their hair long and shave the whole of their bodies except the head and the upper lip.'

The awkward term tribe (Latin *tribus*) used by Caesar has misleading modern associations. It has been related to the Celtic *tref*, or *treb*, populations who had cleared and worked ground and who were ruled by a king (or queen). More than twelve tribes have been identified for England at the time of the Roman conquest, some of which, like the Atrebates, had a tribal centre – theirs was at Calleva (known to us as Silchester, Berkshire) – and others of which, like the Dumnonii in Devon and Cornwall, did not. Camulodunum (Colchester), which was to become the first Roman capital, was the capital of the Trinovantes. Written evidence about customs and institutions is scanty. Within each tribe there was at one end of the social spectrum an 'aristocracy', which might be separated from the daily routines of agriculture, and at the other, slaves. There were also – and this particularly interested Caesar – the Druids, a 'priesthood' of wise men or soothsayers who, beside teaching the young, might be called upon to judge in disputes between adults. They thus had a public role and received dues in money and kind. Caesar believed that they originated in Britain and that they had shrines in the country in 'groves of oak', where the moon as well as the trees (and the occasional mistletoe on them) played a part in their rites. The moon dictated *their* calendar, and their time unit, the fortnight, still survives. The Romans disliked what they heard of the bloodthirst-iness of the Druid religion, but before the advent of Christianity their gods very quickly became confused with those of the Romans.

Caesar was the first writer to describe women as well as men, claiming that wives were 'shared between groups of ten or twelve men, especially fathers and sons'. The Romans also met tribal armies led by women, some of them, like Boudicca, memorable enough to stand out as individuals, though subject to many subsequent reinterpretations. We know that many Celtic women were eventually to marry soldiers in the Roman armies, but, tantalizingly, we do not know a great deal about Celtic family patterns or population. As far as the latter is concerned,

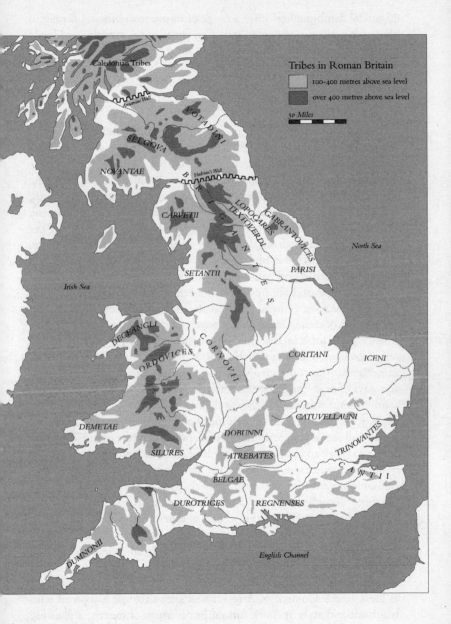

Tribes in Roman Britain

100–400 metres above sea level

over 400 metres above sea level

50 Miles

Caledonian Tribes

Antonine Wall

VOTADINI

SELGOVAE

NOVANTAE

Hadrian's Wall

CARVETII

LOPOCARES

TEXTOVERDI

GABRANTOVICES

BRIGANTES

North Sea

SETANTII

PARISI

Irish Sea

DECEANGLI

CORNOVII

ORDOVICES

CORITANI

ICENI

DEMETAE

CATUVELLAUNI

TRINOVANTES

SILURES

DOBUNNI

ATREBATES

CANTII

BELGAE

DUROTRIGES

REGNENSES

DUMNONII

English Channel

historical demographers offer a range of ingenious estimates similar to those for prehistoric peoples, based on agricultural capacity and likely density of settlement. The peak figure for Roman Britain, which was once set as low as 500,000 to one million, has more recently been calculated as four to six million, a far higher total than most of the estimates for England after the Norman Conquest in 1066 or for the England of Henry III.

During the century between Caesar's expeditions and the successful invasion by Claudius in AD 43 the habits of the Celtic people continued to change and the links between some of the British tribes and the Romans were strengthened. Trade with the Roman world, including the export of slaves from Britain and import of wine from the south, had also increased. Yet when Claudius mounted his invasion, his army was reluctant to sail into a land of mystery beyond the limits of the world. 'Men coming from these remote regions', Tacitus was to write, 'told strange stories – of hurricanes, unknown birds, sea monsters, and shapes half-human and half-animal.'

The victory of Claudius won him the proud inscription on his triumphal arch in Rome, 'He was the first to subject the barbarian peoples beyond the Ocean to the power of the Roman state.' Roman poets eagerly took up the same imperial theme. 'Forget not, Roman,' Virgil exclaimed in lines which were to appeal centuries later to British imperialists, 'that it is your special genius to rule the peoples, to impose the ways of peace, to spare the defeated, and to crush those proud men who will not submit.' Whatever their economic or political motives, the Romans made much of their mission to 'civilize', or, as Tacitus put it, 'to induce a people hitherto scattered, uncivilized and therefore prone to fight, to grow pleasurably broken in to peace and ease'.

What actually happened during the 'civilizing process' and an occupation of four centuries, inevitably with many changes within them, was far more complicated than Tacitus suggested, particularly after the advent of Christianity in the second century. Already by the fourth century there had been one Christian soldier martyr in England, Alban; and within two years of Constantine's recognition as 'Augustus of all the West' in 312 – he had been hailed as Emperor six years earlier by Roman soldiers at York – three bishops from Britain were to appear at the Church Council of Arles. It was after this that a woman who was buried in style at York carried her earrings, a mirror, a glass jug and a piece of bone pierced with the Christian motto, 'Sister, hail! May you live in God!' Christians ceased to be persecuted in Britain several decades before Constantine became a Christian, but there were few of them even after his conversion. Christianity seems to have been most actively practised by a small but influential group of 'civilized' aristocrats, and a strong indigenous pagan element still persisted. No large Roman church structures have been identified; the biggest, at Silchester, held no more than sixty people.

Doubtless other buildings were used for Christian worship: in 1975 a remarkable collection of Christian liturgical vessels, the earliest surviving church plate from the whole Roman Empire, was discovered at Durobrivae (Water Newton, Cambridgeshire) in the highly populated Nene valley. The earliest known portrait of Christ in Britain was found in a villa at Hinton St Mary in Dorset. Such limited survivals do not suggest the existence of a widespread Romano-British ecclesiastical art. A flourishing Celtic Christian culture did, however, exist in Ireland in the time of Patrick (the son of an English landowner who had first gone to Ireland as the captive of slave-traders), and Celtic Christians brought both the Christian message and the inspiration of the Celtic Christian culture over to western England in the fifth century.

Because there was more effective communication both inside the country and with other parts of the Empire, the civilizing process was usually associated as much with travel and trade as with ideas and beliefs. The great Roman roads, designed for military purposes, carried not only troops but also goods and, equally important, information on which the Empire depended. There were post and relay stations from eight to fifteen miles apart, sometimes with facilities for changing horses and taking hot baths. There were three main arms of road radiating from London – to York and the north; to Chester and Carlisle; and to Gloucester, Wales and the south-west. Roads were one of the most remarkable Roman achievements, as the Romans themselves recognized: an inscription in remote Swaledale in Yorkshire reads simply 'to the god who first thought of roads and paths'. The writer might have added waterways, for river traffic was supplemented by canals, and there were sturdy Roman bridges, docks and aqueducts. The Car Dyke, a series of canals which drained part of the Fens, linked the River Cam at the Waterbeach near Cambridge and Lincoln, which was also connected with the Trent, the Humber and the Ouse.

Roman rule imposed financial and political burdens on the population in cash and kind, but at the same time it was capable of appealing both to the desire to serve and to the profit motive. Taxation, regularly reviewed, was high, and the costs of the army, which provided a substantial indirect employment to serve its wants, were met by the British people. There were as many as 60,000 soldiers in the army, a far larger force, backed by auxiliaries, than medieval kings could have maintained, and it required the produce of 100,000 acres to support it. When Britons joined the army, as with other 'barbarians' from across the Channel and the North Sea, their loyalty to the Emperor carried with it incentives and privileges. After twenty-five years' service there were gratuities and grants of full citizenship. At another level, since there was a relatively small number of paid Roman officials residing in Great Britain, as in British India centuries later, it was in the interests of the Governor – or Governors after Britain was divided into provinces, two in AD 197, four in AD 284 and five in AD 369 – and of the fiscal procurator to turn for support in the governing process to the *curiales*, better-off élites (as they have been called), in the towns. Reliance on these was an economic arrangement for the Romans, but it favoured socially those who took office. There was an element of corruption both in the system of supplies and in the farming out of taxes to individual bidders. At the same time, within an imposed centralized system the main units of local administration corresponded significantly to older divisions, just as tribal divisions were to persist centuries later in the colonies of the British Empire.

As for profit, the establishment of a money economy was an essential feature of Roman Britain, even though there were coins before the Romans arrived and after the Roman money economy was established, the use of money was limited. The economy rested on subsistence agriculture and left an important place for the exchange of gifts and favours. Most of the coinage was imported from Italy and Gaul – and there were frequent debasements – but official mints were set up in Britain itself at various times. The money flow was uneven and at certain times there was considerable inflation, particularly in the early fourth century. There also seems to have been an interest in retaining 'sound' silver currency when debased coins were introduced.

The circulation of small coins has been taken as a sign of vigorous local trade, and numismatic evidence has been employed also to point

Roman Britain

- 100-400 metres above sea level
- over 400 metres above sea level
- marshland
- lowland forest
- ● Municipium ○ town
- ◧ legionary fortress
- ▲ fort ── road
- ▦ other site referred to in text

50 Miles

1 Lindum (Lincoln)
2 Salinae (Droitwich)
3 Glevun (Gloucester)
4 Corinum (Cirencester)
5 Aquae Stills (Bath)
6 Galleva (Silchester)
7 Veralamium (St.Albans)
8 Londinium (London)
9 Durobrivae (Rochester)
10 Durovernum (Canterbury)
11 Venta Icenorum (Caistor)

to wider patterns of trade. Money was used from the beginning of Roman control to buy food – some imported, much home-produced – including salt (some from Droitwich, some from the Lower Rhine), beer (a prized local product), wine, pottery, furnishings and jewellery, not to mention oysters, which, it has been claimed, were prized, with or without pearls, as much in Rome as in England. More distant connections still are suggested by the tombstone of the wife of a merchant of Palmyra at South Shields in Northumberland. Merchants had their guilds, and even before the end of the first century there was a *collegium* of metal craftsmen at Chichester. Similar craftsmen flourished in other towns until the end of Roman control. Mineral wealth was exploited too in widely scattered places.

The changing fortunes of the pottery industry reveal the complexity of the civilizing process and all that went with it. The relationship between sales of pottery made at home and imported pottery has been studied in detail by archaeologists, and it is clear that throughout the Roman period there were both imports and exports, sometimes substantial, tied in with changes in demand and taste. Earlier iron age traditions of production persisted during the first years of Roman rule (in Dorset, for example), but there were huge imports. Meanwhile, the demand for pottery by the army led to the creation of workshops under military supervision. New civilian workshops soon followed, with Durobrivae becoming a specialized centre of large-scale production. There were also large numbers of small potters in the New Forest offering less elaborate wares, so that whenever there were no military or political interruptions to trade and production, there was ample competition and choice. Potters' stalls and shops have been excavated in several Roman towns.

The civilizing process did not affect all people equally, of course, however desirous they may have been to benefit from it, and many people – and districts – were left outside it altogether. There was unevenness of development. Nor did the gap between the haves and have-nots narrow. 'Rufus, son of Callisunus,' we read on a writing tablet found in the River Walbrook in London, 'greetings to Epillicus and all his fellows. I believe you know I am well. Do look after everything carefully. See that you turn the slave girl into cash.' Ninety-seven burials at a villa near Marlow have suggested that there was an 'industry' there, perhaps textiles, employing young female slaves. At the end of the

Roman Empire there were large numbers of slaves in Kent, as there were also in the far west.

History from below is often more forbidding than history from above. In the first Roman campaigns, for example, defenders of Maiden Castle against the able young Roman commander Vespasian, who was later to become Emperor, were slaughtered *en masse* and buried in a cemetery at the east gate. In AD 59–60 there was a revolt in eastern England led by Boudicca, the warrior queen, typically portrayed in her chariot; according to one obviously exaggerated estimate, quoted by Tacitus, as many as 80,000 rebels were killed near Verulamium (modern St Albans, Hertfordshire). Previously, she had devastated Colchester, the first Roman capital, complete with temple and theatre, and St Albans itself. The conquest of the north of England in AD 78 under the governorship of Agricola involved the overthrow but not the final destruction of tribal power. Agricola was the father-in-law of Tacitus who paid proper tribute to his achievements. He praised those Britons who 'responded quickly' to Romanization and 'severely criticized the laggards'.

The greatest surviving Roman landmark of the centuries that followed is Hadrian's Wall, which was begun in AD 122 after the Britons, in the words of Hadrian's biographer, 'could no longer be held under Roman control'. Hadrian was a man of imagination and determination, and his Wall took six years to build, was nearly eighty Roman miles long (a Roman mile was 1,620 yards), and stretched almost from sea to sea. Magnificent though it now seems, its building was greatly resented, and there was hostility from the local population on both sides of it. Turrets served as observation points sufficiently high to protect the sentries from attack. Hadrian's successor built a much shorter Antonine Wall, a barrier of turf further north above the present boundaries between England and Scotland, which is less than half the length of Hadrian's Wall, but this last of the imperial linear frontiers had only a brief history. The Picts were never overcome, and there were further uprisings among the Brigantes. The years from AD 213 to AD 342 have been described as 'years of peace', but there was a continual threat from the sea as well as from the land, first from pirates and later from would-be Saxon settlers; and in the third century powerful forts were constructed on the coast from Brancaster in the north to Portchester in the west. The long coastline was always vulnerable to attack.

It was for such reasons that only a part of Britain was densely populated and that towns were less secure than in many other areas of the Roman Empire. Most Roman towns were not by the sea. Some, like Durovernum (Canterbury) or Calleva (Silchester), were on old sites, while others were on fresh sites not very far away from old ones; a typical prehistoric gully bounding a hut site was found at Canterbury in 1946 and Dorchester (Durnonovaria) was only a few miles away from Maiden Castle. From the start, however, the Romans endowed their bigger towns with a social and cultural significance that was new to England, arranging them in a formal grid pattern, with straight lines and rectangles. Like the straight Roman roads, Roman towns defied all the favourite curves of the Celts. In the twentieth century Lewis Mumford, historian of cities throughout the ages, was to generalize scathingly about Roman towns as 'forum, vomitarium and bath', but he left out the temple and the amphitheatre. In fact, the *civitas* or city-state was thought of as the centre of civilization. Urban buildings mattered less than the sense of citizenship: 'the pleasantest, yes and the most profitable side of city life is society and intercourse.'

Roman towns can be divided into categories, *civitates*, *municipia* (a designation which passed into local government centuries later) and *coloniae*. Whether near to old sites or not, they usually were or had begun as garrison centres like Luguvalium (Carlisle) and Catarectonium (Catterick), the latter still a military camp in the twentieth century. Some of them became *coloniae*. The first of them, Camulodunum, established as such after the first legionaries stationed there had moved to Gloucester, was erected as early as AD 49. Glevum (Gloucester) and Lindum (Lincoln) followed later in the first century. Eboracum (York), military base of the Ninth Legion in their fight against the Brigantes and subsequent headquarters of the Roman Army in the north for more than 300 years, became a *colonia* around AD 213. Some smaller towns had their origins in post-houses along the great roads; they remained after armies had moved on.

Each of the four *coloniae* had its *ordo* or council, modelled on the Roman Senate and elected by citizens (later called *curiales* after the *curia* or council chamber) who were of the right age (the minimum was normally thirty) and who had the necessary property qualifications. The *ordo* chose two pairs of magistrates annually, one pair responsible mainly for the maintenance of public buildings and amenities. The attraction of office diminished during the last years of Roman occupation.

Each town, big or small, had its own history. What buildings have survived or have been excavated is largely a matter of accident, yet patterns of development can be traced. The building of a wall and impressive gateways was deemed important symbolically as well as in terms of defence. So too was the shift from timber to stone. The commonest form of urban house was the strip house, a long, narrow building fronting the street in 'parades' with a gable end. There seem to have been no large multi-storey apartments as there were in Italy. Public buildings were erected at different times as towns grew in size and in wealth, and private housing, with painted walls outside and inside, could reflect this growth. Some towns had an aqueduct; all seem to have had baths and public lavatories. Some had a market hall (*macellum*) as well as a *forum*, which served as a meeting place as well as a market-place. All seem to have had shops. The basilica on one side of the forum was the largest covered meeting hall. The temple in pre-Christian times and the amphitheatre, elliptical in shape, were common features of urban life. The games were part of the calendar. We know little of the balance between public and private, though there were some houses enclosed in gardens. In pre-Christian times each house had its shrine to the household gods, the *lares*.

Plagues and fires were major regular hazards both to private and public buildings, as they were to be for generations to come. Thus, when the forum at Viroconium (Wroxeter), the site of which now consists entirely of ploughed fields, was destroyed by fire at the end of the third century (it was the second great fire in the history of the city), it was not rebuilt. The impressive baths continued in use, however, and were reconstructed later; there was further work on them even at the beginning of the fifth century.

At Verulamium, as at Durovernum, the building of a theatre in the mid-second century must have been a major event: it provided more seating accommodation than any hall in modern St Albans. Nor was it the only point of interest. One of the earliest buildings to be erected was a row of nine shops grouped under one roof. A great fire in the city in AD 155 had destroyed many buildings. Yet the range of civic amenities increased, and the theatre was extended as late as *c.* AD 300, when races, 'beast shows' and gladiatorial contests were popular, not least, perhaps, because admission was free. Later in the second half of the century it went out of use. Verulamium also had a stone market-building and a courtyard.

Eboracum, where walls, burial grounds and religious relics can still be seen, became the provincial capital of Britannia Inferior, with its own governor, after Britain had been divided into two provinces (Britannia Superior was so called because it was nearer to Rome). Two Roman emperors died there: the first, Septimus Severus, in AD 211, the second, Constantine, in AD 306. The importance of Eboracum is attested by its magnificent fortress, completed around AD 300 and said to be the best of its kind in the Empire (the headquarters within it are on the site of the future York Minster). A reredos showing Mithras in the ritual act of slaying a bull has survived. The slaughter was the main feature of pre-Christian Roman religion which had strong appeal for soldiers. Another deity popular among pre-Christian soldiers for less mystical reasons was Fortuna, the goddess of fortune; in different guises she figures in all periods of social history.

Londinium, late to acquire a local *ordo*, had to await twentieth-century bombing for its Roman riches to be revealed. The Thames was important before the Romans came, but Londinium itself was a Roman development on an exceptionally favourable site. There was an early Roman military camp there, but the town grew through commerce rather than through war. When a magnificent forum was laid down there before the end of the first century, an even older building and piazza had to disappear, and there was a succession of massive timber wharves, warehouses and a bridged pier. Londinium was directly linked to the trade of continental Europe. It also became a financial and administrative headquarters, and in the early third century it began to build its walls. In the fourth century it acquired the imperial title Augusta. Its population may have risen to about 30,000, and its area grew to 330 acres, over twice the size of Roman Paris. The stone for its public buildings was brought from many parts of the country: Northamptonshire, for example, and Purbeck in Dorset, together with Aquae Sulis (Bath), itself a small Roman town where stone buildings were constructed around curative hot springs early during the Roman occupation. The bath underwent many changes before becoming disused by the end of the fourth century.

It has been suggested that the importance the Romans attached to

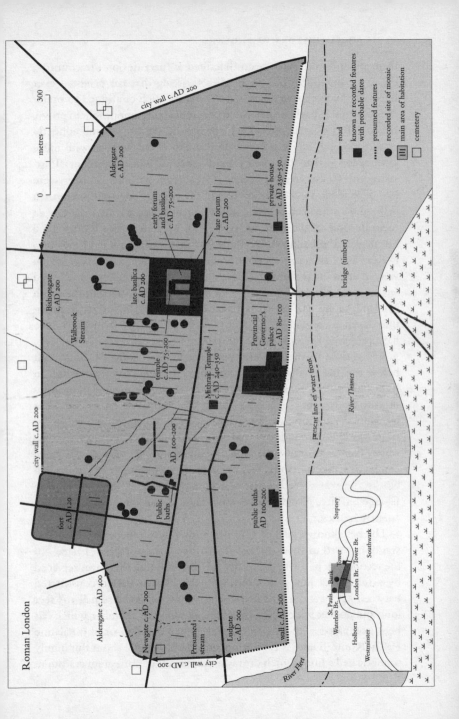

Roman London

city wall c.AD 200

300

metres

0

Aldgate
c.AD 200

early forum
and basilica
c.AD 75-200

late forum
c.AD 200

private house
c.AD 250-350

Bishopsgate
c.AD 200

late basilica
c.AD 200

Walbrook
Stream

temple c.AD 75-200

Mithraic Temple
c.AD 240-350

Provincial
Governor's
palace
c.AD 80-100

AD 100-200

bridge (timber)

present line of water front

River Thames

city wall c.AD 200

fort
c.AD 120

Public
baths

public baths
AD 100-200

Aldersgate c.AD 400

Newgate c.AD 200

Presumed
stream

Ludgate
c.AD 200

city wall c.AD 200

wall c.AD 200

River Fleet

road

known or recorded features
with probable dates

presumed features

recorded site of mosaic

main area of habitation

cemetery

St. Paul's   Bank
Waterloo Br.   Tower
Holborn   London Br.   Tower Br.
Westminster   Southwark

Stepney

their towns, which have been described as 'parasites on the country', led to an anti-urban bias in English thinking that has persisted ever since: the 'native' poor as well as the 'native' rich continued to prefer the countryside to the town. Such continuities are impossible to prove, although R. G. Collingwood, who propounded the thesis, subsequently condemned by J. S. Wacher, believed also – and perhaps with more justification – that 'the dreary mediocrity of Roman provincial art' stifled the Celtic creative spirit. In reality, town and country were interdependent. Few Roman villas in the countryside were more than half a day's ride from a town, and there were apparently very few of them in some of the rural western areas. Moreover, the Romans did not neglect the countryside. They brought much new land into use, in Kent and Essex, for example, and in the eastern Fens, parts of which were drained and reclaimed. There were also large numbers of nucleated settlements, villages as well as hamlets. In the Nene valley in the south Midlands alone 434 of them had been identified by 1972, fourteen times as many as had been identified in 1930. Many farmers seem to have preferred keeping cattle and pigs to sheep.

The earliest of the 600 known Roman villas, some of them built before the end of the first century, were located close to the sea, in Kent and Sussex. Some were comparatively unsophisticated bungalows of six to ten rooms; others were enlarged or improved as the years went by, with the addition of, for example, baths and accommodation for estate workers. Around towns like Verulamium and Corinium (Cirencester) there was large-scale villa development. One villa near Winchcombe in Gloucestershire was made of Cotswold stone cut into small blocks and was roofed with local Stonesfield slates. Another one in Gloucestershire, Woodchester, was as large as many eighteenth-century country houses.

The best-known villa of all, Fishbourne, near Chichester in Sussex, was discovered in 1960 and has rightly been described as a 'palace'. In the second half of the first century the timber house there was replaced by a substantial house in stone, and the Flavian Palace constructed between AD 75 and AD 80 featured an imposing entrance hall 105 feet long and 60 feet wide and a magnificent audience chamber which has been compared with that in the Palace of Domitian on the Palatine Hill in Rome. There was nothing 'drearily mediocre' about this highly sophisticated edifice which drew on the services of immigrant craftsmen and may have been occupied by Cogidubnus, a client Celtic king who was also made a Roman citizen. One of his coins bore the inscription *Rex Magnus*, 'great king'.

Smaller objects found at Fishbourne make it possible to recapture aspects of everyday Roman life, or at least that of the well off. The absence of brooches amongst the objects suggests that togas and not Celtic garments, which had to be fastened together, were the form of dress; leather shoes were worn. Textile fabrics have disappeared, but there is evidence of the use of cosmetics. And a gold earring and other rings point to the privileges of rank. In the kitchen are pottery jars, which may have contained honey, the only sweetener of the time, and a jar of lentils, all that has survived from a vegetable larder that probably once contained imported figs and poppy seeds, cabbage, lettuce, peas, beans and root crops (but no potatoes, of course, for they were to come to England many centuries later). Fish sauce was particularly prized. Professor Barry Cunliffe, who has catalogued the objects at Fishbourne, has drawn attention also to small pebbles for counting; and although there are no written records, ink wells survive, as do a bronze stylus case and styli for writing on wax tablets. Such artefacts survive from many other Roman towns.

Parts of Fishbourne were destroyed by fire during a time of unrest towards the end of the second century, and the construction of coastline fortifications is evidence of a threat to order elsewhere during the early third century. Yet it is a measure of the extent of regional differences that during this same period the Vale of York was enjoying the full benefits of the *pax Romana* for the first time. Farms there were prospering and the first stone buildings began to appear. It was during the early fourth century that some of the greatest Roman villas were built or extended by landed proprietors who were prepared to spend money lavishly. There was a favourable balance of trade, and exports included woollens as well as corn. Woollen rugs were exported and duffel coats (*byrri Britannici*).

Important legal and constitutional changes separated military and civil structures and had broadened citizenship. They had not, however, reduced social inequalities. Although in 197 serving soldiers were allowed to live with their wives, and fifteen years after that Roman citizenship was granted to all free inhabitants of the Empire, there was an increase later in the number of *equites*, 'equestrians' (the term derives from *equus*, a horse), people enjoying the privileges of the highest Roman rank. The *equites* were people able to pass on to their sons as of right a place in the *ordo equester*; these were the spenders.

As the integrity of the Roman Empire was challenged in the fourth century, the situation favoured not only the lawless, but the rich and the ambitious; and Britain, described by the monk Gildas as 'a stiff-necked and stubborn island', was not alone among the western provinces in displaying what has been called a remarkable 'propensity to produce usurpers'. It is necessary to look back before the fourth century, for example to the rebel naval commander, Carausius, who took possession of Britain following earlier disorders and declared himself Emperor in 286, using sea power to support him. Yet his rule may have been welcomed by people in Britain, who felt that the island on the periphery could be more peaceful than the Empire as a whole: his coins bore the inscription *Genius Britanniae*.

In 367, a brief, but alarming and unprecedented barbarian coalition that included Franks and Saxons from across the North Sea as well as Picts and Scots, required the intervention of an able commander, Theodosius, father of the emperor of the same name, to discipline the Roman troops and pacify the island. Yet there was little he could do to guarantee the security of the long, always vulnerable coastline. No coins were minted in Britain after 326 and imports of coins minted in Rome fell in the late fourth century.

Very few coins were in use by the time of Honorius (395–423), 'the weakest of all Roman emperors', when the situation in Britain was irretrievably transformed. By 401 Roman troops were being withdrawn from Britain for the defence of Italy against Alaric's Goths; and over the next decade, during which troops in Britain proclaimed no fewer than three usurpers, Roman control of western Europe broke down and Alaric sacked Rome itself. Britons were now left to look after their own interests, and Honorius was free from illusions when he wrote not to Roman officials but to the *curiales* in 410 telling them to undertake their own defence. We know from the biographer of St Germanus of Auxerre, who visited Britain four decades later, that by the middle of the fifth century all direct links between Britain and Rome had long since been broken. We know little, however, of who held power.

The biographer of St Germanus, who had come to Britain to preach to Christians attracted by the heresy of Pelagius, Britain's first (or first-remembered) heretic, and who met the *curiales* and prayed at the tomb of St Alban in Verulamium, recorded raids by Saxons from Germany and Picts from north of Hadrian's Wall during his visit. There was nothing new about such raids. The best evidence of them, and of early Saxon settlement, is archaeological. We know more about things than about events, even though they are often difficult to interpret.

The years between 410 and 600, during which Roman control ended and the Saxons settled throughout eastern England, have been described as 'lost centuries' and it is impossible at our distance to judge where history ends and myth begins. There has been as much argument as to who Vortigern, the 'proud tyrant' who, it was claimed, summoned the Saxons in, really was as there has been about the role of Arthur, the reputed hero of the resistance to the Saxon invaders. We do know of their defeat, however, in at least one great battle, Mount Badon, *c.* 520, which temporarily checked their move westwards. The appeal of the Arthurian legend, of a 'once and future king', as Sir Thomas Malory described him in his fifteenth-century *Morte d'Arthur*, has lasted to our own day: in the nineteenth century a symbolic Camelot was created by Tennyson's *Idylls of the King*, and in the twentieth century the name was given to President Kennedy's 'court' in Washington.

Latin culture did not collapse all at once in the sixth century, nor the Christianity which came to enshrine it. Yet, in the face of successive invasions from across the North Sea, society was severely strained. The Roman roads were not maintained; the towns languished and their internal order broke down, although not everywhere at the same time; villas were abandoned, although not necessarily all work on their estates; industries, like the iron industry of the Weald, which had sustained Roman fleets, collapsed, although again not necessarily all at once; and there was no longer a money economy, although coins might be prized as ornaments when they had ceased to be a medium of exchange or a unit of account. Nearly all the issues that concern the social historian of the fifth and sixth centuries centre on the extent of these continuities and discontinuities. Recently there has been a search for social continuities, particularly in the English countryside.

The end of Roman control brought with it very different patterns of life, although it is difficult to identify patterns of authority. They varied from one part of the country to another. The Saxons used knives and spears and made metal ornaments, including brooches and beads, although they did not build in stone or use the potter's wheel until the seventh century. It was not until early in the eighth century that runic characters they brought with them gave way to an alphabet. By then authority was clearly in the hands of 'kings', documented by Church chroniclers, and the rural resources of England seem to have been almost as fully exploited by a relatively mobile population as they were to be in the eleventh century. Light sandy soils tended to be rejected, however, and marshlands went undrained. The most common cereals were barley, oats and wheat, although no ploughs and only a few ploughshares have survived.

Housing was simple, and most of the Saxons lived in very small houses with sunken floors. If Mucking in Essex, a commanding site over a bend in the Thames estuary, is typical, there were no street lines. Yet there were boundary ditches at West Stow in Suffolk. As settlement became more permanent and authority established, impressive royal sites were developed, as at Yeavering in Northumbria. Great mead halls, several of them between eighty and ninety feet long, high ceilinged and made of wood, with walls hung with shields and tapestries – so different from tiny cottages with sunken floors – were at the centre of royal life. The 'joys of the hall' included noisy junketing at festival times and in celebration of great events. Ornamental drinking horns figure prominently in Saxon wills, valuable for the interpretation of later Saxon history, as do silver cups and tapestries. Within the hall minstrels would often be in attendance with their harps – 'singers of men' who, like Christian missionaries, were often 'destined to wander through many lands'.

The great Saxon oral tradition first expressed in the sagas reveals something of early Saxon culture. In the beginning were the gods – Woden and Thor – to whom the names of the days of the week are a continuing testimony. The poem *Beowulf*, of uncertain date, tells us of evil monsters descending 'from crags of mist across the moor', of nature's beauty and power, of the ties of kinship, of ring-givers, of royal deeds of fearless valour and of treachery and feud. Another poet was to note how 'each of us must experience an end to life in this world' and to add 'let him who can achieve glory before he die'. Nonetheless, poets knew that epidemics and famine often came in the aftermath of fighting, and they tell us also of the bands of men who travelled in wooden ships across 'the tempest and terrible toil of the deep' and of the land, the source through toil of a new livelihood.

English land had to be worked in English weather. It was farmed laboriously and passed down from one generation to another through different inheritance customs. Historians are ignorant of the origins of the common-field system, which was to dominate medieval agriculture, although most evidence of land worked in strips in great open fields, and of co-operation between neighbours, comes from later Saxon England. It has been suggested that the oldest element of the common-field system was the right of common grazing on pasture and waste land. Some farmers were pastoralists, and while cattle were most prized, sheep provided milk, meat and wool. Pigs were ubiquitous, but there were few goat herds. Arable farming – mainly of wheat and barley – itself depended on animals, not only for power but for fertilization. Heavy ploughing did not become common until the tenth century.

While settlement continued, there were ebbs and flows of power between one part of the country and another as different kingdoms, some of them British, battled with each other in contests for supremacy which the seventeenth-century poet John Milton was to call the 'wars of kites and crows'. Yet he knew nothing of Saxon treasure. The wealth, power and trading contacts of some of the kingly contestants were revealed in 1939 when a seventh-century East Anglian king's grave was discovered at Sutton Hoo, near Woodbridge in Suffolk. All that remained of the boat in which the king was buried at sea were marks of decayed wood in the sand, but the treasure which went with him included a great silver dish from Byzantium, a jewelled Rhenish sword, an even more elaborate shield with bird and dragon figures, a magnificent helmet, cloisonné shoulder straps, flamboyant polychrome jewellery, coins (before they had come back in to general use) and a unique whetstone sceptre.

The king was a convert to Christianity, but the new religion did nothing to change the basic economics and demography of Saxon England: individual lives were short and personal bonds mattered more than abstract argument. The significance of conversion depended on status and experience. When it was conversion from above, it did not quickly destroy old habits. Kings themselves could abjure their faith, and long after Christianity was taken for granted they could behave in old ways in their marriage and burial arrangements. It is clear also that conversion never dispelled belief in 'magic': it could even lend it new dimensions. Magical wells could become Christian shrines; old oaths, which now might be taken on holy relics or the Bible, and potions drunk out of church bells were believed to be especially efficacious.

The first Saxon king about whom much is known is Aethelbert of Kent, who married a Christian princess and himself converted to Christianity. He was one of many kings, however, some of whom were rich and strong, but only one of whom had widely recognized general authority as *bretwalda* (a kind of 'overlord'). Sussex and Wessex figure in lists of *bretwaldas* before Aethelbert, East Anglia comes in rather later, and Northumbria later still in the seventh century with Edwin, Oswald and Oswy. Each Saxon king traced his ancestry back to the gods, either Woden or Saxneat. Pedigrees mattered. One king of East Anglia felt it expedient to include Caesar among his ancestors, and in Christian times Adam, too, could be added to the list.

Aethelbert's conversion to Christianity came at a time when Kent was a rich kingdom, the importance of which was recognized by Gregory I, the Pope, who sent St Augustine to Canterbury at the head of forty missionaries. Equal importance was attached to the conversion of Edwin in Northumbria, and it was at Yeavering that the Italian monk Paulinus baptized thousands on his first mission in the north. Although Edwin's immediate successor apostatized (like Aethelbert's successor, Eadbald), Northumbria – and the island of Lindisfarne, in particular – very soon became a centre of Christian light and learning. In 664 at Whitby on the Yorkshire coast an important religious synod resolved sharply contested differences between Celtic Christians, whose Christian activity had preceded the Saxon conversion and who had developed their own form of ecclesiastical monastic organization, and Roman Christians, who looked directly to the Pope. The decision went in favour of the latter. Thereafter, before there was one kingdom there was now to be one church. Five years after Whitby an outstanding new 'pastor of flocks', Theodore of Tarsus, Archbishop of Canterbury from 668 to 690, who arrived in England from Asia Minor, did much to create and consolidate its diocesan structure. In Northumbria another pastor of flocks, Benedict Biscop, founded monastic churches at Monkwearmouth and Jarrow, decorating their walls with Roman paintings. Some of them revealed how the events of the New Testament had been foretold in the Old.

Oswy, the king of Northumbria, defeated Penda, the pagan king of Mercia (the middle kingdom), who is said to have given his name to the penny, in 655, but soon afterwards Mercia enjoyed a period of supremacy (670–796) with a royal centre at Tamworth and authority over people as different as the hill-folk of the Peak District, Shropshire and the Chilterns and the plains-dwellers of Lindsey and the Fens. Indeed, Wulfhere, the Mercian king who broke Northumbrian supremacy, was even in a position to sell the bishopric of London, dispose of the Isle of Wight and control Hastings in Sussex. A later Mercian king, Offa (757–96), was described in his time as *Rex Anglorum*. Later chroniclers claimed that he founded St Albans Abbey and a short-lived archbishopric: with its centre not at Canterbury but at Lichfield. It has a special place in the social history of England. The distribution of his coins suggests widespread, if small-scale, trade; and one gold coin, his dinar, indicates that it extended even beyond Europe to the distant Caliphate. (The word 'mint' had been borrowed by the Saxons from the Latin of the Roman Empire before they invaded England. So had the word 'street'.) Offa is also known for his great dyke, over seventy miles in length, which provided a line of defence against the Celts, often through mountainous country from the Irish Sea to the Bristol Channel. It has been called the greatest public work of the Saxon age.

While the power of kings was apparent both in their trading contacts and in their deeds, the power of bishops was obvious, too, in the eighth century. A gallery of Saxon saints figures prominently in the great history concluded in 731 by the Venerable Bede, who spent most of his life at Monkwearmouth and Jarrow – in his own words 'almost under the north pole'. Bede (672/3?-735) was a great historian, unwilling to use his powerful imagination to fill in gaps in the available historical evidence ('it is said that' was one of his favourite prefixes). Like many of his contemporaries, he was fascinated by surviving prehistoric remains, which were thought of as the work of 'cunning giants'. The Anglo-Saxon language had no future tense. Bede was not, however, writing 'simple ecclesiastical history', the title of his book, but a species of chronicle and hagiography, in which the English people are sometimes described in the same terms St Paul used about the people of Israel.

The late eighth century was a peaceful period of cultural vitality, particularly impressive in the 'age of Alcuin', as it has been called. Alcuin of York (c. 735–804) was educated in the cathedral school there, but spent much of his life in Charlemagne's Europe. He was a prolific letter writer as well as a theologian, and his letters (very few of them in English) covered an immense range of subjects from law to chant, natural history and astronomy. His was also the age of the superbly illuminated gospels, the famous crosses at Bewcastle and Ruthwell, and the first royal charters (not from Northumbria but from Kent and Sussex). Meanwhile, in the south, the first codes of laws had been drafted: that of Ine of Wessex dates back to the late sixth century. The power of Wessex began to increase and under Alfred in the ninth century it was to prove the winner in the contests for kingly supremacy.

We know most about Saxon society from its codes of law, although, as historians have pointed out, they may be suspected of revealing more about society as it should have been than as it actually was. There is no doubt, however, about the appeal of surviving cultural evidence. The Lindisfarne Gospels, written and illuminated in the half-century before Alcuin, are only one magnificent example. The beauty of Saxon script was in marked contrast to the formality of Roman inscription.

All the many signs of cultural renaissance were overshadowed, however, by 'dire portents' which began to appear over Northumbria in the late eighth century: 'immense whirlwinds . . . flashes of lightning . . . and fiery dragons . . . flying in the air'. The Viking raids had begun. The earliest raids were not carried out by Norsemen we know as Danes but by Norwegians. Their immediate consequences were beyond dispute: material loss, humiliation for men and women (rape figures in the accounts as well as murder), a threat to precariously established 'civilization' (already of a very different kind from Roman civilization) and, following the first raids on the north of England, a geographical switch in power from north to south that was not to shift back until the industrial revolution of the eighteenth and early nineteenth centuries. Lindisfarne was sacked in 793, York was taken, 'the sanctuaries of God' were desecrated, 'the bodies of the saints trampled on like dung in the street'. No fewer than three bishoprics disappeared.

It has been pointed out recently that since many accounts of Viking attacks were written by monks or priests – they wrote little or nothing about themselves – the size of their attacking fleets and the violence of their assaults, particularly on churches and holy places, may well have been exaggerated. Yet while it was in part the paganism of the Vikings which led them to assume the character of a scourge – they were even

The Anglo-Saxons and the Danes

described as the anti-Christ – the exceptional violence of their raids is difficult to dispute. They themselves were silent about their hopes and fears. At first, they may have cared more for loot than for land, but, unlike the first Saxon invaders, they were interested also in trade. Their land hunger was noted by King Alfred. He was once told by a Viking guest how the lands from which he came in the north of Europe were 'very long and very narrow', and that all that could either be pastured or ploughed lay by the sea, 'though it is in some parts very rocky'. The guest, Alfred noted, was 'one of the first men in that country, yet he had not more than twenty horned cattle, twenty sheep and twenty swine, and the little that he ploughed he ploughed with horses'.

It is the Danes, drawn to lowland England, who have passed into English history. They came in different kinds of ships to meet different needs, all requiring remarkable skills to handle them, many carrying large numbers of armed men and, sometimes, horses. They continued to fight after they began to settle in the north and the east, and soon conquered Northumbria, Mercia and East Anglia, thus breaking down the old, if loose, divisions of the Saxon kingdoms. Alfred, who became King of Wessex in 849, was the first king able to withstand them after they had sent a great army in 865. 'With a small company he moved into inaccessible places . . . and continued fighting against the Viking host.' Having fought them to a standstill, he thereby established the power of a West Saxon dynasty which was to last for nearly 200 years, and a reputation as a hero that was to appeal even longer: later generations, including the Victorian, were to bracket his name with that of Arthur. At the time not all Englishmen thought of him as a supreme leader, but his achievements were immediately manifest, and most of them had substantial social implications. He was one of the few kings in any age to write books. He designed candles marked to tell the time. His is the first surviving code of law in its original form. By building ships, by reconstructing his army or *fyrd*, by erecting fortified towns or *burghs* (some of them on or near the sites of iron age or Roman forts), and by defining boundaries, one of which ran for fifty miles along the old Roman road, Watling Street, Alfred ensured that the Danes were contained in a huge region of their own, which in the eleventh century became known as Danelaw. The imposition of Danish law in large parts of this region did not mean, however, that the whole area was colonized by Danes: their main settlements were in Leicestershire, Lincolnshire, Nottinghamshire and Yorkshire.

An important element in Viking activities was the extortion of payments of treasure from the Saxons. From 991 (under King Ethelred) such payments were made at frequent intervals, and for a long time they achieved their immediate object, so that Alfred's successors, from whichever part of England they came, benefited from years of peace. Indeed, the greatest of them, Ethelred's father, Edgar, who died in 975, had already earned the title the 'Peaceable'. He was crowned at Bath in 973 as King of all England, and when he held court at Chester in the north, eight lesser kings rowed him up the Dee. He had been crowned by a saintly monk, Dunstan, who was born near Glastonbury, was related to the royal family, and was later to become first Abbot of Glastonbury and in 960 Archbishop of Canterbury. Edgar himself was deeply devoted to a monastic ideal that gripped many of his contemporaries, women as well as men, after a period when the first monasteries had declined. He is known for his coins, however, as well as for his prayers: one of them showed the Hand of Providence emerging from a cloud.

On Edgar's death further internal 'strife threw the kingdom into turmoil, shire against shire', and a further series of Viking raids culminated in the taking over of the whole country by the Danish King Cnut (1017–35). The fact that in 1012 the Danegeld, a term not used at the time, had begun to be collected on a regular basis as an organized land tax had not saved the Saxons; and the tax continued to be levied on a regular basis on into the twelfth century long after Cnut's conquest. It was calculated, like earlier Saxon taxes (and claims on military service), on the basis of the hide as a land unit. Church taxes took the form of tithes (a tenth of income in cash or kind) with additional payments at particular times of the year, beginning with 'plough alms'.

Measurement obviously mattered increasingly to Saxons and Danes alike – to rulers and ruled – by the eleventh century. Although units like the hide were not uniform in all parts of England, all Englishmen were made to know very early in their history precisely what taxes meant. Thus, in 1041 King Harthacnut ordered the whole of Worcestershire to be punished because two of his thanes had been murdered in Worcester Cathedral when they were collecting taxes.

Hides were thought of imprecisely at first as the amounts of land necessary to support one labourer's family. By the eleventh century there were far bigger land units as well, for already England had been divided into shires, also unequal in size and wealth, later to be called counties. Some were ancient kingdoms, like Kent; most were to remain as territorial units into the twentieth century. In late Saxon England each shire had a court which met twice a year and was presided over by the king's representative, the shire-reeve (sheriff), and the shires in their turn were divided into hundreds (or in the lands of the Danes, wapentakes), again unequal in size and each with its own court. The shire court was the court most used by the rural population who lived in villages or in scattered countryside.

The urban population remained small, although there had been trading centres in each of the major Saxon kingdoms from the seventh century onwards, some of them relatively large, like Southampton (seventy-two acres). Not far away, Winchester, the Roman city which retained its pre-Roman name, *Venta Belgarum*, was refounded in the ninth century, and may have had 10,000 inhabitants. There were a number of primary centres inland such as Banbury and Melton Mowbray in the Midlands and Maidstone in Kent, where there might also be links with older settlements, both Roman and pre-Roman. York had at least 8,000 and Norwich and Lincoln 5,000 inhabitants. At the far end of the scale, London, which had been described by Bede as an 'emporium' for people coming by sea as well as by land and which was already capital of a religious see, may have had more than 12,000 inhabitants by the eleventh century. It had twenty 'moneyers' simultaneously minting coins in 1042.

In all the larger towns there was an interest in mercantile contacts which had nothing to do with older ties to kinsmen; in finance, which meant making money as well as coining it; and in order, which could only be deemed secure if there were conditions of internal and external peace.

Danish kings, like Saxon kings, thought of themselves as unifiers and as lawgivers, and Cnut's 'dooms' or laws were the most advanced in Europe. There was an obvious irony here: the word 'law', which implies the very reverse of arbitrary violence, is a Danish word by origin, as the great historian Maitland pointed out, so that 'if we can today distinguish between *law* and *right*, we are debtors to the Danes.' Kings were expounding the law, not inventing it; and the oldest law was the best. By the tenth century the laws reveal a carefully defined hierarchy, although a man's position in society was determined not only by the law but also by custom and titles, which differed from one part of the country to another. Kindred was still the basis of status, and freedom itself was divisible. At the base were the completely unfree, the slaves, some of them descendants of pre-Saxon peoples, some victims of individual or family misfortune. Above them were large numbers of half-free people, cottagers who were closely tied in their work and obligation to their lord's will; they were not paid, nor did they pay rent, and the Normans were to call them villeins. At the top were magnates, warriors or descendants of warriors. The bond between man and lord, expressed in different ways, was paramount, and men without lords were outside the basic social structures, unless they were lords themselves.

As lesser men came to depend more on their lords than on their kinsmen, the fact of lordship came to be given greater prominence than the fact of kinship. Thus, the laws of Alfred laid down that 'a man may fight on behalf of his lord if the lord is being attacked without incurring a vendetta' and that 'a man may fight on behalf of his born kinsman, if he is being wrongly attacked, except against his lord; that we do not allow'. Kinship language had its limits. The word 'mann' could be used of both genders, just as the word 'bearn' ('bairn') could be used of both boys and girls. The old English word 'wif' means 'woman': its compound 'witman' is the word from which 'woman' derives. It is etymologically related to the word for weaving. Meanwhile, the first spinsters were the women who spun. The word 'husbandry' leads back to the land.

A tenth-century monk, Aelfric, 'Aelfric Grammaticus', Abbot of Eynsham, an early master of English prose, simplified the reality of the social structure as Alfred himself had done in an aside to one of his translations. He explained that the throne stood upon 'three supports': *laboratores, oratores* and *bellatores*.

> *Laboratores* are they who provide us with sustenance, ploughmen and husbandmen devoted to that alone.
>
> *Oratores* are they who intercede for us to God and promote Christianity among Christian peoples in the service of God, as spiritual toil devoted to that alone for the benefit of us all.
>
> *Bellatores* are they who guard our boroughs and also our land, fighting with weapons against the oncoming army.

This three-fold division, inadequate and incomplete though it was –
and it became increasingly so – was to be taken for granted for centuries,
as the later three-fold division into lower, middle and upper ranks or
classes was to be. So too was the lack of freedom at the base. Aelfric's
ploughman ended his complaint with the simple words, 'It is very hard
work because I am not free.' Aelfric also gave a vivid description of
what the ploughman had to do.

> I work very hard. I go out at dawn and I drive the oxen in the field and
> yoke them to the plough. However stark the winter is, I dare not stay
> at home, for fear of my lord. I have to yoke the oxen and fasten the
> share and coulter to the plough, and every day I have to plough a full
> acre or more. I have a boy who drives the oxen with a goad, and even
> now he is hoarse from cold and shouting. I fill the ox-bins with hay and
> water and I clear out the dung.

Aelfric's capacity for empathy introduces a new kind of input into
English social history, something very different from classification.
Observers could be both interested in and concerned for the experience
of people very different from themselves.

Later generations were to simplify these structures in a different way
from Aelfric, distinguishing simply between *eorls*, men with authority,
and *ceorls* (churls), the simple: the rhyming was irresistible. In fact, there
were as many divisions among the *ceorls* as there were among the *eorls*
or *thegas* (thanes), men who had originally been the king's companions
(*gesiths*). In the eleventh century some *ceorls* moved upwards, but more
moved downwards, augmenting the ranks of the half-free. Many of
them passed on their land as husbandmen from one generation to
another, but in Kent, from the start a kingdom with a difference, it was
divided into portions. Moreover, the proportions and status of people
in different social groups varied from one part of the country to another.
Some *ceorls* could be slave-owners in Kent, but in Wessex, even if they
were rich, their wealth could not secure them the highest social status
unless they owned the land. The average landholding of a *ceorl*, however,
was small.

There was no pretence of equality. Stag-hunting, fox-hunting and
hawking were reserved for the lords, who did not work with their
hands; and some parish priests were treated as household servants by
lords who had themselves set up the parish churches. If families which

owned an abbey had no eligible candidate to be abbot, the right of promotion could be sold and bought. Nonetheless, through Church poverty there could be avenues of individual mobility. Kings might deliberately prefer priests as their advisers to the kinsmen of great families. They were in a strong position to introduce reforms from above, for only they could guarantee the donation of land to the Church or secure its retention.

Women occupied a formal place within the Saxon social system, as they did in the system of work. They cleaned and cooked, but they also milked goats and ewes, sheared sheep and made clothes. They had figured in the earliest law code, that of Aethelbert of Kent (c. 600), when widows' compensation was specified carefully but cryptically: 'if a woman bear a living child, she shall have half the goods left by her husband if he dies first.' In many ways women were highly privileged in this period, as they had been at times in pre-Roman Britain, compared to later centuries: they could not be compelled to marry a man they disliked: divorce was easy; in the higher ranks of society they could own land and other property, receive gifts on marriage, including furniture and houses, and make wills; there are seven instances of women disinheriting their sons. Their influence could be substantial.

The last successful invaders of England, the Normans, who came in 1066, were to introduce new features into the social structure, which they tightened and formalized. Yet they were of Viking stock, and their adoption of French had only recently been completed. Moreover, the Norman invasion itself was immediately preceded by a Scandinavian invasion: the last Saxon king, Harold II (1066), had been victorious in a bloody and decisive battle against the Norwegian leader Harold Hardrada near Stamford Bridge in Yorkshire immediately before he was defeated by the Normans near Hastings. William, 'the Conqueror', moved on to London and was crowned King by the Archbishop of York (Ealdred) at Westminster on Christmas Day 1066.

The Norman victory has been seen by a historian of medieval technology as a triumph of the military methods of the eleventh century over those of the seventh: Harold fought without cavalry, with a few archers and with a shield wall: William the Conqueror had employed shod and stirruped horses and bowmen. This, however, was not the contemporary interpretation. Instead, a feeling of guilt and divine retribution was strong. The biographer of a supporter of William I (1066–87), Bishop Wulfstan, was to write angrily, for example:

> Such was the feebleness of the wretched people that after the first battle they never attempted to rise up for liberty behind a common shield. It was as though with Harold had fallen also the whole strength of the country.

Anger – or contempt – shapes historical judgements more often than empathy.

The long-term consequences of the Norman invasion have been much debated, Some historians have opted retrospectively for the benefits derived from the arrival of the 'constructive' Normans, drawn from Europe's mainland and facing south rather than north. Other historians have extolled the 'free' Saxons, struggling against what proved to be a 'Norman yoke'. Most historians, however, have emphasized the continuities, following the example of William himself, who promised to respect and maintain ancient customs. He had crossed the sea to become king, not unjustly by force of arms alone, but, so he claimed, 'in defence of right', promised the crown by Edward the Confessor (1042–66).

The Normans were to prove effective colonizers, endowed with a 'habit of authority', but critical voices were never entirely silenced, and a myth was sustained that there had been a golden age before they arrived and imposed their yoke. Even in Mrs Markham's highly popular *History of England*, published in 1823, two children who have been reading about Saxon England are reminded by their mother, 'As the Saxons continued in the country after the Conquest, and were much more numerous than the Norman settlers, we are still almost all of us chiefly of Saxon descent; and our language, and many of our habits and customs sufficiently declare our origin.'

3 DEPENDENCE, EXPANSION AND CULTURE

Norman saw on English oak
On English neck a Norman yoke;
Norman spoon in English dish,
And England ruled as Normans wish:
Blithe world to England never will be more
Till England's rid of all the four.

Wamba in Sir Walter Scott, *Ivanhoe*, 1820

What concern is it of monks – men who have resolved to flee the world – what does it matter to them, who serves in the world, or under what name? Is not every man born to labour as a bird in flight?

St Anselm, *Letter to Two Monks*, 1081

Servitude is ordained by God, either because of the sins of those who become serfs, or as a trial, in order that those who are thus humbled may be made better.

Twelfth-century theological fragment

The framework of institutions which governs a society can in the last resort be understood only through a knowledge of the whole human environment.

Marc Bloch, *Feudal Society*, 1961

Domesday Book, meticulously drawn up for William I county by county twenty years after the Conquest, was an invaluable, although incomplete, survey (*descriptio*) of England's land and people. Its compilers set out to register on sheepskin pages 'what or how much everybody had who was occupying land in England in land or cattle, and how much it was worth'. As a written record, produced in a society which was largely oral in its modes of communication, the Domesday Book was used practically for reference, often reverentially, in subsequent centuries after economy, society and administration had substantially changed, and at the time it confirmed land tenure – and was followed by a great oath-taking. Yet it was not called the Domesday Book until the twelfth century, and it was not published in book form until 1783. It was a survey without precedent, and in the late twentieth century the material that it contains lends itself to computer analysis.

F. W. Maitland, the great late nineteenth-century historian of the Domesday Book, predicted correctly in 1897, without thought of computers, that 'a century hence' the 'substance' of Domesday Book would have been rearranged. 'Those villages and hundreds which the Norman clerks tore into shreds' would have been 'reconstituted'. The computer has made this possible. At the time a chronicler put it very differently. Awed but shocked by the formidable effort behind the survey, he complained that 'it was a shame to tell, though he [William] thought it no shame to do, [that] there was not even an ox or a cow or a pig left that was not set down in writing.' The inquest, as it has also been called, revealed great local variations both in population and in customs and procedures. Population was very unevenly distributed. The north was particularly thinly settled and the east densely populated, but even in counties like Warwickshire, where there were substantial numbers of people, some woodland areas were sparsely peopled. There was already relatively dense settlement in the prime arable areas of the country like Norfolk, Suffolk and Leicestershire. Modern estimates of England's total population, extrapolated from Domesday patterns, vary between one and three million. The extent of such variations reflects the disagreement among experts concerning the multiplier that should be used to convert entries in Domesday Book into a population census.

The Conquest had immediate economic, social and cultural implications, yet William expressed his desire for counsel, and on the eve of the survey 'had deep speech with his wise men about this land, how it was peopled, and by what sort of men'. By then the old English thanes had lost their land and, therefore, their influence, and a new, tough and resilient aristocracy, which took over some of the Saxon estates intact, had acquired power. By 1100 there were five hundred Norman castles, symbols of power, scattered throughout the English countryside at strategic points – among them Windsor Castle, scanning the Thames Valley. There was a break in the Church too. Saxon bishops were either deposed or replaced by Normans after their deaths, and the organization of the Church, both monasteries and cathedrals, was reshaped. By 1080 only one of the sixteen Saxon bishoprics was held by a native Englishman, and six of the diocesan centres had been moved to bigger towns.

England was drawn at once into close cultural links with the other side of the Channel. Lanfranc, for example, the new Archbishop of Canterbury in 1070, was a former Prior of Bec and Abbot of Caen; he was also a former teacher of the Pope. And many monks followed in his wake. At first, they were Benedictine 'black monks' who came from the great reformed abbeys in Normandy and went on to establish themselves in English towns, many of them cathedral sees: there were already thirty-five Benedictine monasteries when the Normans arrived. Half a century later the Cistercian 'white monks' arrived. Unlike the Benedictines, they founded their monasteries – and these were soon numerous – in secluded places far from centres of population. Rievaulx, Fountains and Byland Abbeys, for example, were built by them within a century of the Conquest. The years from 1070 to 1216 have been described as 'the monastic period of English spirituality', but while monks were living a life apart, new Norman barons were helping in the process of ecclesiastical reorganization.

There was a language gap between the local population and the new landowners, both churchmen and aristocracy. Latin was a language of mysteries; Norman French was now the language of law and authority, and the first 'loan words' into English included castle and prison, cardinal and prior. Inflected English, spoken differently in the various regions of the country, a legacy of earlier settlement patterns, remained the language of the people. It was not displaced, and the *Anglo-Saxon Chronicle* was continued for nearly half a century after the Conquest. (Soon many of the inflections were to disappear.) The novelist Sir Walter Scott was to suggest centuries later that in Norman times 'Old Alderman Ox continues to hold his Saxon epithet while he is under the charge of serfs and bondsmen, but becomes Beef, a fiery French gallant, when he arrives before the worshipful jaws that are to consume him.' The suggestion was wrong, however, for it was not until the eighteenth century that differences between the words for animals in the field and on the plate became generalized. Until then, a farmer could graze 'muttons' and eat mutton. Language develops in complex ways, yet precisely because English was neither spoken by the colonists nor taught in the schools, it developed from below as a particularly rich language, taking time to move up the social scale.

Norman society rested, as Saxon society had done, on 'lordship', secular and spiritual, and the king, wise or foolish, was the lord of lords, with only the Lord in Heaven and the saints above him. Abbot Walter of Evesham claimed that the Norman victory in 1066 had demonstrated the inadequacy of prayers addressed to the old English saints. William, pressing for continuity and consent, developed the custom of wearing his crown in three of the important towns of southern England on the greatest feast days of the Church. In the north of England, however, he was to reveal his power in different fashion: there he laid waste to vast stretches of Yorkshire.

Because the crown was his by conquest, William was able to acquire a huge royal demesne for himself, in size double that of Edward the Confessor. All land belonged to the crown, and all the great landholders to whom William directly parcelled out land, were his tenants-in-chief. Bishops and abbots received 26 per cent of the land, lay barons 49 per cent. There were 170 tenants-in-chief, holding their land at William's gift and in return for specified services. There were no absolute freeholds, secular or ecclesiastical, and the tenants-in-chief parcelled out land in their own demesnes to their own tenants. They also required knightly service from them. During William's reign they were owed service by at least 4,000 knights, who were distinguishable as a social group from their lords. The two groups have sometimes been lumped together as 'powerful men' as opposed to 'poor men', both by historians and in medieval schemes of classification, but neither group was homogeneous. Each included great and small.

Historians have introduced into their interpretation of Norman (and other European) lordships the term 'feudalism', first employed during the seventeenth century by lawyers, and William was himself a feudatory of the King of France. The term 'feudalism' may be set alongside 'capitalism' and 'imperialism', other 'isms' which have acquired an overextended use in relation to all societies and which invite comparisons between them at different periods of time and at different 'stages' of development. Since Karl Marx first discussed 'the transition from feudalism to capitalism' as one of these 'stages', much has been written about feudalism by social and political historians. They have emphasized that feudalism was neither a static nor a uniform system, and they have used the term in both a broad and a narrow sense. Narrowly, it has been related to military (knightly) service as a condition of tenure of land. Broadly, it has been related to the tenure of the land itself, to obligation and dependence, as expressed in the concept of vassalage. The first relationship focuses on warfare in an age of violence, the second on the use as well as on the tenure of land in an age when possession of land was the key to a position in society.

Both interpretations have their point, even though there was no 'feudal revolution' in 1066 or later. Between the Norman Conquest and the Black Death of 1348 there was only one period of domestic peace in England lasting more than thirty years, and for much of the time Englishmen were involved in wars across the Channel. There was little new immigration into England, and Normandy was lost in 1204, but a new and bigger English stake in France was secured when Henry II (1154–89), who had married Eleanor of Aquitaine in 1152, acquired territories in the south and west of France, including Bordeaux, and founded 'the Angevin Empire'. The military service and dues owed to the crown therefore mattered profoundly throughout the period, both when the king was in command, as William I or Henry I (1100–35) were, and when there was baronial anarchy, as there was under Stephen (1135–54).

Permission to build a castle, a licence to crenellate, had to be secured from the king, and the king had the right to garrison men there in case of need. Yet rivalry between tenants-in-chief could be endemic, and 'adulterine castles' were built which had no royal warrant. The chronicler William of Malmesbury, writing from the vantage point of a monastery, claimed, not without irony, that many castles nominally 'defending their neighbourhoods' were 'more probably speaking, laying them to waste': 'the garrisons drove off from the fields both sheep and cattle, nor did they abstain from churches or church yards.' It was a sign of the effective power of Henry II, Stephen's great successor, who reconstructed law and government, that while he destroyed large numbers of adulterine castles, he built only one completely new castle for himself. It was at Orford in Suffolk and it had a magnificent polygonal keep.

By making justice available to all free men Henry II laid the foundations of the common law which derived from older customary law, but was capable of evolution through judgements reached in particular cases. This was to have long-term consequences since Roman law remained the law in many other European countries, including Scotland. Meanwhile, the criminal law was tightened up and more severely enforced in the interest of order. English feudalism did not involve, therefore, a general fragmentation of public authority. An apparatus of centralized government was created which has been praised for its 'rationality'. Royal revenues were carefully accounted and new administrative procedures introduced even before the Exchequer moved to Westminster under John (1199–1216), Henry's youngest son. It was also under John that Normandy was lost in war by the English crown.

The loss of Normandy broke many family links, and the fortunes of William's first great tenants-in-chief subsequently diverged. Two of the first substantial beneficiaries, both of whom had fought at Hastings and both of whom retained lands and influence in Normandy as well as England, had been William Fitz Osbern, who was given a new base at Winchester, the old capital of Wessex, and William de Warenne, who acquired huge and widely scattered estates in Normandy as well as England. Following the loss of Normandy the fortunes of the Fitz Osberns went rapidly down, while those of the de Warennes stayed up. By the end of the twelfth century many of the leading Domesday families had already disappeared. Only thirty-six of the English tenancies-in-chief, or baronies, remained within the same male line for the period from 1066 to 1327.

In each new generation new families regularly emerged, often 'raised from the dust' by royal favour: they consolidated their position by the right marriages to the right heiresses at the right time. The wheel of fortune continued to turn. The Lisles, for example, benefited greatly from a series of successful marriages that led from knighthood to nobility, while the Peverels suffered from a succession of daughters as heiresses. Conscious marriage strategy became a necessary means to the hereditary transmission of estates, for, if it failed, land reverted to the crown through escheat. Nonetheless, whichever families prospered, the gap between the many and the few remained as wide as ever. On the one side were the *pauperes*, poor people; on the other the powerful, the *potentes*.

English radicals in succeeding centuries were to complain, therefore, not only of a loss of native freedom in 1066, but of a continuing 'rain of locusts' generation by generation: Tom Paine, the eighteenth-century radical inspired by the French Revolution, was to suggest that, despite Magna Carta, 'the country is yet disfigured with the marks' of Norman-imposed authority. A century later, however, a diametrically opposed view was expressed by Sir John Fortescue, historian of the British army. England had passed, he observed of the country after 1066, 'to her great good fortune, under the sway of a race that could teach her to obey'; and he saw the strengthening of lineage as a strengthening of the nation.

Such sharply contrasting verdicts reflect significant differences in Englishmen's approach to the whole shape of English social history. Radicals were to condemn privilege and, with Church as well as State in mind, to welcome dissent; conservatives were to praise deference and to defend obedience. In time, of course, all these qualities were deemed to be distinctively 'English'. So too, in most, but not all, generations, was consensus. Incompatibilities could be conveniently treated as complementarities.

In fact, lords themselves, big or small, cultivated only one-third to two-fifths of the arable land in use. The rest outside their demesnes, which they reserved for their own use, was cultivated by various kinds of 'peasants', although this was a controversial term not in use at the time. The contemporary terms were *villani*, villeins (41 per cent of the total group, holding 45 per cent of the land); *bordarii*, cottagers or small householders (32 per cent of the total group, holding 5 per cent of the land); *liberi homines*, free men (14 per cent of the total group, holding 20 per cent of the land); and *servi*, serfs (10 per cent of the total group with no land at all). Work on the lord's demesne itself was a feudal obligation; it varied in scale and scope from one part of the country to another.

Taking the country as a whole there was a great variety of status relationships, few of them completely fixed. For this reason the initial proportions of the different social groups did not hold: there is evidence, for example, that the number of *servi* fell even between 1066 and 1086, when the Domesday Book was commissioned. The basic distinction between free and unfree, which was tersely expressed in a lawyer's dictum of the twelfth century that 'all men are either free or serfs', as simple as a modern economist's dictum that all men are rich or poor, did not save society from continuing argument or litigation. There were always many intermediate status grades, some surviving from Saxon England, and great regional variations, all with their own history. There were, for example, significant differences between Sussex and Kent, where gavelkind, the inheritance system under which land was divided between heirs, was perpetuated and seemed to go with freedom. In the old northern Danelaw, too, free tenants were sometimes a majority of the village population. During the second half of the twelfth century social grades were more sharply defined as the legal system took shape. In the process, however, dependence also was more clearly articulated. 'Unfreedom' could be proved by 'suit of kin', the witness of relatives; and while the law insisted that tenants be dealt with justly 'in accordance with the judgement and reasonable custom of the lord's court', it also offered assistance to a lord who was not 'powerful enough to constrain his tenant in respect of his services or customs'.

Complexities were accentuated by the fact that rural England was divided into both villages (or hamlets) and manors, the latter basic economic units like factories in 'modern times'. They did not necessarily share the same boundaries. A village might be divided between two or more manors, and a lord might hold manors in several villages. Such differences sprang from the fact that while a manor was a piece of landed property held by a lord and managed, at least in the first instance, from a single centre, the village was a community of people living side by side, with or without a lord in residence: at its centre was the parish church, a place of recreation as well as prayer. Two adjacent manors might be quite different in their organization and customs, therefore, just as two adjacent villages might be quite different in their size, appearance, social composition and wealth. Manorial records, among them the records of the manorial court, are an invaluable historical source.

Leicestershire, where W. G. Hoskins has traced the history of the village of Wigston Magna through the centuries, provides good examples of these complexities. In Wigston there was an absentee landlord and nearly half the land in the village, which had grown in size and numbers under the Danelaw, was owned – a term which was beginning to count for more by the thirteenth century – by smaller landlords 'of free condition'. But other Leicestershire villages were in a quite different position, dominated by particular families over a long period of time. Yet even in manors like those, where there was an active landlord in residence, service in kind required of the bondsmen could vary substantially, the heaviest services tending to be demanded on the estates that were of largest or of oldest formation. It is impossible to generalize. The heaviest labour obligation, 'weekwork' (regular work for the lord on his land), was required in some villages and not in others.

One of the most important general points about the Domesday pattern, much of which was to change drastically between the eleventh century and the end of the thirteenth, was that nine out of ten people still lived in completely rural communities. The remaining people were not necessarily 'urban' dwellers. Only one out of twenty-five people lived in the ten towns with over 2,000 residents – they included York, Norwich, Lincoln, Stamford and Leicester – and nearly half of this group lived in London. There are many references to 'boroughs' in Domesday, but they were places of quite different kinds. The large boroughs (burghs) were fortified, with markets and with courts. The rest were centres where farming prevailed, but where other occupations were represented; a bishop, for example, might work in such a centre, or a sheriff, the royal official in the shire on whom the king initially depended. There could also be craftsmen, among them masons, potters, weavers and tanners. Rural craftsmen included potters in Wiltshire, smiths in several counties, and ironworkers in Devon and the West Riding of Yorkshire. Some occupations were clearly not represented in the returns: only one carpenter was mentioned in the whole of the countryside (in Herefordshire), and in a country where much fish was eaten, there were far too few fishermen in the count to have satisfied their fellow countrymen except by a miracle.

One of the surprising facts in Domesday Book, which gave no details of the yield of crops – or of communications, is that a large proportion of the land under the plough in 1914 was already being tilled in 1086. Moreover, daily life in the fields was going on as it had done before the Conquest, although the increased use of heavy ploughs made it easier to reclaim land and to extend cultivation. Unlike the Anglo-Saxons and the Danes, the Normans were not drawn to England by a desire to farm land, and their arrival brought no changes in farming practices, except, perhaps, for the laying down of vineyards, some of which, after a long interlude, have been restored in recent years. The fields were dug in the autumn, harrowed in winter and sown in spring, but the busiest time of the year was the late-summer harvest. Every year much of the land was left fallow. If too much land was cultivated, the number of livestock maintained would fall. By the thirteenth century, however, after protracted expansion of the area of land under cultivation, careful attention, well documented, was being paid to the economics of farming.

The full implications of the intricate social, political and cultural changes following the Norman Conquest took time to work themselves out. Nor did all the changes point in the same direction. Constitutional and administrative historians have focused on the development of strong royal government and the emergence of English common law, moving, unlike the Roman law, from precedent to precedent, before turning to the sometimes stormy relationship between the king and the barons and the making of Parliament. Economic historians have focused on a striking growth in population – with short-term set-backs – which may have raised it at its peak to well above four million, and on an expansion of cultivation, often by small men without power, towards and into poorer marginal lands. They have also examined in some detail the development, marked from the twelfth century onwards, of trade, commerce and urbanization.

Both constitutional and economic themes have their social dimensions. Thus the presence in Parliament in the reign of Edward I (1272–1307) not only of lords, bishops and great abbots but also of a 'commons' demonstrated the increasing wealth of townsmen and knights of the shire and their growing consequence in the local communities which they represented, while the fact that townsmen and knights sat together encouraged the merchants and feudal elements, divided in many political societies, to think of their common interests. Parliament was a new device before it became an established institution. It was a device to secure consent, particularly to collect taxes, but inevitably it involved processes of bargaining.

The levying of taxation was regarded as 'the hardest task which the king and his advisors could undergo'. William I had levied heavy 'gelds' which hit surviving Saxon landowners hard: he once besieged Exeter, which had refused to pay, for eighteen days. One of the most interesting books written in the reign of Henry II is Richard Fitzneale's *Dialogue of the Exchequer*, completed around 1179, in which the author describes the working of the king's Exchequer, complete with its abacus, the computer of the age, brought in, like the system of numerals, from the distant Arab world. Fitzneale stated categorically that the 'state of the realm' depended on the wealth of the king. The king's subjects might look at the matter differently. Taxation, particularly for war, was the hardest burden imposed upon them.

It was largely because of disputes about taxation that John was forced by his barons in 1215 to seal Magna Carta, which linked taxation with consent. Pressure on the pocket (though there were no pockets in men's clothes at this time) is more quickly felt than pressure on the mind. Already it was possible through 'fines' for barons to substitute cash for feudal military service, and this could be a mutually acceptable device. It was also possible for barons to secure cash from knights who did not wish to serve through 'scutage'. To carry out his policies John had been forced to look for additional funds. For example, he added extra charges to marriage and wardship dues. Harassed as most kings were – and were to be – by the demands of war, he had extorted maximum feudal payments, thereby irritating many of his most powerful subjects, who had many valuable privileges of their own *vis-à-vis* those dependent on themselves. He had extended further more novel taxes on incomes (thirtieths, sevenths and even fourths). Opposition was inevitable, and Magna Carta was a somewhat hastily drafted document dealing essentially with the privileges claimed by Norman barons. Nonetheless, over the years, while tax systems were to change, it was to become part of the English constitutional inheritance, because the claims for privileges set out in its clauses could in time be translated into a universal language of freedom and justice.

Later medieval kings were to rely increasingly not only on feudal dues but on what were in effect general property taxes levied on people in towns as well as people in the country, and, from the reign of Edward I (1272–1307) on levies on trade and customs duties. Once again there was a link between economics and politics, since in order to secure necessary assent the king was forced to turn increasingly to 'parliaments'. As early as the 1240s chroniclers wrote of 'most general' or 'great' parliaments to which prelates, earls and barons were summoned by the king's sealed writ, and in 1265 the 'commons' began to be summoned to some of them too. They attended only one in eight parliaments before 1284, but one in three in the later years of Edward I's reign. From Edward I's reign onwards kings were able to tax the clergy without the Pope's permission and to share in the levies imposed upon the clergy by the Pope.

Alongside changes in taxation and the making of Parliament, a continuing process, it is possible to trace the gradual development in the twelfth and thirteenth centuries of a more complex society with far more organized institutions than there had been in 1066. The kind of society described in terms of the human body in 1159 by John of Salisbury, perhaps the most learned classical writer of medieval times, in his *Policraticus* (1159) did not include alongside the *bellatores* (warriors), *oratores* (clergy) and *laboratores* (workers) either townsmen, who were increasing in numbers and wealth, or administrators and courtiers. Yet, sticking to his imagery, he called judges 'eyes' and tax-gatherers 'intestines'. By the end of the thirteenth century we can identify, at least in the largest towns, a complex urban social structure with marked inequalities of income, dress, status and power. The ways of the merchant, uncategorized in surveys of society, diverged sharply from the ways of the *oratores* and the *bellatores*, although the former might develop substantial mercantile enterprises of their own and the latter were prepared to send their children to the city. There was also a growing number of literate laymen, although the *laboratores* and the *bellatores*, many of whom were now speaking English, remained largely illiterate throughout this period.

John of Salisbury also failed to note the inadequacy of the designation *oratores*. They now fell into quite different groups (indeed, there could be conflict between various orders of monks who stressed different values and who assumed different roles in society) and they included teachers (the Church had a monopoly of education), administrators and scholars, prophets and philosophers, artists and musicians. (Descants were introduced in the twelfth century, ornamental variations above the plainsong which had been sung for centuries.) This was a period of intellectual as well as artistic renaissance; the scholars employed Latin as their language and were now passing far beyond literacy into realms of intricate analysis and speculation. New learning about the ancients arrived from the Arab world, and soon English philosophers would read Thomas Aquinas, born in 1225, who looked back to Aristotle as he set out to harmonize faith and reason. The scholars were creating new institutions of their own – universities – where they could meet together, learn and dispute.

The story of Oxford illustrates the sequence of development. The Normans had begun with a castle there in 1071. Forty years later they built a priory, and soon afterwards a hospital and a nunnery. (Nearby was a hunting-lodge at Woodstock.) The town acquired a charter in 1155 and a common seal in 1191. Scholars were lecturing in the town by the late twelfth century and a small community of students was also beginning to be built up; in 1209 a number of them moved east to Cambridge. The impulse to congregate students as well as scholars quickened following the arrival of representatives of the new thirteenth-century religious orders. Dominicans first, Franciscan friars second, and by the end of the century the older orders of monks, the Benedictines and the Cistercians, had all established institutions in the town. Tales of miracles abounded, and there was a cult of relics. Yet one notable thirteenth-century Franciscan scholar in medieval Oxford, Roger Bacon, described mathematics as the only discipline by which truth could be established without fear of error, and he looked outside his time to envisage a future which included spectacles, submarines and flying machines.

Meanwhile, the *bellatores* also developed their own culture. When William the Conqueror dubbed his son a knight at Whitsuntide 1086, the year when Domesday Book was commissioned, it was in a far simpler ceremony than those of the thirteenth century, which included purification, confession and communion. By the latter date the *bellatores* were drawn to elaborate codes of honour (a word of Norman–French origin) that focused on loyalty and prowess, a combination of strength, daring, courage and skill and on armoured display. The codes of chivalry were aristocratic, crossed geographical and dynastic divides, contained a religious element, were nourished by romance and even by fantasy, and in time were to seem 'four parts in five illusion', but they belonged unmistakably, like the tournament, to the pattern of the age. 'What is the function of orderly knighthood?' John of Salisbury asked, giving as his answer 'to protect the Church, to fight against treachery, to reverence the priesthood, to fend off injustice from the poor, to make peace in your own province, to shed blood for your brethren, and, if needs must, to lay down your own life'. Only a few people could share such an ideal. Even fewer could follow it. Yet the ideal was a necessary feature of the culture; it influenced the way in which privileged children were brought up.

The *bellatores* did not fight only in Europe. Some of them also sought through crusades, the first of which was organized in 1095, to 'reconquer and redeem' parts of the Arab world; and two English kings, Richard I, Coeur de Lion (1157–99), son of Henry II and older brother of John, and Edward I went on crusades, the first in 1190, the second in 1270. Neither the realities of war, nor the ribaldry that went with it, easily fitted the codes of chivalry. The crusades themselves were at times as barbarous as the Viking raids had been – and far more calculated in their barbarity – while war in France always involved plunder and often treachery. Ravaging lands and burning villages figured more in warfare than set battles. Of England itself, Peter of Blois, writing in Henry II's reign soon after the murder of Archbishop Thomas Becket in 1170 by four knights at the altar of his own cathedral at Canterbury, observed that 'in these days of ours the order of chivalry is mere disorder. For he is accounted stoutest and most illustrious among knights whose mouth is defiled with the most filthy language, whose oaths are most abominable, and who most despises good.'

If some changes in culture, including literature and art, seem to have been superimposed on a rough society through royal and aristocratic patronage, and even more were imported from France and Burgundy, others, including architecture, obviously reflected domestic social change. Comparing 1086 and 1300, castles, cathedrals and towns now looked quite different. The first castles had been of a 'motte and bailey' type, the motte being a mound at the centre of the castle, either a natural hilly feature or earth thrown up during the course of digging a deep circular ditch, and the bailey an open space at the base encircled by a ditch. The later castles were deliberately imposing with stone towers and keeps. They could look, and sometimes still do, like magic castles in a romance. It must have been a new and exciting experience for people to see castles change or to take part in the work of changing them. At Norwich, for example, workmen in the reign of Henry I replaced a timber castle with a great stone edifice and a novel rectangular keep, and more than a century later the baronial leader Simon de Montfort built elaborate water defences at Kenilworth.

There was even more visual change to note in cathedral towns for, like Stonehenge before them, most English cathedrals belong to different dates in their construction. At Durham, work on the cathedral on the hill began in 1093; it proceeded fast after Ranulph Flambard, one of

William's trusted military advisers in a struggle between the king and his brother, became bishop. The powerful columns and magnificent nave carry a continuing sense of Norman energy and of the will to dominate. Far to the south, the cathedral of Rochester was rebuilt by its bishop, Gundulf, a great builder of castles and architect of the White Tower in London. Cathedral building, like the construction of castles, was seldom a single, consecutive process, and only Salisbury, built between 1220 and 1266 (except for its fine fourteenth-century steeple), was constructed in this way. Most English medieval cathedrals belong to a number of different periods, with significant differences in architecture between one period and another. Thus, between 1170 and 1200, rounded Norman arches gave way to pointed Gothic architecture, with a remarkable burst of further elaboration in 'decorated styles' imported from France and popular between 1250 and 1330. (The ribbed vaulting in the choir of Ely Cathedral is a good example. So also is the Angel Choir at Lincoln.)

Later generations, particularly those guided by A. W. Pugin and John Ruskin in the nineteenth century, were eventually to claim not only that Gothic was the supreme architecture, but also that the men who created it had belonged to an organic society and culture, the secrets of which had been lost or deliberately destroyed following the rise of trade and industry. A similar view was shared by the American writer Henry Adams, who compared the inspiration provided by the thirteenth-century cult of the Virgin with that of the twentieth-century cult of the dynamo. There were in fact two focal points in many cathedrals – the high altar and the shrine. In St Albans Cathedral the shrine of Saint Alban dates back to the first decade of the fourteenth century.

This was a society where the rites of the Church, a universal Church, encompassed all the main events in the local life of the individual and the family. Birth, marriage and death all had their rituals. The calendar was a calendar of fasts and feasts. Whatever messages the villager or townsman, simple or relatively sophisticated, might receive about history or beauty, morality or eternity, came through the Church, and at a local level the parish priest as shepherd was the intermediary between the villagers, his sheep, and their Maker, the Good Shepherd. And the boundaries between the religious and the secular were always blurred. It was through the building itself as much as the services that took place inside it that the Church exercised such a pervasive influence: it spoke through its images – stained-glass windows, wall paintings, stone statues and carved fonts (in Edward I's reign some of these were eight-sided with carvings on each side) – and through its monumental brasses, which date back to before 1300. It spoke also through its graveyards, monuments and crosses. Inside the church communication by word mattered less than communication by eye: there are no pulpits in England which can be ascribed to an earlier date than 1340. Preaching outside the church by friars, God's minstrels, men who lacked the privileges of cloistered monks, was a different matter. Their sermons were deliberately homely in their themes and images. They looked forward, however, as monks did, to an after-life where the righteous would be at peace. In the eleventh century the doctrine of purgatory changed the picture: it allowed for expiation of the consequences of sin.

Religious ritual gained its significance from the fact that confession and penance were a necessary part of the pattern. Wrong doing needed to be redressed. It would be a mistake, however, to consider the Church as a 'kindly mother waiting for the coming of her children'. It enforced its claims as vigorously as it organized its festivals. It had a monitorial function too. As a poem in 1303, entitled *Handlyng Synne*, warned:

> Karolles, wrestlyinges, or somour games,
> Who so ever haunteth any swyche shames
> Yn cherche, other yn chercheyerde
> Of sacrylage, he may be a ferde.

The sheep had their mastiffs as well as their shepherds, although the shepherds themselves might wander astray.

There may have been as many as 40,000 ordained priests during the thirteenth century, a sizeable group recruited from all sections of society including the poorest. While inside church they might 'recite the words of others without knowing in the least what they mean, like parrots and magpies', as Roger Bacon once put it from the vantage point of Oxford, outside church they often had children, got drunk or went poaching. They were increasingly warned, however, not to do these things, and to set a good example. When John Peckham, the Franciscan Archbishop of Canterbury of Bacon's own day, himself the son of a farmer, carried out visitations to try to discover exactly what was going on in all the parishes under his care, he even found it necessary to prescribe that priests' children should not succeed to their fathers' benefices.

The parish church came to handle sin as actively as it fostered virtue. Lay proprietors of church benefices (endowments) often conceived of them as a piece of property. The Church continued to benefit from lay giving until the Statutes of Mortmain of 1279 and 1290 forbade all men to give or bequeath land to the 'dead hand' of a religious body without a royal licence. The religious orders, which controlled a quarter of the parish churches of England in 1200, were also jealous of their rights. Indeed, the history of land use was influenced by bishops and abbots as much as by lay lords, and here religious and secular interests become indistinct. The friars, who preached poverty and were pledged not to 'make anything their own, neither house, nor place, nor any other thing', themselves benefited from lay giving. Houses could be 'thrust upon them', by Henry III at Reading, for example, and by the burgesses at Southampton.

The boundaries between the religious and the superstitious, between the Christian and the pagan, were equally indistinct. Why, for instance, did provincial constitutions drawn up in 1236 lay down that 'fonts are to be kept closed by locks because of witchcraft'? Images were often believed to have magical efficacy, and the Lateran Council in distant Rome ruled that the elements of the Eucharist and the holy oil should always be kept under lock and key. The parish church was a familiar feature of the rural landscape, but its teaching was still mingled with old beliefs and adapted to the felt needs of everyday life.

There is considerable disagreement among historians about the basic question of the standard of living of the majority of the population – Aelfric's *laboratores* – by the end of the thirteenth century. By that time population had probably more than doubled since Domesday, from around one and a quarter million to over four million, and this was bound to have far-reaching effects. For some historians most Englishmen at that time were struggling to exist on inadequate smallholdings. For others England was essentially a prosperous country except in certain crisis years. While there is agreement that there was an expansion of trade during the twelfth and thirteenth centuries, some historians suggest that the chief explanation is that people were being pushed out of an over-populated countryside. Indeed, it has been argued that, at the end of the period it was the poverty of villagers which encouraged the important new economic development, the growth of the worsted trade.

The scarcity of good land led to a significant further expansion of cultivation during the twelfth and thirteenth centuries into less favourable lands: woodland, moorland, fenland and marshland. The 'wastes' of Dartmoor, for example, were cultivated; terraced hillsides, once thought to be prehistoric, were farmed at Mere in Wiltshire and in Dorset; the monks of Battle Abbey in Sussex constructed successive sea walls to reclaim the marshes. By the late thirteenth century a bigger area was cultivated than at any period before the wars of the twentieth century. Development was, as always, uneven and locally determined, but expansion of cultivation, whether carried out by lords, priors or peasants, was the dominant factor of social life. There was significant urban expansion too. Many new towns appeared in the twelfth and thirteenth centuries, among them ports like Newcastle, Hull, Lynn and Boston which thrived on growing foreign trade, and a number of 'planned' or 'planted' towns, of which no less than 172 have been identified. A classic example of the latter was 'new' Winchelsea in Sussex, laid out between 1281 and 1288 in thirty-nine rectangular lots: its chequerboard pattern of streets is still visible, preserved by the misfortunes in its later history. Other new towns included Stony Stratford and Devizes. Meanwhile, older centres, like Higham Ferrers, often acquired new features.

Nevertheless, country rather than town rhythms continued to dictate the pace of life during the twelfth and thirteenth centuries. Some of the most important trading activities took place at country fairs, glorified markets which involved the same medieval mix of activity and conviviality as did the guilds inside the towns. Domesday Book itself has practically nothing at all to say about fairs – only one, Aspall in Suffolk, is mentioned specifically – but by the end of the thirteenth century there were many of them, including the well-documented St Ives fair, founded by Henry I, and the great Stourbridge Fair near Cambridge, founded in the reign of John, which every September lasted for three weeks. Some fairs were, of course, held in towns, like the great Winchester St Giles Fair, with one section famous for its wines and spices, and Bartholomew Fair in London, held in Smithfield. Religion directly influenced the location of fairs: the booths were often grouped around the church. It also determined their timing on days of festival. St Ives fair was held at Easter. Such great fairs promoted commerce between countries, but they also included a local element. In towns without fairs, most weekly markets flourished largely on the basis of local produce.

Villages, the everyday life of which still centred on the seasons, varied like towns in site, size, appearance and fortunes – there were 13,000 of them already recorded in Domesday Book – and by the end of the thirteenth century compact village settlements were to be found in most of lowland England. A few were new, like Fleet in Lincolnshire; most were old. They were often physically unattractive settlements with rough-and-ready cottage dwellings, sparsely furnished inside and filthy outside, but there were also gardens and fruit trees. The simplest dwellings would be made of mud and clay with a thatched roof, but by the thirteenth century the manor house might be built of stone, as might the barn. It was a sign of luxury when the lord of the manor installed better quality roofs, ornamental tiles and floors, strewn with rushes or straw, and cobbled yards; he would often plan expensive enclosed deer parks as well. One at Cold Overton in Leicestershire, first mentioned in 1269, covered 200 acres and had banks 30 feet in width. Inside the manor the great hall was still the centre of life for much of the year, a place for meeting and even sleeping, as well as eating and feasting. Windows were small and high, and glass was used in churches before it was used in domestic buildings. There was little furniture except for wood-framed beds, benches and chests.

In some parts of the country, such as the Lake District and Cornwall, most of the population lived in scattered small hamlets rather than villages. Wherever there was a village, however, it was taken for granted that the individual's interests would in certain respects be subordinated to those of the community. The village, like the town, was not simply a collection of individuals or of families of unequal status and wealth. Community obligations, such as road and bridge maintenance, were taken for granted. In the thirteenth century, under Henry III and his son Edward I, villages were required also to mount watches to protect life and property, and later they were also called upon to provide one man for the army and to pay his wages. Villagers might reach common decisions enshrined in their own by-laws about access to land or the use of the meadows without any pressure from above, or join together in raising funds for a new church. It has been suggested, indeed, that the dynamic element in village life in some parts of the country was more often the community than the lord.

The picture of social order in the medieval village of the thirteenth century has recently been redrawn by the social anthropologist Alan Macfarlane, among others, who have argued that 'the majority of ordinary people in England from at least the thirteenth century were rampant individualists, highly mobile both geographically and socially, economically rational, market-orientated and acquisitive, ego-centred in kinship and social life.' Tied though villagers were to the land, they were not, according to Macfarlane, peasants of the kind to be found in contemporary peasant societies: custom was not all-powerful, kinship under patriarchal direction was not the main social bond. The family was a nuclear, not extended, family. Villagers bought and sold land, there was no rigid division between villeins and non-villeins in the holding of their land, and, according to the law, women were able to carry out transactions as well as men.

Macfarlane implies, in the tradition of the great nineteenth-century historian Maitland, that many legal statements of the time corroborate aspects of his suggested sociology, economics and psychology. Thus, he argues, there was no link between family and land under common law; 'peasant land charters' reveal that there was an extensive land market in some parts of the country in the late twelfth and thirteenth centuries; and the great thirteenth-century lawyer Bracton could assert that 'a citizen could scarcely be found who would undertake a greater enterprise in his life-time, if, at his death, he was compelled against his will to leave his estate to ignorant and extravagant children and undeserving wives.'

While there is ample evidence of both social and geographical mobility, this stimulating alternative picture, relating also to later centuries and in sharp contrast to that of historians like Rodney Hilton, begs many questions. If it is sensible to be sceptical about calling English villagers peasants, it is equally sensible to be sceptical about the attribution to medieval Englishmen and English women of qualities like 'rampant individualism', 'market orientation' and 'ego-centricity', terms derived from the relatively recent language of sociology, economics and psychology. The word 'individual' itself did not emerge in its contemporary sense until the late seventeenth century; in the thirteenth century it meant indivisible. And the raising of the family and the maintenance of the household always mattered as the main preoccupations.

There were, in fact, many medieval constraints on the individual. The social nexus was tightly conceived at the time and status was carefully nuanced, so much so that two recent historians were able to list no less than twenty-one status terms within a group of Cambridgeshire villages in the year 1279. Nor was status the only constraint. The king's courts would not afford the villein protection against eviction, nor award him damages against his lord; and he had no standing in the public courts against the lord unless the latter's actions went beyond all reason (for example, maiming and killing).

Economic and social historians have argued also about the implications of change within the village and the manor between the Norman Conquest and the end of the thirteenth century, focusing more on the attitudes of the lord than on those of his dependants. During most of the twelfth century many lords ceased to manage their land directly and rented it out. During most of the thirteenth century, by contrast, many lords managed their demesne land directly in order to secure the greatest returns from it. Such shifts of policy were influenced by demand, which was itself influenced by population, but inevitably supply factors – the quality of land and the costs of labour – came into the reckoning. So too did prices, which reflected these different forces, for there was rapid inflation between 1160 and 1220, and during the thirteenth century as a whole prices almost quadrupled while wages remained static.

Whatever the circumstances – and most people in the countryside were living on the edge of subsistence – this was a period of substantial economic activity. Wheat was actually shipped overseas from Ipswich, and wool was such an overwhelmingly important national export that when the barons were arguing with Edward I in 1297 about taxation and government, they could claim, with some exaggeration, that half the country's wealth derived from it. Thirty thousand sacks were shipped abroad every year, nearly all to Flanders, where there was a highly developed cloth industry dependent upon English wool. The trade had begun to prosper during the previous century, and several great English estates, like Crowland Abbey, specialized in sheep farming: the flocks there increased from 4,000 to 7,000 between 1276 and 1313.

The special place of wool in English history was to be recognized in many ways. The first customs duty levied on its export in 1275 became known as the *Antiqua Custuma*, and already at that time control of wool was a political weapon. Judges and the Lord Chancellor in the Great Council sat on a wool sack. It is not surprising that the first chapter of the much used early twentieth-century school textbook *The Golden Fleece* was called 'The Wool Pack in the Making of England'.

Furthermore, when wool began to be made into cloth in England rather than exported as raw material, it stimulated the growth of what came to be called 'industry'. England was far behind Flanders in the production of cloth in the late thirteenth century, but there was enough development, including the building of new fulling mills worked by water power to shrink felt and to scour cloth, for a distinguished scholar to suggest that there was an 'industrial revolution' in the thirteenth century. The industry was spread through the countryside rather than concentrated in the towns, and the sources for its early history are, therefore, manorial rather than borough records. One of the first mills at work, as early as the reign of John, was at Elcot, near Marlborough; and by the end of the thirteenth century there were significant concentrations in West Yorkshire, the Lake District, Cornwall, Devon, Somerset, Wiltshire and the Cotswolds.

Despite this marked surge of economic development, most economic historians have argued forcefully that the expansion and the population growth which it supported could not last. Problems multiplied more than opportunities. In particular, landlords' appropriation of land on the commons (to which all villagers held grazing rights) for arable farming raised complex questions of common rights, while the extension of cultivation carried with it economic penalties, notably exhausted land and falling yields. The first of these issues was clearly decided in favour of the lords by the Statute of Merton of 1235, which laid down that a lord was entitled to appropriate the whole of the commons provided he left sufficient grazing for any freeholders who pastured their animals there. But the second, agricultural productivity, was beyond the reach of the law, just as industrial productivity in the twentieth century has remained beyond the reach of politicians. If and when soil became exhausted and the supply of animal manure dropped because there was less land available for animal pasturing, high farming was bound to be in trouble.

The theory that soils became exhausted and agricultural yields began to decline during the last years of the thirteenth century has been seriously questioned in the light of recent detailed evidence, and a number of historians have disputed the conclusion that England (along with other European countries) was over-populated at the end of the thirteenth century in relation to its resources and technology, with the kind of consequences that Thomas Malthus was to identify in the late eighteenth century – growth checked by famine. There were densely populated parts of the country with large numbers of smallholdings where there were no signs of a Malthusian outcome (fenland communities, for example, with a population density comparable to that of the twentieth century) and which remained prosperous into the fourteenth century. Furthermore, the level of rents did not suddenly and generally begin to fall at the end of the thirteenth century. Much depended on the state of the annual harvest, but there was no general day of reckoning with nature.

There were two new features in thirteenth-century experience which, while they did not yet contribute significantly to economic output, were later to become of vital importance in the English economy. In different ways they suggested that nature might even be tamed. First, the burst of new industrial activity in the countryside offered a supplementary or alternative livelihood to that derived from the land. It depended on a new power-driven technology: fulling mills superseded fulling 'under the feet of men', as one contemporary expressed it. It raised questions about the ownership of power that were to be raised again 500 years later with the development of steam power; the Dean in a story of Jocelin de Brakeland argued that 'the profit which may come from the wind ought to be denied to no man.'

Second, throughout the thirteenth century there was increasing interest in agricultural improvement. Careful attention began to be paid to the technology and economics of farming, partly under the pressures of inflation and shortage of land and partly encouraged by the incentive of rising incomes. In consequence, there were many switches from a two- to a three-field rotation system, both to accommodate new land brought into cultivation and to reduce the amount of land under fallow. In addition, there were changes in cropping, including marling (fertilizing) the soil, substituting new seed corn each year and growing more peas, beans and vetches. 'Change your seed every year at Michaelmas,' wrote Walter of Henley in his influential thirteenth-century textbook on stewardship and husbandry, 'for seed grown on other ground will bring more profit than that which is grown on your own. Will you see to this?'

The last question was a pertinent one. Walter of Henley was anxious not only to give advice, but also to ensure that it was followed. Good management, including auditing, mattered as much as new techniques. 'The hayward', he emphasized, 'ought to be an active and sharp man, for he must, early and late, look after and go round and keep the woods, corn and meadows and other things belonging to his office.' Duties were clearly set out for every specialized office, and their number and range were increasing in the thirteenth century. On the negative side, it was stressed that cheating had to stop. On the positive side, production targets could be fixed. Monasteries sometimes led the way in good management, and it is interesting that Walter was writing in Canterbury: Henry of Eastry, the Prior of Christ Church, Canterbury, was one of the most astute stock-keepers and managers of his day.

Walter was concerned with workers as well as with managers, and his advice touched all aspects of farming at every level. 'The dairymaid', he observed for example, 'ought to be faithful and of good repute, and keep herself clean . . . She ought not to allow any under dairymaid or another to take or carry away milk or butter or cream, by which the cheese shall be less and the dairy impoverished.' Dairying was never the only female occupation in the countryside. Women carried out other work on the farm, including hoeing.

There were women, too, who supervised landed estates, as well as household servants, with great ability. A monastic chronicler wrote of Hawisa, a countess in her own right, who in 1180 married the Earl of Essex, that she was 'almost a man to whom nothing masculine is lacking save virility'. Other women were surgeons, receiving substantial fees, or physicians. Some occupations were purely female, including midwives ('wise women') and nuns, and widows enjoyed considerable independence and discharged a wide range of responsibilities. Nonetheless, the formal position of women within society, as laid down by law, had been considerably eroded since the Norman Conquest. Adam had sinned, it was maintained, because of Eve's pressure. Women in both canon and civil law were deemed to be 'under the rod' of their husbands, and canon law specifically permitted wife-beating. Their chattels were the property of their husbands while he lived.

Much information about thirteenth-century social life comes from monastic chroniclers, like Matthew Paris who claimed in 1250 that the wonders of the previous fifty years had been unequalled since Christ. Yet there were other records. There was no single inquiry comparable to Domesday in the thirteenth century, but regular and systematic records multiply, among them court rolls, chancery records, account books and pipe rolls, originally long rolls of sheepskin, recording moneys received by the Treasury from the shires: they go back to 1129-30 and as a complete series to 1154. Chancery records included details of charters, wills and contracts. The Curia Regis rolls were the records of the highly organized system of law which rested firmly on the king's authority: they covered cases in which the king was not a party. Manorial courts continued to dispense feudal justice and ecclesiastical courts universal canon law (with the power of excommunication), while borough courts had local urban jurisdiction. Yet it was the king's courts, including the high court of Parliament, which upheld the law of the land. There was also a system of judicial visitation, and Edward I's reign began with an Eyre of 1274, an itinerant inquiry into royal estates and royal rights, which has been compared with Domesday. Important statutes were enacted in his reign. Among these were the Statutes of Westminster, which fixed three yearly assizes, and of Winchester, which tightened the machinery of law and order, including a jury system. There was still a basic emphasis on old law, however, rather than new, and complaints about the law were always conservative in nature: either that the law was not being observed or that it had fallen into disuse.

There are four surviving originals of the most famous thirteenth-century document, Magna Carta, sealed – not signed – by John in 1215. (Seals, like coins, provide valuable historical evidence.) Two copies are in the British Museum, but the best copy is in Lincoln Cathedral. Its reissue in 1225, when it was cut down in size by a third, and its confirmation by Edward I in 1297, when it was enrolled in a new series of statute rolls, recall the frequent struggles between king and barons during the twelfth and thirteenth centuries. Kings had patronage at their disposal, but when they were felt to have distributed it unwisely they could be under threat. In 1264 Henry III, unpopular because of his foreign expeditions, was actually defeated by Simon de Montfort, Earl of Leicester, at the Battle of Lewes, although in his turn Edward

I, a tough ruler, raised an army, defeated Simon's forces at Evesham, killed him, and erased 'the viper's brood' of the de Montforts from the list of great landlords.

Simon de Montfort's wife, Eleanor, sister of Henry III, who married for the first time at the age of nine, left a fascinating household account. It not only gives careful details of supplies and their prices, but notes frequent changes in the personnel of the household. It is the kind of source, therefore, which enables us to reconstruct past ways of life. We can study the elaborate hierarchy of household servants, who included Simon the cook, Andrew the butler and Ralph the baker, compare the items in daily household fare, and journey with Eleanor from one great house to another. The fare is particularly interesting. While the poor were living very simply, eating daily (at best) up to five pounds of coarse (but nutritious) bread made out of wholemeal barley or maslin (wheat and rye or beans), together with some meat, cheese, milk and butter, vegetables and lots of weak ale, the de Montfort household, which also consumed vast quantities of bread, was supplementing it amply with meat, fowl of all kinds, and fish of even more kinds. There were no forks or earthenware plates.

Rice was so special that it was kept under lock and key. Spices were expensive (the price of pepper fluctuated from 10d. to 2s. 4d. a pound and that of ginger from 10d. to 1s. 6d.) but were considered necessary. (The Crusades had added to their range and to the range of fruits.) The price of sugar could fluctuate from month to month. Meanwhile, the weight of sugar consumed in a year was only just larger than the weight of pepper. Many of the dishes on the table at this time were not only highly flavoured, with vinegar as well as spices as an active ingredient, but also highly coloured, either by bright yellow saffron or, perhaps less attractive, crimson blood. Pastry was predominant. Gascon wine, which was imported in very large quantities from England's empire in France, with Bordeaux as the great port, was a major drink, and while households brewed their own ale, hops were not used in ale-making as early as the thirteenth century. Fruit and vegetables from the orchard and garden were not itemized in the accounts: they were taken for granted. It is interesting to note that while the price of luxuries varied so much, the prices of bread and ale, the two staple commodities for both rich and poor, were controlled (with reference to grain prices), as were standard weights and measures.

Monastic records, including account rolls, are packed with information of every kind and cover far more topics than the monastic chroniclers selected for attention. At their best, they reveal much about the use of time, about rents and yields of crops, labour services and wages, and about their variations from season to season and from place to place. At Canterbury, for example, Archbishop Peckham's archives might suggest that he was as interested in the rent rolls as in the spiritual welfare of priests, and by the thirteenth century there were less well-known abbots who were efficient managers of estates. Yet it was always stressed that the monastery existed for the 'government of souls', not for good management, and that the abbot would be called to account, both for his own teaching and for 'the obedience of his disciples', for prayer as well as for work.

The earliest municipal records date back to the end of the twelfth century, with nearly fifty charters going back to the reign of Henry II. They were no more standard in form than towns were standard in size, but they usually involved the privilege of appointing municipal officials and organizing markets. Freedom from tolls was a major privilege. However, it was through their own organization, different from the countryside though dependent upon it, that the towns reinforced their authority. In 1200, for instance, the congregation of citizens of Ipswich elected two bailiffs, four coroners and 'twelve chief portmen' to manage the town's affairs. The bailiffs were to be replaced later by a single magistrate called a mayor. Unlike bailiffs and reeves, mayors had responsibilities to no one but the citizens of their own community.

London was by far the biggest and wealthiest town both at the time Domesday Book was drawn up and in 1300. It had its liberties confirmed in Magna Carta, although Henry III suspended them in 1239 and dismissed the mayor. The first mention that we have of a Mayor of London is an accusation in the last decade of the twelfth century that one of its citizens claimed, 'Come what may, London will never have any king but the Mayor of London.' With liberties went problems. There were already complaints in the late thirteenth century that London buildings were so close together in many cases that there was 'no vacant land' and that some occupied 'a neighbour's walls where they have no right at all'.

The biggest towns could be turbulent as well as busy places. In 1202 there were around 430 reported cases of crime in Lincoln, including

114 cases of homicide and 45 of rape. A little earlier, the Jew in Richard of Devizes's *Chronicle* (1193–8) had advised a Christian French boy that if he went to London, he should 'quickly pass through it': it was full of 'stage-players, buffoons . . . musical girls, druggists, lustful persons, fortune-tellers, extortionists, nightly strollers, magicians, mimics, common beggars, tatterdemalions'. They were particularly prominent on holy days. May Day was one. At Candlemas there might be a week's holiday and at Christmas twelve days. Richard of Devizes's account was one-sided. It omitted both the clergy, who held substantial estates in London, and the two key groups in the towns – merchants and craftsmen.

There were foreign communities also with privileges of their own in the larger towns; Henry II, for example, allowed the merchants of Cologne to have a guildhall in London as early as 1157, and in 1283 the Statute of Markets gave further encouragement to foreigners to settle and set up in business. There were many signs, however, of anti-foreign and, in particular, anti-Semitic feeling. The first Jewish communities, as dependent on the king for security as he was on them for capital (at high rates of interest), were established in the reign of William I, and by 1200 there were probably a total of 2,500 Jews. In the thirteenth century they were to suffer appallingly from the anti-Semitic pogroms that followed accusations of ritual murder at Lincoln, York and Stamford; and in 1290 they were expelled.

The guild merchant was a characteristic medieval institution, at once a group protecting the economic interests of the merchants in a particular town and a fraternity offering all the pleasures of conviviality. It inspected markets and measures, judged the quality of merchandise and laid down rules both of business and manners, while always protecting and, in so doing, restricting, local trade. It also often maintained a school, some-times to become a grammar school in later centuries. One of the first recorded guild merchants set up by charter was in the now small and beautiful Oxfordshire town of Burford, whose lord granted the charter along the same lines as 'the burgesses of Oxford have in the guild merchant'. But the guild was not identical with the borough authority: there could be burgesses who were not members of the guild, as at Ipswich, and guildsmen who were not burgesses. And it did not exist everywhere; there was no guild merchant in London or Norwich, for example. The trade controlled by a guild might be very small or great, and where it was great the restrictions would be very precise. Thus, at Southampton, it was laid down that 'no one shall bring into the town of Southampton to sell again in the same town unless he be of the guild merchant or of the franchise', while at Shrewsbury no one was allowed to erect booths or to adopt other devices whereby 'to have better sale than any of the other combrethren'.

The idea of fair or just prices for traded products, reasonable alike to buyer and seller, was fundamental to medieval thought, although there was, as always, a gap between theory and practice. The frequency with which middlemen were attacked for forestalling (intercepting goods before they reached the open market), engrossing (cornering by buying up large quantities) and regrating (buying wholesale to sell retail) shows how wide the gap could be. Indeed, it was difficult to draw the line between legitimate and unreasonable business activities. Nor was it always easy to deal with the differences between crafts, which were concentrated in particular streets often named after them – the names have survived – and which in some towns had separate guilds of their own; London led the way as early as the 1260s. Craft guilds were to regulate not only standards and prices but apprentices and wages as well: in most crafts a seven-year period of apprenticeship was deemed to be essential for the 'mystery' of a craft to be acquired.

The language of apprentices' oaths could be French or English, for the third and fourth generations of Normans were bilingual. Richard Fitzneale claimed that 'with the English and Normans dwelling together and marrying, the races have become so fused that it can scarcely be discerned at the present day – I speak of freemen alone – who is English and who is Norman by race.' Nevertheless, Norman French and Latin were, at the end of the thirteenth century, still the languages of the law, of the court and of education, and a proclamation on the Provisions of Oxford of Henry III, circulated in English in 1258, was picked out in a Victorian account of the Middle Ages as 'our one native oasis in a howling wilderness of French and Latin'. Yet English dialects continued to thrive, some of them working their way up the social scale. The future was not clear. A Song of Lewes in support of Simon de Montfort and claiming that 'England breathes again, hoping for liberty', might be written in Latin, but Englishmen were already singing, in English, 'Sumer is icumen in.'

4 ORDER AND CONFLICT

And I have dreamt a marvellous dream. I saw a fair field full of folks poor and rich . . . The commons pursued different occupations, and in particular they produced ploughmen, who were to labour and till the ground for the good of the whole community.

William Langland, *Piers the Plowman, c.* 1372–89

It was a marvellous and terrifying thing to hear the thundering of horses' hooves, the cries of the wounded, the sound of the trumpets and clarions and the shouting of the war cries. .

Sir John Chandos on the Battle of Poitiers, 1356

O just God, mighty judge, the game was not fairly divided between them and us. Their surfeit was our famine: their jousts and tournaments were our torments: . . . their feasts . . . our fasting.

John de Bromyarde, Dominican Friar, *c.* 1420

I was so high upon my whele,
Myne owne estate I cowd not know,
Therfor the gospelle seyth fulle welle
Who wille be high, he shall be low
The whele of fortune, who may it trow,
All is but veyn and vanitye.

Lament of the Duchess of Gloucester, 1441

William Morris, the nineteenth-century poet, designer and socialist, looked back longingly to the fourteenth century when he conceived of his late-Victorian utopia in his *News from Nowhere*, and good words were written also about the fifteenth century by his liberal contemporary, the economic historian Thorold Rogers. In recent years, however, historians (with notable exceptions) have laid their emphasis on the tearing apart of the social tissue in a calamitous fourteenth century, when, as William Langland's poem *The Vision of Piers the Plowman* implied, the world was coming to an end, and a bizarre fifteenth century, which has been said to bear 'the mixed smell of blood and roses'. 'Wherever we look,' one historian, Barbara Tuchman, has recently written in her *Distant Mirror*, a study of fourteenth-century Europe, we see 'panic, brutality, violence in the streets. This was an upside-down world, a troubled, feverish world.' 'Right wild' was how one fifteenth-century gentleman put it at the time.

Any account of the 'waning of the Middle Ages' usually starts with the Black Death, the 'Great Pestilence' of 1348 and 1349, a bubonic plague carried by fleas from diseased black rats. It arrived by ship in the south of England from continental Europe, and was followed by further pestilences in 1361–2, 1369 and 1374–5. The most important effects of the Black Death were on population: within the space of a single generation probably between a third and a half of the population was wiped out. And there is evidence from this time and later too that young people were particularly vulnerable to the plague: indeed, the second plague of 1361–2 was known as the 'pestilence of the children'. The total population of England may have fallen to around two million by the end of the century. There were probably no more people in 1500 than there had been in 1200 and no more in 1600 than in 1300. Historians have written of a 'fertility' crisis as the rate of population replacement declined.

The Black Death was a sequence of visitations of exceptional catastrophe. Yet some of the consequences attributed to the first plague were apparent before it took place. Population, for example, which had grown throughout the thirteenth century, may have ceased to grow earlier in the fourteenth century; moreover, the resistance to epidemic disease, including the plague, may have been lowered by chronic undernourishment. Society was vulnerable, not least to the weather. There was a marked fall in temperatures at the beginning of the century, which produced what has been called 'a little ice age', and between 1315 and 1317 there were great floods, compared by contemporaries with the biblical Flood. Harvests failed, and there were also sheep and cattle plagues, the former beginning in 1313, the latter in 1319, when it is said that in some places horses, which were immune to the plague, had to be substituted for oxen to draw the ploughs. Together these disasters caused what some historians have considered to be the worst agrarian crisis since the Norman Conquest. Scarcity affected the towns as well as the country. The chronicler of the *Annals of Bermondsey* told how in 1348 the poor ate dogs, cats, the dung of doves and their own children. And matters were made worse by the fact that alms were reduced. The supply of charity dried up.

A movement from arable cultivation to pasture and a retreat from marginal lands that characterized the post-plague years were apparent in various places before 1348 in counties as far apart as Shropshire and Sussex, although, as always, the pattern varied from one part of the country to another. A deserted windmill at the village of Ibstone on the Chiltern hills was a symbol of the times: the Fellows of Merton College, Oxford, had invested in it during the 1290s, but thirty years later it was derelict. Deserted villages were not a new phenomenon in the fourteenth and fifteenth centuries, but there were now far more of them. The processes of desertion can again be traced back to pre-plague years: in 1334 the tax assessments (which reflect the size of population) in four Norfolk villages were less than one-fifth of those paid by their neighbours, and when the church in one of these villages, Pudding Norton, eventually fell into disuse in 1401, 'the fewness and the poverty of the parishioners' was blamed not on epidemics but on the soil. Villages were safe only if they had quality corn land, or if their economy depended on other products besides corn, notably wool.

Difficult economic problems were revealed even in the first decade of the fourteenth century, although their extent has been vigorously debated. The main initial problem was inflation, for in some places both grain and livestock prices almost doubled between 1305 and 1310 and went on to reach new heights between 1315 and 1321. It is only with the invaluable help of a price index computed in the twentieth century that we can estimate its impact, since contemporary memories of an earlier period of inflation between 1180 and 1220, described by William Beveridge as the most alarming inflation of the Middle Ages, had gone. Prices (with 1415 as a base line of 100), which stood at 83 in 1264 and 105 in 1310, reached peaks of 216 and 215 in 1316 and 1317 respectively. These were higher than the post-plague figures.

Whatever its causes (one of them was said to be an influx of foreign silver), inflation added to the burdens of the poor, who were already suffering from increased tax demands generated by an unsuccessful war in Scotland, culminating in the defeat of Edward II (1307–27) by Robert Bruce at Bannockburn in 1314. Many prices remained high until 1337, then dropped and stayed low for twenty years, during which lords of the manor complained just as bitterly of deflation as the poor had complained earlier of inflation: goods, although abundant, could not then be sold. There was a shortage of coin, and even though the harvest of 1339 was the worst since 1315 prices did not rise. They rose for another twenty years, however, in the third quarter of the century, within an extraordinarily wide range of local fluctuations. The state of the harvest remained the main fact of life, and following two poor harvests in 1362 and 1363 four good harvests produced the first price falls for a decade.

The biggest landlords, of course, were always in a far more powerful position to complain than the poor. So too were the knights, and their complaints were heard in Parliament. Politics were as confused as economics during the unhappy reign of Edward II which ended in his deposition, the first since 1066, and in his murder at Berkeley Castle. Under Edward III (1327–77), however, after a difficult start, when the king was a minor, there was a long period after 1330 when institutions worked effectively, despite plague, economic upheaval and war. At the county level, justices of the peace were given a wider range of enhanced responsibilities alongside the king's agents, the sheriffs, who collected revenues, including fines, executed writs, presided over the county courts, empanelled juries and guarded prisoners. The number of officials increased also, but it still remained difficult to enforce law and order – crime was widespread – and to eliminate corruption.

Civil strife was as 'vicious and violent' as it had been in the reign of Stephen in the twelfth century or during the barons' war of the mid-thirteenth century. There was urban discontent as well. There had been townsmen's risings, for example, in 1327 in Bury St Edmunds, a monastic town where there had been a long history of conflict between Church and citizens. Edward, however, anxious to win consent (and money) for his costly policies, encouraged townsmen to participate in Parliament alongside knights of the shire. Some of the Commons delegates were mayors and aldermen, like William de la Pole, who represented Hull in 1332, 1334, 1336 and 1337. They too increasingly needed consent from their communities, and in 1339, for example, the Commons refused to grant Edward a tax until they had consulted their fellow townsmen.

The main reason why Edward's policies were costly was war. In 1337 he proudly laid claim to the French throne, challenging 'Philip of Valois who calls himself King of France', thereby starting what came to be known in the nineteenth century as the Hundred Years War. It was, in fact, a series of wars, beginning with brilliant victories, but ending with a series of 'various adversities . . . long undergone'. The cost of the Hundred Years War was fully appreciated outside as well as inside Parliament, provoking *The Song against the King's Taxes* with its bitter message 'people are reduced to such ill plight they can give no more. I fear if they had a leader they would rebel.'

Nonetheless, war could appeal to landlords and knights as an escape from the bewildering economic and social circumstances at home and as a possible, even likely, means of personal profit through plunder. It was attractive for other reasons too, personal and public, since it both promoted individual mobility in society and sharpened the sense of national feeling.

Edward created twenty-four new knights in 1337 when he invaded France, along with six new earls, 'each one content with his rank under the king'. He also created a new order of chivalry, the Knights of the Garter, of whom he himself was one. The first meeting of the first twenty-six knights, including the king, was held on St George's Day in a newly built 'noble hall' at Windsor, where it was claimed that Arthur, whom Edward greatly admired, had founded his great castle with its Round Table. Like the king and knights of lesser status, almost all the magnates were caught up in pride of precedence and in the heraldic arms and codes of chivalry – loyalty, honour, valour and courtesy – that went with it. Society was becoming more ostentatiously hierarchical, more fascinated by 'descent' at the same time as war – and economic change – offered new means of 'ascent'.

In August 1346, on the eve of the Black Death, which challenged all hierarchies, one of the greatest victories the English ever achieved in France was won at Crécy in Picardy, where the full array of French chivalry was destroyed by Edward's archers. It was a triumph of infantry over cavalry, a victory of the longbow against the newly introduced gun, which had also been used by the French during their sack of

Southampton in 1338. In 1347 the town of Calais, which had been besieged for a year, fell to the English too. And in 1356 the French king was brought back as a prisoner to London after the victory at the battle of Poitiers of Edward III's formidable son, 'the stern and gloomy Black Prince'. Jean Froissart, the great chronicler of chivalry, believed Poitiers to have been an even greater victory than Crécy because there were greater feats of arms, 'with the result that fewer great men were killed'. Certainly at Crécy, where many men were 'slaughtered regardless of their rank . . . the number of dead lords was very great'.

To his contemporaries the Black Prince, who was only sixteen years old when he fought at Crécy, was at the same time both 'fell and cruel' and 'the flower of earthly chivalry'. 'To serve him as a knight', wrote one chronicler, 'was to be a lord.' Another outstanding warrior magnate was Henry of Grosmont, the first Duke of Lancaster, a founder Knight of the Garter, who had joined crusades which took him to Lithuania and Spain as well as the Holy Land. Posterity remembers him less for his 'war-like deeds and great exertions', highly estimated by his contemporaries, or for his diplomatic skills, than for his remarkable book of meditations and confessions, *Le livre de seyntz medicines*, which treats Christ as a physician. Henry was renowned for his charity and was the main founder of Corpus Christi College, Cambridge.

The Black Death proved more 'fell and cruel' than any prince, nor was it under the control of any human physicians. As it made its way inland from Southampton and Bristol, it killed nine out of ten of its victims. Wherever it moved, it was a 'wretched, fierce, violent' pestilence. In the vivid and revealing words of an inscription in Ashwell Church, only the 'dregs of . . . a people survive to witness'.

People with power and influence suffered as much as the rest. The newly appointed Archbishop of Canterbury, a distinguished scholar, died within six days of his consecration (one of three archbishops to die within a year) and two out of five beneficed clergymen in the huge diocese of Lincoln were stricken down. Monks and priests suffered in other ways too, since the plague was also thought of as a scourge of God:

> God is deaf now-a-days and deigneth not to hear us,
> And prayers have no power the Plague to stay.

A widely circulated Latin tract raised a different point, as later 'plagues' were to do. Clean-living 'that shall be pleasing to God' was the only true safeguard. The point was difficult to sustain, and a thanksgiving service for the end of the plague at Yeovil was interrupted by restless 'sons of perdition' who kept the Bishop of Bath and Wells besieged in church.

While England's chivalry and the leaders of the mercantile community were among the victims, the biggest direct impact of the plague was on people without power. At Cuxham, a much studied manor in Oxfordshire, all twelve of the lord's villeins died within one year and two-thirds of his tenants, while at Tusmore in the same county the lord of the manor was granted permission to turn his fields into a park since every villein was dead.

Inevitably, therefore, there was a shortage of labour; and although surviving lords of the manor might try to overcome the problem by seeking to reinstate labour services, they could not do so for long. Release from labour dues became as regular and frequent as in the twelfth century. Moreover attempts by manorial lords or smaller landowners to keep down by law the wages for those farm workers whose labour services had been commuted could not work indefinitely. A royal ordinance of 1349, followed by a Statute of Labourers in 1351, which tried to prohibit wages in excess of those paid before the Black Death and to lay down that alms should not be given to able-bodied beggars, was rigorously enforced, but by the end of the century the statute was as unsuccessful as twentieth-century wages and income policies. It encouraged greater social cohesion on the part of agricultural workers who according to the statute were to be paid no more than a penny a day at haymaking time. (As a point of comparison, a trained war-horse, fit for a knight, at that time cost almost £100, the equivalent of a lifetime's earnings for a labourer.)

However energetic the attempts to hold back commutation might be, they failed. Competition between employers for labour was one cause of non-implementation, but effective protest was another: villeins destroyed manorial records which carefully listed laws and obligations. There were signs too that the position of women was changing. Labour shortages gave them new opportunities. The age of marriage rose. As villeinage was being shorn of many of its most cramping features and the relative economic position of the male and female labourer was improving, the revenues accruing to many lords of the manor, lay and ecclesiastical, fell. For instance, the monks of Battle Abbey, near

Hastings, lost 20 per cent of their revenues between 1347 and 1351, and another 7 per cent in the 1380s.

In such circumstances small men might prosper by buying and selling land, often in small parcels, from the lord of the manor or from fellow villagers. There was considerable variation, therefore, in the wealth of smallholders: at Frisby in Lincolnshire, for example, where there were sixteen tenant families in 1381, the richest were reckoned to be two or three times wealthier than the poorest. There is also evidence that the average smallholding became larger and better. But after a period when the claims of the poor were little heeded and there was what one recent historian has called an 'Indian summer' of landlord high farming, there was a wave of unrest. As the poet William Langland noted, the way of a poor man was hard, particularly if he held no land of his own and was 'charged with a crew of children and a landlord's rent'.

Society as well as the economy was deeply disturbed in the late fourteenth century, not only by obvious inequalities but by changes in the facts of inequality. Proportionately at first, the biggest increases in wages often went to the humblest. Thus, a thatcher and his helper, who earned a penny a day before the Black Death, received two-and-a-half times that modest sum twenty years later. And although the price of horses, and the oats on which they were fed, remained stationary, payments to the threshers increased sharply. Market forces were at work, and it is not surprising, given the framework of society and the increased element of mobility within it, that even before unrest burst out the Black Death was followed by a great deal of moralizing and a preoccupation with social status. It was this, rather than 'economic analysis', a term used by a completely different generation, that coloured political speeches and acts of parliament. Above all, the poor were expected to keep their place. It was doubtless to try, through improved communication, to maintain law and order (a coupling of words which still survives) that in 1362 Parliament ordered all pleas to be conducted in English. The voice of tradition had strong social and cultural supports. *The Mirror for Magistrates* stated orthodox opinion clearly:

> No subject ought for any kind of course
> To force the lord, but yield him to the laws.

Worried 'poor tenants' were supposed instead to appeal in their petitions to 'their very dear, honourable and rightful lord'.

Evidence of increasing concern for status among all groups, including the upper ranks of society, is apparent in the 'sumptuary legislation' of 1363, which prescribed the clothing to be worn by different social ranks. Even earlier, indeed, 1336 guidelines had laid down that only the royal family, earls, prelates, barons, knights and ladies with an income of at least £100 a year could wear fur. As the century went by, dress became more ostentatious and more influenced by fashion; and who wore what was deemed significant. Earls and barons were clearly distinguished from knights, and knights from 'gentlemen', 'yeomen' and 'husbandmen'.

Moralists might denounce the extravagance of fashion, but it became even more extravagant in the fifteenth century both for men and women. Meanwhile, shifts in legal terminology continued through the fifteenth and sixteenth centuries as, for example, copyholders, who held customary tenancies from their lords on a lifelong or continuing basis on terms set out in copies of entries in the old manorial rolls, became identified as a legal group with distinct interests. Meanwhile, 'yeomen', the most prosperous – and the smallest – of the groups, were already being pulled away from the life of the village community into the life of 'the county'.

The more talk there was of subordination in the mid-fourteenth century, the more tension and conflict were being generated; and there was a violent, though short-lived, riotous protest, the so-called Peasants' Revolt of 1381, which began in the remote countryside but went on to threaten the Court. It was not given this name at the time, and it was precipitated not by general discontent but, very specifically, by Parliament's attempt to levy a poll tax (a tax per head of population) that fell on all sections of the community. This was the third such tax that had been levied between 1377 and 1381, and the fact that in 1381 it tripled in size and was not graded by rank in refined fashion, as the 1379 tax had been, was bound to generate protest, as a twentieth-century local poll tax was to do in 1988. Significantly, the Parliament that levied the fourteenth-century tax met not in London but in Northampton, because officials feared popular reactions in the capital.

There were other discontents in the background. When the war with France was renewed in 1369 after the brief and unpopular peace of Brétigny in 1360, it was no longer a war of victories. Much of the rich land in Gascony was lost, and in 1372 there was a naval defeat at

La Rochelle. For these reasons the long reign of Edward III, who was by now senile, closed as turbulently as it had begun. In 1376 two of his 'evil councillors' were impeached by the House of Commons, and the death of the Black Prince in the same year added to the gloom. The throne now passed to the Black Prince's son, Richard, born in Bordeaux, a boy not yet eleven years old. It was more in melancholy than in anger that on Edward's death in 1377 an unnamed poet compared England to a once noble ship – with the Commons as the mast – which was now drifting, and asked rhetorically,

> Ah, dear God, what may this be
> That all things wears and wastes away.

In the same year there were French raids on the south coast, and in 1380, on the eve of the Peasants' Revolt, there was fear of a large-scale invasion.

Alarm about the possibility and likely effect of social unrest was well expressed by John Gower, one of the finest poets of his age, a conservative in temperament and outlook, who almost forecast the revolt when he wrote:

> It seems to me that lethargy has put the lords to sleep so they do not guard against the folly of the common people, but they allow that nettle to grow which is too violent in its nature.

'If God does not provide His help,' Gower concluded, 'this impotent nettle will very suddenly sting us.'

It was young Richard II (1377–99), only fifteen years old at the time, who ultimately had to deal with the Peasants' Revolt, which started with risings against the third poll tax in Essex, Kent, Norfolk, Suffolk and Hertfordshire. Three marshland villages near Brentwood in Essex led the way, with other villages soon following. The revolt quickly collected long-standing complaints and stimulated sweeping invective, both radical and conservative. Its Kentish leader Wat Tyler was, in the eyes of authority, 'a king of the ruffians and idol of the rustics'. In his eyes, however, 'We are men formed in Christ's likeness', but 'kept like beasts'. The rebels marched on London, and the revolt reached its climax in three stormy days, the first of them, Corpus Christi Day, 13 June. The Kent contingent had travelled to the capital through Canterbury and Rochester and camped at Blackheath; the Essex contingent was lodged north of the river. Boy king and rebels eventually met near the Tower at Smithfield, London's future meat-market.

Many essential features of the three days are lost. It is not clear, for example, though rumours abounded, how much support the rebels actually secured from the faction-torn citizens of London. There is enough recorded incident, however, to permit reconstruction of the events and even to catch glimpses of individual personalities. The one specific and consistent demand was that the legal bond of villeinage should be broken. One rebel clergyman, John Ball, also demanded that the country should be rid not only of lords but of archbishops, bishops, abbots and priors. Both the Archbishop of Canterbury (who was also Chancellor) and the Treasurer of England were murdered. Richard proved his bravery when he met the rebels face to face, and Wat Tyler was killed by the sword of the Lord Mayor of London.

The surviving rebels were punished severely, and villeinage, the burdens of which were lightest in the north and east of England, was not abolished. Yet it was soon to lose most of its economic backing, while the poll tax was dropped. Thereafter the Commons came to argue even more strongly than before that 'the king should live of his own', by which they meant – and the emphasis, if not the phrase, was new – that he should live on the known revenues of his hereditary rights and properties, supplemented only in exceptional circumstances, for policy reasons and if Parliament approved, by customs duties, subsidies and levies. The political necessity of keeping within this framework was to impose long-term difficulties on royal government and was to be an important contributory factor to the late sixteenth- and seventeenth-century conflicts which culminated not in another peasants' revolt but in civil war.

There are several vivid accounts of the 1381 revolt, each with its own gloss on the events. 'The rebels, who had formerly belonged to the most lowly condition of serfs,' wrote Thomas of Walsingham, 'went in and out like lords; and swineherds set themselves above soldiers, although not knights but rustics.' There is mixed evidence, however, on such matters. While there were demands that 'no lord should have lordship, but that it should be divided among all men, except for the king's own lordship', in many places the rebels tried to secure the support of the gentry. The gentleman, as such, was never the prime target of peasant hostility in 1381. Froissart, the chronicler of chivalry, surveying events at a distance, was interested more in the vicissitudes of personal fortune epitomized by the revolt: 'how wonderful and strange are the fortunes of this world.'

It is impossible to understand the social issues of the fourteenth century without bringing in the Church, increasingly referred to as 'the Church of England', at every point, not only because of the moralizing framework of reference or the fact that there were priests like John Ball who were capable of rebellion, but because at the very centre of power there were often clerical ministers governing the kingdom. The Church itself was a hierarchy composed of its own great lords, some of them combining spiritual authority with administrative, political and economic power; below them came lesser lords, who were influential in their own areas, with large numbers of liveried attendants; archdeacons ('bishops' eyes') carrying out the orders of the bishops who had appointed them; and at the base the clergy, the underprivileged priesthood and the mendicant orders, who still favoured, in theory at least, a return to the simple poverty of the Apostles. There were approximately 9,500 parishes scattered throughout England, with many of the priests in charge of them better trained than their predecessors. Some of them had been to the Universities of Oxford and Cambridge. The mendicant orders, the Franciscans and Dominicans, who played an important part in urban life, also had schools of their own.

It was the wealth of the Church and the fiscal demands that it made on all sections of the population that stimulated both anti-papal and anti-clerical feeling, not least in Parliament, where in 1371, ten years before the Peasants' Revolt, there was a sharp conflict about taxation of the clergy following the dismissal from the Chancellorship of the powerful prelate, William of Wykeham, founder of a college at Winchester and of New College in Oxford. There was even talk at that time of confiscating Church lands, and there was to be a further scandal in 1378 when the Church divided, leaving two popes, one in Rome and one in Avignon in enemy France. It was against this background that in 1393 the Statute of Praemunire insisted that the Crown had 'no earthly master'. There was radical anti-clericalism too: thus, in *The Complaint of the Ploughman*, a poem shot through with social criticism, the anonymous poet criticized 'Peter's successors', 'high on horse', for changing their clothes every day and for punishing the poor:

Of holy church make they an hore
And filleth her wombe with wine and ale.

The most organized late fourteenth-century religious protest was Lollardy, although it had many different strands. In 1372 the first Lollard, John Wycliffe, had taken a Doctorate of Divinity at Oxford, where he had learned much from critical scholars, but he did not begin preaching what were considered heretical ideas until 1378. Going far beyond chauvinistic anti-clericalism, he focused on the Bible as the one sure foundation of belief, urging that it should be placed, in English, in the hands of everyone, clerk or layman. Other points followed from this: he questioned the doctrines of the Mass (the central service of the Church), he demanded a dissolution of its corporate wealth, he condemned monasticism, and he advocated the marriage of the clergy. He stopped short of a broader critique of contemporary society and government, however, because he was most concerned with pressing spiritual matters, because he believed that 'all things not to the will of the Lord must end miserably' (a good motto for his age), and because he placed great trust in 'the Prince'. In his translation of the Book of Genesis, where the seventeenth-century Authorized Version of the Bible was to read 'chief captain of his host', Wycliffe had 'prince of all his chyvalrye'.

It was inevitable that Wycliffe's ideas should be condemned, and by 1411 academic heresy was stamped out in Oxford where it had originated. The Archbishop of Canterbury warned that if Lollardy was not eradicated there would be further social disturbance, but, in fact, while the Lollards wanted to see far-reaching changes in ways of thinking and behaving, like Wycliffe few of them were identified with social revolt. The rebels of 1381 did not share many of Wycliffe's religious views: indeed, his ideas had more support in the Parliament that had provoked the Peasants' Revolt.

It was in the fifteenth century, not the fourteenth, that Wycliffe's ideas took root among small radical minorities, attracting disciples not just in anti-clerical London but in country areas like the Chilterns in Buckinghamshire and the villages around Tenterden in Kent. In Berkshire too there was 'a glorious and secret society of faithful followers'. The demand for an open Bible, in English, was at the heart of what became a Lollard heritage, and, despite all efforts to suppress

Wycliffe's Bible, the first complete Bible in English, over a hundred copies survived. Although Lollardy had not achieved any of its immediate aims, it prepared the way for – even anticipated – the popular dissent that was to figure in the background of the sixteenth-century Reformation.

The fifteenth-century suppression of Lollardy left behind it heroes. One of them was the warrior knight Sir John Oldcastle, a friend of Henry V (1413–22) before he came to the throne. Oldcastle was an intrepid character, and when the Archbishop of Canterbury tried in 1413 to serve him with a final summons to trial as 'the principal harbourer, promoter, protector and defender of heretics', Oldcastle shut the gates of his castle. Tried and convicted, he escaped, unsuccessfully attempted rebellion with the help of craftsmen and ploughmen, went underground, was captured late in 1417 and after appearing before Parliament was hanged and burnt at the Tower of London.

There are elements in the story of Oldcastle which throw light both on men of power, ecclesiastical and lay, and on the medieval 'underground'. Becoming an outlaw, whatever the cause, was a popular theme in the late fourteenth and early fifteenth centuries. These were the years when Robin Hood and other similar legends circulated widely; as early as 1377, the poem *The Vision of Piers the Plowman* refers to 'rymes of Robin Hood'. Several of them hold him up as the upholder of justice who is seeking not to destroy society but to redress its manifest wrongs; but there have been suggestions that he was the hero of the gentry rather than the poor and that his 'merry men' were poaching not for food but for sport. Yet his advice was plain enough. 'Do no husbande harm, that tilleth with his ploughe.'

Most outlaws were clearly not of this kind; the reality of their existence was as far removed from romance as the facts of war in France were at odds with the language of chivalry. The preamble to a 1378 statute described how armed bands were taking possession of houses and manors, 'having no consideration of God, nor to the laws of the Holy Church, nor of the land, nor to right, nor justice'. And the lord of the manor himself might employ, in the right circumstances, the same methods as the outlaw. Not very far from Nottingham, for example, Eustace Folville, one of seven sons of the lord of the manor of Ashby Folville in Leicestershire, had been involved in gang crimes that included robbery, kidnapping, rape and murder, the success of most of which depended not only on team effort, but on support in higher places. Folville was, in fact, pardoned three times because he had fought against the king's enemies (for which he was knighted), and on more than one occasion he was hired by local people with power, including Church canons.

As the Hundred Years War continued, straddling the fourteenth and fifteenth centuries, it was seen increasingly as perpetuating a sense of disorder at home rather than diverting violence to France. Other factors were at work also, for there were dramatic domestic events between 1381 and 1413. Even in 1381 feuding between great magnates loomed larger than peasant protests, and there were two great shifts of power later in the reign of Richard II, in 1388 and 1397 (the latter involving the redistribution of estates by the crown on a huge scale) before the king was deposed and replaced by the Lancastrian Henry IV (1399–1413), who spoke English as his first language. The manner of Richard's deposition suggested injustice – for a brief moment there was a chillingly empty throne – and the reign of Henry IV, thought of by many as a usurper, was an uneasy one. The chronicler Adam of Usk's claim that the sacred chrism used at Henry's coronation produced in the king's hair a crop of tenacious lice and his interpretation of this as an evil omen throw an interesting sidelight on the insecurities and fears of the age.

Under Henry V, who was to be treated in later generations as a war hero, the English won great victories in France, one of them in 1415 at Agincourt, where English bowmen triumphed against overwhelming odds; and in the years that followed lands in France were distributed among great English magnates in a kind of Norman Conquest in reverse. Henry's two-year-old son Henry VI (1422–61) was nominally king of both England and France after victory at the Battle of Vermeil in 1424, as a result of which Sir John Falstaff was said to have won 20,000 marks by 'the fortune of war'. But this was the last significant English victory in the Hundred Years War. The subsequent story is that of Joan of Arc, the rehabilitation of the French monarchy, the growing strength of French cannon and gunpowder, the French recovery of Normandy, and the loss of the whole of France by the English (except for Calais) by 1453, the year of the fall of Constantinople to the Turks.

The story in England itself was also a sad one from the English point of view. In 1450 there was another rural revolt, this time in Kent, led by Jack Cade, who claimed to be a cousin of the Duke of York. For its leadership it drew on esquires and gentlemen rather than on peasants, but Cade's demands included the abolition of the Statute of Labourers and the resumption into the king's own hands of royal lands which had been granted away. The rebels entered London and executed the Lord Treasurer before being dispersed, and Cade was killed. Twenty-one years later sporadic dynastic wars, which had their distant origin in the succession of Henry IV, split the aristocracy between support for the Houses of Lancaster and York and weakened the monarchy. There was more talk while they lasted of 'false authority', as a contemporary poem, *On the Corruption of the Times*, put it, than of order. The impressively tall Yorkist Edward IV (1461–83) won the throne through rebellion, and the first of his Parliaments passed acts of attainder for treason against no fewer than 113 people, including 13 peers.

During the Wars of the Roses, great men attached lesser men to their service by life indentures: the second Duke of Lancaster, John of Gaunt, father of Henry IV, who was given the title in 1362 at the age of twenty-two, had pointed the way in the late fourteenth century when he indentured large numbers of knights and esquires, most of them retained for life in his service in war and in peace. Such 'bastard feudalism', as this 'system' has been called, was quite different from earlier feudalism. The retainer was not a vassal who received land from his lord, owed loyalty to him and was linked to him through ties of mutual obligation. He rather looked to his lord as his patron. He was his lord's follower, wearing his livery and being maintained by him in return for a contract to serve for life or for a fixed period under stipulated conditions. Payment for service in instalments was the quintessence of the system, and there were men, often veterans of the Hundred Years War, who preferred service under a lord of their own choosing, sometimes a soldier of fortune but more often a great lord of their own locality. Once the maintained men put on their lord's livery, they demonstrated his power, and one lord could vie with another in the numbers of his retainers and display.

There was an unavoidable element of instability – or fluidity – in the 'system', even though most lords did not retain huge followings. Retainers could change from a losing lord to a winning one – the deals were not all one-way – and a strong king could control through balancing one side against another. This was a restless society which, for all its attachment to heraldry and to 'honour', favoured ambitious men – those who, in the words of a contemporary, were able to seize their opportunities, 'some by their prudence, some by their energy, some by their valour and some by other virtues which . . . enoble men'. The Paston letters, much quoted by historians, describe three occasions on which members of the Paston family, who lived in East Anglia, were besieged in their own homes by armed bands despatched by members of the peerage.

Nonetheless, the extent of both unrest and revolt in the fifteenth century can be greatly exaggerated. The Pastons were not a typical family, even if their preoccupation with property was widely shared. Nor was everyone driven by ruthless ambition. Religious devotion was at the centre of many people's lives as the well-documented story of Margery Kempe, 'mystic and pilgrim', reveals. Many of the key events of the century are surrounded by myths that originated under the Tudors after Henry VII (1485–1509) came to the throne following his defeat of Richard III at the battle of Bosworth Field, and after Henry VIII's Reformation. There was less bloodshed in the late fifteenth than there had been in the mid-thirteenth century or, earlier still, in the reign of Stephen; and the Wars of the Roses did not directly affect large sections of the population. Towns were not sacked, nor were churches desecrated. The appeal of Lancastrian and Yorkist claims in different places and at different times can be understood only in terms of local family feuds which drew in dependants as well as relatives in what was called at the time 'vicious fellowship'. Moreover, the numbers involved in the battles were small. At St Albans in 1455, for instance, when the Duke of York defeated the forces of Henry VI (1422–71) under the command of the Duke of Somerset, York had only 3,000 men under his command and Somerset, who was killed, about 2,000. The best description of the battle is brief – 'a short scuffle in a street'. A French observer of the wars noted that it was 'a custom in England that victors in battle kill nobody, especially none of the ordinary soldiers, because everyone wants to please them'.

Many people were able to stay out of the turmoil and the feuding, and for them life could be agreeable. In one of the few friendly accounts of the fifteenth century written in the 1920s, C. L. Kingsford described in detail Sir William Stonor's life as a country gentleman, busy with the management of his estates, taking his share in the work of local administration, living in friendly intercourse with neighbours in like circumstances to himself, growing rich with his profits as a sheep grazier, and spending money on the rebuilding of his house and the laying out of his garden. Another section of the community, the monks and the clergy, were less harassed in the fifteenth century than they had been in the fourteenth. Moreover, although Rome demanded a subsidy from the English clergy on twelve occasions between 1450 and 1530, they responded only twice through their assembly, Convocation. While the number of monks fell, their standard of living often rose: early in the sixteenth century the Cistercians at Whalley Abbey in Lancashire were spending two-thirds of their income on food and drink. At St Albans, lying on the main road to the north, there was lavish hospitality. Two Dukes were entertained there, each with 300 attendants, in 1423–4 and in 1436, and in the last of these years nine bishops and the whole of Convocation. The young Henry VI stayed there for nine days with his mother in 1427–8.

Wage labourers, many of them employed by abbeys, were a third section of the population who were certainly better off than at any other time during the Middle Ages. Since population did not recover in the fifteenth century, the wages of both farm workers and urban craftsmen rose faster than the prices of the goods they demanded. Indeed, real wages in the building industry doubled between the Black Death and Agincourt and remained high throughout the fifteenth century. Meat was in plentiful supply, as was poultry. Cereal prices remained low and steady until a series of bad harvests in the 1480s broke the pattern, as a result of which the price of wheat leapt 74.7 per cent in 1482. In the 1470s the lawyer and writer Sir John Fortescue described the Commons in England as 'the best fed and the best clad' of 'any Natyon crystyn or hethen'. They were able to buy new things besides food and clothes: brass pots and pewter candlesticks were in great demand. There was a real, if limited, improvement in the material standard of life. When fifteenth-century Parliaments resisted taxation or granted particular towns exemption from it, this reflected Englishmen's desire to keep their money in their pockets rather than their inability to pay. Fortescue went on to compare the English favourably with the French: in France the king could levy taxes as he pleased, nobles and clergy were not taxed and the necessities – food – were.

Ecclesiastical England, 1450

- - - - boundary of sees
(date of foundation shown)
- - - boundary of Provinces of
York and Canterbury
■ seat of archbishopric
● seat of bishopric
▲ important monastery or abbey

50 Miles

Holy Isle
▲ Lindisfarne

North Sea

DURHAM
995
(to York)

● Carlisle
CARLISLE
1133
● Durham
R. Tees

Whitby ▲

Jervaulx ▲   ▲ Rievaulx
Y O R K   ▲ Byland
625
Bolton ▲ Fountains ▲ ■ York
R. Ouse
▲ Selby
R. Humber

▲ Pontefract

Lincoln ●
Bardney ▲

Irish Sea

Bangor ● St.
Asaph ●
BANGOR (to Bangor)
c.550

St. ▲ Asaph
ST ● (to Bangor)
ASAPH
c.550   Shrewsbury ▲

LICHFIELD
669

▲ Lichfield
● Coventry
Kenilworth ▲

LINCOLN
1067

Crowland ▲
▲ Thorney   The
Wash

Norwich ●
NORWICH
1094

Holme ▲

● Ely
ELY
1109

HEREFORD
676
● Hereford
● Worcester
▲ Pershore

Ramsey ▲
Cambridge ▲

Bury St Edmunds ▲

ST DAVID'S
c.550

● St. Davids

WORCESTER
c.680

Gloucester ●
Tintern ▲

Woburn ▲

Oxford ▲

St Albans ▲

Colchester ▲

LLANDAFF
c.550

● Llandaff

Malmesbury ▲

● Abingdon

LONDON
605
Waltham ▲

● Bath
BATH AND
WELLS
1139
● Wells

Glastonbury ▲
▲ Salisbury
Westminster ▲ ● London
R. Thames
ROCHESTER
Rochester ● 604

Leeds ▲ ■ Canterbury

WINCHESTER c.650
● Winchester

CANTERBURY
597

EXETER
1050

Launceston ▲
● Exeter

Sherborne ▲

SALISBURY 1075

Romsey ▲
Southampton

CHICHESTER
1075 (to Canterbury)
● Chichester
(to Canterbury)

Dover ▲

English Channel

Nor had the prosperity been bought entirely at the expense of the landlords, who were sometimes critical of it. Landlords' fortunes were in fact mixed, even in the same county. Some faced difficulties; others prospered. The most able of them watched their estates extremely carefully, although the biggest estates were now mainly leased out to others. Other landlords lost income, however, at least until the last decades of the century, particularly in the grain-growing districts of the Midlands, and more villages were deserted.

There was one important incentive for farmers of ability and drive: the profitability of sheep farming, which required less labour than wheat and in which transport costs were lower too. Seven years after the Black Death 40,000 sacks of wool were exported annually, and a century later there were sheep farms with 8,000 or 9,000 sheep. Exports of raw wool fell during the fifteenth century, but exports of cloth rose four-fold. Indeed, by 1450 cloth not wool was England's greatest export. Exporting a finished product brought with it more profit – and employment – than exporting a raw material.

Complaints of sheep 'devouring' men as arable land was replaced by pasture were to be more vociferous and numerous in the sixteenth than the fifteenth century. This may have been because the process was further advanced. It may, however, have been influenced by the printing press, introduced into England by William Caxton in 1476. Certainly, the complaints had been heard in the fifteenth century before the printing press diffused them. 'What shall be said of the modern destruction of villages?' a well-known Warwickshire antiquary asked, and he could answer himself with confidence. 'The root of this evil is greed. The plague of avarice infects these times and it blinds men.' It was a charge that was often to be made throughout the long history of the fencing-in of land to consolidate and control its use, a process known later as enclosure.

Obvious conflicts of interest in the sheep fields were reflected in poetry and prose. A contented clothier could declare,

> I thank God and ever shall
> It was the sheep that payed for all.

But neither shepherds nor clothworkers were necessarily quite so contented. In an early fifteenth-century nativity play the shepherd complains,

> But we silly husbands that walk on the moor,
> In faith, we are nearhands out of the door;
> No wonder, as it stands, if we be poor,
> For the tilth of our lands lies fallow as the floor
> We are so hammed
> For taxed and rammed
> We are made hand-tamed
> With these gentlery-men.

The way of life of the shepherd, and of the ploughman, did not change much in the fifteenth century, but that of the clothworker did. There could be as big an economic gulf between the great clothier and the journeyman as there was between the lord and the farm labourer. There was also an argument about the number of apprentices a master might employ and about access to the trade. An act of 1388 had laid down that all who served in husbandry until the age of twelve should not be permitted entry to a 'mystery', and an act of 1406 stipulated that no one might send his son to be apprenticed 'except he have land or rent to the value of twenty shillings a year at the least'. Once in the trade, an apprentice could look forward to becoming a journeyman, and a journeyman to becoming a master (or at least this was the approved pattern), yet there were also permanent groups of wage earners who had 'sufficient cunning and understanding in the occupation and exercise of their craft' but who lacked the financial means to progress in the trade.

Few towns gained in importance during the fifteenth century, although the population of Norwich doubled and its wealth increased. Some old towns like Lincoln and Winchester decayed. 'Here cometh no repair of lords nor other gentlemen', the citizens of Lincoln complained in 1486, 'wherethrough the craftsmen and victuallers are departed out of your city.' Forty years earlier the citizens of Winchester had complained of the ruin of their city, 'which in ancient times was chosen out for the coronations and burials of kings'. It had been beset by 'pestilence and loss of trade'. Historians have talked, indeed, of 'urban malaise', even of an 'urban crisis', affecting old cities like York, Canterbury and Coventry. They have noted particularly that the urban centres of the wool trade which prospered most did not have a municipal constitution. Among them was Lavenham in Suffolk, an insignificant village which suddenly became one of the fifteen richest places in the country: constitutionally it was still a village governed through a manorial court.

Early in the following century Thomas Spring, a Lavenham clothier, was the richest man in Suffolk after the Duke of Norfolk. And not far away from Lavenham, which was virtually rebuilt in a single architectural style, were other great cloth centres such as Long Melford, also dominated by its wonderful parish church. There were great churches also in the Cotswolds, another important wool area, which from 1399 was linked with Calais, then the wool-staple town (the authorized entrepôt for all wool passing to the continent), by a route that followed the ancient Ridgeway to Sandwich. There were links also with Southampton, where there was a great Wool House which was to survive even the bombing of the city in the Second World War.

Non-ecclesiastical architecture flourished in all these areas. Thus, William Grevel, 'the flower of the wool merchants of all England', who contributed generously to his parish church, built an imposing house for himself at Chipping Campden, and William Browne of Stamford, 'a merchant of very wonderful richness', built a 'hospital' for the poor brethren. They each have their brasses in their local churches. It was the new churches, designed as they often were in an English style, 'perpendicular', that could produce the most magnificent effects. This was a century when there was persistent preoccupation with death (plagues continued to rack town and country alike), and masses for the dead were a preferred religious endowment. And recently deceased 'holy men' were venerated along with the old saints, while rood screens, often with complex images, carry the sense of fifteenth-century devotion. Yet perpendicular architecture let in grace and light. St Mary Redcliffe, Bristol, vaulted throughout, has been described as 'the most splendid of all parish churches', and the chapel of King's College, Cambridge (Henry VI was the king), carried to its logical end what has been described as an architectural revolution, begun by monks at Gloucester. There was light too in Nottingham's carved alabasters, which were bought as eagerly abroad as at home.

Meanwhile, castles, of which the last examples were concerned with prestige, not with defence, were giving way to country houses everywhere at the end of the fifteenth century, and greatly improved farmhouses were dotting many rural landscapes. In the port towns there were new wharves, and at Southampton a new guildhall; in some favoured older towns there were whole new groups of houses, as at Norwich. In London there was the magnificent Guildhall, parts of which were to survive the great seventeenth-century fire and to be embellished in medieval fashion in the nineteenth century.

As in the twelfth and thirteenth centuries, only one in ten of the population lived in towns. They were expensive places to govern (which made some businesses move out of them) since they had to maintain lavish traditions of ceremony and hospitality – particularly true in the case of London, which remained far bigger and richer than any other town – and they were characterized by increasingly complex patterns of urban control. Even in small towns like Beverley, there were street and traffic laws to protect the streets, laying down, for instance, that 'no cart shod with iron be driven or enter the town by any burgess', while in London it was ordered that 'no carter within the liberties shall drive his cart more quickly when it is unloaded than when it is loaded.' At Scarborough there were complaints that a private solar overhung the road 'so low that it is an obstruction', while a later rule of 1467 at Beverley anticipated nineteenth- and twentieth-century by-laws and legislation to deal with air pollution. It laid down that 'no one henceforth here to build any kiln for burning brick . . . under penalty of 100s.', because of the danger of attendant fumes. The injunction spoke frankly of 'the stink and badness of the air to the destruction of fruit trees'.

The recognition of such problems and pressure for controls often came from below. Thus, in London, where there were still fields between the city and Westminster, with its great abbey building, a citizens' petition of 1444 complained of 'swannes, gees, herons, and ewes and other pultrie whereof the ordure and standing of them is of grate stenche and so evel savour that it causeth grete and parlous inffecting of the people and long hath done'. The petition may be compared with a writ from above, sent in 1372 by Edward III to the Mayor and Sheriffs, ordering them to keep Tower Hill free from dung and filth and noting that he had been told it was in such a state as 'to fill those dwelling about with disgust and loathing'. The Abbey records have been explored systematically by Barbara Harvey and illuminate most aspects of social life from birth to death. They also reveal the role of late medieval charity.

Towns, which unlike continental cities could afford to neglect their walls, were often thought of as places of greater social division inside rather than of more generous charity or tighter social control. Craft guilds, which became increasingly important during the fifteenth century, did not necessarily share the same interest as merchant guilds. Thus, there were open conflicts during the 1440s between merchant drapers and artisan tailors, in London, Coventry and Norwich, for example. There were other divisions also. As livery companies developed, distinctions began to be drawn between those who were allowed to wear the livery and those whose lack of means excluded them. Journeymen often began to organize themselves separately. At Coventry a brotherhood of St Anne formed by journeymen was repressed but revived again under a different name, and even in the late fourteenth century a journeyman cordwainer who refused to join a journeymen's guild had been so violently assaulted that he had barely escaped with his life.

A further source of division was conflict between the organized economic interests of the guilds and civic and county authorities. Economic ordinances could be highly restrictive, as in the past, like the rule of the cordwainers and cobblers that no person who 'meddled with old shoes' should sell new ones. Legislation was passed in 1437, ordering 'the masters, warden and people of the guilds' to submit their ordinances to the justices of the peace in the counties or to the 'chief governors of cities and towns', and a further act of 1504 was to refer backwards to the many times in the past when guilds had 'made themselves many unlawful and unreasonable ordinances as well in prices of wares as other things, for their own singular profit and to the common hurt and damage of the people'.

Guild life in the fifteenth century expressed itself culturally, and alarm was sometimes expressed at the expense of the often elaborate plays and pageants, which were held on special feast days, particularly at the great midsummer festival of Corpus Christi, first established as a feast in 1311. Such regular and recurring events have been called 'mirrors of the community' and they were great urban occasions, the organizing of which had by the mid-fifteenth century often passed from the clergy to the laity. They were performed in different parts of the cities with musicians also taking part. Organization was complex, but the aim was simple enough – to present a moving Christian vision of the fall and redemption of man. At York, for instance, where there was a cycle of mystery plays, as at Chester and Coventry, the 'Shipwrights' presented the building of Noah's Ark and the 'Fishery and Mariners' the Flood. The Shepherds' plays, in particular, passed from the simplicities of existence – 'Lord, what these weathers are cold' – to the raptures of assured faith: 'Hail, sovereign Saviour, for thou hast us sought!'

Other medieval drama included miracle plays dealing with the lives of saints and, in the late fifteenth century, morality plays, of which the most famous was *Everyman*, the great allegory which was first to be printed early in the following century. Everyman is stripped of all his Good Deeds in order to be saved at the reckoning:

> And he that hath his account whole and sound,
> High in Heaven shall he be crowned.

We now classify *Everyman*, along with *The Vision of Piers the Plowman* as 'literature'. In the fourteenth century, however, when the term was first used, it had the sense of learning from reading and was close in meaning to the twentieth-century word literacy. ('He has not sufficient literature to understand the scripture', we read as late as 1581.) *Everyman* was for every man, and it was spoken in an English that could be generally understood, grammatically far simpler than that of earlier generations, but at the same time far richer in its vocabulary.

Increasing numbers of private letters survive, signs of the spread of literacy, the most important of them a collection of over 1,000 letters, written in English, that illuminate the lives of the Paston family between 1420 and 1503. The remarkable level of linguistic competence that they display seems to have been shared by the members of the family who had been to university or an Inn of Court and those, including Margaret Paston, who had not. 'Right reverend and worshipful husband', she would begin her letters, but what she had to say was often close to direct speech. 'I may more leisure have to do writen half a quarter so much as I should sayn to you if I might speak with you.' 'I suppose the writing was more ease to you,' she adds generously. We can almost hear the Pastons talking in their letters, just as we can hear the talk of the Celys, wool-staplers who lived in Essex and ran their business in Mark Lane, London, through their correspondence.

It is Geoffrey Chaucer's poems, however, which introduce English literature as most people know it – fresh, bright, pictorial, packed with memorable characters, bristling with humour. If we were to rely on documentary evidence other than the poems, we would have little reason to believe that Chaucer had written them. Chaucer, whose father had been in attendance on Edward III, was born around 1343 in London's Vintry, the quarter of the wine dealers, a thriving group when London was directly linked with Bordeaux, and his own fortunes, as a page who became a civil servant, followed the political fortunes of those on whom he depended:

> This wretched worlde's transmutacioun,
> As wele or wo, now povre and now honour,
> Withouten ordre or wyse discrecioun
> Governed is by Fortunes errour.

Although Chaucer was deeply read in Latin, French (both of France and of Stratford-atte-Bowe) and Italian, it is through his mastery of English – and he knew many of its regional variants – that he can still draw us back to his own century.

Chaucer has left us not only with *The Canterbury Tales*, a collection of pilgrims' tales, but with a gallery of unforgettable (and diverse) profiles of particular people. They also evoke the atmosphere of pilgrimages, some of them linked to holy days, all of them to sacred sites. 'Then longen folk to goon on pilgrimages', Chaucer noted, to Canterbury and, further afield, to Santiago de Compostela and Jerusalem. It is often forgotten how frequently, and how far, medieval Englishmen travelled on pilgrimages. 'Right heartily beloved wife', one real pilgrim wrote in 1456, 'I greet you with a thousand times, letting you wish that at the making of this letter I was in good health, blessed by God, and that is great wonder, for there was never men that had so perilous a way as we had.'

The perils of pilgrimages were real enough. The keynote of *The Canterbury Tales*, however, is jollity. Chaucer's pilgrims could forget any hazards there might have been as they listened to the Prioress or the Wife of Bath, the Franklin or the Pardoner:

> This pardoner had hair as yellow as wax,
> But smooth it hung, as doth a strike of flax . . .
> And in a glass he had pigs' bones,
> But with these relics, when that he found

> A poor person dwelling upon land
> Upon a day he got more money
> Than that the parson got in two months . . .
> He made the parson and the people his apes . . .

Among the pilgrims, the idealized medieval knight lives today more in Chaucer's words than through any real knight's chivalrous deeds:

> A knight there was, and that a worthy man
> That from the time that he first began
> To ride abroad, he loved chivalry
> Truth and honour, freedom and courtesy.

For other pictures of knights we can turn to the springy, alliterative metres of *Gawain and the Green Knight*, which was written by an anonymous author in the dialect of the North West Midlands area, and to the direct and simple prose of Malory; his *Morte d'Arthur*, written in 1469, was printed by William Caxton, whose first patron was Edward IV's sister, in 1485. 'I, William Caxton, simple parson, present this book following which I have emprised t'imprint', Caxton wrote in the preface. He had started his career as a merchant in Bruges, for many years a foreign staple town of the English wool trade. The first book that he printed, in Cologne, was a *Histories of Troy*, but by 1478 he offered *The Canterbury Tales*. Caxton's self-styled 'simplicity' is suspect, and as a translator and critic he could get things wrong (he praised Chaucer, for example, for his 'ornate' eloquence), but the books he printed in whatever language (and many were translations from Norman French) reveal as much about the age as they do about printing. It was an age when new social groups were emerging. Already in 1379, when Richard II had levied his graded poll tax, justices of the bench were charged more than earls, and junior barristers the same as knights.

Like all major inventions, printing was controversial and its effects are as difficult to disentangle as those of television in the twentieth century. 'The art of Printing will so spread knowledge', it was to be argued later (in 1642), 'that the common people, knowing their own rights and liberties, will not be governed by way of oppression.' That comment, however, was made in a century not of limited social conflict but of civil war. In the fifteenth century, when printing was new, it speeded production and widened distribution: a press was more effective than a *scriptorium*, where texts were laboriously, but often lovingly, copied by hand. More information was stored as script gave way to print. Nonetheless, diffusion was of greater importance even in the short run. Old books as well as new books reached more readers.

Most other generalizations about printing are suspect: the image, for instance, was not immediately overcome by the word, nor the pulpit by the press. Moreover, during the first years of printing it had as strong an influence on 'the home', a developing concept, as on public events. The family, if it could afford books, was now open to books on manners and morals (Caxton translated a French text on the first of these in 1487), on health (his *Journals of Health* appeared four years later) and, above all, on religion. Priests and members of universities might lose ancient privileges of access to knowledge, although universities as institutions were soon to be given new rights as printers and publishers. Meanwhile, the social perceptions of those who could read were bound to diverge from those who could not; in other words, a new inequality was added to all the existing inequalities of lay society.

One of Caxton's books, *A Description of Britain*, was extracted from John de Trevisa's translation of Ranulf Higden's *Polychronicon*, and he rearranged Higden's order of the British realms in it so that England, rather than Ireland, came first. It not only included familiar complaints that 'a yeoman arrays himself as a squire, a squire as a knight, a knight as a duke and a duke as a king', but went on to argue that the unity of the English people still seemed incomplete. 'Men of the South beeth esier and more mylde; and men of the North be more unstable, more cruel and more uneasy; the myddel men beeth some dele partners with bothe.' This picture of the Kingdom of England was to change radically during the next century, when foreign as well as regional comparisons abounded. By 1559, John Aylmer, later Bishop of London, could write from exile with a firm sense of national identity.

> Oh, if thou knewst thou Englishman in what wealth thou livest, and in how plentiful a country: Thou wouldest VII times a day fall flat on thy face before God and give him thanks that thou were born an Englishman, and not a French peasant, nor an Italian, nor German.

5 PROBLEMS, OPPORTUNITIES AND ACHIEVEMENTS

> We Englishmen beholde
> Our auncient customs bolde,
> More preciouser than golde
> Be clene cast away
> And other now be fownd
> The which (ye may understand)
> That causeth all your land
> So greatly to decay . . .
>
> From *Now A Dayes*, a ballad of 1520

> Have mind, therefore, thyself to hold
> Within the bounds of thy degree
> And then thou mayest ever be bold
> That God thy Lord will prosper thee.
>
> Robert Crowley, *Advice to a Yeoman*, 1550

> We were just in a financial position to afford Shakespeare at the moment when he presented himself.
>
> J. M. Keynes, *A Treatise on Money*, VOL. II, 1930

> Elizabethan Englishmen were conspicuous for some of the qualities that we nowadays associate with the Japanese.
>
> C. M. Cipolla, *Clocks and Culture*, 1965

It was a generation later, in 1587, a year of strange 'pre-ordained' eclipses and conjunctions of the planets, that an Elizabethan prayer, uttered on the eve of the Spanish Armada, referred proudly to 'the Commonwealth of England, a corner of the world, O Lord, which thou hast singled out for the magnifying of thy majesty'. The prayer and the sentiments it expressed were very similar to the one offered up at the opening of the Crystal Palace in 1851 in the reign of Queen Victoria. Both monarchs drew deeply on the loyalty of self-confident and divinely blessed Englishmen, many of whom thought of themselves as a chosen people. Nonetheless, the differences between the two centuries were as great as those between the two queens. Victoria was the mother of a large family, married to a German: Elizabeth, who had been hailed at first as a second Deborah, a 'swete virgin pure' who would 'restore the rule of Christ to her people', went on to be hailed also as Gloriana, the imperial virgin of classical myth, 'the phoenix of the world'. In 1851, England was the workshop of the world: in 1603 the Dutch were far ahead in economic strength. In the nineteenth century there was a *pax Britannica*: in the sixteenth century Englishmen were fighting at various times on the soil of continental Europe, and at the time of the Armada were threatened also by invasion. Tudor England did not, like Victorian England, profit from strength through peace. Nor for dynastic, religious and other reasons was internal peace secure. Yet there were echoes across the centuries: Victoria lived in an age of increasing democracy, while the Tudor monarchs, in particular Elizabeth I (1558–1603), were increasingly forced to recognize the role of Parliaments. Moreover, both centuries witnessed extraordinary population growth, and in both there was a heightened sense of national identity. In present perspective both seem very different from the twentieth century, although in the first year of Elizabeth II's reign (1953) there was talk of creating 'new Elizabethans' and during Margaret Thatcher's prime ministership (1979–91) there was talk of returning to 'Victorian values'.

It is important to go beyond Victorian interpretations of Tudor history, which reveal as much about the Victorians as about the Elizabethans, in order to explain the history of what has been called 'the century of the Reformation'. It is important too, given the extent of change, to break down that century – and the long reigns of Henry VIII (1509–47) and Elizabeth – into smaller units. Throughout the century Tudor sovereigns, from Henry VII, who won his crown by force at Bosworth Field and whose reign saw no sharp break with fifteenth-century values, to Elizabeth I, who reached the throne precariously after being locked away from public view, hoped for consent –

or set out to engineer it. At the same time they always expected obedience. They regarded rebellion as the greatest danger to society as well as to their dynasty, whether it was provoked by 'over mighty subjects' or fermented by discontented priests or rural labourers. Order was considered essential to the stability and security of the state. The belief that the law of nature itself lay behind the one law of the realm lent sanctity to the whole system. Richard Hooker's *The Laws of Ecclesiastical Polity* (1593), the great Elizabethan work on Church and State, which was to become influential in the seventeenth century, summed up in magisterial style philosophies that had emerged intact from the hot crucible of sixteenth-century experience. Hooker was in no doubt, first, that 'obedience of creatures to law of nature' was 'the stay of the whole world' and, second, that 'all things do work after a sort according to law.' The laws of society therefore required that 'every part do obey one head or governor' and that 'order, moderation and reason' should 'bridle the affections'.

The laws were reinforced by paternal authority within the family and by the preaching of the Church, however much it might change in liturgy or doctrine. Each household, like society as a whole, had its 'head' who, in theory at least, expected obedience in his small realm. Wives, by law as well as by custom, were held to be subordinate to their husbands. So, also, were children to parents. Indeed, in 1590, according to William Perkins, who wrote one of a number of 'domestic conduct' books on the subject, the definition of a husband was 'he that hath authority over the wife' and of parents 'they which hath power and authority over children'. The Bible was held to justify this natural 'order', although for dissenters it set forth quite different interpretation. It was preached every Sunday from the pulpit. Official print carried the same message.

Order was deemed to lie at the centre of all things. 'Take away order from things,' wrote Sir Thomas Elyot in his *Boke Named the Governour*, which went through ten editions between 1531 and 1600, 'what then should remain?' Many of Shakespeare's most rousing passages deal with dynastic, social and natural order, like the often quoted lines in *Troilus and Cressida*:

> The heavens themselves, the planets, and this centre
> Observe degree, priority and place . . .
> . . . But when the planets

In evil mixture to disorder wander,
What plagues and what portents! what mutiny!
What raging of the sea! shaking of the earth! . . .
Take but degree away, untune that string
And hark, what discord follows! Each thing melts
In mere oppugnancy.

When Elizabethans wrote like this, directly linking the order of nature – God's dispensation – with the order of men, they were not merely expressing an ideal. They also had in mind the experience of their immediate ancestors and remote forebears (real or legendary) in whom they were increasingly interested. 'During the last twenty years', wrote a Venetian observer of early Tudor England, 'three Princes of the blood, four Dukes, forty Earls, and more than three hundred other persons have died by violent death.' Statecraft demanded careful calculation. Henry VII married Elizabeth of York and in 1499 disposed of the last Yorkist with a title to the throne that was better than his own; Henry VIII, whose divorce from Katharine of Aragon and marriage to Anne Boleyn in 1529 reflected anxiety to secure a male heir, disposed of many other people with royal ancestry – and nine treason laws were passed in his reign; Elizabeth was in 1587 reluctantly forced to sign the warrant for the execution of her cousin, Mary Queen of Scots, after her involvement in a Catholic conspiracy against the throne. In fact, Henry VIII's three children, Edward, Mary and Elizabeth, were to follow him in natural, if contrasting, succession. Under Mary (1554–7) three hundred people 'perished in the flames for religious opinions'.

Violence was present in the sixteenth century at every level. Indeed, it was part of the texture of everyday life. Private armouries and armed gangs were taken for granted. Non-political brutal crime and equally brutal punishment were commonplace, homicide rates were high, and in the prisons people were kept 'lying in filthy straw, worse than any dog'. There were frequent local riots and disturbances, both in the countryside and in the towns, and intermittent large-scale rebellions. In 1536–7 the Pilgrimage of Grace associated in uneasy alliance peers, gentry, yeomen, peasants and clothiers in the north of England, groups with diverse interests; and in 1549 two separate rebel armies were in the field, one in the west, the other, Robert Kett's in East Anglia, urging relief for 'your poor Commons'. Five years later, Sir Thomas

Wyatt led rebels from Kent across the river at Kingston and reached Charing Cross. Oxfordshire villagers rioted against enclosure in 1596 at the same time as London apprentices were rioting against the City government. Nonetheless, the 1570s and 1580s were relatively orderly, despite or because of the Spanish Armada scare, and there were fewer disorders than might have been anticipated during the crisis years of the 1590s. In 1601 the rebellion of the Earl of Essex, who 'concentrated the pride, the quarrels, and the popularity of the age', had no aftermath of violence. After his peers condemned him to death it was left to the ballad writers to lament his loss.

The loss of direct control over arms and men by the nobility restricted chain reactions. As courtier and navigator Sir Walter Raleigh, himself tried and found guilty of treason in 1603, described it,

> the lords in former times were far stronger, more warlike . . . than they are now. There were many Earls who could bring into the field a thousand barbed horses; whereas now very few of them can furnish twenty to service the king

The fourteenth- and fifteenth-century retaining system had survived the reign of Henry VII, but a Statute of Liveries of 1504 directed that persons practising livery and maintenance should be summoned before the Council in Star Chamber, a new prerogative court in which defendants might be found guilty by 'confession, examination, proofs, or otherwise'. Such a measure enacted before the Reformation was crucial in the creation of the Tudor State since it drastically reduced the number of the crown's subjects answerable to lords other than the monarch. The Act lapsed in 1509, but by then it and a series of other measures had achieved their object. Henry VIII appointed Lord Lieutenants to supervise the military organization of the realm: their powers were continued by statute under Edward VI (1547–53), Mary and Elizabeth. Below the Lord Lieutenants were the unpaid justices of the peace who exercised both administrative and judicial functions. The Tudors' increasing use of the local gentry as justices should be seen not as a concession to a new and increasingly important social group, but as an attempt to maintain order effectively and cheaply: they were used to keep an eye on 'disorderly alehouses' and 'unlawful games' as much as to watch for signs of social and political protest. Meanwhile, at the centre of government, sovereigns sought out talented public servants, irrespective of their social origins. Thomas Wolsey, Thomas Cromwell and William Cecil, different though they were in temperament, outlook and policy, all came from the middle ranks of society.

Whoever the agents of government were (and the number of permanent salaried officials of the crown remained small), the law, and the lawyers, were always in the background. Admission figures to the Inns of Court, a distinctive English institution, multiplied by five in the sixteenth century to reach a figure of 200. The law itself was venerated even if it was not always observed or enforced; and if it sometimes lagged behind social facts, its strength lay in its uniformity, whether it was dispensed by the local justices of the peace or by the judges in the higher courts of the realm. There were still manorial courts (although their jurisdiction was limited) and ecclesiastical courts, which dealt *inter alia* with sex offences, even after the break with Rome, but canon law no longer figured in the curriculum of universities. The only real challenge to the common law came from new prerogative bodies which included the Council in Star Chamber, the Court of Requests, deputed to deal speedily with cases affecting poor men, the Court of Wards, which extorted large sums of money from reluctant landowners, and the regional Councils of the North and Wales. Each of these bodies was to be attacked bitterly by defenders of the common law, but the main challenge was to come later. The efficiency and speediness of their procedures was an early recommendation for the Crown and its agents.

The laws of nature and society required respect both for 'authority' and for social 'degree, priority or place', although the relationship between the system of ranking and the mobility of individuals within it is difficult to establish. The numbers of 'gentry' increased, but at this level of society there were considerable variations in numbers and background from place to place, even within the same county, as there were in most matters. In parts of Kent near London only one-third of the late seventeenth-century gentry were indigenous, but in East Kent only 3 per cent were not of native stock. In Leicestershire the leading families of the gentry were well established, but in neighbouring Northamptonshire, which, according to William Camden, one of the great scholars of his age, was 'everywhere adorned with noblemen's and gentlemen's houses', 'only the slenderest thread of blue blood flowed through county society from its medieval sources.' Half the county had formerly been royal forest, and many of the new estates with their great houses were in or near the old forest areas.

At the lower levels of society there was enough social mobility in some parts of the country, particularly in and around the metropolis, for hierarchy itself to be difficult to buttress. Of 881 persons admitted as freemen of London in the years 1551 and 1553, 46 were the sons of gentlemen, 136 the sons of yeomen and 289 the sons of husbandmen. Some people, as always, were coming down, others were going up. Both processes require more complex imagery than that of the social ladder. A younger son apparently coming down might often become his elder brother's master, or at least his better, in wealth if not in honour and reputation. Those who were successfully going up might move from commerce to landowning or seek to ensure that their children did so once they had accumulated sufficient wealth. There was relatively flexible entry into the ranks of the gentry, if not into the ranks of the higher aristocracy.

Since the ownership of land continued to confer the greatest social status and the greatest influence over others, the effects of social mobility on the hierarchical system of society were obviously just as apparent in the countryside as in the towns. The dissolution of the monasteries (1536–40), a decisive move in the process of Reformation, widened the land market in many parts of the country to the benefit of the gentry, and the market undoubtedly boomed again from the 1580s onwards. Of course, there were obvious manifestations of degree other than ownership of land. To whom did you raise your hat? Where did you sit in church? What clothes did you wear? It was always difficult in Tudor times to enforce sumptuary laws which prescribed what different groups could or could not wear. When one *arriviste*, Thomas Dolman, chose to display classical mottoes over the entrance of his new mansion, he selected a revealing self-confident text, 'the toothless envies the eater's teeth.'

Given the welter of examples of individual *arrivisme*, there was ample scope for contemporaries to generalize about upward mobility. Thus, Sir Thomas Smith, lawyer and government official, stated tersely in 1560 that 'gentlemen be made good cheap in England' – 'whosoever . . . can live idly and without manual labour, and will bear the port, charge and countenance of a gentleman, he shall be called master.' For Smith and many others what was happening was not amiss. But the process had its critics. Edward VI, for example, referred to 'merchants become landed men' who called themselves 'gentlemen though they be churles'.

One of the best-known expositions of the framework of social hierarchy was that of the country parson William Harrison, who later became Canon of Windsor. 'We divide our people commonly into four sorts,' he wrote in 1577. The first sort were gentlemen, with 'the prince at the head . . . the nobility next . . . and next to them knights, esquires and simple gentlemen'. Second came 'citizens and burgesses . . . of some substance to bear office' and third 'yeomen' of the country-side. At the base were members of the fourth group, people 'to be ruled and not to rule others' – 'day labourers, poor husbandmen, and all artificers, as tailors, shoemakers, carpenters'. 'These', Harrison went on, 'have no voice or authority in our commonwealth.'

Harrison, who allowed for wealth as well as birth in the determination of his hierarchy, left out professional people and the clergy, and he was less interested in what was happening at the lower end of the social scale than what was happening at the top. Here he recognized homogeneity: peers had legal identities since they received individual writs of summons to Parliament. They had no special judicial or territorial powers, how-ever, and their fortunes varied. The numbers of the high aristocracy – dukes, marquesses, earls, viscounts and barons – remained constant during the sixteenth century. (There were fifty-five peers in 1485 and the same number, though with many new names, in 1597.)

'Gentlemen' accounted for around only 2 per cent of the population of two counties as widely separated as Kent and Lancashire in the early seventeenth century, although their numbers there too were increasing. They were not a legally defined group, yet the distinction between 'gentlemen' and the rest was for Harrison the crucial one. Their strength lay in their ownership of land and the social and economic influence that went with it. They too, however, did not all share the same fortunes or outlook. It is not possible to generalize about the 6,000 men to whom the College of Heralds, the guardian of titled status, granted arms between 1560 and 1640. Some of the gentry, old or new, stayed at home; others were drawn into the life of London and the Court. After 1611 some of them were to become baronets, hereditary knights granted a new title. And while some of the gentry felt special concern for the 'meaner sorte', others lacked any sense of obligation.

The yeoman, who ranked next to the gentleman, like him did not have a legally defined rank and, unlike him, did not bear a coat of arms, but he could be richer, and he too could be called to public service as constable, churchwarden or juror. Below the yeomen were working husbandmen, with land of their own, descendants, romantic legend was to have it, of the archers of Crécy and Poitiers, although their numbers were decreasing. And alongside and below the working husbandmen there were many varieties of powerless poor men, dependent at best on wage labouring. The worst-off were survivors from older systems. Thus, three bondsmen or villeins on one Norfolk manor provided feudal services until 1575, and the last case concerning villeinage was handled in the royal courts as late as 1618.

Harrison had nothing to say about other distinctions within the fourth of his social groups, although it had its own hierarchies. It seemed enough to comment simply that these people were left out of government. 'The meaner sorte' were clearly a huge majority of the population, but they were at best a chorus, with individuals rising occasionally to sing unrehearsed parts of their own. Their economic powerlessness was as striking at all times as their political powerlessness:

> From pillar to post
> The poor man he was tossed:
> I mean the labouring man,
> I mean the ploughman,
> I mean the handycraft man,
> I mean the victualling man
> And also the good yeoman.

The lament for the plight of the poor, missing for much of the fifteenth century, was a recurring theme in the sixteenth century. So too was vagrancy, which was a perpetual concern of the justices of the peace. Indeed, in 1548 branding by hot iron with 'V' for 'Vagrant' was enacted. Before the Reformation the Church, through the monasteries and urban charity, had concerned itself directly, if not systematically, with provisions for the poor. So too had the guilds. While charitable giving may have declined in real terms after the Reformation, relief provided by public authority at a local level increased. It was often initiated by local justices of the peace and town councils before Parliament itself introduced major legislation in 1572, imposing compulsory poor rates.

York, for example, levied a compulsory rate as early as 1561. Between 1546 and 1557 London, which had taken the lead with a poor relief scheme of 1552, also reorganized its hospitals: St Bartholomew's was for the 'impotent poor' and Bethlehem (Bedlam) was for the insane.

National legislation on the subject became increasingly sophisticated. Thus, a statute of 1531 distinguished between vagrants and the sick and unemployed poor, only the latter being allowed to beg in their own parishes, while a statute of 1552 ordered parishes to register their poor and to meet their responsibilities in relation to the local resources available. Evolving policies culminated in important acts in 1597 and 1601 recognizing that the poor did not all belong to one category, confirming the parish as the unit of poor law administration, and empowering justices of the peace to levy poor rates and to pay for work provided for the able-bodied poor. This Elizabethan legislation became known as 'the old poor law', and it remained in force with changes (some of them substantial) until 1834. Overseers of the Poor were now appointed annually by the local justices, under penalty of fine, and took their place alongside churchwardens as busy, unpaid and necessary local officials.

In some earlier Tudor poor law legislation there had been a harshness of tone which reflected both the fear that the numbers of the poor were increasing in town and countryside and the belief that they were a threat to public order because they included 'rogues and vagabonds' as well as 'impotent poor' (the contemporary term for people of good character and goodwill who were sick or could not find employment). It also reflected in part, however, the sense that there were limits to what government could do to alleviate the problem of poverty. It is to this period that we can trace back a clear awareness that economic and social policy might not always move in the same direction.

Ideal and practice could clash in other ways. In theory, according to the laws of natural and mutual obligation, the community, local or national, was one. 'Note', the early sixteenth-century preacher Hugh Latimer told his congregation, 'that our Saviour biddeth us to say "us".' The use of the word 'Commonwealth' was as common as the use of the word 'Empire', and Elizabeth herself stressed that 'it was the duty of a prince to hold an equal hand over the highest and the lowest.' Shakespeare was not alone in pointing out that in death all trappings and ceremony disappeared and all people were in the same condition.

'Lordes, ladies and gentlemen, learned or unlearned of what estate or degree so ever you be of,' Andrew Boord told his readers in his *Breviary of Health* (1547), 'think not that no man can be holpen by no manner of medicines, if so be God do send the sickness, for he hath put a time to every man.'

Boord was aware, however, as Latimer was, that as long as people lived, some could get all manner of medicines and others could not: 'at our tyme physic is a remedy only for rich folks.' Theories of obligation did not necessarily work easily in practice, for, in fact, inequality expressed itself in contrasts that started with chances of life and death and extended through gender, work, diet, clothes and shelter to education and taste. Natural order could be used also as an argument against government intervention. As one sceptic argued in 1550, when an attempt was made to regulate prices of cheese and butter by proclamation, 'Nature will bear her course . . . and never shall you drive her to consent that a *penny-worth* of . . . shall be sold for a farthing.' Thomas Nashe, late sixteenth-century poet, pamphleteer and dramatist, expressed similar scepticism about the way theories of natural obligations worked in practice.

> In London the rich disdain the poor. The courtier the citizen. The citizen the countryman. One occupation disdaineth another. The merchant the retailer. The retailer the craftsman. The better sort of craftsman the baser. The shoemaker the cobbler.

Social contrasts were obvious enough, even on the surface. One of the most obvious was pointed out by Harrison. The 'gentilitie' ate wheaten bread; 'their household and poor neighbours rye or barley bread, and in time of dearth bread made . . . of beans, peas or oats'. Moreover, as the sixteenth century went by, this particular contrast was sharpened. Clothes were another obvious contrast. Only a small section of the population could contrive to wear (let alone pay for) starched ruffs, padded doublets and farthingales (framed hoops worn under the skirt). The best wool, fine linen and silk were worn at one end of the scale, and leather and rags at the other – and this in an age when bright clothes were particularly prized. Houses contrasted equally sharply. The differences were there too in hours of eating. The nobility and gentry, according to Harrison, dined and supped earlier than the merchants, and the husbandmen dined 'at high noon as they call it' and 'supped at seven or eight . . . As for the poorest sort,' he concluded, 'they generally dine and sup when they may, so that to talk of their order to repast, it was but a needless matter.'

One of the courtiers of Philip of Spain (Mary Tudor's husband) was struck by the contrast between English labourers' 'large diet' and their houses 'made of sticks and durte', while at the other end of the scale, for Harrison 'every man almost' was 'a builder' and 'the basest house of a baron dooth often match in our daies with some honours of princes in old time.' Indeed, it is to the builders of this period that we owe some of our most characteristic English domestic buildings. There was a competitive spirit behind much of the building, and it is significant that in four widely separated counties – Derbyshire, Essex, Somerset and Shropshire – more new country houses were built between 1570 and 1620 than in any other half-century. The size and management of large households changed less than might have been expected, but there were physical changes, like the introduction of galleries and lodges. There were also signs of an increasing desire for privacy, impossible for the poor.

Education, like diet, costume and shelter, was socially and culturally stratified, and the proliferation after the Reformation of a wide range of educational institutions, from small private establishments, often kept by a single master, to often well-endowed grammar schools – over 300 new schools were founded between 1500 and 1620 – on the whole exaggerated rather than reduced inequalities. Literacy, however, increased during the 1560s and 1570s, and although the rate of growth may have slackened off between then and the end of the century, there is evidence that 47 per cent of at least one major social group, the criminal class of London, could read soon after the beginning of the next. The book trade expanded – 259 books were published in the year 1600 alone – as did the business of printing broadsheets. Yet there was a substratum of illiteracy. It is interesting to note, for example, that Shakespeare's father always marked rather than signed documents.

There was also a distinct increase – with a setback in the last decade of the sixteenth century – in the total number of undergraduates receiving university education. They included parish priests – uneducated resident parish priests became less common – and laymen who could see new opportunities for themselves in administration. Yet access to the universities was not easy, for the education offered was costly.

As Harrison put it in 1577, 'it is in my time an hard matter for a poore man's child to come by a fellowship (though he be never so good a scholer).' The Inns of Court were even more exclusive, since they offered no scholarships, and in the early seventeenth century nine out of ten of the students there came from the aristocracy and the gentry.

Shared education, if only for the exclusive few, brought with it both increased cultural cohesion and a widening of interests among the gentry and the aristocracy; and although there were local variations in culture and style, there were now country gentlemen who through their literary and artistic interests could form something of a 'dispersed university'. Non-verbal culture was not despised: the complete 'Renaissance man', epitomized by Sir Philip Sidney, was expected to combine bodily and verbal skills – to dance as well as to read, to use the bow as well as the pen. Roger Ascham, who was to serve as a tutor to the young Elizabeth, had described in 1530 what the education of privileged young males implied – 'to ride comely, to run fair at the tilt or ring, to play at all weapons, to shoot fair in bow or surely in gun, to vault lustily, to run, to leap, to wrestle, to swim, to dance comely, to sing and play of instruments cunningly, to hawk, to hunt, to play at tennis and all pastimes generally which be joined with labour, used in open place and in the daylight, containing either some fit exercise for war or some pleasant pastime for peace.'

Ascham, nonetheless, enjoyed what were in time to be regarded as unpleasant pastimes like cockfighting, and Sir Thomas Elyot, an admirer of horsemanship but not of fox hunting, considered that 'daunting fierce and cruel beasts' was a spectacle that 'imparteth a majesty and dred to inferior persons'. (He did not add that Elizabeth herself had a private bear garden or that the savaging of bears was often arranged to delight her.) Despite shared interests across the social divides – horse racing was another – there were already 'high' and 'low' elements in the national culture. Musicians, writers and painters sought patronage from courtiers and gentlemen, either in London or in the great new country houses. Neither music nor painting were thought of as arts in the modern sense, but as they began to secure new influence outside the Church or the City they were now fitted into a privileged social context. The fashionable Elizabethan lute was an expensive instrument: so, too, were the virginals. Painting from Hans Holbein onwards was for kings, courtiers and gentlemen, and Nicholas Hilliard, official miniaturist to Elizabeth (himself the son of a sheriff of Exeter), expressed the wish that 'none should meddle' with limning (miniature painting) but 'gentlemen alone'. Within this increasingly distinct 'high culture' there was always a dividing line between the artist as gentleman, including gentleman-author, and the artist as craftsman, whatever the art, or as performer. Thus, Queen Elizabeth would admire the dancing of a courtier, but not of a professional dancing master. 'I will not see your man,' she once told the Earl of Leicester, who invited her to watch his dancing master dance. 'It is his trade.'

Literature, architecture and gardening, as well as music and painting, explored the language of allegory. The poet Edmund Spenser introduced many allegorical devices into his ingenious *Epithalamion*, describing in twenty-four stanzas the twenty-four hours of his wedding day, and the Roman Catholic recusant Sir Thomas Tresham (who had the number *tres*, representing the Trinity, concealed in his name) built a three-storey triangular lodge at Rushton in Northamptonshire, each side of which measured thirty-three feet, had nine windows (three in each storey) and bore an inscription of thirty-three letters.

Popular culture in small towns and villages still had its roots in tradition. Once Latimer could not preach in a village because the parishioners were celebrating 'Robin Hoode's day', while the Eliza-bethan Puritan Phillip Stubbes watched with horror parishioners gathering round 'their Maie pole, which they bring home with great veneration'. There were also new leisure pursuits to enjoy or to condemn. Organized horse racing, for example, began at York in 1530, and bowls was becoming more common by the end of the century. Stubbes thought that football was more 'a freendly kynde of fight' than a recreation, but he was biased. He was anticipated by Elyot who dismissed it as 'nothing but beastly fury and extreme violence'. Nonetheless, football was never stamped out, and a new boys' pastime was recorded also in 1598 – 'crickette' (along with other 'plaies') on a disputed piece of land at Guildford in Surrey.

Authority tried to regulate sports more than it was ever capable of doing. An act of 1504, for example, restricted the use of crossbows to the nobility and gentry, while insisting that longbow archery should be practised by the 'lower orders'. An act of 1526 permitted entry into private houses to search for illicit crossbows and to 'take and burn . . . tables, dice, cards, bowls, closhes, tenis balls'. There was to be one set of sports for the poor and one for the rich. Yet it was not so much private houses, or indeed alleys, but 'dissolute places' like alehouses which alarmed authority. They multiplied at a time when hops, dismissed earlier as a 'wicked and pernicious weed', became a staple ingredient of what became 'the national drink'. Their use was criticized by Conservatives:

> Hops, Reformation, Beys and Beer
> Came to England in one bad year.

The Reformation, the biggest of three major agencies of change, gave a new significance to change in the sixteenth century. Population growth, also clearly visible at the time through its effects, was the second agent of major change; the third, which most puzzled contemporaries, was inflation. Religious change was most direct: one Venetian observer described it as 'the greatest alteration that could possibly arise in the nation because a revolution in customs, laws, obedience and, lastly, in the very nature of the State itself, necessarily follows'.

With the political changes of the Reformation there were changes in the constitution, in the 'very State itself', for the king through Parliament now became Supreme Head of the Church of England, which was deemed sufficient of itself 'without the intermeddling of any exterior person'. Henceforth, Church and State were one. Church property, too, was transferred to the State, although much of it soon made its way from the Crown into the hands of the laity. Critics then and later called it 'plunder'. Yet even during the first phase of the Reformation, when sweeping changes in the power and position of the Church were masterminded by Thomas Cromwell, merchant and soldier before he became an administrator, the Reformation had other dimensions. The changes were carried through on a ground-swell of anti-clericalism, and there were imported influences, too, for Calvinism and Lutheranism, which Henry VIII had opposed, already had their adherents in England. Nonetheless, in most parts of the country there was a strong attachment to what has been called 'traditional religion'.

While most, but not all, of the clergy were prepared to accept the change, the views of the laity were inevitably divided, and the Church of England was not to become firmly established for another thirty years. Cromwell himself was to lose his head in 1540, and there were further religious struggles during the reigns of Henry's Protestant son,

Edward, and his Roman Catholic daughter, Mary. The Mass became the Holy Communion only in Edward's reign, when Archbishop Thomas Cranmer's new Prayer Book was introduced with its beautiful haunting English, threatened in the late twentieth century, but there were many people who opposed the change, like the disgruntled Cornishman who complained to Cranmer that the new service was 'but a Christmas game'. Mary's attempts to restore the Catholic faith were, however, doomed to failure by her determination to re-impose papal authority.

It was only with the Elizabethan settlement of 1558, initially a compromise between contending forces, that the Church of England found the basis on which it could acquire enduring support and, even then, despite the stress on 'uniformity', there were always parties within it. Religion could be no more completely controlled from above than sports or pastimes, and the desire for religious change to complete an unfinished Reformation continued to serve as a driving force for Puritans – the word, which was to extend its meaning in the seventeenth century, was current by the 1560s – pushing the Church further in a reformed direction with a different pattern of government and administration, different church interiors, and an open Bible in every home.

The biggest economic change resulting from the Reformation, directly affecting not only the State but the balance of social forces inside it, was the dissolution of the monasteries, a two-stage operation beginning in 1536 with 374 lesser houses with an annual income of less than £200,000, and continuing in 1538–40 with the 186 'great and solemn monasteries'. The object of this Cromwellian exercise was to enrich the crown. The monastic houses, which collected about half the total income of the Church, were an obvious target even though there were striking variations between rich and poor monasteries, just as there were between rich and poor dioceses. The first effect of the dissolution was to augment substantially royal annual income from monastic lands, and it needed a new agency, the Court of Augmentations, to deal with it. The assets could have provided a long-term relief to royal revenues, although the social consequences would have been uncertain.

But the crown did not keep all the land it had acquired: a small part was given away subject to feudal service, more was exchanged, and a large part was leased or sold at market prices, fixed at a minimum of twenty times the annual rent. Two out of every three peers were either granted or purchased monastic estates, and by the end of Henry VIII's reign two-thirds of the new wealth had been alienated in land market operations of unprecedented scale and speed. The freed lands passed for the most part not into the hands or pockets of 'new men' and speculators, but into the hands of existing local landowners, the peerage and gentry. In Yorkshire, for example, where, as in other counties, there were marked local variations between one part of the county and another, over a quarter of the gentry families of 1642 owned property which before 1540 had been held by the monasteries.

Once seized, there was no chance that the property would revert to the monasteries again; old believers were just as unwilling to part with their acquisitions as Protestants. Naves speedily became farmhouses, chantries became parlours and towers became kitchens. A Gloucester clothier, Thomas Bell, turned a Dominican priory into a factory; a furnace and forge were set up on the site of a Sussex monastery at Robertsbridge; and the end of the Black Friars' franchise in London released properties for use as theatres. Where monastic land continued to be leased under lay hands, shortened leases, racked rents and evicted tenants were common. Thus, the properties of St Albans Abbey were a century later worth eighty times their value at the time of dissolution.

A further dissolution of chantries, chapels, colleges, hospitals, fraternities and guilds in the reign of Edward VI completed the process of property transfer, although some of these institutions suffered more than others. Chantries, a favourite form of late medieval endowment, suffered more than guilds. Some of the income from this second dissolution was used to found grammar schools, hospitals and almshouses. Yet much land passed on to the market, and private individuals benefited directly as they had done during the 1530s.

Inevitably, the dissolution of the monasteries led also to social unrest, since the monasteries had been important employers and exercised many charitable functions, particularly in rural areas. The Pilgrimage of Grace had its origins, in part at least, in the closure of the great monasteries in the north of England. And if economic change brought with it social discontent, doctrinal change brought with it social division. The Reformation had both Catholic and Protestant martyrs: on the one side Sir Thomas More and Cardinal Fisher, who were executed in the reign of Henry VIII, and, on the other, Latimer, Ridley and Cranmer, burnt at the stake during Mary's reign and commemorated in John Foxe's widely read *Book of Martyrs*. Less well remembered, but just as significant, shires, villages and families were divided. In the reign of Mary, who was admired by the Holy Roman Emperor as '*une bonne anglaise*', many Protestants of all ranks moved into exile: of 472 people known to have fled, 166 were gentry, 67 clergy, 40 merchants, 119 students, 32 artisans and 13 servants. Some of them were zealously firm that 'the walls of Jerusalem should be built again in England'.

In earlier and in later years 'idolatrous' church images were destroyed, religious texts replaced medieval paintings on church walls, church plate was sold, altars gave way to communion tables, marriage was legalized for priests (in 1547 and again in 1559) and the Mass was no longer said in Latin. Yet, however great the zeal of reformers, much was carried over from the past, especially in the 'dark corners of the land', as the Puritans called them, counties like Lancashire and Shropshire. Elizabeth herself kept candles and a crucifix in her private chapel. The hierarchy of the Church – from bishops to parish priests – survived everywhere and retained much of its influence: five new dioceses – for a time six – were created following the dissolution of the monasteries. The ecclesiastical courts and Convocation kept their influence, too. The clergy never became a salaried body as they did in many other European Protestant countries, and they continued to be supported by tithes, endowments and income from their glebe lands.

Some lay patrons chose clergy for the colour of their churchmanship, but in much of the countryside old religious beliefs and customs prevailed. There were still services in the fields, for example, at Rogation Tide, and the parish boundaries were still perambulated. Screens which separated ministers and the people might be destroyed in Edward VI's reign, but in the reign of Elizabeth some of them returned despite Protestant objections. A 'witchcraze' in England began while the Reformation was still in progress – around 1550 – and continued for a century. Between 1563 and Elizabeth's death in 1603, in the county of Essex alone, 174 persons were indicted for 'black witchcraft', which was a capital offence, although only half that number were executed. 'White witchcraft' was generally acceptable, as were the 'cunning' men and women who practised it. Awe and superstition did not disappear from the society or the culture.

During the first phase of the Henrician Reformation, Thomas Cromwell ordered parish priests to keep registers of marriages, baptisms and deaths, a measure that was resented by many of the gentry as an infringement of individual liberties. Through systematic analysis of these registers, dating from 1538, historical demographers have been able to determine more accurately than for any previous period population trends and patterns during this period, and it is clear that the sixteenth century saw a dramatic growth in population which was to have far-reaching effects. By the 1470s population had started rising for the first time since the Black Death. Growth continued throughout the sixteenth and early seventeenth centuries, although there was a setback in 1557–9, years of epidemic disease, when burials were more than double the annual average, and there was also some slackening off of growth during the 1590s. By 1603, the population of England had probably passed the four million mark and was still growing. Rates of growth were not equal, of course, throughout the country, but to take one main farming county, Leicestershire, as an example of a not uncharacteristic scale of growth, population increased by 58 per cent between 1563 and 1603.

In the early sixteenth century there had been talk of depopulation. Now there was talk of over-population. For the geographer and historian Richard Hakluyt, writing in 1584, 'wee are growen more populous than ever heretofore.' For Sir Humphrey Gilbert, who wanted people to emigrate, England was 'pestered with people'. Local migration, particularly to places where there seemed to be available common land, and there was much of this, could lead to bitter litigation as well as sad complaint. Yet there was no serious Malthusian problem of mass starvation and unemployment, since the Tudor economy successfully absorbed the rise in population which was markedly less than that in many twentieth-century developing countries. As the number of people increased – and the numbers of cattle, sheep, horses and pigs – there was less vulnerability to famine than there had been earlier. Yet the great dearth of 1596 and 1597 was serious enough for a preacher to complain that 'our summers are no summers; our harvests are no harvests; our seed-times are no seed-times.' The price of flour tripled and real wages fell by about 20 per cent.

Fluctuations in rates of population growth can be traced back to bad harvests and to epidemics, and the two were still closely related to one another: 'first dearth and then plague'. If dearth was diminishing, so also was the intensity of plague. In 1499/1500 the plague had been so severe in London that Henry VII and his Court had moved to Calais to escape it. There was no such escape route in Elizabethan England. Nor was there ever for most royal subjects. There seems to have been relatively little change in the underlying patterns of demography at the time, although the expectation of life may have risen and the age of marriage was one or two years lower than it was a century later.

Analysis of the parish registers offers a unique insight into the structure of the population and household and family patterns. Families were not large, and they were nuclear (consisting of parents and children) rather than extended (hosts of relatives living together). Infant and child mortality rates were high, although there were marked differences between parishes. Over half the population was under the age of twenty-five while only 8–10 per cent were over sixty. Expectations of life were low: so also was the span of working life. Very young children from poorer families were expected to work from the age of six or seven.

Marriages in families of status and wealth, often involving property deals, were usually arranged, but there were arranged marriages at other levels of society as well. The wedding ceremony itself was a festive and public occasion. Marriage practices were localized, and while there were contemporary complaints of early and hasty marriages, most people, either ordinary or privileged, did not marry much younger than in the late twentieth century; they were, indeed, much older in relation to their expectation of life. At the same time, illegitimacy rates were low until the last years of the sixteenth century, when limited evidence suggests a sharp rise continuing into the seventeenth century. There was a large minority of unmarried people and of children with only one parent alive.

The family was the basic unit of production, although viewed within the context of Western European countries there was a relatively high number of family groups which were not production units. Within a household there were non-members of the family, servants and dependants, the number varying with wealth and status so that the poorest households tended to be the smallest. The more children, the greater the strain. Not surprisingly, there was considerable migration of the landless poor. The areas to which they migrated were more 'open' in social atmosphere than the old 'fielden' areas of the Midlands. Trade was a magnet.

It is far more difficult to generalize about actual behaviour within families, particularly among poor families, than it is to identify demographic trends. The marriage system allowed for a considerable play of personalities, although always within the context of the authority of the head of the household. There is ample evidence from Shakespeare's plays of individual women who ruled their husbands, and servants might rule men too. Likewise, while girls were in general not as well educated as boys, there were significant exceptions, including Anne Boleyn and the learned daughters of Sir Anthony Cooke, one of whom married William Cecil. The beating of children by their parents could be recommended or frowned upon even in books of guidance, and there were many examples in practice of parents actually demonstrating signs of love for their children. There were also examples both of generational conflict, not surprising in an age which flaunted youth and venerated age, and of cross-generational sympathy. Apprentices were often considered to be one of the hopes for the future. 'If there were any good to be done in these days,' wrote an Elizabethan minister, 'it is the young men that must do it, for the old men are out of date.'

Contemporary generalizations about the balance of the population were often linked to lively and concerned comment about the price rise, the third major agent of change in this period, particularly during the decades in which prices rose most rapidly: the 1540s, 1550s and 1590s. Prices rose throughout Western Europe, starting with Spain, following a period of stability in the fifteenth century. Taking a selective Phelps Brown/Hopkins price index for England, with 1451–75 prices as the base line of 100, the index had risen to over 160 by 1520 and to 170 by 1555. And there were two extraordinary years in the middle of the century: in 1556 the index reached 370 and in 1557 a peak of 409. The index had dropped back to 281 by 1594, but rose to 505 two years later and to 685 in 1597. The trough never fell below 400 again and was to reach a mid-seventeenth-century peak of 839 in 1650.

When compared with late twentieth-century continuing inflation, this upward movement may seem mild rather than revolutionary, but it has been identified, nonetheless, as the highest between 1250 and 1900, and it significantly disrupted social relationships. Economic historians have argued as much about its causes as social historians have about its consequences, but there is now common recognition that the economy still included a large subsistence sector which was affected by the change only to a limited extent; that there were marked geographical differences in its incidence; that the prices of different commodities did not move uniformly; and also that movements of wages and rents, as well as movements of prices, have to be taken into the reckoning at every stage.

No simple explanation seems adequate. Contemporaries attached special significance to the import of large quantities of Spanish treasure from across the Atlantic and to the debasement of the coinage; and while emphasis has shifted recently to the influence of the growth of population on demand, the fact that far more spectacular population growth two centuries later did not produce a comparable increase in prices over a long period suggests that this alone cannot have been responsible. And if debasement was more a symptom of trouble than a cause, it is nonetheless true that the velocity of circulation of money was speeded up by Henry VIII's debasements of 1526 and 1544–6, which broke a long tradition of standard metal coins and reduced the fineness of silver first by a half and next by two-thirds. Later debasements by Protector Somerset reduced the proportion of silver to a quarter.

The fiscal policies of the crown were of direct influence also, as in later inflations. Henry VII combined parsimony with lavish spending on buildings and ceremonies. Henry VIII's army in France in 1544 was bigger than any earlier English army that had set foot on the Continent, and this time there was no plunder to collect. During the last eight years of his reign Henry spent more on futile war than the total yield of taxes and loans. Meanwhile, the demand for monastic lands, stimulated after the dissolution of the monasteries, pushed up land prices and rents: meadow land in Derbyshire fetched a rent in 1584 four times that of 1543, while rents in parts of Kent near to the growing metropolis rose sharply enough for William Lambarde to anticipate later theories of rent as an unearned surplus. It was not 'the quantity of their possessions or the fertility of their soil' which enriched the gentry there, Lambarde suggested, but 'the benefit of the situation of the country itself'.

There has been protracted debate about the effects of price and rent rises on the different orders of society. The fortunes of the landowners, including the high aristocracy, varied and so did their expenditures. Some peers spent ostentatiously on building, clothes, food or drink and got into aristocratic debt, although this was not always a sign of poverty.

A few peers of ancient lineage, like the Berkeleys, found themselves in serious difficulties, selling manors and dismissing servants; their plight was explained by their inefficiency as much as by their extravagance. Others, like the Spencers of Althorp and the Russells of Woburn, built up their estates and their wealth with them. Older landlords with scattered estates were often able to balance profits from some against losses from others.

These were times when the industrious, the enterprising and the lucky (to be found in every generation) – and above all, the lawyers – could exploit the situation, justifying John Stow's generalization that 'there was no want of anything to him that wanted not money.' The unlucky victims, however, were not necessarily unindustrious or unenterprising. They included people with fixed incomes, or income from tithes expressed in kind, and people with insecure land tenures. Cottagers and wage workers, both in the countryside and in the towns, suffered seriously since wages lagged behind prices, and usually they had no other ways of supplementing their meagre incomes. Furthermore, with the rise in population, labour lost the bargaining advantage it had enjoyed during the late fourteenth and fifteenth centuries: the Phelps Brown/Hopkins real wages index reached its lowest point in seven centuries in 1597, the year of Shakespeare's *A Midsummer Night's Dream*.

For the Crown there were major financial problems. As in the thirteenth and fourteenth centuries, monarchs found it difficult to live on their own. Wars had become costly because of gunpowder and changes in the techniques of warfare. Henry VIII was forced to raise a 'subsidy' in 1512, a Parliamentary tax based on an assessment of individual wealth and Wolsey extorted an 'amicable grant' in 1525. Although Elizabeth's reign began peacefully – and the costs of government fell – she too had to turn to Parliament for financial support increasingly as her reign went by. Her ministers and her taxpayers were at one in economizing; in 1576 the Speaker of the Commons congratulated her on having 'most carefully and providentially delivered this kingdom from a great and weighty debt . . . a cancer able to eat up not only private men and their patrimonies . . . but also princes and their estates'. Yet while as late as 1597 her Chancellor of the Exchequer could congratulate her – and himself – for keeping the country free from 'extreme and miserable taxes', when Elizabeth died the country was left with a debt equivalent to more than one year's income.

The quest of the Crown for new sources of income was bound to provoke argument with Parliament, and, as in earlier centuries, it raised constitutional issues both of political representation and of individual rights. The House of Commons was always suspicious of extended feudal dues and it did not easily yield to demands for extraordinary purposes through subsidies; at no time did it offer financial support for a standing army in peacetime. It was also suspicious of any new forms of taxation. The most important of these were monopolies, which were conferred on successful applicants by the Crown in return for cash, a device originally introduced by Henry VIII to protect skill and to encourage innovation. Ship money, an extension to the whole country of a fourteenth-century impost to outfit ships for the protection of the coasts, originally only levied on port towns, was revived by Elizabeth, and also became a bone of contention in the next century. It was in Elizabeth's reign that the attack on monopolies began; and she faced critical Parliaments in 1593, 1597 and 1601 when she tried to get increased support from them. In 1601, for example, when Members of Parliament were told that the Crown had granted monopoly patents for a long list of items ranging from currants to playing cards (the latter a monopoly enjoyed by Sir Walter Raleigh), one Member provoked a memorable exchange when he called out, 'Is not bread there?' 'Bread?' asked other Members. 'No,' replied the first, 'but if order be not taken for these, bread will be there, before the next Parliament.'

The relationship between the income of the Crown and the income of its subjects was bound to change in a period of economic and social change, and in Tudor times the changes began not with playing cards or with currants – or for that matter with bread – but with wool. 'The web of our life', wrote Shakespeare, 'is a mingled yarn, good and ill together,' and in sheep farming there was ample evidence of both.

It was a rise in the price of wool that encouraged the first sixteenth-century expansion in flocks and pasturage between 1510 and 1520, and after a contraction there was a further burst which lasted until 1551: 'of all stock the rearing of sheep is most profitable,' wrote Fitzherbert in his Book of Husbandry in 1579. (By then the Spencers had 13,000 sheep.) Yet there was a serious enough contraction of demand for wool after 1551 to lead to considerable unemployment in the clothing industry, a fall in the sheep population and a shift among sheep farmers to meat and cheese production. Grain prices too rose faster than wool prices between 1548 and 1600.

The protracted argument about enclosures revealed the same sharp differences of values as in the fifteenth century, particularly in the Midland counties in the heart of 'open-field' England. A statute of 1489, often echoed in later statutes, had forbidden all depopulation and conversion of arable to pasture, but it could not be enforced, and Leicestershire, where some 140 villages or hamlets out of a total of 270 were partially or completely enclosed between 1485 and 1607, was one of the main storm centres.

Already in 1520 a ballad described how:

> Gret men makyth now a dayes
> A shepecott in the churche.

And a generation later complaints could be heard that there were men 'that live as though there were no God at all'. 'They take our houses over our heads, they buy our grounds out of our hands, they raise our rents, they levy great (yea unreasonable) fines, they enclose our commons. No custom, no law or statute can keep them from oppressing us.'

Thoughtful contemporaries were at pains to distinguish between a farmer's enclosure of his land for 'improvement' and rich men's enclosure of 'other men's commons'. They also drew distinctions between enclosure by force and enclosure by consent. But as common rights were lost, 'greed' often seemed more in evidence than the desire to improve the land, evident in books like Thomas Tusser's *A Hundred Good Points of Husbandry* (later expanded to 500 points, few of which were original), that first appeared in 1557. Not surprisingly, there were serious anti-enclosure riots, for example in 1548–9.

The increasing prevalence of usury (lending, usually at high rates of interest) seemed to be a related problem, and after Parliament had legalized it in 1571, reviving an act of Henry VII repealed in 1552, Harrison could observe that 'usury, a trade brought in by the Jews, was now perfectly practised almost by every Christian and so commonly, that he is accounted for a fool that doth lend his money for nothing.' There were forces restraining as well as sharpening economic appetites: thus, Sir John Gostwick, a Bedfordshire squire, who benefited from monastic spoils in Henry VIII's reign, could advise his heirs 'to heighten no rent unless your farmers have heightened theirs to subtenants'. Yet by the end of the century there was increasing resistance to interference from government in matters like enclosure and usury, although dislike of 'middle men' was as strong as ever. Sir Walter Raleigh was not alone in urging that every man should be left free, 'which is the desire of a true Englishman'.

This cry was to be raised in the future mainly in relation to industry, a term not yet used in its modern sense in the sixteenth century, when most 'industries' were still linked with agriculture, operated on a small scale and were at a craft stage.

Textiles were still the biggest of them. Camden called their manufacture 'one of the pillars of commonwealth', and they were the main source of livelihood. They flourished now not so much in the most important wool-growing areas as in parts of western England and the north, where there was a reserve of labour and cloth could be made more cheaply. The expansion of the market led not to the concentration of production in factories – these were a phenomenon of the future – but to work being 'put out': clothiers with sufficient capital collected orders, hired out looms and depended on the manufacture of others for their sales. English cloth remained the country's most valuable export, with a steady overseas level of demand from 1559 to 1603, followed in the early sixteenth century by a further boom that generated rapid economic growth. This was the period when immigrant craftsmen, a source of strength to the Tudor economy in this as in other industries, introduced the so-called 'new draperies' with names like 'beys', 'perpetuonos' and 'shaloons', fabrics which were cheaper, lighter, and less durable, and highly amenable, therefore, to changes of fashion. Fashion might be dismissed by Harrison as 'a fantastical folly', but its exploitation could be highly profitable and the new draperies were there to stay. So also were the immigrants who first made that manufacture possible. 'What country in the world is there,' a Member of Parliament asked in 1596, 'that nourisheth so many aliens from all parts of the world as England doth?'

In one flourishing branch of the textile industry, hosiery, there was one indigenous invention that was a portent of things to come. A clergyman, William Lee, 'the first English mechanician of his own or any preceding age', invented a knitting frame in the late sixteenth century, and it was quickly adopted in the flourishing hosiery industry in the East Midlands. There are many myths about Lee's invention and the motives which inspired it: one was that he was distressed to see his wife endlessly knitting stockings by hand to supplement his meagre income. There was no myth, however, in the misfortunes of his later career, which anticipated those of later inventors. He died in poverty in France in 1610.

Other genuine 'new industries' were assisted by foreign immigrants: they included paper making, printing, gun founding and the manufacture of gunpowder. (Francis Bacon was to describe gunpowder and printing as two of the three great inventions of his age, the mariner's compass being the third.) Development in these industries was overshadowed, however, by the substantial growth of the lead, copper and iron industries. There was a growing demand for products made out of all these metals from cast-iron cannons to pots and pans. One of the most important suppliers was not a new man but the sixth Earl of Shrewsbury who also opened glass works and coal mines.

The introduction of the blast furnace at the very end of the fifteenth century had been a significant new technical development in the iron industry, and a century later there were more than sixty furnaces in operation, most of them alongside finery forges in the forest of the Weald in Kent and Sussex. It was in that area too, where iron had been produced for centuries, that steel was first produced (with the help of German craftsmen) in 1565, and a slitting mill opened in 1588. Whether or not iron production was already beginning to be held back by lack of the timber necessary for the charcoal used in the bloomeries and blast furnaces has been much disputed. It has been persuasively argued that the extent of woodland did not, in fact, diminish as the result of the ironmasters' operations. Timber prices actually rose more slowly than those of any other agricultural product.

Harrison, who rued the 'rewmes' and 'catarres' caused by the smoke-carrying chimneys of London, wondered why the Weald did not use coal, the product of the biggest and most concentrated of the mining industries. The increase in coal output, with Durham and Northumberland in the lead in distribution, was big enough for some historians to write again of an 'industrial revolution'; and while coal was not yet directly associated with the iron industry, as it was to be in the eighteenth and nineteenth centuries, its domestic use was already darkening the skies of London. In 1563–4, 33,000 tons were shipped to London from

Newcastle (Shakespeare's grubby 'Master Seacole') and in 1597-8 163,000 tons. In the absence of the steam engine, which both depended on coal for fuel and enabled deeper coal mines to be pumped and brought into use, there were, however, inevitable limits to growth.

The working lives of miners and their feelings as communities reveal continuities both before and after the advent of the steam engine, particularly in the north-east. They were already a tightly knit group in Tudor times, as conscious of their bargaining power as they were of the risks of their occupation. Coal was their life.

Yet coal mining was not the only industry to flourish outside the towns. The woollen industry too was not as closely associated with towns as it had been in the Middle Ages and was to be again in later centuries: Worcester was quite exceptional in having almost half its identified craftsmen working in the textile industry in the second half of the sixteenth century. Some old corporate towns, like Coventry, were shrinking in size and losing in economic importance in relation to the countryside or to smaller unincorporated towns like Birmingham; and there were public complaints in York that weavers were moving across the moors to Halifax, where there was abundant water power. The economic historian Sir John Clapham, himself from the north, suggested that water power was 'a solvent of guild power from the days of the first fulling mill', although there is little evidence that the craft guilds of York or those of Norwich, England's second city in population, were a brake on progress during the sixteenth century. Norwich, however, had an immigrant population of about one-third as early as the 1570s.

Some historians, seizing on observers' comments or complaints from the towns themselves and on expressions of concern on the part of central government, have discerned an intensification of urban crisis during the period from 1520 to 1570 or even later. Others have spotlighted the oligarchic character of urban government which excluded the many and carried with it costly obligations for the few. Once again, however, they have confronted a complex and variegated pattern of problem and opportunity.

The decline of Winchester and Lincoln, which had started in earlier centuries, was associated in part, at least, with the Reformation. Yet cities like York and Norwich, where there were the same sharp breaks, soon took on new functions and acquired new activities. York was the headquarters of the Council of the North, Norwich a centre of the new draperies. Each of them began to exert an increasingly strong pull on the local gentry and the aristocracy through the provision of leisure facilities, shops and even of town houses. And while Southampton was declining in size, Newcastle was emerging as a thriving port. Manchester was already described by the writer John Leland, an active explorer of his own country, as 'the fairest, best builded, quickest and most populous town of all Lancashire'. It remained under the control of a manor court, however, while smaller and commercially unimportant places, like Grampound in Cornwall, became new parliamentary boroughs.

There was much new urban building, along with other improvements like paving, lighting and 'scavenging', in smaller towns as well as in regional capitals and county towns. Leland used the term 'suburbs' when he was describing urban expansion; and for one writer in 1579 these were no longer simply places for the poor to live 'outside the walls' but for the rich who were seeking fresh air and less noise. The centres of towns were still crowded places where different social groups lived in close proximity and where different economic and social activities were carried out in juxtaposition, in churches and markets, houses and warehouses, shops and brothels. But there was a rural flavour too. Gardens were common and pigs could still wander through the streets. The framework of control was, of course, being further extended – with a multiplicity of provisions. Thus, as a fire precaution, the use of thatch was banned in Norwich in 1509 and in Bristol in 1574, and in Leicester it was enacted that no person of whatever degree, except officers and the watch should be abroad in the streets after nine o'clock at night.

One city in England was still growing and increasingly dwarfed all others. London, five times as populous as Norwich in Henry VIII's reign, was twelve to fourteen times as large by 1600. In the early 1520s its population was probably about 70,000, but by 1600 it had probably passed 200,000. The first panoramic view of it was drawn in 1588, and forty years later John Stow's magnificent *Survey* of the city penetrated behind the panorama to the people and forces responsible for its change. Stow himself was seventy years old when he wrote it, so he could remember how things had changed. Not surprisingly, London, like all great cities, inspired and provoked contradictory reactions. Edmund Spenser penned the immortal line 'Sweet Thames! run softly till I end my song,' but a foreign ambassador maintained that the city stank and was 'the filthiest in the world'.

The main complaint about London was that it was 'swallowing up all the other towns and cities', particularly the other ports. 'Soon,' Elizabeth's Scots successor James I (1603–25) was to remark, 'London will be all England.' The complaint was exaggerated, but the fear that the city would serve as a centre of crime, disorder and disease, all of which would spread, was real enough. At least one-third of London's immigrants were scraping a bare subsistence there. Proclamations of 1580 and 1602 banning further building within three miles of the gates of the City of London, prohibiting multiple occupation of existing properties and ordering lodgers who had arrived during the previous seven years to leave could not hold in check the human flow.

Towards the end of the Tudor period there were signs of increasing, though still incomplete, national integration. Local economies were becoming more specialized and more complementary, although in general the richer south and east were drawn into the emerging unified pattern more than the poorer north and west. Increasingly, different parts of the island were being linked by the expanding coastal trade. Nonetheless, parts of the Midlands far from the sea, including, for example, Wigston Magna, were still tied essentially to subsistence rather than to exchange, and in the most flourishing section of the coastal trade, different measures for weighing coal were still used in London and Newcastle. Standardization was only beginning.

The surge of exploration and discovery, heralded by Henry VIII's development of the navy, which led Elizabethans like Martin Frobisher and Francis Drake to cross the oceans, began in England itself as a growing interest in its geography and history. Interest in the kingdom as a whole is apparent in every page of John Leland's *Itinerary*. 'I was totally inflamed', Leland had told Henry VIII, 'with a love to see thoroughly all those parts of your opulent and ample realm that I had read of . . .' Half a century later, Christopher Saxton produced his first county maps and historians began to produce county histories.

Under Elizabeth the Church once more became an agent of national integration: it was 'by law established', that is by the Second Act of Supremacy in 1559, that the unity of the Church and of the realm were deemed to be not complementary but identical. Elizabeth's birthday became a holy day of the Church in 1568, and the royal arms were displayed in every church. At Tivetshall in Norfolk, where they still survive, they were painted perhaps significantly on the reverse side of a medieval Doom picture. After 1559 attendance at church was compulsory by statute and non-attendance punishable by fine and imprisonment; outward conformity rather than inner belief was the crucial factor. As Camden put it, 'there can be no separation between religion and the commonwealth.'

Language also was becoming more standardized, partly as a result of the development of poetry, although Cornish continued to be spoken and different words continued to be used in different parts of the country (sometimes even in the same county) for cattle, clothes and domestic objects. The power of language in Elizabethan prose owed much to its closeness to folk speech, 'to the English of ploughing, carting, selling and small town gossip', as one historian has put it. But that was only one of its debts. The boy who drove the plough might well have turned for his imagery to the Great Bible of 1539 or the Book of Common Prayer, and the merchant might have picked up words like chocolate, tobacco and potato from across the Atlantic. Shakespeare himself, who could coin unforgettable phrases, each of which was to have its own later history (like 'we have seen better days' or 'brave new world'), turned often to the law. Scholars were among the enthusiasts for the language: 'Why not all in English?' asked Richard Mulcaster, who became High Master of St Paul's. The English tongue was 'no whit behind either the subtle Greek for couching close or the stately Latin for spreading fair'.

Social integration was expressed in the new art of the theatre, which brought together different sections of the population. There were links between Elizabethan drama and medieval miracle and morality plays, but there was one great difference: Tudor drama was essentially secular. In 1545 the Master of the Revels became responsible for overseeing players and playhouses and soon found himself responsible – under the Lord Chamberlain – for the censorship of plays. In this way a lay officer took over a function hitherto exercised by the Church. By the end of the century the most famous actors were being condemned by both their religious and their lay critics for dealing in 'profane fables'. It was in London in particular that a new theatre-going public emerged. In 1576 James Burbage built 'The Theater' in Finsbury Fields, and other theatres like the Swan and the Globe, most famous of all playhouses, in Southwark, followed in its wake (to be rebuilt in the late twentieth century). Actors were acquiring social status and, in a few cases, fortune. Richard Burbage left a large sum at his death; Edward Alleyn, who retired before he was forty, bought a manor and founded a college at Dulwich.

The Elizabethan world often seemed to contemporaries less like a 'scene' or a 'world picture', as scholars have seen it subsequently, and more like a performance on a stage. Most famous of all such images are Shakespeare's lines from *As You Like It*:

> This wide and universal theatre
> Presents more woeful pageants than the scene
> Wherein we play in.

But it was Raleigh, historian and poet as well as courtier and navigator, who carried it furthest:

> What is our life? A play of passion:
> Our mirth? the music of division.
> Our mothers' wombs the tiring-houses be
> Where we are dressed for life's short comedy.
> Heaven the judicious sharp spectator is,
> That sits and marks still who doth act amiss:
> Our graves that hide us from the searching sun
> Are like drawn curtains when the play is done.

Social historians recognize the value of reactions of poets – and later of novelists – to their society as historical evidence. They appreciate also, however, that they need close critical scrutiny. They may encompass uncommon views of common experience and common views uncommonly, even dazzlingly, expressed. But they may also register unique experience. It is a mistake, then, to use labels like 'the age of Shakespeare'. Shakespeare belonged to more than one world. He was a man of his time, but he was not limited by it, and his plays, which draw deeply from a quarry of historical as well as current material, have meant new things for new generations.

In his own generation, he could appeal to the same English pride that Elizabeth stirred. No other sovereign since 1066 had so little foreign blood, and she was so much at the centre of the stage, claiming her subjects' love as well as their obedience, that if any label is to be attached to the age it must be that of 'the age of Elizabeth'. She left no heir. When Henry VII, her grandfather, had crossed into England from Wales with a small army, carrying Cadwaladr's red dragon on his banner to defeat Richard III and to found the Tudor dynasty, he had come as an illegal claimant, but when James VI of Scotland marched south from Scotland, it was at the invitation of the English Parliament.

6 REVOLUTION, RESTORATION AND SETTLEMENT

These are times for historians to write who seek to avoid all calm narrations as a dead water, to fill their volumes with cruell wars and seditions. I desire not employment at these times.

Sir Henry Slingsby, 1643

We found that we that till that hour lived in great plenty and great order found ourselves alike fishes out of the water, and the same so changed, that we knew not at all how to act any part but obedience.

Anne, Lady Fanshawe, *Memoirs*, 1600–1672

What will not all oppressed, rich and religious people do to be delivered from all kinds of oppression, both spiritual and temporal, and to be restored to purity and freedom in religion, and to the just liberty of their persons and estates?

Richard Overton, *A Remonstrance of Many Thousand Citizens*, 1646

I cannot forbear carrying my watch in my hand in the coach this afternoon, and seeing what o'clock it is one hundred times and am apt to think with myself, how could I be so long without one.

Samuel Pepys, *Diary*, 13 May 1665

The English Parliament did not then include 'the poorer sort'. Nor did it three centuries later. Yet Robert Royce in an account of Suffolk, which appeared in 1618, thought it 'fit' to begin his observations with 'the poorer sort from whom all other . . . sorts take their beginning'. 'As well the poor as the rich proceed from the Lord . . . The rich cannot stand without the poor . . . and the humblest thoughts which smoke from a poor man's cottage are as sweet a sacrifice unto the Lord as the costly perfumes of the prince's palace.'

Both the content and language belong unmistakably to the seventeenth century. The poor were often to be heard, asserting claims of their own, not always humble in tone, during the late 1640s and 1650s, and religion, usually more militant than consoling, was to colour most of the social comment and almost all of the social protest then and earlier. The magnificent Authorized Version of the English Bible of 1611 preceded by thirty years the most unauthorized uses made of it, and it was to survive them all. Yet the century was not all of one piece. Long before it ended, the demands of the poor were no longer heard so loudly. Indeed, they were often not heard at all. Nor was radical religion any longer a major driving force 'turning the world upside down'. There had been restoration following revolution, a revolution which according to a recent historian of the period, Conrad Russell, was the product of an 'unrevolutionary people'. Taking the seventeenth century as a whole, economic progress rather than the force of religion was the major determinant of social change. Another historian has concluded that 'for all save the "Poor" who benefited relatively little from economic progress – and their numbers remained very large – life was a little more varied, a little less primitive' in 1700 than in 1600. The generalization was true: the qualification was necessary.

It would be misleading to try to write the social history of the seventeenth century entirely in terms of social structures and social processes, for, above all else, this was a century of dramatic and unprecedented events: a civil war which drew in broad sections of the population; the execution of Charles I (1625–49) and the rule of and offer of the kingship to Oliver Cromwell, born a farmer; the return of Charles I's heir from foreign exile in 1660. Even then there were still unprecedented events in the offing. Edward Hyde, first Earl of Clarendon, told a new Parliament at the beginning of Charles II's reign (1660–85) that he hoped it would join in restoring 'the whole nation to its primitive temper and integrity, to its good old manners, its good old humour and its good old nature', but twenty-eight years later there was a second 'revolution'. After Charles II's brother James II (1685–8) had tried to rule the country not through Anglican squires and parsons but through Roman Catholics and dissenters – and the effort was possible – a new king, William III (1688–1702), married to James

II's daughter, was brought in from Holland – a Protestant country
against which England had fought earlier in the century, and England
was thrust into a protracted European war.

For contemporaries the 'Glorious Revolution' of 1688 did not require
the kind of explanation Clarendon had offered for the Civil War – that
it was influenced by so many 'miraculous circumstances' that 'men
might well think that heaven and earth and the stars designed it.' To
most men in the know, and to many who were not, the revolution of
1688 was a victory of pragmatism and human reason responding to a
clearly perceived threat to 'the Protestant religion and the laws and
liberties of this kingdom', and its effect was to settle issues of contention
that had profoundly disturbed earlier generations. A 'balance' was
established which was to be maintained for years to come. During the
nineteenth century, the historian T. B. Macaulay, presenting a Whig
interpretation of history and tracing connections across the centuries,
was to speak of it as making Englishmen 'different from others': 'because
we had a preserving revolution in the seventeenth century . . . we
have not had a destroying revolution in the nineteenth.' For some
twentieth-century historians of the seventeenth century, however, it
marked the end of 'the heroic age' of English politics.

Not surprisingly, the events of the seventeenth century, more dramatic than anything on the Tudor stage, left vivid memories. They
could also leave people breathless, even exhausted. Thus, Sir John
Reresby, member of the established landed gentry, could write in the
1690s that he had seen so many changes 'and so many great and little
men removed in my time, that I confess it began to cool my ambition,
and I began to think there was a time when every thinking man would
choose to retire and to be content with his own rather than venture
that and his conscience for the getting of more.' He concluded with
the conviction 'that safety was better [than] greatness'.

All the great events, particularly those leading up to the Civil War,
had provoked argument, sometimes fundamental argument; or rather,
perhaps, the events themselves were the outcomes of argument, not all
of it resolved or even exhausted, much of it conducted from the pulpit
or through the medium of the printed word. This was a reflection of
the greatly increased literacy of the period. 'When there is much desire
to learn,' wrote John Milton, the great Puritan poet, a pioneer of free
speech, 'there will of necessity be much arguing, much writing, many

opinions; for opinion in good men is but knowledge in the making.' There was vigorous censorship of the printed word during the 1630s, but the authorities could never control completely either pulpit or tavern; and when censorship ended briefly in 1641 the great age of the pamphlet followed. Twenty-two pamphlets were published in 1640, 1,996 in 1642. This application of the printing press to the requirements of social and political struggle enlivened both religion and politics. It also provided massive material for historians.

The argument ranged widely over taxation, the law and the liberties of the subject, religion, land and trade, authority and property. Many of the economic arguments early in the century originated in the financial difficulties of the Crown, which, never easy since the late Middle Ages, now became increasingly awkward because the sixteenth-century price rise, a European phenomenon, was slow to come to an end. Indeed, when prices flattened out in the 1620s, this was a sign not of stability nor of improvement but of economic strain. The highest recorded exports of cloth were in 1614, but eight years later the figure had been cut to a half. These were years of an adverse balance of trade, frequent bad harvests, and distress, particularly in the woollen industry. Jacobean houses and furniture might impress their own and future generations by their weight and permanence, but the economy was volatile even when it was not under pressure. There were 'seven fat years' from 1629 to 1635, but many hard times thereafter. The years 1642, when the Civil War began, and 1649, when the king was executed, were particularly bad years, for example, as was 1659, the year before Charles II returned to the throne.

Economic historians have noted 'a real and prolonged crisis arising from a radical readjustment of England's foreign trade', but contemporaries blamed the plague and the bad harvests, which for obvious economic reasons reduced home demand and led to a withdrawal of gold specie to pay for grain imports. 'Scarcity of money' was another regular complaint. There were personal villains too, perhaps most notably Alderman William Cockayne and his partners, who, having promised much in an attempt to win over the cloth finishing trade from the Dutch, failed disastrously. The land of Cockayne, which had long meant a land of make-believe, acquired a new contemporary relevance.

James I was aware from the time of his succession to the English throne of what he called 'the canker of want'. Yet in 1610, when the

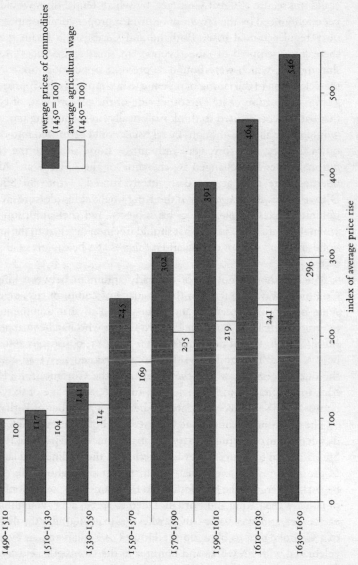

Price rises, 1490–1650

- average prices of commodities (1450=100)
- average agricultural wage (1450=100)

index of average price rise

years

years	prices of commodities	agricultural wage
1490–1510	100	100
1510–1530	117	104
1530–1550	141	114
1550–1570	245	169
1570–1590	302	205
1590–1610	391	219
1610–1630	404	241
1630–1650	546	296

debt which he inherited from Elizabeth had increased three-fold, he could not secure a 'Great Contract' by which feudal dues would have been renounced by the crown in return for proper fiscal compensation on a regular annual basis. Both he and Charles I, a lavish spender, thereafter attempted to raise revenue by 'shifts and devices', such as ship money, which were bound to provoke opposition. So, too, was the delegation of the raising of revenue to tax-farmers who appropriated a large proportion of it. The other side of the picture was, of course, that parliaments refused to think realistically: in accounting terms they would never allocate enough. Fiscal issues could be turned into constitutional issues, therefore, very early in the story, although the constitutional issues had changed by the time of the Civil War. 'All our liberties were now at one dash utterly ruined,' wrote Sir Simonds D'Ewes in his *Autobiography*, 'if the King might at his pleasure lay what unlimited taxes he pleased on his subjects, and then imprison them when they refused to pay. What should freemen differ from the ancient bondsmen and villeins of England if their estates be subject of arbitrary taxes?'

Much, although not all, of the early argument between king and Commons was conducted in the language of common law, especially since matters of precedent and rights raised in that argument were referred to the law courts. Sir Edward Coke, who had been appointed Lord Chief Justice of the King's Bench in 1613, obstinately refused to behave like a 'lion under the throne'. Concerned above all else with the due process of law and the liberties of the Commons, he looked back for inspiration to Magna Carta. In 1616, at the age of sixty-four, he was dismissed. Five years later he became a Member of Parliament.

The accession of James I had been seen by both Puritan and Catholic dissidents as an opportunity to try to win the concessions they had wanted but had failed to secure under Elizabeth; and the outlines and language of the religious argument that was to persist throughout the century began to emerge in the first decade. At the Hampton Court Conference of January 1604 King and Puritans failed to agree, after wrangling with each other, and a year later Guy Fawkes was executed after the discovery of a Catholic plot to blow up the Houses of Parliament, an event still celebrated with fireworks and bonfires in the twentieth century. The Puritans, who were the bigger and more dangerous group, well represented in Parliament itself, demanded that 'God, that chose this corner of the earth to plant his truth in' be besought to preserve it.

As the century went by, the variety of extant Protestant versions of the truth, most of them claiming the authority of the Bible, and the number of Protestant sects, not all of them with a long-term future, increased sensationally. They included Independents, Presbyterians, Baptists and Quakers and radical Millenarians and other groups with still more exotic names, like Ranters, Seekers and Muggletonians, who have long since passed into oblivion. The 'womb of teeming birth', as John Milton chose to call it, could not be sealed. The sense of truth versus error remained dominant on both sides. For Milton, as for many of those participating in the Civil War on the Parliamentary side, the war when it came was essentially a war of good against evil, not of one set of interests or even of opinions against another. 'God may leave a nation that is but in outward covenant with him, and why not England?' the preacher Thomas Hooker had warned his congregation in a farewell sermon of 1641. 'The Word and the Sword must be joined,' a Puritan preacher thundered in 1645. There were equally strong views on the other side, too. Charles I could be – and has been – treated as a saint.

Historians at different periods have concentrated on the constitutional debates in Parliament and on the religious ferment in the country in their attempts to analyse the causes of the Civil War, but they have also raised questions of social and economic interest and traced continuities before and after 1660. It was members of the nobility and gentry who drew England into the Civil War; and while many would have preferred to stay out of it, it was they who often profited from it. Indeed, Parliament's confirmation after the Civil War of the abolition of institutions like the Court of Wards, 'that great bridle of feudality' which had been abolished by the Long Parliament before the Civil War, has been described as 'probably the most important single event in the history of English landowning'. Landowners were now free not only from the burdens of feudal service but from monetary substitutes for it; and by the end of the century, when all barriers to hereditary title had disappeared, the claims of private property, and of large estates in particular, were more firmly established than they had been at the beginning of it. By then, there were also new theories to justify the claims of property and new legal defences to protect them. In fact, they needed no protection. As Bernard Mandeville put it succinctly in the early eighteenth century, 'Dominion follows property.'

The earliest explanation of the eventual line-up in the Civil War as a conflict of social and economic interests was that of a contemporary, James Harrington, in his book *Oceana* (1656), which claimed that war had broken out because of shifts in the ownership of land from the Crown and Lords to the Commons, resulting in a transfer of power. In the nineteenth century he was followed by Karl Marx. Under the Tudors, in Harrington's words, 'the nobility being abated, the balance fell into the power of the people'. According to Marx, the English struggle was that of bourgeois against feudal England. 'Power follows property.'

Harrington included the gentry in his 'nobility', but historians of the 1940s and 1950s often sharply distinguished between the two, referring to 'the crisis of the aristocracy' and 'the rise of the gentry'. They examined closely and compared in detail the fortunes and attitudes of both 'nobility' and 'gentry' between the death of Queen Elizabeth and the outbreak of the Civil War. After fierce historical debate (as fierce at times as the seventeenth-century debates in Parliament) it is plain that there were no significant economic differences between landowners on the two sides in the Civil War. It was 'caused' neither by the rise of the gentry nor by the economic decline of a part of the gentry. It is difficult, indeed, to classify Roundheads and Cavaliers in terms of rising or declining gentry or of 'feudal' and 'bourgeois' landholders.

Argument still continues, however, about Marx's concept of a 'bourgeois revolution' led by 'progressive' elements in society, and, in particular, about the extent to which merchant interests supported Parliament against the king. There were certainly links through London and the ports, and through the printing press, with the politically conscious bourgeoisie of Geneva, Strasbourg and Amsterdam, but English merchants did not always share the political awareness of their continental counterparts: there were always divisions within their ranks. People from the same background took up different political – and religious – positions. Those who had a voice in Parliament were a minority there, sitting alongside the gentry from the shires. The merchant classes may have been particularly inclined towards the adoption of Puritan values – to 'inveighing against idleness', for instance, and to believing in their occupations as a divine 'calling' – and some, at least, of them had long shown that they had little patience with hierarchy in Church or in State, but there were divisions within the mercantile community which persisted after the Civil War broke out. While, then, the economically 'advanced' south and east of the country supported Parliament more firmly than the economically 'backward' north and west, within each of these regions there were forces on the other side. Thus, there were Roundhead enclaves in the royalist textiles district of West Yorkshire and there was a Cavalier uprising in King's Lynn, Norfolk, in Parliamentary territory.

It was, nonetheless, of crucial and unquestionable importance to the success of the Parliamentary cause that rich London was behind it from the start and remained so. Some London merchants had earlier had strong links with the Crown, but if we leave on one side the twelve 'monopolist' Members of Parliament who were expelled in 1641, eighteen of the nineteen remaining London MPs supported Parliament in 1642. They provided backing at crucial times.

Other historians have taken a different angle of approach to the problems of 'causation', recognizing that while social and economic groups defend their interests, however they perceive them, there are other differences of perception also. They have seen tension between Court and Country as a widening and eventually unbridgeable divide that was to lead to civil war. That tension had certainly existed from the beginning of the reign of James I. The Puritan Lucy Hutchinson described James's court as 'a nursery of lust and intemperance', and Sir Walter Raleigh, who was in a position to know, condemned it just as strongly:

> Say to the Court it glows
> And shines like rotten wood

'Alien' influences there were attacked too; and there were certainly stronger continental links in politics and in style in James I's and Charles I's courts than in that of Elizabeth. The great Whitehall Banqueting House and the Queen's House at Greenwich, the work of Inigo Jones, were directly inspired by the classicism of Palladio. So too was Covent Garden, London's first square.

The Court then and later was sustained by an intricate network of courtiers, ministers and officials – with no distinction between civil servants and politicians – and although for financial reasons it should have economized, as Elizabeth had tried to do, it often spent money conspicuously, both at home and abroad. James I's favourite, George

Villiers, the first Duke of Buckingham, impeached in 1626, was a collector as well as a key figure in foreign policy, and Charles himself was a great patron of foreign art. The Country too had its own tangle of families and connections at the county level and its own chains of influence and dependence – and some members of the aristocracy and gentry were themselves influenced by foreign styles – but it did not usually have the same messy entanglements with finance and business. Lionel Cranfield, for example, one of James's most able ministers, struggled hard to curtail waste, but he had accumulated a private fortune as a trader and speculator before becoming a state servant, and he continued his business activities throughout his career until it ended in impeachment, imprisonment, release and retirement.

The Court offered all the opportunities of Place, the Country all the satisfaction of Independence. Not all Place was highly lucrative, but all Place carried with it status, much of which was secured, in Francis Bacon's telling phrase – and he knew from experience – by 'a winding stair'. Not all Independence was shabby, for there was a rise in landed income both from direct farming and from rents in the early seventeenth century. Most country gentlemen fared well, but they did not have to be in straitened circumstances to dislike bitterly the way in which Property could follow Place.

During Charles I's reign there were increasing signs of the cultural gap between Court and Country. The arts of the Court were for the few – and all were expensive. Science, a subject of practical as well as of speculative interest among the gentry and in the towns, was kept out. Satire was too. The formal masque was preferred, with 'ingenious speeches', 'melodious music' and 'delicate devices', much to Ben Jonson's distaste (though he wrote masques himself, designed by Inigo Jones).

> Painting and carpentry are the soul of masque!
> Pack with your piddling poetry to the stage!
> This is the money-get mechanic age!

It is difficult to claim, nonetheless, that when the Civil War came it could be explained simply in terms of Court versus Country or for that matter 'ins' versus 'outs'. Motives were complex, and they were certainly not always dominated by a sense of envy or distaste or by a feeling of exclusion. There were shifts of opinion too, so that political forces were

aligned in different ways in the years 1625 and 1640 and in the years
1640 and 1642. What happened between mattered crucially. Situations
and choices need to be examined in detail, as they do, of course, in all
political history. Explanations are misleading that take the inevitability
of war for granted. For this reason alone a step-by-step analysis of what
happened is just as necessary for the social historian elucidating shifts
in social relationships as it is for the political historian tracing sequences
of events. One stage has often been regarded as being of crucial importance in relation both to social alignments and the unfolding of events.
Following the framing by the Commons of a Petition of Right in
1628, cataloguing grievances and demanding an end to unparliamentary
taxation, martial law and unregulated powers of imprisonment, which
Charles was forced to accept because of his financial difficulties, he
insisted in 1629 that he would grant no new liberties but only confirm
ancient ones. The House of Commons went on forcibly to assert its
claims by pinning the Speaker to his chair when he refused to adjourn.
As a result, between 1629 and 1640 Charles I ruled for eleven years
without Parliament. The two chief agents whom he then called upon
were Archbishop Laud, born in 1573 and promoted to the see of
Canterbury in 1633, and Thomas Wentworth, whom he created Earl
of Strafford in 1640. Laud's coherent views both on Church doctrine
and Church (and university) order were diametrically opposed to those
of the Puritans long before he was appointed, but Wentworth, who
had sat in every Parliament since 1621, had hitherto been a critic of the
king acting without Parliament's assent.

The two men had to fall back now on the king's authority, enforcing
policies which were often unpopular by methods which were often
arbitrary. Laud's call to establish Church discipline in the name of
'the beauty of holiness' provoked a display of revenge on the part of
Puritans, who objected to railing off a communion table to make an
altar and to bowing to it as evidence of 'Popery'; while Wentworth's
paternalistic economic and social policies alienated both men of enterprise in the City of London and country gentlemen and yeomen who
objected to paying more tithes. Above all, tough censorship and the
muzzling of critics repressed opposition without suppressing it. The
lawyer and pamphleteer William Prynne, a critic both of bishops and
of stage plays, lost his ears in 1634 and was put in the pillory for his
book on stage plays, seen by Laud to reflect badly on the queen; John

Hampden, a wealthy gentleman, became a national hero through his opposition to paying ship money in 1636. And since the king lacked the apparatus of bureaucratic support which the kings of France and Spain had at their disposal, he was forced to find his civil servants among the bishops, disparagingly satirized by their contemporaries as 'stall-fed doctors' and 'crown'd divines'. In consequence, they became more unpopular than they had been in James I's reign. It was at this point that the regime became offensive to many persons of 'honour and quality', as Clarendon was to describe them.

There was a consequent loss of moral authority at a time when there were many other signs, local as well as national, of cultural fragmentation and of the erosion of middle ground that men of moderation and goodwill had once occupied. Because there were determined people at each extreme who were wary of compromises the two cultures eventually became two warring camps. Strafford could speak contemptuously of 'your Prynnes Pyms and Bens [sic] with the rest of that generation of odd names and natures', while Lucy Hutchinson on the opposite side could refer to 'needy courtiers', 'proud encroaching priests', 'thieving projectors' and 'lewd nobility'.

Even in 1640, however, the die was not cast, and Scottish history has to be considered in detail in relation to English history in order to explain the subsequent chronology. It was in 1640 that Charles sacrificed Laud and Strafford after being forced to summon the so-called Short Parliament, which lasted for three weeks before being controversially dissolved, and a second Parliament, subsequently to be known as the Long Parliament, which was to continue formally until 1660. But the effect of the execution of Strafford in 1641 and of the impeachment of Laud (who was himself to be executed five years later) was the opposite of that intended, as Cardinal Mazarin noted across the Channel. Parliament went on to take control of taxation, to abolish the prerogative courts and the episcopacy.

Although some of the men who had been Strafford's sharpest critics dissociated themselves from what had become a divided Parliament, it went on to pass a Triennial Act and an Act Against (its own) Dissolution. The Scots had insisted on the last two measures. A 'Grand Remonstrance' was published and distributed in 1641 and directly attacked Charles I. It was passed by only eleven votes, and one of those who opposed it exclaimed:

When I first heard of a Remonstrance, I thought to represent unto the King the wicked counsels of pernicious Councillors, the treachery of false judges. I did not dream that we should remonstrate downwards, tell stories to the people and talk of the King as a third person, I neither look for the cure of our complaints from the common people nor desire to be eased by them.

By then it did not need 'remonstration downward' to mobilize the discontented forces in the country. When, following the Grand Remonstrance, the king failed in his attempt to arrest five Members of Parliament (among them Hampden and Pym) and moved out of London, there were many people psychologically and morally prepared for the fray, if still reluctant to start it. And there were enough divisions, not only between different parts of the country but even within families in the same areas, to ensure that if and when war came it would not be won easily.

The battles of the Civil War, fought as three military campaigns, took place not in London but in the counties. The king's standard was first raised at Nottingham in 1642, and when he could not get to London, he made Oxford his temporary capital. It did not fall until 1646, but by then Charles had already surrendered and had passed into the hands of the victorious New Model Army, 22,000 strong, which went on to take possession of London, installing its commander Sir Thomas Fairfax as Governor of the Tower. Fairfax's second-in-command was Oliver Cromwell, who was to prove himself a great military leader and who was to become Lord Protector after the execution of Charles in 1649. England now became a republic, the House of Lords was abolished and religious toleration proclaimed.

All in all, in four years of struggle around 100,000 Englishmen had been killed. Yet most Englishmen had not taken part in the military campaigns, and as they continued there had been signs of war-weariness. There were many signs of ignorance too. At Marston Moor, where parliamentary forces won an important victory in July 1644, it is said that a husbandman, warned off the field because battle was about to begin, asked, 'What! Has them two fallen out then?' Nevertheless, feelings could run high, and extraordinarily radical and violent opinions were expressed both during and after the Civil War. 'I hope', said one Northamptonshire rebel, for example, 'within this year to see never a gentleman in England.' The true colour of the unique political and religious radicalism of the 1640s is best revealed by the series of debates at Putney in 1647 during which a congregation of soldiers from the New Model Army, fresh from the experience of civil war and free from local attachments and social restraints, hammered out sharply contrasting propositions about religion, government and property. 'God hath appeared with us and led us and taken delight in the work by us,' the soldiers believed, but that did not stop them from differing radically with each other not only about the social significance of the war which they had just fought but even about the social and political significance of the Norman Conquest.

Some of the views expressed came from the lips of men without social and political power. 'It seems now,' one speaker complained, for example, that, 'except a man hath a fixed estate in this kingdom he hath no right in this kingdom. I wonder we were so much deceived. If we had not a right in this kingdom we were mere mercenary soldiers.' A second speaker, Henry Ireton, Cromwell's son-in-law, replied to him equally frankly, putting forward a different point of view. 'No person has a right to an interest or share in determining or choosing those that shall determine what laws we shall be ruled by here . . . that hath not a permanent fixed interest in the kingdom.' It was the second view that was to prevail.

The more extreme republicans in the New Model Army, the 'Levellers' as they were called, were, however, in full agreement with the first speaker. They had their manifesto, the Agreement of the People, and they rallied together to defend the rights of 'hobnails, clouted shoes and woollen aprons', to press for manhood suffrage, which might have made Parliament a very different (possibly at that time a more conservative) place, and to demand the abolition of tithes, which would have broken the power of any established Church – with or without bishops. 'If we take not advantage of this time,' they urged, 'we shall never have the opportunity again.'

The Diggers, a far smaller and still more radical group, opposed the private ownership of property altogether and struggled to 'set the land free'. And they did not stop at words. They squatted on manorial common lands and felled feudal trees. Charles I, they maintained, had been the legatee of William the Conqueror. 'If the common people have no more freedom in England but to live among their elder brothers

Civil War Battles, 1643–5

50 Miles

Newcastle
Carlisle
Appleby
Richmond
Bolton Castle Thirsk
York
Preston MARSTON MOOR Hull
Manchester Sheffield
ROWTON HEATH
Chester Lincoln
Montgomery Lichfield Ashby-de-la-Zouch Norwich
Birmingham NASEBY
Leominster Northampton Cambridge
EDGEHILL
Gloucester Oxford Chelmsford
Malmesbury
Bath Devizes NEWBURY Reading
Wardour Castle Salisbury Reigate Canterbury
LANGPORT Winchester
Taunton
Exeter
Launceston
Lostwithiel Plymouth
Truro

and work for hire,' asked Gerrard Winstanley, one of their chief spokesmen, 'what freedom can they have in England more than they can have in Turkey or France?' 'The poorest man', the Diggers insisted, 'hath as true a title and just right to the land as the richest man.'

The language of radicalism which burst out between 1640 and 1645 alarmed conservatives of all kinds. Decades before the Civil War fear had been expressed by influential, if not 'average', men that 'the loose and needy multitude' might all too easily be transformed into a 'senseless and furious beast . . . with many heads'; and at least one critic of the king changed sides before the Civil War because he believed that 'the necessitous people of the whole kingdom' would 'presently rise in mighty numbers' and 'within a while' would 'set up for themselves to the ruin of all the Nobility and Gentry in the Kingdom'. Indeed, once war had begun, radical outbursts tapped veins of conservatism in people who were not conservative by the standards of the early century and who themselves sometimes held radical religious convictions. 'If the unruly rout have once cast the rider,' it was claimed, 'it will run like wildfire through all the counties of England.' Cromwell himself, 'the constable in the parish', a 'Root and Branch man' in religion, was a reluctant republican, anxious to preserve 'the ranks and orders of men whereby England hath been known for hundreds of years: a nobleman, a gentleman, a yeoman'. And in this, as in so many things, he may simply have been showing his 'resemblance to the average man'. S. R. Gardiner, the late nineteenth-century historian, called him the most typical Englishman of all time.

It was not 'the beast with many heads' but the 'Nobility and Gentry' who eventually profited from the Civil War and the Interregnum between 1649 and 1660. The Diggers failed in all their ventures and the Levellers were suppressed in 1649 after a rebellion. Nor did radical religious groups like the Ranters create a new Sion. There were some notable innovations: religious toleration was extended to a large number of the less radical Puritan sects, enormous areas of confiscated ecclesiastical and royalist lands changed hands, Cromwell welcomed Jews back into the country (although they did not receive citizens' rights), and there were legal reforms. Parliament continued to have a chequered history, purged, nominated, dissolved, reformed. But there was certainly no appreciable change in the condition of the have-nots.

From 1655 England was divided not only into its traditional parishes, but into districts, each with a soldier Major-General exercising authority in the name of 'godliness and virtue'. In the country and the town alike, successive regimes enforced Sabbath Day protection and anti-gambling rules (introduced under the Tudors), closed alehouses and, for several years, theatres, banned race meetings as well as cock fights and duels, exercised censorship, severely punished those people found guilty of immorality (or swearing), and suppressed 'rowdy' or 'superstitious' practices like dancing round the maypole or celebrating Christmas. 'Who would have thought to have seen in England the churches shut and the shops open on Christmas Day?' we read in a letter of 1646. But the Puritan excesses of the Major-Generals and their unpopularity can be exaggerated. Many of the bans were not new, while Cromwell himself, who was born at Huntingdon not far from the Fens, loved horses and hawking, and although he served 'plain fare' at his table, he and his household consumed substantial quantities of wine – and listened to music (except in church).

It proved difficult to suppress 'custom' and to turn England into 'a land of saints and a pattern of holiness to the world', as the Puritan Richard Baxter had hoped. Alehouses might be described, again not for the first time, as 'nests of Satan', but in the attempt to suppress them the gap between 'local notables' and 'common people' widened, as it often did when the same notables tried to get the 'common people' into church to listen to sermons which they might not understand. 'Not one in twenty . . . go to any place of worship on the Lord's Day, but sit in their own houses,' complained one minister to his Major-General. In some places, indeed, the attempt which followed similar attempts in the sixteenth century to insist upon religious observance as a public duty, was abandoned; and the services, which followed no uniform pattern, became exclusive to small groups of believers.

The existence of voluntary religious groups was to remain a feature of English society in the future, but many of the changes of the Interregnum were short-lived and did not survive Cromwell's death in 1658 and the restoration of Charles II two years later. The ecclesiastical and royalist lands confiscated by Parliament during and after the Civil War were for the most part regained by their owners – some before, but most after the Restoration. There were, therefore, no profound long-term shifts in the pattern of land ownership as there had been and were to be in other national revolutions. By the end of the century, indeed, the great estates were getting bigger, and systematic attempts were being made to exploit them through their tenants. According to the pioneer statistician Gregory King, landlords' rents and farmers' profits then accounted for about half the country's income, a figure close to recent twentieth-century estimates of 43 per cent. He estimated the cultivated land, including woods, orchards and gardens, at 25 million acres, which, he calculated, maintained 12 million sheep, 4.5 million cattle and 2 million pigs, worth together about £15,000,000, and base crops worth about £9,000,000.

Interest in agricultural improvement, with some of the methods taken from Holland, was expressed in a wide range of books on profitable husbandry; and it was Holland too which provided the know-how for the draining of the Fens. Yet the game laws (the successors of the old forest law) were tightened up in the interests of privilege. The so-called Cavalier Parliament of 1671 prevented all freeholders of less than £100 a year (the great majority of them) from killing game even on their own property. The use of the shot-gun, which was to supersede hawking, was to be restricted to their 'betters'. The landed interest was secure and well established.

At the peak of the social pyramid were 160 peers. Their numbers had been increased by James I in inflationary fashion from 55 to 126, and were now to be stable for a century. Below them there were another 80–100 non-noble families owning 10,000 acres or more. The greatest landed families could benefit directly from marriages outside their privileged rural circle. Thus, in 1695 the fortunes of the Russells, Dukes of Bedford, were powerfully reinforced when the young Marquis of Tavistock married Elizabeth Howland, the daughter of a wealthy London merchant. The social and political influence of merchants varied as did their wealth, but in most parts of the country the gentry were now beginning to be thought of as a 'squirearchy' with substantial power. They owned about half the land in the country, and when they served as justices of the peace they exercised an even greater degree of local power between 1660 and 1685 than they had done before 1640. The justices were also in charge of the local militia, the only substantial armed force in the country.

Gregory King demonstrated also that in 1688, while the power of property was being consolidated after the Revolution, about half the families in England were not earning 'a subsistence'. And long before then, the poor law and the poor rate had become accepted facts of life at all times, not just in emergencies. An Act of Settlement, passed in 1662, empowered any justices of the peace, upon complaint to the Overseers of the Poor, to eject any newcomer to a parish who had no means of his own to return to the parish where he was last settled, a measure intended to deal with the whole population of the poor as only rogues and vagrants had been dealt with previously.

That old contrasts of circumstance were sharpening is revealed by the fact that the poor, who had suffered appallingly in the dearth of 1659, suffered even more during the last years of the century when bread prices doubled between 1693 and 1699. (Thomas Muffett had written in 1655 that 'Bread and Cheese be the two targets against Death.') These were exceptional years in a period of agricultural improvement. When corn yields were increasing and marginal lands brought into cultivation, there was a downward trend in grain prices. Agriculture was second in its techniques only to that of the Low Countries, but prevailing attitudes towards the social contrast demonstrated little sense of common interest let alone of commonwealth. As the better off discovered new luxuries, the poor were condemned as idle, vicious and irreligious.

It was only a limited consolation for the poor to be told by Edward Chamberlayne in 1687 that lack of food might be compensated for by a 'variety of divertissements, sports and recreation'. Indeed, those 'divertissements' which were encouraged had another purpose. A series of notes prepared by the Duke of Newcastle, a survivor from the reign of Charles I, suggested that the revival of Shrove Tuesday festivities, 'May games, Morris dances, the Lord of the May and the Lady of the May, the fool and the Hobby Horse, Whitsun Lord and Lady, carols and wassails at Christmas, with good plum porridge and pies', which had been 'forbidden as profane', would 'amuse the people's thoughts and keep them in harmless actions which will free your Majesty from faction and rebellion'. Charles himself enjoyed riding and won the Newmarket races twice. By the end of the century, however, there was a reaction in attitudes. The pendulum had swung. Societies for the Reformation of Manners were being set to 'bring to justice' men and women (almost always men) found guilty of drunkenness, breaking the Sabbath or 'any other dissolute, immoral or disorderly practice'.

The politicians of Charles II's and James II's reigns had their own 'divertissements'. Like revellers in a carnival, they were frequently assumed to be wearing masks to conceal their features: 'sham' was a favourite new word of the period, another was 'plot'. It was applied in 1678, for example, to the Popish Plot, when Titus Oates alleged that Jesuits were planning to murder Charles II and install his brother James, and in 1683 to the Rye House Plot, another alleged conspiracy to assassinate the king. The word 'cabal' also originated in this period; it was an acronym for the group of ministers in power from 1667 to 1673, derived from the initial letters of their five surnames.

Given that one of the main fears throughout the period was Popery (it roused even the poet Milton from his retirement), there was an element of sham at the very centre of society, for Charles II, the Defender of the Faith, was a secret Roman Catholic, and James II was an open Roman Catholic, who, after getting into difficulty with his first Parliament, did not summon a second. Looking for effective political alliances, he replaced nearly half the justices of the peace by his own nominees, a more drastic change of office holders than any attempted earlier in the century. If James had succeeded in establishing royal absolutism, supported by a strong army, while relying in the process on people outside the Church of England, Puritans as well as Roman Catholics – an outcome that has been considered feasible – then independent country gentlemen would have been at the mercy of salaried officials and England would have become more like some other European monarchies. But he did not succeed. The Anglican gentry in alliance with the landed aristocracy rejected him. The Church of England had the substantial backing of property. It was to survive both fundamental social changes and later the erosion of the view that Protestantism was an essential part of the constitution and that Church and State were one; and significantly it is the 1662 edition of the Common Prayer Book to which devoted Anglicans, faced with alternative rites, still turn.

Nonetheless, the fact that it proved impossible for the post-Restoration Church of England to retain within it the comprehensiveness of religious outlook that it had maintained with difficulty until the Civil War implied that thereafter in English social history there would be a divide – and a contrast – between Anglicans and dissenters, or Nonconformists, a divide which was to seem as important at times as that between rich and poor. The third Act of Uniformity of 1662, which laid down that all priests who did not conform to the Prayer Book liturgy by St Bartholomew's Day would be deprived of their livings, ensured the secession of nearly 1,000 'Bartholomewmen', but the dissenters were strong enough to withstand persecution and other measures, like the suppression of unauthorized religious meetings in conventicles and restrictions on their freedom to operate in incorporated towns.

'Fanatical opinions' were out of fashion after 1660, and the new dissenters, who, like Roman Catholics, were excluded from public office in 1663, turned increasingly to trade and industry. They were not, however, 'excluded from the nobility', wrote John Corbett in 1667, and among the gentry 'they are not a few'. The most important were those who were 'in the trading part of the people, and those that live by industry, upon whose hands the business of the nation lies much'. They were 'patient men', wrote Sir William Petty, 'and such as believe that labour and industry is their duty to God'.

The most democratic dissenters were the Quakers who addressed people, whatever their rank, as 'thou' and refused to doff their hats. They were to create a small but effective national network of organization to be copied by others in the eighteenth century; they were also to repudiate violence and, in time, to become renowned for their philanthropy. The Independents, to whom Cromwell had belonged, were locally based, with each congregation choosing its minister; they were to become Congregationalists. The Baptists were to split into 'closed' and 'open' congregations. The Presbyterians, who were strongly represented in the Long Parliament – and who retained control of the church in Scotland – had their own Calvinistic system of church order. They were never to have the influence they exercised in Scotland, although they continued to dream of a comprehensive Church of England until 1689. Some of them were to reject the doctrine of the Trinity in the eighteenth century and to become Unitarians, thereby gaining influence of a different, predominantly secular, often cultural, kind, largely in urban society.

The Toleration Act of 1689, part of the settlement of the 'Glorious Revolution', was to allow all Nonconformists, except Unitarians, freedom of worship; and although they were not to secure their full religious and civil freedom until the nineteenth century (they were still to be excluded from public life unless they were prepared to communicate once a year in their parish church), in most places they did not suffer as keenly as Roman Catholics did from the interplay of increasingly strong popular prejudice and the penal laws. They became one among a broad spectrum of economic and social interests in society, represented both in London and in the provinces.

There was a place in that spectrum – before and after 1689 – for the sciences and the arts. Indeed, before 1660 it could be claimed that the sciences, in particular, had benefited during the Interregnum both because there were Puritans who had long been drawn to science and, more generally, because men's minds had become more 'active, industrious and inquisitive'. As for the arts, the portrait painter and connoisseur Peter Lely, who had painted Charles I and was to flourish after the Restoration, was told by the Protector not to leave out the 'roughnesses, pimples, warts and everything' in the picture which he painted of him. He had been able to secure many commissions during the Interregnum. Literature too had scarcely suffered. Nor did it necessarily focus on religious themes. Thus in 1653 Izaak Walton 'for whom England was brooks, not agonies', published his *The Compleat Angler*. In 1651, but abroad in Paris, Thomas Hobbes, tutor to Charles II, had published his *Leviathan*, a profound book, shot through with fear of civil disorder and bound to provoke conflict because of its absolutist tendencies. It had an interesting future. In September 1668 Samuel Pepys recorded in his *Diary* that he had paid three times the publisher's price for a second-hand copy ('the bishops will not let it be printed again'), and eleven years after that copies were burned publicly in Oxford.

Two of the greatest works of the seventeenth century date from immediately after the Restoration: Milton, who had used his talents for political purposes during the Interregnum and who was now blind, published his *Paradise Lost* in 1667, and in the following decades John Bunyan, who had been swept up into the Civil War, wrote his great Puritan work, *The Pilgrim's Progress*, which has often been described as England's most powerful allegory. Bunyan had spent more than twelve years in gaol for his faith, and his book gave a new dimension to the idea of pilgrimage presented centuries earlier by Langland and Chaucer.

Bunyan's Christian had to resist the snares of the city and 'the merchandise of the fair' which included not only debauchery but stage plays. While Restoration comedy was much appreciated by Charles II, who encouraged rhyming verse in drama (and 'clear, plain and short sermons' in church), it was particularly repugnant to Puritans. The language of the Restoration dramatists, like their themes, was polite and witty on the surface, but it was underscored by an often bawdy muse of comedy and it focused on deceit and intrigue. They themselves participated in the society that they portrayed. 'Our way of living became more free,' commented the poet John Dryden, who approved of the change, 'and the fire of the English wit, which was being stifled under a constrained, melancholy way of breeding, began first to display its force, by mixing the solidity of our nation with the air and gaiety of our neighbours.' There was more than an undercurrent of violence, however, and there were complaints from audiences that too much attention was being paid to effects or tricks – 'that which makes our Stage the better makes our Players the worse.' Much comment has survived. Thus, in a diary of November 1661 we read, 'I saw Hamlet, Prince of Denmark, played; but now the old plays begin to disgust this refined age.' By 1701 there was still greater refinement and a new playwright William Congreve who wrote all his plays between 1693 and 1700 – the year of *The Way of the World*.

The personal diary had come into its own as a literary form in the middle and late seventeenth century. Indeed, diarists have left us some of the most memorable accounts of life in England after 1660. Pepys, who was born in 1633, rose to be Secretary of the Admiralty and was elected to Parliament in 1673, but it is the directness of immediate comment in the diary, which he kept in shorthand between 1660 and 1669 and which was first published in an abbreviated form in 1825, rather than his knowledge of the workings of government, which won him immortality. Another diarist, John Evelyn, a voluminous correspondent, left to posterity a life-long calendar, describing vividly all the striking events of the day, such as the removal of the bodies of the Commonwealth leaders from their tombs to be hanged again on the gallows of Tyburn in 1661.

But Evelyn and Pepys did more than recount events. They caught the changing ways of life and thought of their country. Evelyn was a founder member of the Royal Society, and Pepys joined it in 1665. The Society, incorporated in 1662 with the king's blessing, aimed to 'promote the welfare of the arts and sciences' and to 'make faithful Records of all the Works of Nature or of Art'; and its prose, in contrast with that of Restoration comedy, was plain, direct and deliberately designed to avoid 'fulsome metaphors'. Yet one experimental 'natural philosopher' could write in the same year of 'Philosophy' coming 'in with a spring-tide' and 'all the old Rubbish' being 'thrown away'. As new 'sciences' evolved there was a strong sense of change. Isaac Newton, who was to produce a new system, worked away from the centre. Indeed, he spent his *annus mirabilis* in 1665–6 sheltering from the plague in his home in rural Lincolnshire. It was years later that Samuel Johnson was to say of him that 'he stood alone because he left the rest of mankind behind him.'

Evelyn and Pepys catch the immediate tempo of the age from London. Time was acquiring a new significance in the late seventeenth century: it mattered as much to businessmen as to diarists and historians. Business – and much of secular life – began to follow the clock as relentlessly as the Church had followed the bell and agriculture still followed the seasons. Pepys was not alone in being proud of his watch and in treating it increasingly as a necessity. It was Bunyan who wrote in a *Book for Boys and Girls*:

> Behold this Post-boy, with what haste and speed
> He travels on the Board; and there is need
> That so he does, his Business calls for haste.

Puritans made more of the importance of 'time well spent' than any other section of the community. The clock pendulum and the balance spring, which enabled minute-hands to be added to hour-hands, both belong to the Restoration period.

All sectors of the community – at least of the urban community – were becoming more interested in news. English newsbooks and *corantos*, imitations of earlier Dutch innovations (like so much else), had first appeared during the early 1620s, but under the tight censorship of both the Commonwealth and Restoration there had been strict licensing regulations, with the government seeking to treat news as a monopoly, against which Milton had argued in *Areopagitica*. The twice-weekly *London Gazette* was established in 1665 as an official vehicle for news, but by the end of the century, when news sheets were appearing in single-leaf layout, it was clear that the demand for unofficial news was increasing rapidly. As far as books were concerned – and their numbers and influence were increasing – the system of licensing, which had been in operation since 1557 when the Stationers' Company was incorporated, was allowed to lapse in 1695. And as William's wars were fought at great expense (greater expense than that in many seventeenth-century wars) there was an avalanche of new publications.

The increased demand for the written word reflected changes in population and in urbanization. An article in the thrice-weekly *British Mercury*, published by the thriving Sun Fire Insurance Company, was to claim in retrospect that urban population was growing proportionately as the rate of increase in national population slackened off (with local variations) until the 1690s. By 1700 16 per cent of the national population lived in towns of 5,000 people or more. There were then seven towns with a population of more than 10,000, and twenty-three towns with a population of more than 5,000. Some of these provincial towns greatly impressed the traveller Celia Fiennes, who visited them in the 1690s, a quarter of a century before the journalist Daniel Defoe published his *Tour through the Whole Island of Great Britain*. Nottingham was the 'neatest' town she saw, Leeds 'the wealthiest town of its bigness', Norwich 'a rich thriveing industrious place', and Liverpool, which had begun as a row of fishermen's houses, was 'very handsome', a 'London in miniature'.

London stood out, dominating economy and society, although throughout the seventeenth century it was a crowded, unhealthy and dangerous place as well as a centre of wealth, associated both with production and trade. Its population doubled between 1600 and 1650, and by 1700, when it had reached over half a million, one in nine of the English population lived there as against one in twenty in 1600. It was the largest city in Europe except for Constantinople.

London, with a pall of smoke usually hanging over it like a canopy, was compared in 1703 with 'the head of a rickety child which becomes so overcharged that frenzy and death inevitably result'. Yet during its social season, when large numbers of temporary residents patronized its shops as well as its performances, it was a place of gaiety and scandal as well. It was also the place of events. Charles I had been executed at Whitehall in London, and Cromwell's severed head had been placed on a pole above Westminster Hall. For Bunyan, 'he that will go to the [celestial] city and not pass through this town must needs go out of the world.'

We can turn to Evelyn and Pepys for the accounts of the two most dramatic events in the London of the 1660s: the 'great plague' and the 'great fire', which came within a year of each other, in 1665 and 1666, when England was involved in a difficult (second) war against the Dutch. 'Everybody talking of the dead,' Pepys wrote simply of the first; it made 'a noise like the waves of the sea'. The antiquary Anthony Wood wrote memorably of the second, a fire which raged for four days and destroyed 13,200 houses, 87 churches and 44 of the City of London's great livery halls.

Plague and fire together, in Wood's words, left the city 'much impoverished, discontented, afflicted, cast downe'. Yet, just as revolution had been followed by restoration, so fire was followed by rapid and imposing reconstruction. Old London disappeared; a new London was born. Christopher Wren, a member of the Royal Society, gave London a new look as he rebuilt, or superintended the rebuilding of, fifty-one of the City churches which had been burnt. His St Stephen's in Walbrook should be set alongside his new St Paul's, which, according to Evelyn, made Westminster Abbey Gothic look like 'crinkle-crankle'. Who, Evelyn asked, could deny the superiority of the great domed building 'which strikes the understanding as well as the eye with the more majesty and solemn greatness'? Gothic was all 'turrets and pinnacles, thickset with monkeys and chimeras'.

There were many obvious contrasts between the taste and the mood of the early years of the century and those of the period after the Fire, which provides a prelude rather than a climax. Changes in costume were noted most, however, just after the Restoration. The critics were scathing. 'A strange effeminate age when men strive to imitate women in their apparel', wrote Anthony Wood in 1663, 'viz, long periwigs, patches in their faces, painting, short wide breeches like petticoats, muffs, and their clothes highly scented, bedecked with ribbons of all colours'. Two years earlier, Evelyn had watched a man strolling through Westminster Hall with 'as much Ribbon about him as would have plundered six shops and set up twenty Country Pedlars: All his Body was dres't like a Maypole or a Tom-a-Bedlam Cap.' The king himself complained to Parliament in 1662 that 'the whole nation seemed to him a little corrupted in their excess of living. All men spend much more in their clothes, in their diet, in all their expenses than they need to do.' However, it was Charles who set the fashions, and they were not cheap.

Diet was certainly becoming more sophisticated – for the well-to-do. Old recipes were being collected, while new foods and drinks were being imported, including coffee, 'heretofore in use amongst the Arabians and Egyptians', and chocolate, 'lately much used in England'. Soon the coffee house, the first of which was opened in 1650 (in Oxford), was to become a new social rendezvous, not only in the capital but in provincial towns too: Bristol came second to London in variety of them. The number of places to dine increased also, particularly in London, some of them patronized by members of the Royal Society. The cult of claret belongs to this period, although during the last years of the century the consumption of French wines declined drastically as a result of heavy taxation, generated by war, while the consumption of spirits and beer increased. Drinking was one of London's great occupations, with the places that offered drink often offering other forms of entertainment as well. In the 1680s the Belle Sauvage, a great coaching inn on Ludgate Hill, was charging its customers one shilling for a look at and two shillings for a ride on a rhinoceros.

The scope and scale of dining at home can be best appreciated not from life in great noble households but from Pepys's diary. At a New Year's breakfast in 1661 (still taken early in the day), he offered his guests a barrel of oysters, a dish of meat, some tongues and a plate of anchovies, and at a special dinner in 1663 he presented them with

> a fricassee of rabbit and chickens, a leg of mutton boiled, three carps in a dish, a great dish of a side of lamb, a dish of roasted pigeons, a dish of four lobsters, three tarts, a lamprey pie, a most rare pie, a dish of anchovies, good wine of several sorts, and all things mighty noble, and to my great content.

There were many great dinners in 1688 to celebrate the arrival in London of William and Mary, and the event was to be celebrated equally enthusiastically a century later.

William and Mary were to be rulers not by divine right but on the invitation of Parliament and people. Indeed, they were presented with a Declaration of Rights before they accepted the crown. This was the essence of the 'Glorious Revolution' of 1688. Royal powers, now limited, were never explicitly defined, but the Bill of Rights, professing to declare ancient rights rather than create new or abstract ones, declared, *inter alia*, that extra-parliamentary taxation was illegal (Charles II had ruled without Parliament between 1682 and 1685) and required explicitly that Parliament must approve any peacetime standing army. The role of Parliament was further emphasized by the Triennial Act of 1694, which laid down that Parliament must be summoned at general elections to be held at least once every three years. Finally, the Act of Settlement of 1701, which required that the king should be an Anglican, sought to perpetuate the settlement: it was sub-titled 'an act for the further limitation of the Crown and the better preserving the liberties of the subject'.

If the bloodless revolution was to be remembered as 'glorious', the constitution was hailed as 'the most beautiful constitution that was ever framed', and it soon began to be revered as a landmark. There would have been less reverence, however, had there been no earlier record of disturbance and conflict, and there would have been no 'Whig interpretation' of English history without the struggles earlier in the century. The experience of the whole century was relevant to its eventual outcome.

In the final years of the seventeenth and early years of the eighteenth centuries a financial settlement also was reached which was directly related to the constitutional settlement and which emerged out of a longer experience than that of the last decade of a stormy century. During the Civil War it had been possible for Parliament to introduce in 1643 two new taxes, which the king would not have been able to secure before the war began. The first was a land tax which replaced the old parliamentary subsidy and the dues of wardship. The second was the excise, a tax on consumption introduced by Pym to pay for the Civil War: it was modelled on a Dutch tax. The wide range of articles on which it was levied was narrowed after 1660 to beer, cider and spirits (on which it is still levied in the twentieth century) and tea, coffee and chocolate, but it was widened again between 1688 and 1713 to cover malt and hops, salt, candles, soap, leather and paper. If the burdens of the land tax fell on the propertied, landed interest, many of the burdens of excise fell on the poor. At the same time, import duties multiplied by four between 1690 and 1704 in order to pay for the long European wars in which England was engaged after 1688, for the first time as a major European power. The continuing debate on such subjects, which encompassed the study of private and public wealth as well as the structure of 'interests', was now free from all 'feudal' undertones. The old idea that within a complex society the king might continue to 'live on his own' had been dead already by the 1640s, when a wide range of pamphlets had been published on trade.

Even with the benefit of new taxes, Cromwell had left a bigger debt than James I, and Charles II turned to his powerful and unpopular neighbour Louis XIV, King of France, for secret subsidies. More important in the long run, however, he, like Cromwell, turned also for loans to merchants and bankers, thereby strengthening the 'City interest', even though such loans involved risk and difficulties, as in 1672 when the Crown repudiated a part of its debt in the much criticized 'Stop of the Exchequer'. Banking was developing in London as a profitable activity before the Bank of England was set up by Charter in 1694 – with the king and queen heading the subscription list, but with Parliament, not the king and queen, now underwriting public borrowing.

The effects of these important fiscal and financial changes were wide-reaching. As contemporaries fully appreciated, the growing variety of 'interests' made for a much more complex society. Yet while one pamphleteer could argue that trade and commerce are 'nowhere to be found but in the regions of freedom, where the lives and properties of the subjects are served by wholesome laws', the expanded mercantile interest, representing 'the great Sinews of Trade', and the City interest, concerned with credit in both private and public funds, often met with suspicion and resentment. Trade and Credit, it was claimed, were less solid than Land, and it was 'the Landed Gentlemen, Yeomen and Farmers, whose Substance is fixed in this particular part of the globe' who were 'the most settled inhabitants and the Bulk of the Nation'. Only two peers figured among the initial holders of Bank of England stock. The early eighteenth-century politician Henry St John, first Viscount Bolingbroke, was to pass on to posterity – not least to the nineteenth-century politician Benjamin Disraeli – a Tory version of English history in which the growth of the institutions and credit structures of the City of London had destroyed rather than strengthened the country. He was to put it memorably in 1749: 'the landed men are the true owners of our political vessel, the money'd men are no more than mere passengers in it.'

After the revolution of 1688, the intricate system of public borrow-ing, based on the Dutch, gave government a new fiscal base, whichever government was in power. Over £14 million was borrowed (along with £45 million raised in taxes) between 1690 and 1700 to pay for the costs of European wars. Within a hundred years Lord North, Prime Minister during the American War of Independence, was to call the Bank of England a part of the constitution. 'It acts not only as an ordinary bank,' wrote Adam Smith – and by then there were many 'ordinary' banks, in the country as well as in London – 'but as a great engine of State.'

Nonetheless, the seventeenth century did not end quite as neatly as such comments might suggest. It was a sign of the restless spirit of the age that the Bank of England was founded a month before the Cabinet had passed a bill for a £1,000,000 national lottery with £10 tickets. (Dealers were soon to sell smaller shares. They were sold. The smaller prizes were sums of around £1 a year for sixteen years: the larger sums of £1,000, then a very substantial figure, guaranteed far more than financial independence.) The passion for gambling was at least as strong at this time as the pursuit of industry, and during the next twenty years there were to be more 'projects' – projects of every kind, some based on new inventions – than in any previous period of English history. Moreover, the constitutional settlement did not dampen political argu-ment. During the reign of James II's second daughter, Anne (1702–14), both political and religious argument was often strident: elections were keenly contested, and sermons were as polemical as political speeches. If England was to move into an 'age of stability' in the 1730s and 1740s, it was to do it noisily, not quietly. Indeed, Daniel Defoe was to write in 1701 that 'whether we speak of differences in opinion or differences in interest, we must own we are the most divided quarrelsome nation under the sun.'

Six years later, the 'perfect union' of England and Scotland, for which James I had expressed hopes when he became King of England in 1603, was realized through the Act of Union of 1707. There was now to be one Parliament and one Union Jack; and although there was to be open rebellion by loyal supporters of the Stuarts north of the border before union was fully established, a new sense of Britain was to be forged by the last decade of the eighteenth century. A succession of wars with Catholic France helped the forging. So too did the creation of overseas empire, which owed much to Scotland. Union, to be challenged in the twentieth century, was to come about not through political and constitutional change but through the continuing quest for wealth and power which both countries shared.

7 THE QUEST FOR WEALTH, POWER AND PLEASURE

Men are gaining possession without your knowledge ... Merchants
ignore the interests of their sovereign, and are concerned only with their
own commercial profit.

> Tsar of Russia, Ivan the Terrible, to Queen Elizabeth, 1571

When Britain first at Heaven's command
Arose from out of the azure main,
This was the charter of the land,
And guardian angels sang the strain:
'Rule Britannia, rule the waves;
Britons never will be slaves.'

> James Thomson, *Rule Britannia*, 1740

England purchased for some of her subjects, who found themselves
uneasy at home, a great estate in a distant country.

> Adam Smith, *The Wealth of Nations*, 1776

Happiness is the only thing of real value in existence: neither riches, nor
power, nor wisdom, nor learning, nor strength, nor beauty, nor virtue,
nor religion, nor even life itself, being of any importance but as they
contribute to its production.

> Soame Jenyns, 1765

The seventeenth century had ended in war, as the eighteenth century
was to do. England's entry into long wars against Louis XIV's France,
which were not to end until 1713, raised public expenditure between
two and three times and increased the national debt from £11,000,000
to over £40,000,000. Yet national wealth increased rapidly at the same

time: in 1701 it was believed to have risen by 20 per cent since 1688. This wealth was in large part generated at home, but some derived from the quest for wealth and power abroad. There is much that is distinctive and ironical in the story of that quest, and much also that influenced the social history of other continents, among them Asia and Africa. And because the story is bound up with rivalry – sometimes war – with other European countries, the context of Europe is also relevant to an understanding of the processes of expansion. In 1700 the European market still accounted for 85 per cent of both English exports and re-exports, while two-thirds of the nation's imports (£0.67 for each man, woman and child) came from the same source. By 1722–4, 42 per cent of British exports were crossing the Atlantic.

The achievements – and the ironies, not to speak of the tragedies for the victims – began in the sixteenth century, the age of discovery; there were many signs of a greatly enhanced sense of opportunity. While Richard Hakluyt was cataloguing a wide range of exports, including needles, soap, glue and locks, and advocated colonization in his *Discourse of Western Planting* (1584), his compatriot John Hawkins was trading in African slaves. English coal too was in active demand abroad, while cloth still deserved its name 'the golden fleece'. The explorers led the way further afield: Francis Drake in his *Golden Hind*, a ship weighing less than 150 tons, completed his circumnavigation of the globe in 1580 after a voyage of nearly three years, and in 1600, William Adams, a far less well-known figure in England, reached Japan and helped the Japanese to found a navy.

As horizons were widened attitudes were being transformed. It was not a sailor but the astrologer/scientist John Dee who as early as 1577 predicted the growth of an 'incomparable British Empire'; and it was Francis Bacon, prophet of New Atlantis, who carried the idea of the map into learning itself, breaking with the traditions of scholasticism. Bacon, who was deeply and realistically concerned with 'the Greatness of Kingdoms and Estates', was also an advocate of emigration, although he warned that 'planting of countries is like planting of woods' and would take time to produce results. He was frank about the motives behind early discovery and colonization, and claimed that they did not centre on the 'propagation of the Christian faith', but on 'gold and silver, and temporal profit and glory'.

The cluster of regulated trading companies that had already come into existence by the end of the sixteenth century probably emerged not from an expansion of trade, but from its stagnation in Europe. Even if trading activities of 'interlopers', 'outleapers' and 'pirates' are taken into the reckoning, the much-noted growth of Elizabethan trade was something of a myth. Political barriers in Europe and limits to economic opportunity there pushed English merchants further across the seas. Thus, for example, it was after the cloth trade collapsed at the end of its greatest boom period in the middle of the sixteenth century and after Antwerp began to lose its dominance in the European trading network to Amsterdam that new English trade with Morocco was opened up. The first voyage to Guinea was made in 1553, and in the same year English voyagers reached the White Sea and travelled by land to Moscow. The Muscovy Company was set up by royal charter in 1555. Later in the same decade England lost Calais, its last possession on the European mainland.

Holland and Germany remained by far the biggest, if often precarious, markets for cloth, but trade with the Baltic and the Mediterranean was extended. An Eastland Company had been incorporated in 1579, followed two years later by a Turkey Company, which was to become part of a bigger Levant Company in 1592. They all had a monopoly of trade in their area, but merchants traded on their own – for a fee – and not for their own profit. This was not true of the new joint stock companies, the most important of which were the Royal Africa Company, launched in 1588, and the East India Company, created on the last day of 1600. These were run by a salaried staff at home and abroad.

The biggest profits from overseas trade came not from exports or re-exports, but imports: wax, tallow, furs and hides from Russia; pitch and tar along with timber, hemp and flax from the Baltic (and in one year, 1595, sizeable quantities of grain); wine from France, where the loss of Bordeaux had not destroyed the trade; and fruit from the Mediterranean; silks, spices and perfumes from the East; sugar from Morocco, before it was grown in the West Indies; and tobacco, a new crop in 1585, from Virginia. While many of the individual items in this list excited Tudor consumers, the size of the import bill and its effect on the balance of trade worried some contemporaries, as did the monopolistic organization of the companies. 'We brought in more foreign wares than we vended commodities,' suggested a Member of Parliament, not for the first or last time, in 1593.

Economic analysis does not do justice to the excitement of the quest for either wealth or power (they were usually the same) during the late sixteenth century, when 'all perils and misadventures' were accepted as 'tolerable' and all acts of piracy were welcomed as 'adventurous'. To catch in words the flavour of the times centuries later, it is revealing to turn back the pages of Hakluyt's massive *Principall Navigations, Voyages and Discoveries of the English Nation*, the first volume of which appeared in 1589 and the last in 1600, the year of the foundation of the East India Company. The English, Hakluyt proudly claimed, had 'excelled all the nations and peoples of the earth' in 'searching the most opposite corners and quarters of the world and . . . in compassing the vast globe'; and a viceroy of New Spain said of Drake that he is 'one of the greatest mariners that sail the seas'. 'He drinks and sups to the music of viols.'

In the age of discovery, daring should not be confused with foolhardiness. Navigation rested on science and on scientific instruments: science was more to the point than art, for among the necessary inventions of the time were the mariner's compass and a new sea quadrant, which was invented by an Englishman, John Davis. Meanwhile, maps recorded the charting of what had hitherto been uncharted. It was not until 1767, however, that John Harrison invented a chronometer that 'solved' the problem of longitude.

By 1640, shipping tonnage had more than doubled in sixty years and there were English footholds of empire in Asia, where Surat on the north-west coast of India became the first base of the East India Company (with access to Agra), and in the West Indies, where St Christopher was settled in 1624. The uninhabited island of Barbados was claimed three years later, Nevis in 1628 and Montserrat and Antigua in the 1630s. There was as much of a 'fashion for islands' at this time as there was for gardens. Further north, Bermuda, 'God's perfect garden', had already inspired Shakespeare (*The Tempest*) and the poet Andrew Marvell:

> He gave us this eternal spring
> Which there enamels everything.

The biggest early mainland plantations were in Virginia, named after the Virgin Queen. They were set in countryside often resembling that of England: the ideal of the gentleman could be exported, although increasingly it could be maintained only with the help of black slaves.

'In the beginning,' wrote William Byrd, 'all America was Virginia.' Yet the first settlers there faced hardship and danger: of 104 men and boys who travelled there in 1607, fifty-one were dead by the following spring. In 1632 the sponsors of the enterprise complained of 'the extreme beastly idleness' of their fellow countrymen because they did not back the venture strongly enough; indeed, they suggested that the English were 'wedded to their native soil like a snail to his shell'. Nonetheless, Virginia, centre of the tobacco trade, soon flourished, as did Maryland, which began to be settled in 1622.

As the years went by, slaves provided the work, and substantial profits were made out of their acquisition and transport by the Royal Africa Company and subsequently by shipowners and by sugar and tobacco merchants themselves. Excitement had given way to exploitation. The first Englishman to 'plant' Barbados took with him ten negroes and thirty-two Indians, and although few black slaves were imported, by 1660 there were as many blacks as whites – 20,000 of each – in Barbados, with a population density higher than that in most parts of England. The gulf in lifestyles widened as the planters grew rich: indeed, five of them were to receive baronetcies between 1658 and 1665.

Very different colonies were created further north in the colder climes of 'New England'. There was little publicity for the voyagers on the *Mayflower*, a vessel of only 180 tons, which landed at New Plymouth in 1620 after a voyage of nearly two and a half months, although the fact that forty of them died during the first hard winter has kept the memory of the journey alive on every subsequent Thanksgiving Day. These first pilgrims were Independents, and there were to be further Puritan reinforcements for 'New England' before the Massachusetts Bay Company received its charter in 1629 and Providence Island its charter in 1630.

New England was deliberately different from old England: in the words of John Winthrop, an emigrant from Suffolk, who had one son in Barbados, it was 'a shelter and a hiding place for us and ours, as Zoar for Lot'. Yet it was not democratic. Winthrop called democracy 'the meanest and worste of all forms of government', while Edward Winslow, one of the first pilgrims, stated tersely that America was a place where 'religion and profit jump together'. In fact, religion was the point of departure and no more; above all else, the immigrants *had* to be practical, and while there were to be many cultural and economic links with

England – the first magistrates printed the main provisions of Magna Carta alongside their own 'fundamentals' – the American colonial experience was always sufficiently distinct to create a separate, if related, social history. And there were varieties within America, too. The New Englanders had quite different perspectives from the Virginians.

It was while the English Puritans were in command in their own country that the seventeenth-century quest for power and wealth reached its peak. Cromwell was an enthusiast for New England. He sent out convicts rather than pilgrims as colonists, introducing systematic procedures after 1655. English mercantile interests were paramount in the Navigation Act of 1651 (the work of the Long Parliament), which had been foreshadowed in earlier acts, and which laid down that all merchandise imported into England from America, Asia and Africa should be imported in English ships and that all other merchandise should be imported either in English ships or in ships of the country of origin.

The wars of the Interregnum were primarily commercial in motive. That against the Protestant Dutch of 1652–4, the first of three such wars in the seventeenth century, was designed to break their grip on trade in key commodities, and, when it ended, the peace was unpopular with English merchants. Trade, conquest and colonization in the West Indies also figured prominently in the less successful war with Spain, which began in 1656. Jamaica was captured from the Spanish in 1655 – to be completely re-fashioned. Across the Channel, Dunkirk was captured, and across the oceans trade contacts were established with China, despite prejudices in London against the East India Company. Between the two, Admiral Blake, fighting Barbary pirates, bombarded Tangiers, attacked Tunis, and released English captives in Algiers.

Just as important as these victories was a change in attitude towards the making of wealth. The figure of Avarice, which had stalked its way through Ben Jonson's plays and in many places off the stage, lost its dramatic power. The rate of interest, which fell to 6 per cent in 1652, could now move as freely as the rate of profit, whatever the consequences. After 1660, moral or ethical debate on the permissibility of interest gave way to practical discussion concerning the level of the rate of usury and whether there should be any legal limits to it: low interest rates in Holland were judged to be a main factor in that country's prosperity. Thomas Mun's *England's Treasure by Foreign Trade*, published in 1664 but written decades earlier, presented the merchant as master of the 'mysteries of trade', whose frugal lifestyle contrasted with that of his fellow countrymen who spent their days in 'Idleness and Pleasure'. Puritanism emphasized the importance of hard work.

Yet by 1691 Dudley North in his *Discourses upon Trade* could describe as the main spur to 'Industry and Ingenuity' what he called 'the exhorbitant Appetites of Man'. 'Did Men content themselves with bare necessaries', he went on, 'we should have a poor World.' This was the Restoration view. In 1681 John Houghton argued boldly that 'our High-Living, so far from prejudicing the Nation . . . enriches it.' Although the political position of England in Europe weakened substantially after the Restoration of 1660, there was no substantial change in much of the economic policy devised under Cromwell. Indeed, some of the personalities involved were the same. So, too, were the theorists, like Sir William Petty, founder of 'political arithmetic'. The Navigation Code of 1660–63 completed the work begun in 1651, and from 1663 onwards colonists were bound to buy most of the European goods they needed in England. There were further expensive and unsuccessful Dutch Wars which, nonetheless, turned Englishmen's eyes further away from Dutch economic strength in Europe and the role of the French as Charles II's paymasters. The Dutch were able to attack Chatham in Kent in 1667 and to win a great naval battle off the Suffolk coast five years later.

Between these two dates the East India Company acquired the island of Bombay, and by 1680 the Company's annual investment in Bengal was £150,000; its agents there were behaving like English merchant clothiers and ordering silk 'taffeties' and cotton 'ginghams' for the English consumer market. 'The Artists of India out-do all the Ingenuity of Europe,' wrote a clergyman visitor to Surat. A decade later tea had become another favourite commodity, with annual exports to England rising to 100,500 lb by the end of the century. Tea from the East needed sugar from the West, and as the West Indian islands boomed – in particular Barbados, referred to in 1681 as 'one great City adorned with gardens' – imports from the Caribbean more than doubled between 1660 and 1700. At the same time, trade in Newfoundland cod was the main means by which England kept trade with the New World out of rival hands.

Bristol, which was described by Samuel Pepys in the 1660s as 'in every respect another London', was the main English port involved in triangular trade with Africa and across the Atlantic. It had been flourishing even before slaves became a precious cargo in the late seventeenth century, but now it was given a new impetus. 'We merchants', a Bristol merchant exclaims in Richard Steele's *Conscious Lovers* in 1722, 'are a species of gentry that have grown into the world this last century and are as honourable and almost as useful as you landed folk that have always thought yourselves so much above us.' English manufacturers, who did not yet figure on the stage, were also profiting from the African market: between 1690 and 1701, one Birmingham manufacturer shipped over 400,000 knives and 7,000 swords, and by the last quarter of the eighteenth century one-third of Manchester's textile exports were going there too. The Indian textile industry entered a period of decline.

It was as a result of the long Wars of the Spanish Succession, when Marlborough's armies were fighting great battles on European soil, among them Ramillies and Blenheim, that England secured the *Assiento*, or sole right to ship slaves to the Spanish American Empire, in 1713. Ten years earlier Portugal had been drawn into the system by the Methuen Treaty, which also ensured that port as a drink, still not a fortified drink, would become a prized ingredient in the eighteenth-century way of life. Slaves were the key to the system, and more than two million of them were exported to the British colonies alone between 1680 and 1783. The profitability of the different ventures linked to this trade, some of them highly speculative, like the South Sea Company which was set up in 1711 and which took over the *Assiento* rights in 1713, has been the subject of extensive argument, most recently by quantitative economic historians.

The South Sea Bubble, which encouraged every other kind of speculation as well, left many people with nothing but paper when it burst ignominiously in 1720. The historian Edward Gibbon's grandfather was one of them: for him, 'the labours of thirty years were blasted in a single day', and for the politician Sir Robert Walpole it was an experience 'never-to-be forgot or forgiven'. Other enterprises were hit too, but the year of the crash was not a bad year for commercial bankruptcies in general, and the slave trade continued confidently in other hands. 'All this great increase in our treasure', Joshua Gee wrote in 1729, 'proceeds chiefly from the labour of negroes in the plantations.' Many fortunes depended upon it, as some of the richest merchants and the most obscure middlemen both admitted. Thus, the Bristol merchant John Pinney, a great plantation owner in the West Indies, stated frankly that 'negroes are the sinews of a plantation' and that it was 'as impossible for a man to make sugar without the assistance of negroes as to make bricks without straw.' The planters themselves often returned to England like nabobs, displaying their great wealth ostentatiously, sometimes to the distaste of people of more modest temperament. There was also a powerful West India interest at Westminster, which drew its support not only from returning merchants but from members of the English landed interest with West Indian possessions who remained absentee landlords.

Socially, the consequences of West Indian slavery were profound and cast their shadows into the distant future: in the twentieth century English-speaking descendants of the first slaves were to come to England in large numbers and influence contemporary patterns of life, particularly in the large cities, and already in the eighteenth century there were black slaves in London. In the eighteenth century more was made of the difference between black and white than ever before: the novelist Tobias Smollett wrote in 1753 that the 'Africans' had manners 'as wide from ours as we should find in the planetary subjects above could we get there'. Not surprisingly, 'manners' were very different in the Caribbean and in Africa. There was nothing approaching family life, and the growth of a coloured population of mixed stock had its origins not in marriage but concubinage and sexual abuses of various kinds: a law was passed in Jamaica in 1748 limiting the amount of property that could be inherited by a concubine and her issue to £1,200. Yet Smollett also attacked the slave trade, as many other people, particularly Quakers, were to do as the century went by.

Between 1700 and 1780 English foreign trade nearly doubled, and shipping, largely organized through syndicates, doubled with it. Although Europe still accounted for the biggest share of England's trade, the lure of high profits continued to draw Englishmen to all corners of the world; symbolically a new gold coin was called the 'guinea' after the African territory. Nonetheless, there were still many writers who suggested that one of the chief uses of colonies was to provide 'an Outlet, or Issue for the ill Humours which from time to time are engender'd in the Body Politick' or a means 'for employing our poor, and putting hands to work, either at home or in the plantations who cannot support themselves'. General James Oglethorp used the second argument when he urged the case for settlement in Georgia in 1730. Philosophers found other interests in the story. John Locke, who prepared a Fundamental Constitution for Carolina, quoted American experience to support his theory of property.

Although England kept out of war between 1713 and 1739, seen as a whole the eighteenth century was one of war intertwined with diplomacy; and from 1745 Englishmen abroad were deeply involved in action on frontiers far from Europe. Slave colonies were as liable to change hands as European frontier towns. This was a time when open war with France and Spain was popular not only with many merchants and colonists but with the English public, who were roused by chauvinistic journalists – 'literary hacks' as their critics called them. They were now supported by large numbers of Scotsmen, too, for they proved themselves particularly shrewd and energetic merchants and adventurous and hard-working colonists. News of war in 1739 drew the crowds to the streets of London, Bristol and Liverpool to cheer the proclamation. Melodies could stir as much as words: Arne's setting of *Rule Britannia* was published a year later, and *God Save the King* was first printed in 1744.

Four years after the victory of George II's son, the Duke of Cumberland, over the Jacobite Scots in the savage battle of Culloden near Inverness, the poet James Thomson, author of the words of *Rule Britannia*, was extolling England as an 'ever-sacred country':

> It knows no bound: it has a retrospect
> To ages past: it looks on those to come.

And a very different poet and hymn writer, Isaac Watts, produced words which appealed to 'God our help in ages past, our hope for years to come', words which were to acquire similar patriotic connotations in the twentieth century.

The years to come were in one respect different after September 1752, when Britain belatedly adopted the Gregorian calendar, which had been in use in Roman Catholic Europe since 1582. There was popular protest at 'the loss of eleven days' and at the necessary and difficult rescheduling of private as well as public dates. The measure was passed when George II (1727–60) was in Protestant Hanover, from which his father had come to London in 1714. George II was more interested in Hanover's German affairs than in the world of merchants, sailors and colonists. Indicatively, when he led his troops into battle – he was the last English king to do so – it was at Dettingen on European soil. Yet once his dynasty was secured in 1745 against Jacobite armies who mustered in Scotland and marched south into Lancashire, his ministers were drawn increasingly into power struggles on a global scale, involving Europe, North America, the Caribbean, Africa and India.

The hope of many Englishmen in the 1740s and 1750s was William Pitt. 'When trade policy is at stake it is your last retrenchment,' he had proclaimed as a young politician in 1739, 'You must defend it or perish.' In the twentieth century, however, historians have demurred, echoing Samuel Johnson's dictum 'Reason frowns on war's unequal game.' 'If England had enjoyed unbroken peace,' Professor T. S. Ashton used to argue, 'the industrial revolution might have come earlier.' Certainly three major wars of the eighteenth century, those of 1702–13, 1739–48 and 1755–83, led to a sharp contraction in the value of overseas trade, even though they were followed by expansion. Terms of trade moved against the English in wartime as well, and real incomes were depressed.

Other historians have considered war an important spur to technological advance. And 'going to war' had its immediate prizes, particularly for sailors. The scale of naval wages did not increase between 1653 and 1797, and press-ganged sailors were often eager to desert, but everyone shared the booty. 'If these French gentry do not escape me this time,' wrote one admiral to his wife in 1714, 'they will pay for the house and the furniture too, beside something to save hereafter for all our dear children.' There were other inducements. A military recruiting order of 1782 appealed to 'all handsome young Men, whose Hearts beat at the Sound of the Drum, and are Above Mean Employments'; and for those who enjoyed 'active service life' the excitement compensated for the toughness of the initiation and the discipline. That it was not just talk is suggested by the enthusiasm of those like the young countryman William Cobbett, a future radical, who wanted to become a sailor and actually became a soldier. The Forces could attract.

The Navy was the senior service, and more money was spent on it by England than was spent by the French. The seventeenth-century fear of standing armies persisted, and although the number of officers grew with every war, contemporaries considered that the French held the military advantage. 'Though our colonies were superior to those of the enemy in wealth and the number of inhabitants,' Lord Waldegrave noted during the Seven Years War, 'the French were much our superiors in military discipline: almost every man amongst them was a soldier.' There was no compulsory service for the Army, and no adequate peacetime training in England.

Nonetheless it was the English who won the protracted struggle against the French fought in different continents between 1756 and 1763. Naval action was decisive in the capture of Fort St Louis in Senegal in 1758 and the taking of Goree, the other main French settlement in West Africa. James Wolfe's capture of Quebec in 1759, 'a year of victories', called by the actor and dramatist David Garrick a 'wonderful year', signalled the end of French power in Canada in 1760, although not the end there of French language, culture or political aspirations. Wolfe's army was smaller than that of the French, and naval support was again decisive in the victory. The rich island of Guadeloupe in the Caribbean fell in the same year, and at the time it seemed a bigger prize. Two years later, Pondicherry, the French capital in India, fell also, completely ending French power there. Again, Robert Clive, the East India Company's ambitious commander in the field until 1760, had been given valuable additional leeway in his long campaign on land by the defeat of the French fleet in Indian waters during the earlier year of victories.

By this time national pride needed no encouragement from Pitt. In 1757 the clergyman John Brown had published his *Estimate of the Manners and Principles of the Times*, an anatomy of England which accused his fellow countrymen of effeminacy, but a year later he published his *An Explanatory Defence of the Estimate*, praising Pitt's achievements in rousing the nation. A year after that a Sussex shopkeeper, Thomas Turner, was writing proudly that 'no nation had ever greater occasion to adore the Almighty Disposer of all events than Albion, whose forces meet with success, in all quarters of the world'; and in 1774 the name 'The Fortunate Isles' was employed by an author of an article called 'Great Britain superior to every other country'. It was not effortless superiority, however, and the costs were high. Land tax, which under Sir Robert Walpole, Prime Minister from 1721 to 1742, had once stood at a shilling in the pound – he believed in economy, but was, nonetheless, faced with a crisis when he planned a higher inland excise tax in 1733 – now stood at four shillings. Moreover, 200,000 troops were being paid for out of the budget. There were massive loans too. Of £160,000,000 spent by government between 1756 and 1763, £60,000,000 was borrowed. The national debt mounted to more than double that sum, though by this time Parliament had a direct interest in it and in the annual interest repayments. So too did the scattered holders of the new 'consols', the name applied to the consolidated 3 per cent government stock of 1752. The greater part of the small individual holdings, a considerable proportion of them belonging to women, among them spinsters and widows, were held in London and the Home Counties.

Pitt fell from office in 1761, on a dispute about Newfoundland cod, and he was to complain bitterly about many of the features of the first Treaty of Paris made in 1763 at the close of the Seven Years War. Against his wishes Canada was preferred to Guadeloupe, which was restored to the French together with parts of French West Africa, and French fishing rights round Newfoundland were confirmed. Nonetheless, the British Empire reached a new peak as a result of the war. The thirteen American colonies, with far-flung lands to the north in Canada, stretched in the south to Florida and in the west towards the Mississippi. France recovered several of the Caribbean islands that had been seized during the war, but the British secured others, including Grenada, St Vincent and Tobago. Meanwhile, in the East, the riches of Bengal were being exploited as if it was a new El Dorado. Others paid the price: according to Robert Clive's many critics, the increase of 'the London government's share of the spoils' had been bought at the cost of the late famine in Bengal and the loss of three million of inhabitants'. Clive's own advice that the 'sovereignty of India' was 'too large' for a Company did not then greatly appeal to English politicians.

For all the triumphs of war and peace, the Empire as it stood in 1763 had many weaknesses. Its various parts were so different from one another that it was impossible to envisage them in terms of one single design, even a Providential one. It was an empire held together by sea power, but sea power alone was not enough to control it, let alone to govern it. Nor was trading supremacy guaranteed. France remained a strong rival after 1763, although some contemporaries believed that it was in the country's interest to be at continual variance with that restless

The growth of the British Empire, 1763–1914

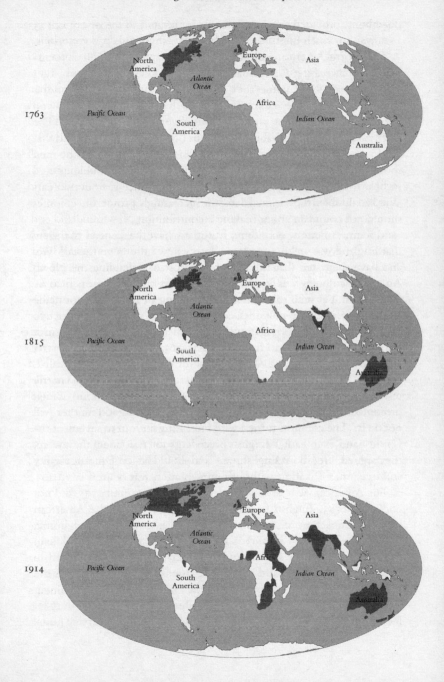

1763

1815

1914

neighbour, provided the contest could be limited to the operations of a sea war, in which England would be always invincible and victorious.

The North American colonies posed other problems. Their population was increasing at a dramatic rate – in 1760 it was six times larger than in 1700 – and while their inhabitants could be as patriotic as Englishmen when they talked about their shared heritage or naval and military victories, there were obvious divergences of interest. The Grenville government that took office in London in 1763 believed that for reasons of defence a permanent standing army of some 10,000 men should be kept in America and that American colonists should be taxed to help to cover the costs. It suggested too that since the Seven Years War had doubled the national debt, the increasingly prosperous colonies should not complain about making a contribution.

Modern American economic historians have challenged the view that England was seeking to place a heavy new burden on the colonies and have suggested that the real annual cost of defending the North American colonies was £400,000, five times the maximum income from them. Yet such calculations, convincing or not, were not made at the time, and the colonists, already chafing under the restrictive seventeenth-century Navigation Acts, felt increasing resentment against the tightening up of British policy after 1763. The Sugar Act of 1764 and American Stamp Act of 1765, both of which were later repealed, and the Tea Act of 1767, which was later modified, were bitterly disliked. There had been too much legislation of the kind which prompted Benjamin Franklin to remark, 'a wise and good mother will not do it.' The colonists turned with increasing fervour to seventeenth-century and even earlier English precedents for resistance; they were, they argued, 'free-born Englishmen' and should be 'co-equal in dignity and freedom'. Taxation without representation was tyranny.

The American War of Independence, which began in 1775, did not end until 1783. English failures were as important as the American victories since they undermined the English government at home; indeed, the debate in England on the war, which, according to William Pitt the Younger (the son of Pitt the Elder), had been 'conceived in injustice' and 'matured and brought forth in fury', was as bitter as the fighting on the other side of the Atlantic. When Lord Cornwallis was finally forced to surrender to George Washington at Yorktown in 1781, his troops recalled the upheavals of the seventeenth century at home when they stacked down their arms to the tune of 'The World Turned Upside Down', and their feelings were echoed in a remark of 1782 that defeat had produced in England 'the strangest, though not unexpected, revolution that has happened in this country for many years'. Lord North, who had been in office since 1770, was replaced as Prime Minister first by the Marquis of Rockingham, his Whig critic, and then on Rockingham's death by Lord Shelburne, who arranged the Second Treaty of Paris. It recognized a new independent America south from the Great Lakes and west to the Mississippi.

A gloomy Samuel Johnson felt that 'we have all the world for our enemies' as an Empire was 'broken down'. Yet as industrial output in England soared during the later 1780s, Englishmen sold more goods to independent America than they had done in colonial days under 'the old colonial system', which was propped up by the Navigation Acts. The value of total exports amounted to £12,500,000 in 1782 and to £20,000,000 by 1790. And when in 1790 constitutional arrangements were introduced in Canada, where large numbers of 'loyalists' had settled after American independence, their effect was to strengthen 'the principle of authority in government and of hierarchy in society'.

The Secretaryship of the Colonies was abolished in 1782, but the Empire was not abolished with it. Indeed, James Cook's discovery of Australia in 1770 added an enormous (although as yet unexplored) territory that would later become an important penal colony. Cook was an enterprising explorer who carried around with him plants and trees; he was killed in Hawaii in 1779. Meanwhile, the Empire was still being extended in India, despite attempts by a series of governments to bring the activities of the East India Company under control. The government of Pitt the Younger, which was formed in 1784, established a Board of Control a year later to scrutinize all the Company's political operations. This was followed by the impeachment and trial of Warren Hastings, the Governor-General, 'an empire builder by design', in which the Marquis of Cornwallis, who broke with the tradition of working in association with Indians, played an unappealing part. 'Though the constitution of our Eastern possessions is arbitrary and despotic,' Pitt explained in 1795, the year Hastings was acquitted, 'still it is the duty of every administration in that country to conduct itself by the rules of justice and liberty.'

India was far away and had its own history. What was crucial in

English social history was that throughout the eighteenth century it had been possible to pursue the quest for wealth as vigorously and profitably inside hierarchical England as outside it. Land remained the major source of wealth and power, and the great landlords continued to improve their economic position: in 1700 peers owned about 15 to 20 per cent of England's landed wealth, and by 1800 they owned between 20 and 25 per cent. In some cases they could increase their wealth, too, from coal and iron royalties, from canals and, above all, from urban properties – with the Bedfords and the Grosvenors leading the way in London. It was their country seats, however, which were both symbols and centres of display and of hospitality. 'Banishment alone will force the French to execute what the English do for pleasure,' Arthur Young was to write. 'Reside and adorn their estates.'

Below the aristocracy, the landed gentry, with diverse properties and varying fortunes, were also in a strong position in an age of 'improving agriculture' to increase their wealth, and a few of them, like Thomas Coke of Holkham, were to improve their status too and become peers. Whatever their titles, their social role as squires was the key role in local society. They determined its patterns of power as justices of the peace, backed by clerks of the peace and unpaid parish officers, churchwardens, overseers and constables. There was no money in such activities, only burdens, but because of local and national influence the gentry were in a position to maintain corn laws and game laws. No fewer than thirty-two game laws were enacted in the reign of George III (1760–1820). They were all designed to reinforce privilege. This was the time when fox hunting became an established country sport.

The composition and wealth of the gentry might be reinforced through links with London and with overseas trade, for in the City there were 'merchant princes' who, as one foreign visitor observed in 1727, were 'far wealthier than many sovereign princes of Germany or Italy'. In the same decade one Lord Mayor of London held £122,000 in South Sea stock and £118,000 in Bank of England stock. The mixture – or 'confusion' – of the nobility and the 'mercantile part of the nation,' wrote P. J. Grosley in his *Tour to London* in 1772, 'is an inexhaustible source of wealth to the state. The nobility having acquired an accession of wealth by marriage, the tradesmen make up for their loss by eager endeavours to make a fortune, and the gentry conspire to the same end by their efforts to raise such an estate as shall procure a peerage for themselves or their children.'

This was an ideal picture, and contrasts with the definition of 'gentlemen' given in 1730 in the dictionary of Samuel Johnson's predecessor, Nathan Bailey: 'In our days all are accounted gentlemen that have money.' In fact, entry to the peerage, in particular, was far more restricted than contemporaries like Grosley (or earlier and later writers) claimed. It was a fact also, however, that marriage remained a main way to wealth: the father of Lord North, for example, married three heiresses. (It should be added that his brother was in turn Bishop of Lichfield, Worcester and Winchester, the last and richest of all the sees.) Neither the aristocracy nor the gentry constituted closed orders of society, and although the former may have been more closed than in many other periods of English social history, contemporaries took pride in what was called in 1757 the 'gradual and easy transition from rank to rank'. 'Merchants are commonly ambitious of becoming country gentlemen,' observed Adam Smith, along with many others, including Daniel Defoe who warned his readers in 'the business of trade' not to be dazzled by thoughts of gentility, but who allowed his character Robinson Crusoe to buy land in Bedfordshire when he returned from his island solitude. Similarly, Pinney, a member of a family that acquired a West Indian fortune, wrote in 1778 that his 'greatest pride is to be considered as a private country gentleman, therefore I am resolved to content myself with a title and shall avoid even the name of a West Indian.'

A 'title' was perhaps too modest. Land values almost doubled between 1700 and 1790 as more land, approximately a further 4,000,000 acres, was brought into cultivation and as agriculture became more productive. At no point did the growth of industry imply that farming languished: 'while manufacturers are flourishing and increasing,' wrote the Reverend John Howlett in 1772, 'agriculture will flourish with them.' There was no spectacular agricultural revolution, and some of the corn-growing areas even faced depression during the 1730s and 1740s, but there were so many changes over the country as a whole, most with their origins in the seventeenth century, that they have rightly been compared to the movement of a tide. 'Move your eyes which side you will,' wrote Arthur Young, eloquent advocate of agricultural improvement, 'you behold nothing but great riches and yet greater resources.' One economic historian has calculated that in 1700 each person engaged in farming fed 1.7 persons, whereas in 1800 each fed 2.5 persons, an increase of 47 per cent. Even so, England ceased to be a regular net exporter of wheat and wheaten flour in 1750 (the peak year for exports), and there were net imports in 1757 and 1758, and regularly after 1767. They were necessary because of the rise in population which can be traced back to the mid-1730s.

The merits of improved farming – better use of soil, crops, tools (like Jethro Tull's famous drill) and farm layout – were much publicized, notably by Arthur Young, who himself was a failure as a farmer; his *Six Weeks' Tour through the Southern Counties of England* appeared in 1768, eight years after the accession of George III, who liked to consider himself a farmer king. Livestock and potatoes were topics of lively conversation, even controversy. Oil paintings of giant bulls, spectacular sheep and, of course, the sleek horses of the period hung alongside portraits and landscapes in large numbers of new eighteenth-century houses, gems of the landscape, many of which had begun as farmhouses. George Stubbs, whose paintings of horses were greatly prized, was the son of an ostler and author of *The Anatomy of the Horse*.

Young began to publish his *Annals of Agriculture* in 1784 and the geographical area he most publicized was the county of Norfolk. It was there that experimenters in crop rotation developed the so-called 'new husbandry' which enabled fields to be cultivated continuously with no years in fallow. They were able to provide hay and winter-feeding stock for sheep and cattle, making possible an increase in the numbers of livestock and thereby in the quantity of manure. 'Half the country of Norfolk within the memory of man had yielded nothing but sheep feed,' but now, it was claimed, 'those very tracts of land are covered with as fine barley and rye as any in the world and great quantities of wheat besides.' Thomas Coke, later Earl of Leicester, the great improver, who enjoyed such financial success that under his management the value of produce from his estate increased four-fold within fifteen years, was the name chiefly associated with the changes in Norfolk, but he had his predecessors, notably 'Turnip Townshend' and Prime Minister Robert Walpole. There were some counties, however, like Gloucester-shire, where Coke could not persuade farmers to change their ways, or Herefordshire, where as late as 1804 Young travelled 'near one hundred miles' without seeing 'drilled crops'. Even as late as the 1840s there were as many acres under fallow as under turnips.

Leicestershire was publicized for its agricultural change at least as much as Norfolk, and visitors from all over Europe visited Robert Bakewell's farm at Dishley Grange, near Loughborough, to admire his horses, cattle and sheep, which he considered as 'machines for turning grass into mutton', although they were dismissed by his critics as 'too dear to buy and too fat to eat'. It was not always big farmers or those who were most publicity-conscious who succeeded in the long run: Bakewell's hospitality was too lavish and he bankrupted himself. Meanwhile, the spread of what became great English breeds, like Herefordshire cattle or Southdown sheep, went on successfully without being a matter of controversy. While counties like Norfolk and Gloucestershire turned increasingly to arable farming, those like Leicestershire were turning increasingly to livestock. Indeed, in 1790 William Marshall could describe Leicestershire as 'a continuous sheet of greensward'. The most flexible system was mixed farming, which had the extra advantage of maintaining soil fertility.

Continuing enclosure was a necessary part of the process of agricultural 'improvement', and following the enclosure of the clay fields of the Midland counties in the earlier part of the century, between 2,000,000 and 3,000,000 acres of open fields and waste lands in the Midlands, south and east, were enclosed between 1760 and 1799. The procedure used was usually enclosure by Act of Parliament rather than by voluntary agreement or pressure. A successful Enclosure Act did not require local unanimity, but it did require enough money to pay for the lawyers' and surveyors' fees and for fences, hedges, roads and drainage after the bill had been passed. This was largely a formality since the Enclosure Commissioners appointed to survey the land invariably favoured the parties wishing to enclose, and so too did Parliament, which passed a general Enclosure Act in 1801 simplifying future procedures. By then more than 1,300 Enclosure Acts had been passed since 1760. Almost 1,000 more were to come between 1800 and 1820.

Contemporaries thought that farmers who favoured enclosure were 'new men in point of knowledge and ideas' (a description suggested by the physical appearance of farmers at Banbury market), while Young believed that enclosure itself quickened enterprise: it 'changed the man as much as it has improved the country'. Inevitably, big men led the way. 'It will at once be apparent,' Young wrote, 'that no small farmers could effect such great things as have been done in Norfolk. Great farms are the soul of Norfolk culture; split them into tenures of an hundred pounds a year, and you will find nothing but beggars and weeds in the whole county.' The demand for enclosure came, however, from their tenant farmers – about three-quarters of English land was cultivated by them at the end of the century – and from small landlords too; there was a drive to consolidate holdings and to eliminate waste. Yeomen who could be tempted to augment their capital by selling their freeholds and go on to become tenant farmers were another category again.

Enclosure and agricultural change transformed the appearance of the rural environment. Even by the 1760s Smollett described it as 'smiling with cultivation . . . parcelled out into beautiful enclosures'. As the fields were enclosed, woodlands and wastes disappeared and a new pattern of hedges, walls, fences and roads took shape. 'I admit I was often amazed,' wrote a German visitor who returned to England in the early nineteenth century, 'to see great uncultivated areas made productive as though through magic and transformed into fine, corn-bearing fields.' Not until the late twentieth century was there to be such a drastic transformation in the appearance of the countryside.

There was certainly wealth to be made out of enclosure: rent rolls rose, farm profits were boosted, and styles of life changed. Yet some of the big men were attacked, as their ancestors had been in previous centuries, as oppressors of the 'indignant many'; and even of lesser men Cobbett could write that 'when farmers become gentlemen their labourers become slaves.' Young himself, often inconsistent, came to feel that enclosure led to human suffering. While he believed that labourers in parishes without enclosure worked 'like negroes and did not live so well as the inhabitants of the poor house', he admitted that, 'by nineteen enclosure bills in twenty, the poor are injured, and in some cases grossly injured.'

Enclosure threatened the independence of a number of people who had previously felt themselves to be independent. Nor did it help when they were told by Sir Frederick Eden, author of an invaluable late eighteenth-century book on the state of the poor, that 'it is one of the natural consequences of freedom that those who are left to shift for themselves must sometimes be reduced to want.' Just as 'independence' was later prized by craftsmen in the age of the machine, so too was it prized by cultivators whose holdings were so small that access to common land was of vital importance to them: they had no capital at their disposal to build fences, drains or barns. Squatters on common land were, of course, those who suffered the most: they had no legal rights and they were often evicted without ceremony. For a time the actual process of enclosure itself might provide them with work, but in the long run it left many of them paupers. Not surprisingly, therefore, they might become disaffected.

> They hang the man and flog the woman
> That steals a goose from off the common
> But leave the greater criminal loose
> That steals the common from the goose.

Political discontent might accompany demoralization. 'The poor . . . may say, and with truth, Parliament may be tender of property; all I know is, I had a cow and an Act of Parliament has taken it from me.' Enclosure turned land into absolute private property and quickened suspicion both of the law which enshrined that process and of the justices of the peace who administered it; it was one more demonstration of Oliver Goldsmith's dictum that 'laws grind the poor and rich men grind the law.' And although what was happening seemed irrevocable, poor men in the nineteenth century might still dream of repossessing the land, and even seek actively to repossess it long after the process of enclosure had been completed.

There had been strains in the village community long before eighteenth-century enclosure and deserted villages long before Oliver Goldsmith wrote about them. But there could now be a sense of crisis. Thus the village of Wigston Magna in Leicestershire, the population of which had tripled between 1524 and 1765, was completely transformed by an enclosure of 1765. The small owner-occupiers (two-thirds of the population owned less than fifty acres) virtually disappeared as a group within sixty or seventy years, becoming instead rural labourers, framework knitters or paupers. In 1754 local poor rate expenditures amounted to £95; in 1802 they amounted to £1,776.

In many parts of the country local magistrates decided to grant outdoor relief allowances to the poor when bad harvests led to soaring wheat prices, and went on to prepare formal scales of wage support even when such peak points of distress were passed. The best-known example was that of Speenhamland, a village in Berkshire which gave its name to such a system of allowances. Yet the 'system' was never universally or consistently applied, and it is wrong to divide England into 'Speenhamland' and 'non-Speenhamland' counties. The number of workhouses enforcing labour on the able-bodied poor also increased between 1776 and 1801. A General Workhouse Act which enabled parishes to build a workhouse if they wished had been passed in 1723, and by 1776 there were almost 2,000 such places, usually with twenty-five to thirty inmates, while a further Act of 1782, Gilbert's Act, permitted parishes to combine into unions to deal with their poor law problems. Such changes, often supported by humanitarians, ushered in the last stage in the history of the 'old poor law'.

It was to become increasingly expensive to operate in the early nineteenth century and increasingly irrelevant to the needs of a more industrialized society. The origins of that society lay in the eighteenth century, which ended with two decades of spectacular industrial advance. Already, however, by the beginning of the century, when the word 'industry' still designated a quality of human beings not a sector of the economy, Defoe had observed that 'an estate is but a pond, but trade is a spring.' His successors might have added that 'industry' could be a fountain. By the end of the century the word was already beginning to suggest fire and smoke.

The Quaker Ambrose Crowley, Tyneside ironmaster, made a fortune out of his great works. By 1760 Ben Truman had a brewing plant valued at £30,000 and a floating capital of over £100,000. Abraham Darby, another Quaker, was the first man to smelt iron with coke, in 1709; he transformed Coalbrookdale in Shropshire. Matthew Boulton, who started business as a button maker, was dealing successfully in all kinds of metal enterprises before he met James Watt in 1769, and his great works at Soho, near Birmingham, were described by a local poet as 'Europe's Wonder and Britannia's pride'. He had 'turned a barren heath into a delightful garden'. Richard Arkwright, who had opened his first factory at Nottingham in 1768, built a handsome new factory at Cromford in Derbyshire three years later, and when he died in 1792 he left many factories, 'the income of which was greater than that of most German principalities'. Josiah Wedgwood, the potter, who had founded the Wedgwood Potteries in 1759, the 'year of victories', was a man of genius, clever enough to be made a Fellow of the Royal Society in 1783. He left a fortune of £500,000.

The politician Edmund Burke, a victim of the political changes of the early 1780s, was to lambast popular English radicals after the French Revolution and in turn be lambasted by them. Yet it was he who suggested that there was another side to the picture, as there was in the village. Indeed, he did not hesitate to draw comparison between English slaves and slaves overseas.

> I suppose that there are in Great Britain upwards of a hundred thousand people employed in lead, tin, iron, copper and coal mines ... An hundred thousand more at least are tortured without remission by the suffocating smoke, intense fires and constant drudgery necessary in refining and managing the production of those mines.

In fact, conditions varied. Crowley's men were given orders to work; those to whom he gave poor relief – and he believed both in that and in health care – had to wear a badge inscribed 'Crowley's Poor'. Arkwright's men were attracted to work at Cromford by good conditions, but they were also expected to sing:

> Come let us all here join in one,
> And thank him for all favours done;
> Let's thank him for all favours still
> Which he hath done beside the mill.

A significant proportion of the new labour force consisted of child pauper apprentices brought in from London parishes; they had no choice in the matter.

The eighteenth century did not create contrasts, but it added to them. There were child chimney sweeps before there were factory children, and disgruntled and unevenly employed craftsmen before there were discontented and unemployed factory workers. It was a tile hewer who complained:

> My trade and occupation
> Was ground for lamentation,
> Which makes me curse my station
> And wish I'd ne'er been born.
> I ne'er can save one shilling
> And must – which is killing
> A pauper die when old.

The sense of 'station' remained strong, and at the base of society were the large numbers of people who in Defoe's phrase were 'the miserable that really pinch and suffer want'. Above them were 'the poor that fare hard'.

Any picture of the eighteenth century that focused exclusively either on poverty or on wealth would be misleading as far as structures or motives were concerned. Between the aristocracy, the gentry, the yeomen, the tenant farmers and the landless labourers on the one hand and the employers, industrial workmen and craftsmen on the other, there were extremely large numbers of 'middling folk', who increased in numbers and income during the eighteenth century, and growing groups of professional people.

The role of the 'middling folk' in work and leisure – with their own gradations of status – has long been recognized; indeed, it was fully recognized at the time. They were involved in a wide variety of occupations, respectable or otherwise, rural or urban (the two were never completely set apart), and all of them 'bearing', in the words of one contemporary, 'the heat of the day'. There were more of them and they had more opportunities of making money than ever before, and like the rich, whom they were often accused of imitating, they had far more opportunities of spending it.

So too had lawyers, who benefited directly from the growing volume of legal business and the delays in settling it. Their professional income came from fees, not from trade, and for this reason, and because many of them came from 'good families', they were clearly distinguished from 'middling folk'. There was no doubt that they, like physicians (if not apothecaries) and army officers, were 'gentlemen', although there were divisions between barristers and the newly emerging group of qualified solicitors. There were even more nuances of status with clergymen, some of whom were very poorly paid; some of the most learned, active and best paid were in London. Surgeons were rising in status, and physicians were secure. Apothecaries were often making large sums of money. 'Men of letters', artists and musicians were whole spectra in themselves, fashionable or 'Bohemian' (the use of the word had not been coined), independent or servile. Samuel Johnson, the best remembered of them, knew well the variety of possible conditions. There was also an 'underground' of vagrants, sharpers, cheats, thieves, prostitutes, the 'upside-down world' of John Gay's *The Beggar's Opera*

(1728). There could be popular heroes in the underground, among poachers and highwaymen in particular. There were also links through gambling and rough sports between the highest and the lowest.

Women have left only a limited record of their own condition. As to male thoughts on women, for Lord Chesterfield they were 'children of a larger growth' and 'a man of sense only trifles with them.' For Johnson himself 'the chastity of women' was of 'all importance since property depends on it'. There were contradictions in male views. Some women were associated with pleasure; married women were associated with family, and respectable unmarried women – the word 'spinster' was used to describe them in 1719 – were associated with charity. In fact, married women lost any financial independence under common law. For the great lawyer Blackstone it was enough to say that 'in marriage husband and wife are one person, and that person is the husband.' Other writers had something different to say. Thus, an article in *The Lady Magazine*, published in 1774, maintained that 'the idea of matrimony' was not 'for man and wife to be always taken up with each other, but jointly to discharge the duties of civil society, to govern their families with prudence and to educate their children with discretion.'

Spending by women and men was in vogue and could benefit artists, men of letters and musicians along with those engaged in service trades of every kind. This was an age when fashion counted, and when considerable effort was being made – successfully – to satisfy wants. Arthur Young, who objected to 'the poor' treating tea as a 'necessary' and to farmers or farmers' wives buying pianos, could talk in 1771, the year of the first coloured fashion-plate (in *The Lady Magazine*), of 'universal luxury'. Handbags had only been introduced during the previous decade, but by the end of the century they were to be called 'indispensables'. So too were umbrellas. By 1800 there were 153 shops in Oxford Street in London, catering for the 'whim-whams and fribble-frabble of fashion'. London was unique – in its growth as well as in its variety: to be 'tired of London' for Johnson was to be 'tired of life'.

One new institution, the British Museum, opened in 1753, was financed by public lottery, but the Royal Academy, founded fifteen years later, was under royal patronage. There was manifest pride in this, and pride too that London 'novelties', and the 'civilization' which went with them, could be shared by the middle ranks of society in the provinces as well as in London. Bath, called by Defoe 'the resort of the sound rather than the sick', grew rapidly during the century, from a population of 2,000 in 1700 to 34,000 in 1800, and as it did so an old town gave way to a sparkling new one. Nearby Bristol prided itself not only on its trade but on the fact that its 'theatrical performances are little inferior (if any) to those in London'. This was the great age of the spa, including the seaside spa, like Scarborough in Yorkshire. Liverpool, a northern port which was to grow at the expense of Bristol and which in 1800 was already the second largest city in the kingdom, prided itself both on its 'elegant houses' and on its imposing public buildings. And even in Leeds, which was becoming an industrial city, an inhabitant noted soon after the beginning of the nineteenth century that whereas he could remember a time when 'there were not seven carriages' kept in the city, 'now there are a hundred'. Birmingham, like many other towns, had its own Assembly Rooms, dignified with the French name of *Hôtel*. It too had its own theatre by 1774.

By then local urban amenities were as much in demand as new country houses with engaging 'prospects' (and new stables and gardens); and in both town and country there were the same aspirations to acquire elegant mahogany furniture made by Chippendale, Sheraton and Hepplewhite, Adam brothers decorations, silver tableware, porcelain tea sets and chinoiserie. For the wealthy who looked further afield it was also the great age of the Grand Tour through France, Italy and Germany, which was thought of by landlords and squires as not the least important stage in education for living:

> His honour posts o'er Italy and France,
> Measures St Peter's dome, and learns to dance

returning home

> Half atheist, papist, forester, bubble, rook,
> Half fiddler, coachman, dancer, groom and cook.

Public school education – and grammar schools – provided for those who had access to it – and in this period they still included poor as well as rich – a necessary classical preparation. It was left to dissenting academies, the most famous of which was at Warrington in the north of England, to pursue scientific education with a practical bent, catering intelligently for Congregationalists, Unitarians and others, and offering a challenging as well as a useful curriculum.

To know the rules of polite taste did not need too much formal education. Richard Steele and Joseph Addison had pointed the way to their definition early in the century in essays in *The Tatler* (1709–11) and *The Spectator* (1711–12); and as the century went by the rules were clearly defined as in the work of the painter Sir Joshua Reynolds, the first President of the Royal Academy; in the design and layout of rural and urban buildings and gardens (the great Capability Brown, redesigner of nature, was the son of a tradesman); in the framing of heroic couplets in 'poetic diction'; in the oratorios of the German-born composer Handel, who arrived from Hanover in 1710 and composed his *Messiah* in 1741; in the formal dance steps of the great ball; and in spelling books and dictionaries, which increasingly standardized the language.

It was a sign of the vitality of the period that none of the rules was universally accepted and that there were significant changes of taste and fashion, including a revival of Gothic. At no time either exuberance or prophecy could be completely constrained within set limits. 'Enthusiasm' always had its devotees, despite Johnson's definition of it as the 'heat of imagination', and 'violence of passion'. The great poet William Blake, a man of genius, hated Reynolds and all that he stood for. Ordering nature (like philosophizing about it) was followed by, sometimes accompanied by, a newly discovered delight in 'the picturesque' – including moors and mountains – and sentimental musing about landscapes and ruins. Gothic buildings were sometimes built near Palladian buildings. There were early stirrings of 'romanticism', which was to blossom in the last decade of the century in the romantic poetry of Wordsworth and Coleridge. *Lyrical Ballads* first appeared – in Bristol – in 1797.

The ordered novels of Jane Austen, who was born in 1775, were admired by the Prince Regent (they did include one gentle satire of a horror tale), but in her own time they never attracted the kind of admiration reserved for men of letters of the early eighteenth century. Yet even then 'Grub Street' had been a subject of satire for Alexander Pope, against whom the romantic poets reacted, while the appeal of the novel itself as a new form, separating itself out from other forms of writing, was itself a matter of controversy at every stage in its evolution. There were, indeed, as many shifts of approval and disapproval in the eighteenth century as in the nineteenth, so that the detailed story of eighteenth-century enjoyment and enrichment demands a carefully compiled chronology which takes account of literary and aesthetic currents and their eddies at every stage. It must also take account of new circumstances affecting patronage and the public, including the rise of publishing, as distinct from printing or bookselling, the spread of circulating libraries, and the growth of a feminine readership. Goldsmith was only one of several writers who objected to 'writing being converted into a mechanic trade' and to booksellers becoming 'the patrons and paymasters of men of genius' 'instead of the great'. Limits were set to development, however, by limits to literacy and to incomes.

One reason why sophistication – and order – were so much asserted throughout the century was that eighteenth-century life could be extremely raw. There was a place in it for buffoons alongside *savants*, roughnecks alongside rakes. Nor were the boundaries always easy to define in practice. Elegance and squalor coexisted. Far more people died young than old, and if there was no plague there was still fever. Medical treatment could be gruesome: bleeding and vomiting were modes of relief. Everyday life could be extremely violent – verbally in the pamphlet and the broadsheet; physically in the ring and in the street – and the boundaries between political demonstration and crime were not always easy to define either. Henry Fielding, author of *Tom Jones*, who was a magistrate as well as a novelist, had strong views about both.

The principles of authority and hierarchy were frequently challenged, not as the result of any faltering of purpose on the part of government, which set out to uphold them with the full force of law (especially during the French Revolution and the wars against Napoleonic France which began in 1793), but by political, religious and economic discontent. In an attempt to deal with crime, rural and urban, the Waltham Black Act of 1724 created no fewer than fifty new capital offences, most of them concerned with attacks on property. There was ample evidence both of judicial leniency and of the arbitrariness of the law. Although there were now nearly a hundred capital offences on the Statute Book, no more than two hundred people a year were actually hanged. One effective statutory intervention was the Gin Act of 1751, which, through heavy taxation, brought to an end a 'gin era' which had begun in 1720 and which inspired Hogarth to present his contrast between what happened in Gin Lane and Beer Lane. At the peak of the era in 1739 William Maitland in his *History and Survey of London* estimated there were 8,659 'dram' shops. There were nearly 6,000 alehouses too, mainly patronized by the 'mechanick part of mankind'.

In the countryside a 'moral economy' was acknowledged which in practice allowed for the expression of discontent through ritualized behaviour (including tolerated but circumscribed violence) when food prices were high; the crowd assumed that popular views of what was right would be appreciated if not shared. In the cities, however, there was already more uncertainty about motivation and behaviour. London, in particular, was a frequent scene of unritualized rioting, most notably in the Wilkes Riots of 1763 and the Gordon Riots of 1780. Indeed, it has been claimed that, in the terms that the flourishing new insurance companies used, ten times as much damage was done to London property during the week of the Gordon Riots as was done to Paris throughout the French Revolution. The riots, provoked by the repeal of some of the penal laws against Roman Catholics (notably concerning the right to acquire and inherit property), began with cries of 'No Popery', but as they went on targets included rich men's houses. Everything was out of control. Nor was there any police force to attempt to control it.

The circulation of radical ideas during the French Revolution further inflamed passions. Thomas Paine's *Rights of Man*, widely circulated and quickly sold out, was the most disturbing book, and led to fierce controversy, stirring into action what Burke called contemptuously 'the swinish multitude', while at the same time encouraging supporters of 'King, Constitution and Country' to create their own organizations. It was in Birmingham, not London, that Paine was burned in effigy in 1793 and a hostile crowd provoked not by radicals but by conservatives attacked the house of Joseph Priestley, the Nonconformist preacher, writer and scientist.

Priestley was a product of the dissenting academies. John Wesley, whose 'enthusiastic' religion was very different from Priestley's 'enlightened' Unitarianism, was a product of Oxford. Priestley seemed far removed from the poor, although he recognized their rights; Wesley appealed to them, although he stressed their duties. In 1738 Wesley had been 'converted' to a 'religion of the heart', open to all, rich or poor, and he preached it fearlessly. The Church of England was dominated at that time by bishops and clergymen who thought of Christianity in terms of virtue and prudence rather than in terms of salvation and judgement. In consequence, Wesley, who remained a member of the Church to his death, was often treated as fiercely as any Unitarian as he travelled 25,000 miles from parish to parish, claiming the whole world as his parish. Telling his own history of personal redemption he made many converts, 'the people called Methodists', who eventually were to form a church of their own and to spawn sects. One of those sects, the 'Primitives', was to produce not only preachers but future radical and labour leaders.

Evangelicalism inside the established Church was a more powerful force even than Methodism, for there were fewer than 100,000 Methodists at the end of the eighteenth century at a time when the so-called 'Saints', with William Wilberforce, a friend of William Pitt, prominent among them, were demanding from places of power a wholesale 'reformation of manners'. Bitterly opposed to the French Revolution, they were concerned at this time too with the struggle to free the slaves overseas, a successful struggle, strongly supported by the Quakers. The trade, with all its entrenched interests, was abolished by Act of Parliament in 1807 in the middle of the wars against Napoleon. Already, by the beginning of the nineteenth century, as G. M. Young has written, 'virtue was advancing on a broad invincible front,' and when Napoleon was defeated in 1815 the Evangelicals were to claim a share in the victory on the grounds that they had provided moral armour for the nation.

Moral armour would not have been enough. The expensive wars against Napoleon could not have been won had England not been a far richer country at the end of the century than it was at the beginning, and the riches were now coming increasingly from the growth of industry. With that growth, the moral economy of the crowd was to give way to the political economy of the market-place and of the factory; and within this new and never static context what was cheap was to matter more in practice than what was elegant or what was fair. At the same time, the fact that England's revolution, unlike the French Revolution of 1789, was industrial not political meant that there was less emphasis on equality than on development. In such a society the pursuit of pleasure, while it continued, became suspect to the 'industrious'. There was little place for it among the smoke.

8 THE EXPERIENCE OF INDUSTRIALIZATION

> Were we required to characterize this age of ours by any single epithet, we should be tempted to call it . . . the Mechanical Age.
>
> Thomas Carlyle, *Signs of the Times*, 1829

> Ingenuity rather than abstention governed the industrial revolution.
>
> D. N. McCloskey, *The Economic History of Britain since 1700*, 1981

> Whilst the engine runs, the people must work – men, women and children are yoked together with iron and steam. The animal machine – breakable in the best case . . . is chained fast to the iron machine, which knows no suffering and no weariness.
>
> J. P. Kay, *Moral and Physical Conditions of the Operatives Employed in the Cotton Manufacture in Manchester*, 1832

> It is a historic irony that the nation that gave birth to the industrial revolution, and exported it throughout the world, should have become embarrassed at the measure of its success.
>
> M. J. Wiener, *English Culture and the Decline of the Industrial Spirit*, 1981

There was a time when the study of the English industrial revolution, the first of its kind in the world, was left almost entirely to social historians. They sympathized deeply with the poor, usually considered the beneficiaries of revolution, who were judged to be its victims in this case. 'The English people never, by any plague, or famine, or war,' wrote the Oxford historian Frederick York Powell in 1901, 'suffered such a deadly blow at its vitality as by the establishment of the factory system without the proper safeguards.'

Values were more prominent than facts in such studies. Thus, when in the 1880s Arnold Toynbee argued that more had been destroyed than created through the smoke of the industrial revolution, he had long historical perspectives in view. For him the essence of the revolution was not the spectacular transformation of the coal, iron and textile industries, nor the development of steam power, but 'the substitution of competition for the medieval regulations which had previously controlled the production and distribution of wealth'. However, although many of these regulations, including those relating to wages and employment, continued to be invoked, they had in fact ceased to be effective *before* the industrial revolution.

The same inadequacies of general explanation are obvious also in a number of more recent interpretations by economic historians, some of whom have been tempted to treat the industrial revolution as a simple success story, others to eliminate altogether the sense of a revolution, even of a break. They have been right, of course, to point out that mechanization was not triumphant until the middle of the nineteenth century and to insist that cumulative economic processes led up to the changes a century earlier. They have been right, also, to take many factors into account: England's (and Britain's) intricate trade connections before the industrial revolution; the large numbers of middlemen; the existence of rural industries before the rise of factories; the developed mechanical skills of many Englishmen; the use of water power before the advent of the steam engine; the increase in population; and the growing demand for a wide range of products, including simple products which could be made cheaper by new forms of processing. Defoe had noted all these aspects of the English economy early in the eighteenth century, and when William Hutton went to busy Birmingham in 1741 he found there a 'vivacity' which he had never seen before. 'I had been among dreamers, but now I saw men awake.'

Nonetheless, there was the sense of a leap forward in the late eighteenth century. Human and animal strength were replaced, or supplemented, by machines and inanimate power. Coal production doubled between 1750 and 1800, then increased twenty-fold in the nineteenth century; within that sequence it was to double between 1800 and 1830 and again between 1830 and 1845. Pig-iron production rose four times between 1740 and 1788 and quadrupled again during the next twenty years; it was to increase more than thirty-fold in the nineteenth century. Raw cotton imports quintupled between 1780 and

1800 and rose thirty-fold during the nineteenth century. Many other indices, notably those relating to the falling proportion of the population involved in agriculture, tell the same story. Neither these quantitative changes, nor the paths of growth themselves, were smooth or continuous, and business rhythms led sometimes to 'boom', sometimes to 'slump', but it was as a result of this massive, if jerky, capitalist development that England produced the kind of society that is only now, belatedly, beginning to seem obsolete. It did not spring into existence fully formed, and it incorporated many elements from the past, but for most people for nearly two centuries since, this is 'where we came in'.

One necessary lever of change, often feared then (as it is today), was invention, without which it would have been impossible to achieve such huge increases in output. Nonetheless, more than half the achieved technical progress between 1780 and 1860, measured in terms of the contribution made to aggregate economic growth, lay with a few sectors of the economy. It owed little directly to science and much to empirical effort, although an interest in science inspired many of the inventors and led them to believe that nothing was impossible. Moreover, bodies like the (Royal) Society for the Encouragement of Arts, Manufacture and Commerce in Great Britain, founded in 1754, directed the spirit of inventiveness into *useful* channels. Ingenuity by itself was not considered enough.

The success of the inventors themselves, who came from varying social backgrounds and ranged from millwrights to clergymen, required qualities other than inventiveness. Business acumen was one of them. The Scotsman James Watt, who revolutionized the use of steam power and died a national hero, though he was never knighted, found a perfect partner in 1773 in Birmingham's Matthew Boulton, who had already boasted that he had 'established a correspondence with almost every mercantile town in Europe which regularly supplies me with orders'. Meanwhile, Henry Cort, the inventor of a crucial puddling and rolling process (1781) that made possible a huge increase in the production of wrought iron, was 'treated shamelessly by the business people, who are ignorant asses one and all', as Watt himself observed. Other inventors fell foul of their fellow workmen: thus, John Kay, inventor of the flying shuttle (1733), had his home attacked and had to flee to France.

Some of the inventors worked in solitude behind the scenes: others, like the businessmen with whom they had to co-operate unless they became businessmen themselves, were publicity-minded, and their skills, like those of the great potter Josiah Wedgwood, turned to marketing and the exploitation of fashion. The enthusiastic foundry-owner John Wilkinson, who helped to make England iron-conscious, had an iron boat, which was as well known as his iron coffin. After his death, the story spread that seven years later he would rise out of the coffin and visit his blast furnaces; a large crowd gathered to witness the resurrection.

It is as much the adoption of technological innovations as the innovations themselves that provides the dynamic in the social history of the industrial revolution. Economic growth may have tended to produce entrepreneurs rather than vice versa, but there had to be capital and there had to be a willingness to take risks. Rags to riches was not the usual story. Legal barriers, notably the patent law, might stand in the way of change: conversely, holding a patent could be a spur to effort and there was frequently an articulate demand for a particular invention. 'We want as many spotted Muslins and Fancy Muslins as you can make,' a northern cotton spinner was informed by his London agent in 1786, 'You must look to Invention, Industry you have in abundance . . . As the sun shines let us make Hay.' More often, one successful invention led to a demand for a complementary invention in a related process (in spinning and weaving, for example). So long as business and consumer expectations were high, one technological change generated another.

Yet there were many economic activities that by 1860 were still relatively little touched by invention: in a labour force which was more specialized than that which had existed in 1780, only three out of ten people were employed in activities that had been radically transformed in technique during the previous eighty years. Human strength had not become completely obsolete, as boilermakers (or dockers) of later generations would testify. Factory workers were in the minority. There were large numbers of out-workers, sub-contractors and, at the base, casual workers, including 'wandering tribes' of migrant labourers; and there were more domestic servants than operatives in the textile industry, more males engaged in building and construction than in mining and quarrying, and still more engaged in agriculture, horticulture and fishing than in construction and mining combined.

Nevertheless, the numbers of miners were increasing: there were 216,000 of them in 1851 and 495,000 thirty years later. Coal was the fuel of the industrial revolution, both metaphorically and literally, while iron was the master material. 'The strength of Britain', declared the railway pioneer George Stephenson, 'lies in her iron and coal beds . . . The Lord Chancellor now sits on a bag of wool, but wool has long ceased to be . . . the staple commodity of England. He ought rather to sit on a bag of coals, though it might not prove so comfortable a seat.' Steam power had been applied in coal mines to pump out water before it was employed to move machines in factories. It was in factories, however, that, following the development of machine tools and precision engineering, what the Conservative Prime Minister Sir Robert Peel called 'an additional race of men' was produced. Apologists of the new factory system took pride in the claim that it was opening up future possibilities of complete automation: Andrew Ure, in his *Philosophy of Manufacture* (1834), called it 'the great minister of civilization to the terraqueous globe'. Ure also argued that 'the most perfect manufacture is that which dispenses entirely with manual labour.' Meanwhile, the many eloquent critics of the factory system – and of the machine – saw it as an agency of social (particularly family) disorganization.

It was success in the 'dynamic' sectors of the economy, notably cotton, which made possible a substantial growth of *per capita* income between the 1780s and the 1860s despite a three-fold increase in population that was related to economic growth in complex and controversial ways. Whereas in previous periods of population growth larger numbers had pressed hard on the means of subsistence – and during the sixteenth and seventeenth centuries may have halved the incomes of the poor – average incomes now rose. Phyllis Deane has calculated that the average *per capita* income of the total population, which had been around £8–9 a year in 1700 and £12–13 fifty years later, rose to £22 by 1800 and doubled again by 1860. Behind this rise in incomes was an increase in capital, although the proportion of national investment to national income was stable at around 13–14 per cent during most decades between 1780 and 1860. On the eve of the industrial revolution, durable national assets other than land, the oldest asset, accounted for less than one-third of the national capital of Great Britain; by 1860 the share had increased to a half.

Not all these relevant statistics of economic growth were known to contemporaries, but those that were fascinated them; the successive editions of statistician G. R. Porter's *Progress of the Nation*, which first appeared in 1836, recorded such rapid change that they were said 'to partake of the nature of a periodical'. The statistics were a matter of widespread (though not universal) pride, particularly when placed in their international context. In 1780 the national output of iron was smaller than that of France; by 1848 it was greater than that of the rest of the world put together. By then, also, coal output was two-thirds, and cotton cloth more than half, that of total world output. In 1851, when the Great Exhibition of all the Nations was held in the Crystal Palace, over half the 14,000 exhibitors represented Great Britain and her colonies. In the 'age of the machine' Britain stood out as 'the workshop of the world'.

The qualitative changes impressed the Victorians even more than the statistics. 'The Crystal Palace', wrote one of them, 'is an outstanding sign of the mind of the age. It could not have taken place half a generation back . . . It could not have been imagined by the chivalry of the middle ages.' The new glass building designed by the Duke of Devonshire's gardener, Joseph Paxton – who was extolled, not surprisingly, as a model of self-help – was often compared with a temple: its length was three times that of St Paul's Cathedral. And the objects exhibited inside conveyed the message of visible 'progress' more eloquently than numbers. A contemporary writer drew the proper lesson – that 'Englishmen employ their capital, but are ever seeking for mechanical means to work it.' It was right and proper, too, that there should be an enormous block of coal, weighing twenty-four tons, at the entrance to the Exhibition (although it was placed next to a statue of King Richard the Lionheart), and that many of the objects on display inside came from distant countries. 'The products of all quarters of the globe are placed at our disposal', wrote Albert, Victoria's Prince Consort, who had much to do with the success of the Exhibition, 'and we have only to choose that which is best and cheapest for our purposes, and the powers of production are entrusted to the stimulus of competition and capital.' Free trade, opened up during the 1840s before and after the repeal of the Corn Laws, was already a gospel.

Yet this was only part of the story. The object of both free trade and free competition, it was claimed, was to lower prices. 'It is very odd,' wrote a French visitor enviously in 1851. 'An aristocratic country like England is successful at supplying the people, whereas France, a democratic country, is only good at producing goods for the aristocracy.' There was certainly a wide repertoire of consumer goods, including matches, a new nineteenth-century invention, steel pens and envelopes, in use and on display at the Exhibition. And the postage stamp, too, was a Victorian invention: the beautiful Penny Black of 1840 was the world's first postage stamp. Later in the century there was to be a striking expansion of mass markets, with new kinds of shops offering a perpetual display: William Whitely, 'the Universal Provider', opened a great department store in London in 1863, while one entertaining retailer in Liverpool, David Lewis, described himself and his staff as 'Friends of the People'. By the end of the century there were also many chains of shops: Jesse Boot, the Nottingham chemist, owned 181 local shops, and Thomas Lipton, the grocer, had more than sixty in London alone.

Optimistic Victorians believed, therefore, that the industrial revolution had made possible for the first time not only 'the conquest of Nature' but also 'the betterment of the species'. In the enthusiastic language of Samuel Smiles, who more than any other nineteenth-century writer popularized the heroes of the industrial revolution and proclaimed their values, there was 'a harvest of wealth and prosperity'. 'We are an old people', he added, 'but a young nation ... The civilization of what we call "the masses" has scarcely begun.' Smiles's sense of newness had been anticipated in 1843 by an earlier writer who stressed that steam power had no precedent and the spinning jenny no ancestry: 'the mule and the power loom entered into no prepared heritage: they sprang into sudden existence like Minerva from the brains of Jupiter.' For Charles Babbage, who invented a mechanical computer that pointed to an age yet to come, steam engines 'furnished the means not only of their support but of their multiplication'. 'They create a vast demand for fuel ... and call into employment multitudes of miners, engineers, shipbuilders and sailors.'

Among these groups the engineers stood out, as the editor of the new periodical *Engineering* wrote in 1866:

> Engineering has done more than war and diplomacy ... more than the Church and the Universities. It has done more than abstract philosophy and literature. It has done ... more than our laws have done ... to change society. We have ... reached an age of luxury, but without effeminacy. Few of our middle class ... could be induced to exchange their homes and appliances for comfort for the noblest villas of ancient Rome.

Smiles was as much interested in civil engineering as he was in mechanical engineering, but he was most interested of all in 'the civilization of what we call "the masses"'. So too was William Whewell, Master of Trinity College, Cambridge, who thought 'useful application' was 'the name of the great engine working on the railway of civilization'. This conception of industrialization was to be taken up in the late twentieth century by Lord Snow, who argued robustly that only machine-breaking 'Luddites, including intellectual Luddites' could condemn it. Yet there is over-simplification in this view. The impact of the industrial revolution on the way people lived, thought and felt was greater than that of most political revolutions, and there never was – nor could have been – one single response to it.

There are two main reasons why the Smiles thesis did not command universal assent at the time and why it has been possible for historians to resist its logic. First, although *per capita* incomes increased substantially, the rich benefited more than the poor. Indeed, there was a contemporary debate, which has been taken up again this century, as to whether the poor benefited at all in the crucial period of early industrialization. And the poor themselves took part in the debate with a new voice.

Critics of industrialization, like the poet Robert Southey, were particularly disturbed by the situation of those workers who were obviously not better off, like the handloom weavers, who had prospered during the early years of the Napoleonic Wars, but who later saw both wages and opportunities for employment fall drastically. There was no question that they were victims of the power loom; the only question was how long it would take them to wither away. In 1820 there were 240,000 of them, nearly half of whom were in Lancashire; there were 123,000 by 1840, and 23,000 by 1856. 'We are shunned by the remainder of society and branded as rogues because we are unable to pay our way', a weaver in Bury, Lancashire, wrote as early as 1818. Ten years later, one-third of the inhabitants of Colne, in the same county, were subsisting on twopence a day: their main fare was meal, buttermilk and potatoes with a few gills of ale on Saturday nights. Yet the position of the handloom weavers was exceptional. Real wages, which declined between the end of the Napoleonic Wars in 1815 and 1820, seem to have increased every decade until the Great Exhibition of 1851. It seems, too, that the earning power of women and children, who were a main source of labour in the factories, kept pace with the increase in the earnings of men. These were years of volatile local prices, however, and of severe unemployment, and the most striking gains to the poor accrued later in the century as prices fell sharply – by 40 per cent between 1875 and 1900.

Much of the early critique of industrialization was moral and socio-logical rather than economic or political, although Marx, who lived in England for thirty-four years and who directly related politics to economics, tried to present a scientific analysis. Thus, Southey compared the rhythms of the seasons with the tempo of the factory, villages with cities, cathedrals with cotton mills, and factory children with Negro slaves. By the end of the century industry had settled down into routines, and while socialists had systematized their analysis, other new critics, like the novelist D. H. Lawrence, born in a coal-mining village, com-plained of the deadening effects of industrialization on the sensibilities and on the imagination.

The second attack on Smiles's interpretation of industrialization came from critics like John Ruskin, who deliberately turned from art and architecture to politics, claiming that industry not only disturbed human relations, but led inevitably to the deterioration of the industrial environ-ment. Ruskin foresaw the possibility of twentieth-century England 'set as thick with chimneys as the masts stand in the docks of Liverpool', with 'no meadows . . . no trees, no gardens'; 'no acre of English ground shall be without its shaft and its engine.' William Morris, convert to a Marxist version of socialism, asked bitterly whether all was 'to end in a counting house on the top of a cinder heap, with the pleasures of the eyes having gone from the world'.

Ruskin, with his theory of 'illth' and wealth, two opposites, was certainly not alone in his response to the industrial landscape. One German visitor, J. G. Kohl, caught the essence of the new environment after a visit to England as early as 1844:

> Imagine black roads winding through verdant fields, the long trains of waggons heavily laden with black treasures . . . burning mounds of coal scattered over the plain, black pit mouths, and here and there an unadorned Methodist chapel or school house, and you will have a tolerable idea of what the English delight to call their 'Black Indies'.

And this picture left out the polluted large industrial towns and cities. In the view of the critics, signs of 'degradation' were never compensated for by canals or railways. 'Here civilization makes its miracles, and civilized man is turned back almost into a savage', wrote de Tocqueville of Manchester. 'From this foul drain the greatest stream of human industry flows out to fertilize the whole world. From this filthy sewer pure gold flows. Here humanity attains its most complete development and its most brutish.' '

During the 1830s and 1840s Manchester was a Mecca for everyone who wished to understand what was happening to society and what would happen to it in the future. Its distinctive characteristics fascinated Marx's close friend Friedrich Engels, who lived there as a businessman and who wrote his *Condition of the Working Class in England* from a Manchester vantage point. In it he drew heavily on official Blue Books, the famous reports of Committees of Enquiry, set up by Parliament, and on earlier writers like Peter Gaskell, who regretted the decay of 'community' and the values that went with it, claiming that 'the domestic manufacturer, as a moral and social being, was infinitely superior to the manufacturer of a later date.' Yet Engels himself drew different conclusions from the same data, for while Gaskell perceived the rise of organized labour as the rise of a dangerous *imperium in imperio*, Engels welcomed it as an inevitable agent of revolution – and therefore of salvation. Moreover, like Marx, he enthused about the increase in output in a way that Gaskell would never have done.

Neither Gaskell nor Engels had grasped the whole truth, for there were more modes of social adaptation at both the local and Parliamentary levels than simplified diagnoses of society suggested. Community did not always lose its integrity in industrial towns and villages, and business paternalism could often flourish. Workmen, who had more often been attracted into the factories and towns by higher wages and greater social opportunities than coerced into them, were more quickly adapted to a new environment than was often thought at the time, while employers were not all ruthless exploiters. It was said, for example, of one Lancashire employer, Hugh Mason of Ashton, that 'it would be impossible for him to buy the labour of his workpeople and for the workpeople to sell him that labour the same as an ordinary commodity over the counter of a shopkeeper. He felt a deep interest in the welfare of his workpeople.'

England was not a society of 'two camps' with the 'millionaire commanding whole industrial armies and the wage-slave living only from hand to mouth', as a contemporary socialist put it. There was still

The Industrial Revolution
in England 1820

Cu Copper mining

Fe Iron ore mining

⋰ Coalfields

Sn Tin mining

Pb Lead mining

Canals

Rivers

50 Miles

1 Leeds
2 Bradford
3 Halifax
4 Rochdale
5 Huddersfield
6 Bolton
7 Manchester
8 Sheffield
9 Chesterfield
10 Stoke on Trent
11 Derby
12 Newcastle under Lyme
13 Birmingham
14 Stourbridge
15 Merthyr Tydfil

Edinburgh

Carlisle

Newcastle
upon Tyne
Sunderland
Durham

Whitehaven

York

Preston
Goole
Hull

Liverpool
Wakefield
Doncaster
Grimsby

Chester
Lincoln

Nottingham

Shrewsbury
Grantham

King's Lynn
Great
Yarmouth

Leicester
Peterborough
Norwich

Worcester
Coventry
Northampton
Cambridge
Ipswich

Hereford
Gloucester
Cirencester

Milford
Haven
Swansea
Oxford
Slough
Hertford
Chelmsford
Ilford

Cardiff
Bristol
Swindon
Reading
London
Gravesend
Chatham

Bridgwater
Basingstoke
Dover

Southampton
Portsmouth

Exeter

Plymouth

Falmouth

North
Sea

Irish
Sea

English
Channel

a governing class as well as an employing class, and large sections of it drew their income not from industry but from the land: squires and aristocrats could sometimes sympathize with industrial workers more than with their employers (and vice versa), while some industrial employers were willing to turn the spotlight on bad living and working conditions in the countryside. A model of social action which leaves out these diagonal links (or the prevailing ideals of private and public conduct which influenced behaviour, if often ambivalently) is misleading rather than inadequate. Religion, too, retained its force − often divisive and cutting across other social divisions. Methodism, particularly Primitive Methodism, could either push working men into, or provide a substitute for, politics.

The new industrial town and city were not the insensate places that some social historians, drawing mainly on secondary evidence, have suggested they were. There was a deep concern about the implications of a huge new population being 'herded' there, but there was city pride too: in freedom from aristocratic influence, in a greater diversity of opinion, in the unprecedented range and vitality of voluntary organization and, finally, in the belief that the city itself was the 'nidus of a new commonwealth', a phrase coined by a Leeds Nonconformist minister who welcomed the rise of the operatives, whom, he believed, it was completely wrong to categorize as 'masses', a term which displayed ignorance of real people.

'Murky Leeds' itself was a lively place, one of the new *genus* of industrial cities, which, in Yorkshire alone, included nearby and rival Bradford and Sheffield, large numbers of smaller factory towns like Huddersfield and industrial villages like Denholme. There were also mining villages and one mining town, Barnsley. At the first census of 1801 (a landmark in social history) there had been only fifteen towns with a population of over 20,000 inhabitants; by 1851 there were twenty-eight and by 1891 sixty-three. Leeds, along with Manchester, Sheffield and Birmingham, experienced a growth rate of over 40 per cent between 1820 and 1830, the decade of most rapid growth, and Manchester's population almost doubled (and that of adjacent Salford almost trebled) again between 1851 and 1901. Meanwhile, old towns grew far more slowly, though there was growth there, too, at differing rates. The population of Oxford, for example, more than doubled between 1801 and 1851, from 12,000 to 28,000, while Winchester increased from 8,171 (which included nearly 2,000 soldiers) to 13,706. York, which had become a great railway centre, increased from 17,000 to 36,000.

Like old towns, industrial towns had different profiles and were not, as the American historian of the city, Lewis Mumford, was to claim, the same place – 'Coketown' – with different aliases. In particular, there were marked differences in the industrial and social structures of Manchester and Birmingham: in the first there were many great 'capitalists' (the term was beginning to be used), some of them in Richard Cobden's phrase 'sturdy veterans with £100.000 in each pocket'; in the second, there were large numbers of small employers. Mercantile Liverpool was different again: here there was a huge floating population of casual workers. Among the smaller towns, there were marked differences between Oldham, Northampton, Barrow-in-Furness and Middlesbrough, a new town, 'the youngest child of England's enterprise'.

At the same time, there were many common features of cities at this stage of their history. Working-class housing with its long rows of terraces, the Coronation Streets of the future, often looked very similar, particularly when they were built in brick. Railway stations and 'pubs' (now a well-established term to cover ale-houses and taverns) might resemble each other too, with great varieties of style. The key problems of public health and order faced all towns and cities, old as well as new, as did those of urban transport. The patterns of local government, reformed by the Municipal Corporations Act of 1835 and far more by late nineteenth-century legislation, provided a common framework to deal with these problems, although the drive behind local politics varied, so that municipal development in fact followed different courses and chronologies. London, the wonder and horror of the age, was the exception to most rules in both government and scale of growth. In most places strict economy was the rule, unwillingness to spend or to invest.

The degree of local determination of policy was substantial enough to persuade city and town councillors that initiative lay with them and not with Parliament in Westminster. 'We have little independent "local authorities", little centres of outlying authority,' wrote Walter Bagehot, editor of the *Economist*, in 1867. 'When the metropolitan executive most wishes to act, it cannot act effectively because these lesser bodies

The growth of London

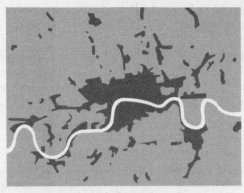

London at the end of the eighteenth century

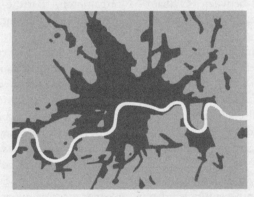

London in the 1830s

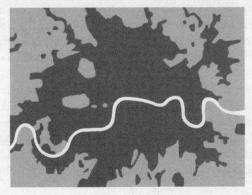

London in the 1870s

hesitate, deliberate, or even disobey.' Bagehot was writing on the eve of a dramatic demonstration of positive and effective local politics in Birmingham. 'Our Corporation', the local Liberal leader Joseph Chamberlain argued forcefully, 'represents the authority of the people'; and another local advocate of a 'civic gospel' claimed that 'a town is a solemn organism through which shall flow, and in which shall be shaped, all the highest, loftiest and truest ends of man's moral nature.' Under the direction of such men Birmingham municipalized gas and water supplies and carried out a huge scheme of urban improvement. A new Corporation Street was the visible result.

Chamberlain, who was a screw manufacturer before he became a politician, was typical of most early entrepreneurs in that he was associated with a small business. Individual ownership or partnership was the key to the manufacturing system, and family businesses were passed on from one generation to the next as if they were landed estates. There was much intermarriage amongst business families, too. The great company growth in manufacturing industry, with steel, shipbuilding and chemicals leading the way, came later. There had been important limited liability acts in 1856 and in 1862 consolidating rules relating to the business company, but as late as the 1880s there were, for example, only four limited liability companies in Birmingham. The separation of ownership from control and the development of increasingly specialized patterns of management were features of the later, not the early, industrial revolution, except in banking – a necessary service in the new industrial society – and in transport. As late as 1882, the paid-up capital of all the companies quoted on the London Stock Exchange was only £64 million out of a total of £5,800 million. Moreover, there was only one significant large-scale amalgamation in England before the 1890s – the Nobel Dynamite Trust of 1886.

In the later industrial revolution, a term applied to the last decades of the nineteenth century only in the twentieth, Britain's lead was cut as other countries, notably Germany and the United States, themselves experienced dramatic industrial revolutions at this time: by 1913 Germany was producing 13,500,000 tons of steel and the United States 31,000,000 as against Britain's 8,000,000 tons. Textiles, too, faced increasing competition: although there was heavy investment in Lancashire between 1895 and 1914, it was largely in what was by then traditional technology. Coal output rose to a peak of over 270,000,000 tons in the years 1910–14 (as against 66,700,000 tons in the years 1855–60) and coal exports to a peak of 62,700,000 tons. Yet productivity was falling, and in newer industries, like chemicals and electrical engineering, other countries were ahead from the start.

It has been claimed late in this century that the Great Exhibition marked the peak of English confidence in the industrial economy and in the technology which made it possible, and that soon afterwards there was a 'decline of the industrial spirit'. Yet during the thirty years between 1851 and 1881 the national product rose from £523 million (£25 *per capita*) to £1,051 million (£75 *per capita*). And exports, on which Britain's international strength depended, rose, too, from £100 million in the decade 1850–59 to £160 million in the following decade and £218 million in the next. The tonnage of British shipping rose from 3,600,000 tons in 1850 to 6,600,000 in 1880, and the production of cast iron increased three-fold between 1850 and 1875. Industry itself was certainly not in decline. The horsepower used in British industry increased from two million in 1870 to ten million in 1907, and in 1901 a higher proportion of the population was engaged in the manufacturing industry than at any date earlier or later. The greatest Victorian boom had ended by 1875, but while it lasted it was striking enough for Disraeli to describe it as a 'convulsion of prosperity'.

There was ample evidence, too, of both technical and entrepreneurial ability late in the century and in the years before 1914, and one important new invention, Charles Parsons' steam turbine of 1884, pointed to the future. William Lever's soap enterprise led him to the jungles of West Africa, and his successors joined hands with the Dutch in the huge Unilever concern of 1929, the first great European multinational. Ludwig Mond, whose chemical business was eventually to become a key component in Imperial Chemical Industries Ltd, was another tycoon, and William Armstrong, later of Vickers Armstrong, who vied with Krupps in the world's armament business, was a third. It was through enterprise as well as hard work that in 1913 Britain still accounted for a quarter of the world's trade in manufactured goods (as against 37 per cent in the early 1880s). Its share of the world's industrial production had fallen from over 30 per cent to 13 per cent, yet the rate of growth of the national income (2.3 per cent) was not very different from that of the mid-Victorian years.

Nonetheless, while the years after 1875 cannot be labelled as years of a 'great depression', as they used to be, they were years of increasing uncertainty. The Cambridge economist Alfred Marshall caught the mood when he wrote in 1908 that, while it had been 'inevitable' that the United States and Germany would oust England from its leadership of many industries, acquired in the previous sixty years, it had not been inevitable 'that she lose so much of it as she has done'. Five main points have been made in relation to this 'decline'.

First, the financial power of the City of London now conveyed more status than the skills and resources of industrial England, and capital which might have been used at home was diverted abroad to countries of formal and informal empire: by 1914 total investment abroad was £4,000 million, a far larger figure than that of any other country. Meanwhile, between 1870 and 1914 the number of provincial stock exchanges fell from ten to two. It was, and is, a matter of argument whether home industry was inadequately re-equipped in consequence and whether new industries developed as quickly as they might have done. 'Plutocrats' who made their money from South African diamonds or mines and city development in Argentina were certainly richer than English industrialists, and, according to one estimate, 'rentier' (that is, primarily unearned) incomes in 1913 surpassed the whole budgetary revenue of France, where the term 'rentier' had originated.

Second, Britain was said to be lagging behind in the 'new industrial revolution' which rested on scientific knowledge and research and which demanded both more standardized equipment and product specification and a more adaptable labour force, able and willing to cope at work with increases in the operating speeds of machinery. There is controversy about this also. Workers themselves complained that their employers would not allow them 'to do their best work, but compel them to take out the finish, smoothness and beauty, in order that they can get into the market cheap'.

Third, statistics seemed to demonstrate the greater productivity of industry in other countries. One estimate for the period from 1870 to 1907 suggested that the annual average rate of increase of productivity in the United States was over twice that of Britain, and the German rate even greater. Yet not all surveys corroborated this. A study of German steelworks in 1910 suggested that three men were carrying out tasks that in England were carried out by one.

Fourth, there were vociferous complaints about management, trade unions and education as agents of retardation. Marshall traced a decline in entrepreneurial vigour (sons were not as good as their fathers), while other critics complained that 'the Gospel of Ease' had 'permeated the nation'. 'England shows traces of American enterprise and German order', wrote Arthur Shadwell in 1906, 'but the enterprise is faded and the order muddled.' Employers blamed trade unions for restrictive practices and trade unions blamed employers for not installing up-to-date machinery, while a few foreign critics, notably the French historian Elie Halévy, blamed a tacit collusion between the 'two sides' of industry for a lack of clarity and drive. His thesis can be illustrated from the Birmingham metal trades or from the Durham coalfields.

The inadequacy of technical education had been a matter of concern since the 1850s, and the Education Act of 1870 introducing 'elementary schools', Board Schools provided for out of local rates, came late in the story of industrialization. When the Education Bill was moved, W. E. Forster, its proposer, MP for Bradford, told the House of Commons:

> We must not delay. Upon the speedy provision of elementary education depends our industrial prosperity . . . If we are to hold our position among . . . the nations of the world, we must make up the smallness of our numbers by increasing the intellectual force of the individual.

By the end of the century, a whole generation had passed through the primary schools, but by then there were additional complaints, to be echoed throughout the twentieth century, not only about inadequate secondary education, but about the classical bias of the public schools, their 'neglect of science' and 'hostility to business'. How could the owners or managers of the future be given the right start there? Meanwhile, grammar schools, it was said, were producing people who did not know how to use their hands.

Fifth, the 'decline' was blamed on a lack of incentives to workers to become 'American minded': wages and expectations were low. There was too much apathy and absenteeism. Good layout of plant, reasonable conditions of work and managerial efficiency were deemed necessary to encourage individual operatives to work hard and to earn as much as they could. Yet English and American (or German) circumstances were different, and American trade unions in particular contrasted with their English equivalents both in leadership and in objectives. There was a stronger sense of class in England too.

It is to the later years of the nineteenth century and the first decade of the twentieth that we should turn for the making – or re-making – of 'the English working class'. The widespread language of class had been a product of early industrialization when, in the words of a contemporary, 'operative workmen being thrown together in great numbers, had their faculties sharpened and improved by constant communication.' It had been then, too, that 'movements' had been formed from below, some dedicated to reform, a few to revolution, all to 'union'. There had long been a working-class version of political economy, pivoting not on competition but on co-operation, not on mobility but on solidarity, not on 'a reserve army of unemployed' but on 'the abolition of poverty'. Labour was the source of all value.

Chartism, led by an Irishman, Feargus O'Connor, had been the first independent working-class movement in the world, a snowball movement of social protest drawing in elements which were to prove incompatible but which were united in pressing for the six points of a political programme set out in the People's Charter of 1838: these included the demand for universal male suffrage. The height of the agitation came in 1842, one of the most difficult 'crisis' years of the early nineteenth century, the fourth year in a run of bad harvests and a year of heavy unemployment when, in the words of Thomas Hood's poem 'The Song of the Shirt', 'bread was dear and flesh and blood were cheap'. Chartism faded during the 1850s after mass demonstration on Kennington Common in 1848, but memories of it were revived a generation later in new circumstances.

It was after 1870 that a new working-class culture with a distinct way of life took shape, the product essentially of segregation. The culture owed less to shared attitudes towards industrial work – these were often contradictory – than it did to attitudes towards life and leisure (although some leisure was directly related to the workplace itself). There were, however, many variables and many differences of both interest and outlook in different occupational groups in different parts of the country. Indeed, there were at least as many differences of fortune and outlook within the working classes as there were in the middle classes (one-sixth of the population); and, in particular, the gulf between skilled and unskilled workers was so great that one acute observer spoke of them as two separate races. Skilled workers – and they themselves fell into many different groups – were often given a privileged position in the workplace, including control of recruitment: unskilled labourers were hired and fired as occasion demanded. Their work was described as 'casual'.

The limits to class-consciousness, which was not the only nor necessarily the main influence on working-class thinking and behaviour in many parts of the country, were revealed at every point in the nineteenth century. Old notions of deference had often survived the deepest crises of early industrialization, and new views of harmony between the 'classes' were advanced during the 1850s and 1860s. Meanwhile, 'the State', a word little used in England, intervened throughout the different phases of industrialization to redress some of the 'abuses' in the industrial system. It was while Lord John Russell, Peel's successor, was Prime Minister, though not at his instigation, that Parliament, after furious agitation from outside, passed the Ten Hours Act of 1847 restricting the working hours of women and children in textile factories. Already, an earlier act of 1833 had introduced the machinery of inspection. The first four factory inspectors, appointed by the end of the year 1833, had at first been viewed with suspicion by masters and workers alike, but as they were drawn into the tasks of enforcement they devoted themselves with remarkable energy and dedication to the task of what one of them described as 'correcting the great moral evils that had taken root and extensively spread in . . . industry'. As the century went by, further factory acts, involving more systematic state intervention in a widening range of industries, were passed, culminating in the consolidated Factory Act of 1901: its 'fine-meshed, wide-cast, "bureaucratic" net', Sir John Clapham has written, was what the men of that day 'were learning to use or tolerate, if not always approve'.

The most important countervailing element in early and mid-nineteenth-century industrial development was not, however, the regulation of wages and hours by the State, but the development of trade-union power. In 1870 only about 4 per cent of the labour force belonged to trade unions, which had been legal since 1824. By the early 1890s, however, there were about 1½ million trade unionists, over 300,000 of them miners, another 300,000 in the retail trade, with an increasing number also in new 'unskilled' unions. The story (or 'march') of trade unionism had been a long one. There had been trade clubs, different in character from the old journeymen's guilds, under the old domestic system. Printers' chapels (the term had no religious significance and was borrowed from France) had been in existence in the seventeenth century, and as early as 1696 journeymen feltmakers in London were involved in a 'combination' to fix wages. In industrial Lancashire machine spinners' unions had been organized in the 1790s, and there was even an attempt at federation in 1792. A general Spinners' Union had organized unsuccessful major 'turn-outs' (strikes) in 1808 and 1810 for 'equalization' to Manchester rates, while Preston weavers had struck for higher wages in 1808, 1818 and 1821. New laws against such combination had been passed in 1799 and 1800, but they did not stop such action.

The social implications of trade unions inspired as much comment on both sides as did their economic implications. By 1824, the year when the combination laws were repealed, the Manchester Chamber of Commerce was not alone in maintaining that 'combinations, whether of masters or workmen, produced a hostile feeling . . . directly opposed to the best interests of society.' Those who supported repeal believed that if the restrictive laws were to go, trade unions would disappear, but in fact the unions went on to gain in strength and ambition, and attempts were made to achieve local, sectional or 'general' unions of workers. Indeed, there was more faith at first in 'general union' than in sectionalism. John Doherty, a young Irishman living in Manchester, created a Grand National Union of the Operative Spinners of Great Britain and Ireland and later a National Association for the Protection of Labour. In 1833, Bronterre O'Brien wrote eloquently that

> a spirit of combination had grown up among the working classes of which there has been no example in former times . . . The object . . . is the sublimest that can be conceived, namely . . . to establish for the productive classes a complete domination over the fruits of their own industry . . . They aspire to be at the top instead of at the bottom of society – or rather that there should be no bottom or top at all.

It was in 1834, before the rise of Chartism, that early trade unionism reached its peak and that the movement found its first martyrs, not in an industrial town or district, but in rural Dorset. Six trade unionists from the small village of Tolpuddle were accused and convicted of administering unlawful oaths under the Mutiny Act of 1749 while their 'combination' held abortive discussions with their employers, who had cut their miserably low wages from nine shillings to six. Their sentence to transportation provoked large-scale demonstrations in London and other cities, and while the judge who sentenced them pointed out that part of the 'object of all legal punishment' was to 'offer an example and a warning', the real significance of the incident was its public warning to society that trade unionism was here to stay. It was as much a by-product of England's industrial experience as smoky towns and polluted rivers, the new financial and service infrastructure, and the limitless hopes of universal free trade among Manchester businessmen.

In its early stages trade unionism was most successful (as in 1834) when business was prosperous and there was a good harvest, and weakest when times were bad, as they were to be in the depression of unprecedented depths which began in 1837. In obverse, political action was related to 'distress'. 'You cannot agitate a man on a full stomach,' declared William Cobbett, in his lifetime one of the most influential of radicals, although he had a Tory frame of mind and looked back to a golden age more than to a new kind of society in the future. During the last years of the nineteenth century, when the future was more clearly in view, the state of the home harvest, which had directly influenced the whole level of economic activity during the 1830s and 1840s, began to count for less than it ever had done before; more food was imported from overseas and bread itself ceased to be the staple of life as it had been for centuries. But this was not all. The forms of capitalism were changing, too, as employers as well as workers began to organize collectively, and there was a far bigger group of professional people inside and outside business. Politics, too, took on a new shape. In the early years of the century political agitation had moved from one platform demonstration to another with landmark dates like the 'Peterloo massacre' in Manchester in 1819 and years of lull between. Now more organized political parties kept politics constantly in movement, particularly after the extension of the suffrage to large numbers of working men in the towns in 1867. And behind the parties were well-organized pressure groups, many of them also operating continuously as part of the rich social and cultural infrastructure.

Within this context, the trade unions became a part of the economic and political system, with a distinctive English style, expressed in well-drafted books of rules, carefully kept minute books and audited sets of accounts. In 1868, when the newly formed Trades Union Congress held its first annual meeting at Manchester, a small affair with only thirty-four delegates present, the new unions, which drew their first main support from relatively well-paid workers, like engineers, carpenters and builders, had only 250,000 members, but within five years (of economic boom) numbers had trebled. They were to drop again soon afterwards when economic conditions deteriorated, but by then some agricultural workers had formed a union during the boom. The main union strength remained in the cities; in some of them there were Trades Councils, like the London Trades Council, founded in 1860.

Mid-Victorian trade unionists have often been described as an 'aristocracy of labour', and even at the time they were accused by other workers of running mere benefit societies (like the other 'friendly societies' which flourished during the period). Yet they were willing to strike when occasion seemed to demand it, and the number of strikes did not diminish between 1850 and 1880. They sometimes took part in political movements too, including the renewed struggle for the suffrage during the 1860s, and they were often active in the co-operative movement, the origins of which were older than the store in Toad Lane opened in 1844 by twenty-eight Rochdale workers who raised an initial capital of £28. By the early 1870s the co-operators had 927 branches and 300,000 members.

It was the skilled trade unionists who, through their organizational strength, secured increased recognition for trade unions under the law during the middle years of the nineteenth century. They gave evidence to a Royal Commission of 1867 and thereafter served as a pressure group to secure the Trade Union Act of 1871, sometimes called the Trade Unionists' Charter, which provided that the purposes of a union should not be regarded as criminal merely because they were in restraint of trade. Trade unions were to be protected by law, but were to be free from the interference of the law in their own internal affairs. This act, passed by a Liberal government, was followed by a still more favourable act introduced by Disraeli's Conservative government in 1875. Breach of contract was no longer to be a criminal offence, and peaceful picketing was legalized.

The legal position of the trade unions was challenged in the early twentieth century when a court decision of 1901 in the Taff Vale case – involving a railway worker – laid down that unions were liable to actions for damages by employers for civil wrongs payable by union funds. By then, however, unskilled workers also had been drawn increasingly into trade unions, pressing for further claims like the eight-hour day (King Alfred, they said, was the first to divide the day into three parts – work, sleep and recreation), and showing themselves willing to turn not to liberal but to socialist politicians who were prepared to use the State to achieve their objectives. It was due to their efforts that the numbers of trade unionists increased from 800,000 to 1,500,000 between 1888 and 1891. Two years later, Keir Hardie, a Scots socialist in a cloth cap, who had emerged from a coal-mining background, became leader of a new Independent Labour Party which was brought into existence in industrial Bradford in 1893. This party joined with other socialist groups, including the Fabian Society, whose famous book of essays appeared in the same year as the great dock strike of 1889, to form the Labour Representation Committee. Under the new name of the Labour Party, it won twenty-nine seats at the general election of 1906, with solid trade-union support from the start, and its long-term life was guaranteed as the number of trade unionists in the country rose to four million by 1914. When Hardie looked into the future, he drew on a metaphor from the industrial past. Within the Labour Party, the ILP would be, he claimed, 'what steam is to machinery, the motive power which keeps all going'. Like many such predictions, it did not come true. Nor, indeed, was steam to be the main motive power of the future.

9 WEBS OF COMMUNICATION

Keep moving! Steam, or Gas, or Stage,
Hold, cabin, steerage, hencoop's cage –
Tour, Journey, Voyage, Lounge, Ride, Walk,
Swim, Sketch, Excursion, Travel-talk –
For move you must! 'Tis now the rage,
The law and fashion of the age.

> Samuel Taylor Coleridge, 1824

'Only fancy, Aunt Helen, that Uncle Henry was in Paris yesterday and
will be at home today. Is it not wonderful? What did men do before
there were railroads and steamboats?'

> Anon, *The Triumph of Steam*, 1859

We have been considering the cases in which independent persons run
motor-car services along the roads to our railway stations. We do not
see why we should not fuel our own railways ourselves by means of
motor cars.

> The Chairman of the Great Western Railway Company, 1903

When flying machines begin to fly
We shall never stay at home,
Away we'll skip on a half-day trip
To Paris, perhaps, or Rome.

> The Musical Comedy, *The Bride of Bath*, 1906

The transformation of England from an agricultural and mercantile
society into an industrial society would have been impossible without
the development of an improved communications system: the more

efficient transport of raw materials and finished products to extended markets and at lower costs was as basic an activity as production itself. Like industrialization, it owed little of its impetus to the State, although the State was drawn in to control it. Like industrialization too, it was not an entirely new phenomenon which began with the industrial revolution. The transformation of transport was preceded by steady, if patchy, improvement.

England's inland transport system had for centuries depended more upon water than land, so that canal building, the first great improvement, seemed a natural rather than a revolutionary development. Inland waterways had been improved more or less continuously from the second half of the sixteenth century. Lighter Canal, paid for and built by the Exeter Corporation in 1564–6, incorporated the first pound lock in England (Italy had led the way). But the rivers, particularly the Severn and the Mersey, remained the main arteries in the seventeenth century. It was at the end of that century that Andrew Yarranton in his book *England's Improvement by Sea and Land* dreamed of a canal system.

The great age of canal building did not begin until the early eighteenth century, and it did not reach its peak until the canal 'rage' of the 1790s, during which a total of forty-two new canals, requiring a capital outlay of £6,500,000, was projected. Indeed, the year 1792 was described by contemporaries as a year of 'canal mania', with 'the passion of speculation spreading like an epidemical disease'. Canal shares, usually in large units, were not quoted on the Stock Exchange until 1811, but they were taken up eagerly by local merchants, manufacturers and landowners.

It was men from the last of these broad groups who had done much to pioneer canals. Thus in 1761 the young Duke of Bridgewater, fresh from the Grand Tour, working with an able, and entirely self-educated engineer named James Brindley, opened a 10.5 mile stretch of canal linking his coal mines at Worsley in Lancashire to the outskirts of Manchester. With an impressive aqueduct and underground canals tunnelled into coal measures, it was described at the time as 'perhaps the greatest artificial curiosity in the world'. Merseyside, where Liverpool was beginning to forge ahead as an ocean port, was already a main area of development, and an even earlier stretch of artificial canal, the Sankey Cut, had been built by a Liverpool engineer in 1759.

The canal system – if it deserved to be called a system – was concerned first with linking the great rivers and then with providing facilities for places that had no water transport. The rivers had many disadvantages for the transport of industrial goods: in 1796, for example, the level of the Severn, which, unlike the Dee, never silted up, was so low that the river was navigable for only two months. A developing industrial area like Coalbrookdale in Shropshire, an industrial showplace then and now, where Abraham Darby first smelted iron with coke in 1709 and where Thomas Telford built the world's first iron bridge over the Severn in 1779, could not operate successfully in such conditions. And there were other industrial areas far less favoured by nature, notably the West Midlands, which lay on the great watershed of central England: traffic to and from there had to use a combination of land and water. There were many other places which were completely landlocked.

James Brindley had dreams of creating a great silver cross of over 260 miles of canal to join up the rivers Mersey, Severn, Thames, Trent and Humber. One canal started in 1766 was called the Great Trunk. In fact, from 1772 the Severn was linked with the Mersey through Stourport, which eclipsed the old river town of Bewdley; and there was a further link with the Thames in 1790, when the first boatload of coal despatched from Coventry reached Oxford. The bells of Oxford rang out in celebration. Other land barriers were pierced later. The Leeds and Liverpool Canal, the most important water route across the Pennines, was begun in 1770 but was not completed until 1816, by which time there were already many other canal links, among them John Rennie's Rochdale Canal with impressive but expensive locks. The system, however, was never completed. There was never any direct canal link between Manchester and Sheffield, and when the Manchester to Liverpool Ship Canal was completed in 1893 the age of canals was long past.

At the peak of the canal enterprise there were 4,000 miles of inland waterways, often built on local initiative (with some London backing) and they had immediate effects on employment and distribution. 'A good canal', said Bridgewater, 'should have coals at the heels of it'; in fact, corn and all kinds of agricultural and industrial products were carried as well as coal. The Potteries, in particular, benefited through the canal transport both of raw materials and finished products, and Wedgwood strongly backed Brindley, claiming that his works would be 'the most lasting memorial to his time'.

People could be carried by canal too, in 'passage' or 'packet' boats, with travellers enjoying the sensation of gliding 'tranquilly onwards through a continuous panorama of cows, cottages and green fields,' as one nineteenth-century traveller described it. The first boats, like the first barges, were often highly decorated, and there were agreeable canal inns with names like The Anchor or The Navigation along the tow paths. There were horses too, and careful calculations were made comparing the size of load a horse could carry using different kinds of transport.

The canal and the machine were to produce quite different responses during the industrial revolution: while the machine inspired or disturbed, the new waterway satisfied men and seemed to complement nature. So, too, did bridges. Mechanical engineering carried with it the idea of conquering nature; civil engineering moulded an environment which already existed. There was one handicap, however. Canal water was usually as 'black as the Styx and absolutely pestiferous'.

The early days of the canal coincided with the great days of coaches. 'Door to door' traffic was still dependent on eighteenth-century English rutted and usually rolling roads, which had a bad reputation with many travellers. Arthur Young, in characteristic vein, described the main road between Preston and Wigan as 'infernal' and to 'be avoided by travellers as they would the Devil'. In London itself the Edgware Road was often deep in sludge, and one irate resident complained that the road from Kensington to Westminster had 'grown so infamously bad that we live here in the same solitude as we would do if stranded on a rock in the middle of the ocean'.

There had been many eighteenth-century improvements in both the roads themselves and the vehicles that carried passengers and other traffic along them. Gated turnpike roads, not all of them of high quality, had begun to be built from 1706 onwards, not by parishes, on which the maintenance of roads had previously depended, but by business trusts, supported by local interests. By Act of Parliament they were individually authorized to borrow money and to levy tolls. (The first Turnpike Act had been passed as early as 1663.) During the second half of the eighteenth century the number of turnpikes increased rapidly (452 Acts were passed between 1760 and 1774 – Horace Walpole claimed that they were the main business of Parliament – and a General Turnpike Act became law in 1773), so that there were 1,600 of them in existence by 1800. There was a further substantial increase in mileage throughout the golden age of coaching which lasted until the 1830s. Great surveyors and engineers, like blind 'Jack' Metcalf of Knaresborough in Yorkshire, who tapped his way along the roads, Thomas Telford, more famous still as a bridge builder, and John Loudon McAdam, who gave his name to a modern road surface, not only improved individual roads but planned, usually abortively, almost on Roman lines, great road systems into which parish roads would serve as feeders.

The number and spread of coaches increased and journey time was cut drastically. In 1754 there were six firms operating wagons from Manchester to London. 'However incredible it may appear,' a newspaper advertisement boasted, 'this coach will actually arrive in London four days after leaving Manchester,' yet thirty years later travel time had been cut by a half. By 1816 there were as many as 200 land carriers transporting goods to and from Manchester in 'wagons or carts', and by 1830 there were 54 passenger coaches per day travelling each way. All in all, the number of stage coach services provided in major urban centres multiplied eight-fold between 1790 and 1836, when 700 mail coaches and 3,300 stage coaches were in regular operation.

Some of the coaches were already beginning to deliver 'royal mail' as well as people. As early as 1784 John Palmer of Bristol had introduced lighter springed vehicles and a combination of relays and stage points on the journey. Very quickly government as well as passengers saw advantages in such improvement, both for the postal services and for the transport of people; coaches were licensed, and mileage was taxed – at increasing rates in 1783 and in 1815. Innkeepers, of course, profited directly from the traffic, and one of them, W. J. Chaplin, manager of The Swan with Two Necks in London, owned no fewer than sixty-eight coaches and 1,800 horses in 1838. Yet there were risks in the business just as there were hazards for the traveller even after highwaymen, a notorious menace in the eighteenth century, had disappeared. Meanwhile, the early rioting against turnpike tolls – some of it, like disturbances in 1753 near Leeds and Bradford, so fierce that it amounted almost to 'rebellion' – had passed, like Dick Turpin, into legend.

Far more daring ways of conveying people and goods were also contemplated during the early canal and great coaching age. Indeed, there was as much talk about improvements as there was about the construction of new kinds of machines in the century to come: 'rowing barges against the stream', 'propelling carriages without horses', balloons (there had been a balloon craze in the 1780s) and even 'conveying Letters and Goods with Great Certainty and Rapidity by Air' were all discussed. Erasmus Darwin, a friend of Wedgwood and Boulton, was daring enough to contemplate carrying people by air in steam-driven 'fiery Chariots'. Nevertheless, the fastest form of travel was still by horse, and the eighteenth century was a great age of the horse for work and play. The Jockey Club dates back to 1752, the St Leger to 1777, and the Derby to 1780.

The first great new development came with the successful introduction of 'iron horses', the railways, which from the start carried far more passengers than had been predicted. The development of the railway was a protracted process, with a long prehistory for each of its different features: the rail track, first called the 'wagon way' and made not in iron but wood; the locomotive and its engines; the movement of goods by rail; and, not least, the movement of passengers. It is not surprising that the mining area of the north east was a centre of innovation, as it was in the development of the pre-Watt Newcomen steam engines, used for pumping.

The name of George Stephenson, a self-made Northumberland engineer who started as a brakesman in a pit and whose engine *The Rocket* won the railway trials between Liverpool and Manchester in 1830, is usually associated with the creation of the railway. Certainly, for Smiles, Stephenson was the 'father of the locomotive'. Yet George Stephenson was only one man out of many: indeed, the engineering contributions of his son Robert were outstanding. The most remarkable of the earlier railway pioneers was a Cornishman, Richard Trevithick, who (against the advice of James Watt) began working successfully with noncondensing high-pressure steam engines, known as 'puffers', in the very early nineteenth century. Trevithick, a believer in 'strong steam', took out his first patent in 1802, and six years later he was tempting Londoners to pay to see his mechanical engine, the 'Catch-me-who-catch-can', outstrip the 'animal speed' of a horse. Already it was being predicted that the number of horses in England would be considerably reduced in the steam-driven future, and already, too, power was being measured in terms of 'horse power' as it was to be in the age of the motor car.

It was not only inventors who were enthusiastic or foresaw future developments. One of the most eloquent assessments of future possibilities was a book with the formidable title *Observations on a General Iron Railway or Land Steam Conveyance; to supersede the Necessity of Horses in all Public Vehicles; showing its vast Superiority in every Respect, over all the Pitiful Methods of Conveyance by Turnpike Roads, Canal and Coasting Traders, Containing every Species of Invention relative to Railroads and Locomotive Engines,* by Thomas Gray, published in 1821. In it Gray predicted many future features of the railway. So too did the Quaker Edward Pease, a Darlington manufacturer and one of Stephenson's backers, who took as the motto of his railway 'At private risk for public service'.

During the years between 1825 and 1835, fifty-four Railway Acts permitting railway building were passed, resulting by the end of 1838 in 500 miles of track, but it was in 1836 and 1837, when forty-four companies concerned with 1,498 miles of track were sanctioned, that there was the first sense of a railway 'boom'. By 1843 there were 2,036 miles in actual use. And the 1830s boom was to be far eclipsed by the 'railway mania' of 1845–7, when 576 companies and a further 8,731 miles of track were sanctioned.

The dimensions of the 'mania' exceeded those of the canal 'rage' of the 1790s, and although there is scanty evidence to suggest that it 'infected all classes from peer to peasant', as one historian has suggested, there is no doubt about the eagerness of the urge to buy shares in railway companies. The promoters were quick to seize on it, knowing that behind steam power there had to be money power. The country gained too. For the first time in modern history an economy was devoting a net tenth or more of its total income to capital accumulation. It is true that English railways were far more costly to build and more wasteful in their duplication than most later systems, but railway building brought England out of a major industrial depression, and once in operation railways widened markets and stimulated industries, not least coal and iron. The private money that was lost during the mania disappeared both through speculation and through peculation. Remarkable characters were involved. The most famous of them, George Hudson, 'the railway king', started in business as a draper in York and his statue still stands there. He had one of the dizziest of all business careers which led him first to Westminster and then to gaol.

Questions of monopoly were raised by the railway, but successive governments were forced to accept company deals rather than unlimited competition. Questions of management soon arose also. The greatest of the railway contractors at home and abroad was Thomas Brassey. He had strong views on labour and the economy, and he left a fortune of £3,200,000 on his death in 1870. Brassey learned better than anyone else how to manage a large, mixed and, at times, awkward labour-force, dismissed by contemporary moralists as 'impetuous, impulsive and brute-like . . . owing no moral law and feeling no social tie'. This was far too comprehensive an indictment. In fact, the contribution made by construction workers, 'navvies', to the transport revolution was crucial. Using picks and shovels – and not machines – they pressed forward relentlessly. Hamilton Ellis, a railway historian, has called them 'a great army, which in other conditions might have carved out a great empire'.

Once the railways began to work, their managers introduced an almost military discipline into the management of their uniformed railway staff (although it was an admiral who is said to have devised buttons and peaked caps). As in the Army, there were differences of status and authority which were carefully devised and quickly became acceptable. 'The man in the lower grade', wrote a worker in a railway goods yard, 'was now regarded as socially superior to the lower grade man [elsewhere]. The goods porter was looked upon as an inferior animal by the shunter. The shunter was tolerated as a necessary evil by the goods guard.' There was no railway trade union until 1872, and then it was called the Amalgamated Society of Railway Servants. Its successors, however, were at the centre of history in 1901 (the Taff Vale case), in 1919 (a great strike) and in 1926 (the General Strike).

In new railway towns like Crewe, which had not even figured as a place name in the 1841 census, and Swindon, there were new social ties between companies and workers which for generations inhibited independent action. A paternalistic community building provided by the London and North Western Railway Directors, who acquired Crewe in 1840, was said to prove that even a railway company, which some critics described as a 'feudal organization with modifications', had 'bowels of compassion', although it was added that they were not 'on public exhibition'. In Swindon (where the first small 'lock-up' had proved too small to contain railway labourers who were drunk or disorderly) it was claimed with exaggeration in the 1870s that 'whatever is good for the company is good for New Swindon.'

Whatever the perils of entrepreneurship or investment, by 1855 there were over 8,000 miles of track, managed by fewer companies than a decade earlier, and all the great cities had long been linked, with Birmingham the first to get two lines to London. In 1845 a Clearing House scheme came into existence, a benefit that the canal companies, now in decline and subject to relentless competition or railway take-over, had never been able to achieve. One of the railway gauges – that of the Great Western, designed by the great engineer Isambard Kingdom Brunel – was broader than the rest, inhibiting the creation of a unified system, but conversion, started in the west, was widespread by the later 1860s and was completed by 1892 at the company's own cost. Financiers might come and go, but the engineers, contractors and navvies stuck to their tasks, and it was soon difficult to remember what the country had looked like and been like before their advent. 'We who lived before railways and survive out of the ancient world,' wrote the novelist William Thackeray, 'are like Father Noah and his family out of the Ark.'

As one excited journalist had commented on the triumph of *The Rocket* in the 1830 trials, 'The victory has established principles which will give a greater impulse to civilization than it has ever received from any single source since the Press first opened the gates of knowledge of the human species at large.' No journalist could have said more. Yet even he did not know how much the future development of the press, described in the 1850s as a 'Fourth Estate', would depend on railway transport. He could not have foreseen the enterprise of W. H. Smith, the great distributor of newspapers, books and periodicals, 'media of communication' as they were to be called in the twentieth century.

By the last decades of the nineteenth century railways, no longer thought of as a novelty, had ceased to capture the imagination of the public. They were taken for granted, not just because what they carried was now deemed commonplace (they quickly revolutionized the distribution of consumer goods, perishable, bulky and fragile, from milk to mail), but because passengers no longer felt that great excitement in speed of movement which the first travellers had done. There had been a time, before time itself was speeded up, when a traveller by rail had noted with pride that 'had the double tailed comet passed that way, the country people could scarcely have been more interested by the spectacle.' He continued:

the men at work in the fields and quarries stood like statues, their pick axes in their hands, in attitudes of fixed attention . . . and women . . . in their best gowns and bonnets fled from the villages and congregated at the corner of every intersecting lane. Neither were the brute creations less animated . . . Every horse was on the alert, viewing the huge moving body as it approached with a mixture of fear and surprise.

Some of the first travellers by rail did not stop at the plain metaphor of the iron horse: they elaborated it. Thus, for the actress Fanny Kemble,

she goes along wheels which are her feet and are moved by bright steel legs called pistons; these are propelled by steam . . . The reins, bit and bridle of this wonderful beast is a small steel handle, which applies or withdraws the steam from its legs or pistons, so that a child might manage it. This snorting little animal . . . I feel rather inclined to pat.

Given that horses had figured so prominently in English life, the arrival of the 'iron horse' was, indeed, a moment of truth. It has been estimated that to keep a single horse on the road for a year in the great coaching age required five acres of hay and oats, not to speak of an army of blacksmiths. Coal, carried everywhere by rail, was a cheaper source of power, although it needed miners (women included among them until 1842) still working in difficult (and often dangerous) conditions underground to produce it. At first children were employed too.

Exhilaration was always only part of the early story. For many nineteenth-century English men and women the railway was contro-versial, and locomotives, in the words of the Tory diarist Thomas Creevey, were 'monsters navigated by a tail of smoke and sulphur'. Charles Dickens, the great popular novelist, in *Dombey and Son* (1849) depicted 'the power that forced itself upon the iron way' as 'a type of the triumphant master Death'. Railway accidents, even those that occurred at the building stage – like the terrible story of death in the construction of the Woodhead Tunnel not far from Sheffield between 1839 and 1845, when at least thirty-two men were killed and many injured – were man-made horrors on a huge and unprecedented scale. 'A railway is long, but life is short,' wrote a critic in *Punch* – 'and generally the longer the railway, the shorter your life.'

Other critics were ambivalent in their attitudes, complaining, as modern critics of motorways do, about the displacement of families and bisection of communities on the two sides of the track. Even those critics who believed that railways might indirectly favour sanitary reform by carving their way through densely packed and unhealthy working-class districts admitted that while the locomotive had 'a giant's strength', he was no better than 'a blind and undistinguishing Polyphemus when he is called in as a sanitary reformer'.

The impact of the railways on Victorian cities, many of them cities of the railway age, was enormous. By 1890 railway companies owned up to 8–10 per cent of central land in the cities and influenced the use made of another 20 per cent, although they did not achieve their ambition of completing a central link through London (there were instead many complex outer links). It was London from which all main lines radiated; there were very few cross-country lines. The great main line stations – the word 'station' was new – were places of pride. Euston had its spectacular Doric arch. Gothic St Pancras, opened in 1868, had a roof span of 360 feet.

The railway could have as marked an effect on smaller communities as on large ones. Thus, Teddington, described in 1837 as a 'quiet rural village, with its "grove", its "Manor", its little waterside church by the Thames, and its broad expanse of open meadows', was completely transformed by 1884. 'Rows of spruce villas and neat terraces' had appeared along with 'grand hotels' and 'magnificent stores' that drove out other hostelries and alarmed small traders.

Even when there were no social displacements or accidents, railway travel was felt by its critics to be breaking the established rhythms of life and challenging accepted social relationships. It seemed to be too 'democratic', as Dr Arnold, Headmaster of Rugby School, put it, 'destroying feudalism for ever'. Some landowners feared its intrusion into their estates and kept it as far as they could from their property. So too did the Provost of Eton and the Vice-Chancellor of the University of Oxford. A stilted dialogue between two aristocrats in Disraeli's novel *Sybil* (1845) caught contemporaries' fears and entanglements.

> *Lord de Mowbray:* You came by railroad?
> *Lady Marney:* From Marham, about ten miles from us.
> *De M:* A great revolution.
> *M:* Isn't it?
> *De M:* I fear it has a dangerous tendency to equality. I suppose your husband gives them all the opposition in his power.

M: There is nobody so violent against the railroads as George . . . he organized the whole of the district against our Marham line.

De M: I rather counted on him to assist me in resisting this joint branch line here, but I was surprised to learn that he had consented.

M: Not until the compensation was settled. George never opposed them after that. He gave up all opposition to the Marham line when they agreed to his terms.

That was the view from above.

From below, many people, particularly businessmen seeking to enlarge their markets, immediately found railways useful, and by 1870 were finding them indispensable. Mass distribution, particularly of perishables, depended on the railway which carried, for example, milk from Newbury, beer from Burton-on-Trent or fish from Grimsby, Hull, Lowestoft and Yarmouth. Between 1849 and 1870, while track mileage doubled, the number of first-class and second-class passengers increased four times and the number of third-class passengers six times. An Act of Parliament of 1844 had obliged railway companies to run at least one train every weekday, except Christmas Day and Good Friday, at fares not exceeding one penny a mile for adults and a halfpenny for children between three and twelve years of age, and although this did not immediately produce a nation of commuters, middle class or working class, it opened up the new system to everyone in the community. 'Does not the railway take the third-class passenger at the same speed at which even royalty travels?' asked the radical politician John Bright in 1879. 'Science as applied to railways has come down to the humblest of the people.'

The railways, like the factory, had certainly sharpened the sense of time. As early as 1839 the first *Bradshaw* had set out regular timetables. You either caught your train or missed it. For many middle-class and professional people railways became essential in the journey to work, but it was not until 1883 that the first extensive Cheap Trains Act was passed. The opening up of suburban routes, separating home and work place, altered all the patterns of everyday life.

Another big change, quicker to take shape, followed the recognition that railways could lead not only to the factory or to the office but also to the seaside and the country. A special train on the Whitby and Pickering Railway in North Yorkshire had carried visitors to a church bazaar in 1839, and in 1841 Thomas Cook, founder of what became a

Railways in 1870

100–400 metres above sea level

over 400 metres above sea level

50 Miles

Glasgow
Edinburgh
Berwick
Hawick
Carlisle
Newcastle-upon-Tyne
Durham
Stockton
Darlington
Whitby
Scarborough
Barrow
Skipton
Bradford
York
Hull
Fleetwood
Preston
Leeds
Liverpool
Manchester
Doncaster
Birkenhead
Holyhead
Sheffield
Lincoln
Chester
Caernarfon
Crewe
Stafford
Derby
King's Lynn
Shrewsbury
Leicester
Norwich
Yarmouth
Birmingham
Peterborough
Ludlow
Rugby
Ely
Worcester
Cambridge
Ipswich
Gloucester
Colchester
Carmarthen
Oxford
Swindon
Reading
Bristol
London
Cardiff
Redhill
Dover
Salisbury
Taunton
Southampton
Exeter
Portsmouth
Brighton
Dorchester
Plymouth
Penzance

huge travel agency, persuaded the Midland Counties Railway to issue cheap tickets to 510 Leicester temperance workers to attend a quarterly delegates' meeting in Loughborough. 'We must have RAILWAYS FOR THE MILLIONS' was Cook's cry. And he got them. Soon afterwards the aristocratic image of Brighton was dented in 1844 by the first day-excursion train from London, and the proletarian image of Blackpool was built up from the time the railway arrived there two years later: before that it had been 'the sweet little village by the sea'. Cook himself became 'so thoroughly imbued with the tourist spirit' that he began to contemplate 'Foreign Trips, including the Continent of Europe, the United States and the Eastern lands of the Bible'.

It took more than a century for the English to follow Cook outside the island in their millions, but already, by the end of the nineteenth century, they were pouring out along the English coast. The Bank Holiday Act of 1871 laid down that certain days in the year should be official holidays, very different in motivation from the old holy days of the Christian calendar, which ensured not only crowded trains but crowded beaches; the picture postcard, a late nineteenth- and early twentieth-century innovation, helps us to recapture the mood. And it was the railways that determined the pattern of holiday geography: the old inland spas declined in importance while the new seaside resorts rose. Both Morecambe to the west and Bridlington to the east were nicknamed Bradford-by-the-Sea. From London there was a choice of Brighton, Eastbourne, Hastings, Worthing or Southend. Each resort had its own history and its own tone.

It took time, however, for railway directors and managers to free themselves fully from the view from above when they considered future prospects. At first, they had been far more concerned with freight than with people and were content, as a Great Western Railway director put it bleakly in 1839, to contemplate for the 'accommodation' of third-class passengers only 'carriages of an inferior description at very slow speed'. One early traveller wrote of such carriages that

> there was a general feeling of bare boards and cheerlessness as you entered them . . . Even the windows were but small apertures [and] the seats were cushionless . . . Trains stopped at every little place on the way; you were shunted here and shunted there, or found yourself resting in some lonely siding for what seemed an age.

Standards of third-class service improved, however, as the nineteenth century went by and 9,000 stations, big and small, were built. The second class disappeared, and even third-class carriages (unlike most of those across the Channel) were fitted with padded seats. Coaches with separate corridors and lavatories had been introduced in 1881 and de luxe Pullman coaches even earlier on some lines.

The opening of Victoria Station in 1860 was of great importance in relation both to the journey to work and the escape from it. In appearance it could not vie with Euston or St Pancras, but it pointed resolutely to the commuter age and it opened up a great new 'gateway to the Continent'. Three years later, London's first underground railway, the Metropolitan, was opened; it ran between Paddington and Farringdon Street, a distance of nearly four miles, and was supported both by the City of London and the Great Western Railway. The District Railway brought Victoria into this system in 1871, and in 1884 the Inner Circle was completed. The underground opened up whole new housing areas in South London and in 'Metroland', which led in turn to early morning and late evening travel rushes. They were to be followed in time by the late twentieth-century traffic jams on overcrowded roads.

The next major development in communication after the railway was the rise of the automobile, which in its beginnings was very different in character. For the well-off traveller it had been a major weakness of the railroad that 'you were shunted here and there' along fixed tracks. You did not know, moreover, whom you would meet when you entered a railway carriage. By contrast, if you had the money, a motor car was your own, and subject to the conditions of the highway you could do what you liked with it. You had 'the freedom of the road'. You would also, it was claimed, find an automobile easy to maintain. 'Looking after a motor car', a speaker told a London audience in 1897, 'is child's play compared to attending to a horse. If you do not use your carriage for a month, it does not cost you anything: there is no horse eating his head off in the stable.' Moreover, 'what pair of horses could carry a load, as my Daimler has done, of 250 pounds of baggage, myself and my man?'

The internal combustion engine supplanted the steam carriage that for more than a century had seemed to offer the best prospect for 'self-propulsion', then a luxury, as this language demonstrates. Unlike the railway – and this was a sign of the times – it was developed not in

England but in France and Germany. It was not until 1888 that Edward Butler, son of a West Country farmer, produced the first English petrol-driven engine capable of being attached to a moving vehicle; and not until 1895 that Frederick Lanchester produced the first English four-wheeler car and Herbert Austin designed a car that was built (this was real continuity) by the Wolseley Sheep Shearing Machine Company in Birmingham. At nearby Coventry, an old city which had switched profitably from silk and watch-making to sewing machines and bicycles, the Daimler Company soon began to manufacture cars in a disused silk factory. The first car seen in England, a Benz, had been imported in 1894. (Its importer, who collected it at the docks, was stopped by the police as he crossed London.) There had already been an increase in the amount of traffic on the roads between 1878 and 1890, but it was horse-driven traffic, mainly 'short-stage'.

Butler's first design for a vehicle had been not for an automobile but for a petro-bicycle. The age of the bicycle (with or without petrol) preceded the age of the automobile. In the history of communications bicycles were significant, therefore, not only in their own right – and they were to have their own continuing history – but as precursors of automobiles. (William Morris, the future Lord Nuffield, repaired bicycles before and after he made cars.) Bicycles revived or created a sense of the 'freedom' of the road; the fact that they were relatively cheap and soon became cheaper (£4.50 in the 1890s) made them popular too, particularly after they had got through their bone-shaker phase. The Rover safety model, devised by J. K. Starkey in 1885, triumphed over all rivals. As early as 1878 a Bicycle Touring Club had been founded, to be renamed the Cyclists' Touring Club five years later, the year when the National Cyclists' Union was founded. Both bodies stressed 'the fellowship of the road' as well as its freedom. Both enjoyed exploring the countryside.

There were many bicycle cultures, some of them associated with youth, a term not then used, some with socialism, a word coming into use, some with 'liberated women', a contemporary phrase; the bicycle did more to encourage 'rational' women's dress than generations of dress reformers. All made as much of the open air as of self-propulsion. The air was in danger of being polluted, however, as a result of the activities of the first motor car owners, a few of them aristocratic, most of them plutocratic. They were the butt of friendly and unfriendly jokes, occasional physical assaults, and numerous witty verses like Hilaire Belloc's well-known lines:

> The rich arrived in pairs
> And also in Rolls-Royces;
> They talked of their affairs
> In loud and strident voices.

Nonetheless, by the time Belloc wrote, there were motor cars of a different kind and price in active use across the Atlantic, where the utility of the automobile in a continent of huge distances was immediately recognized. Henry Ford was at work to lower their costs, and Belloc could add a further verse to his poem:

> The poor arrived in Fords
> Whose features they resembled;
> They laughed to see so many lords
> And ladies all assembled.

Six thousand Ford Model Ts were being produced in Manchester in 1913.

If the 'railway age' had seen a diversion of social capital from such activities as housing to transport, the 'automobile age' saw a diversion of private capital, and incomes, away from necessities to diversion itself. Although the internal combustion engine was introduced 'hesitantly' in London for public buses in 1907, following the earlier introduction of electric trams in the 1890s and the metered motor taxi for the better off in 1905, the private motor car continued to draw most attention. 'Wandering machines, travelling with an incredible rate of speed,' a socially minded Liberal politician called them in 1909. 'You can see them on a Sunday afternoon, piled twenty or thirty deep outside the new popular inns, while their occupants regale themselves within.' Not all the hostile comment was equally polite. 'Your birthright is being taken from you by reckless motorists,' warned a Fulham handbill of 1908. 'Men of England . . . rise up, join together and bring pressure on your representatives in Parliament.' Such opponents of motoring were far less influential, however, than the (Royal) Automobile Club, founded in 1897, and the Automobile Association, established in 1905 after a merger of earlier bodies.

Nevertheless, there were social problems that could not be solved by lobbying. Thus the number of fatal car accidents increased from

373 in 1909 to 1,328 in 1914, by which time there were 132,015 licensed private cars on the roads of Britain, nearly three times as many as in 1909. Of course, the roads had proved inadequate for motor traffic: the age of the turnpikes was past (22,000 miles of road had been turnpiked by 1838, but by 1890 there were only two turnpike trusts left in existence). There were also restrictions on the freedom of the motorists: the Red Flag Act of 1865, extended with limited amendments in 1878, restricted speeds to four miles an hour in the country and two miles an hour in the towns and required every 'road locomotive' to have three attendants, one to walk not less than six yards in front carrying a red flag by day and a lantern by night.

Such irksome restrictions, which were introduced to deal not with motor cars but with older and heavier types of road vehicle, were modified in 1878 and repealed by the Light Locomotives on Highways Act of 1896. Instead, different motoring controls were to take their place: licensing, introduced in 1904 along with number plates; petrol and horse-power taxes, first levied in 1909 (with the promise of a Road Fund); and speed limits – twenty miles was set in 1904 – to be followed decades later by beacons, traffic lights and white lines in the road. These, however, were the product of a new age, not the epilogue of an old one. In 1896, the year in which the magazine *The Autocar*, 'published in the interests of the mechanically propelled carriage', was founded, Harry J. Lawson, patentee of the safety bicycle and would-be George Hudson of the automobile, organized the first London to Brighton motor rally, with the Earl of Winchelsea ceremonially tearing up a red flag to celebrate the occasion.

It would have been difficult to predict in 1896 and 1897 just how popular motor cars were to become in England in the late twentieth century. And this was true also of the cluster of new communication developments (some of them English) that followed on the advent of the telephone, which had been patented by Alexander Graham Bell in 1876, and the phonograph, which had been patented by Thomas Edison in 1877, but was to be much 'improved', mass produced and given a new trade name, 'the gramophone', by Emile Berliner just twenty years later. In 1896 the word 'record' had just come into use, although two-sided records were not to be manufactured until 1904.

The development of the telephone in England was slow: in 1882 *The Times* reported that there was one telephone for every 300 people in Chicago, but only one for every 3,000 people in London. One reason

why the English were as slow to learn to use telephones as they were
to learn how to mass-produce cars was the entrenched strength of the
telegraph system that had been taken over by the Post Office under a
Conservative government in 1868.

The electric telegraph had been developed alongside the railway
under private interests since William Fothergill Cooke had sent the first
telegraphic message to his fellow inventor, Charles Wheatstone, in
1837: he transmitted it from Camden Town station to a dingy office
in Euston. Under Post Office control telegrams were treated like letters:
they played an important part, often alarming, in family history. They
also played a crucial part in the history of the press and of news agencies.
The words 'by telegraph' appeared above many news columns, some
of the information being supplied through Reuters, founded in 1851.
Telephone messages, private or business, were a very different medium,
but in 1892 the Post Office took over the telephone trunk line system
too – the word 'trunk' again stands out – and in 1911 most of the
privately developed local system.

While the history of each of the different means of communication
had its own distinctive features, there were years of convergence,
notably 1896, which stands out in retrospect as a landmark date in the
history of communications as a whole. It was a landmark because it
anticipated the future, although it was not recognized as such at the
time. This was the year not only of the first London to Brighton car
rally, but of the founding of the *Daily Mail* and of the beginning of
regular cinema shows in London's West End. It was also the year when
the young Guglielmo Marconi arrived in London to display his bundle
of wireless patents which he kept in a black box.

The publisher of the halfpenny *Daily Mail*, Alfred Harmsworth, later
Lord Northcliffe, himself an early motorist and future editor of a volume
on *Motors and Motor Driving* (1902), promised the new readers of
the *Daily Mail*, a popular newspaper to which the label of the 'new
journalism' was attached, that 'four leading articles, a page of Parliament,
and columns of speeches' would 'NOT be found' in it. Lord Salisbury,
England's Conservative Prime Minister at the end of the century, might
dismiss the *Daily Mail* as 'a journal produced by office boys for office
boys', but by then nearly a million copies of it were selling, and within
the next decade Harmsworth was to take control of *The Times*, England's
supreme 'quality newspaper', as well; it had first appeared in 1788.

The first regular cinema shows in 1896, in London's Leicester Square, did not seem revolutionary at the time and certainly no one anticipated the huge size of mid-twentieth-century cinema attendances or the glamour of palatial cinema buildings with exotic names, like Granada and Eldorado. There was a long pedigree, however, behind the cinema. The camera had first been demonstrated in 1839 by Fox Talbot in England and Daguerre in France, although it was not until 1888 that the Kodak, which made photography easy and popular, was launched by George Eastman, its American inventor. It was an Englishman, Edward Muggeridge, who produced moving pictures – of horses – in 1872. After 1896 the moving film, pioneered in Brighton, was quickly to become a form of 'mass entertainment' rather than a private diversion: it rapidly supplanted older technologies like the magic lantern, and very soon it was to challenge the theatre.

In Marconi's case, neither the inventor himself nor the Post Office engineers to whom he demonstrated radio looked very far forward. They did not think of 'wireless' as an instrument of broadcasting; indeed, it needed further technical invention to make possible 'wireless telephony', communication by voice rather than by signals. Radio telegraphy was conceived of as a substitute for line-to-line communication by wire, and the 'broadcasting' element was treated as a liability, not an asset. It was impossible to foresee a time when a monarch, George V (1910–36), would talk to his subjects throughout the Empire by radio. Already, however, radio had attracted attention before 1914 when it helped to catch a criminal (the famous Dr Crippen) and when it told the story of the sinking of the liner *Titanic*.

Much in the history of communications seems to move in thirty-year generational cycles, and thirty years later wireless was to become the country's main story-teller. Then it was to have unanticipated economic, social and cultural consequences, serving a great audience and levelling time and place. A British broadcasting handbook was to stress that

> till the advent of this universal and extraordinary cheap medium of communication, a very large proportion of people were shut off from first-hand knowledge of the events which make history . . . Today he who has something to tell his countrymen can command an audience of millions ready to hand.

Communications nationalized the audience.

There was an irony in this in that the 'communications revolution', as it came to take shape in retrospect, was by its nature an international revolution, crossing frontiers. Behind it there were common technologies, which were not distinctively English. Yet the institutional shell devised to handle radio technology in Britain was very specifically British, if not English. John Reith, the first managing director and later Director-General of the BBC, was a Scot, a 'son of the manse', and under his direction broadcasting was to be driven by a sense of service rather than the profit motive: the programming for which the BBC was given a monopoly was to reflect this. This was not true, however, either of the cinema (although British film-making was to be subsidized) or the press, both of which were developed by private entrepreneurs.

No account of the communications revolution before 1914 would be complete without reference both to shipping and the aeroplane. Shipping was thought of as a 'traditional' activity throughout the period, although it was in fact transformed as profoundly as land transport during the steam revolution of the nineteenth century. The change from sail to steam was just as dramatic as the change from stage coach to railway. The record year for the building of new sailing ships, 272,000 tons, was 1864. Fifty years later, sail accounted for 1,205,000 tons and steam for 17,264,000. It is not surprising that a British historian of shipping gave the title *Our Ocean Railways* to his book on nineteenth-century shipping developments.

As in the case of railways, the facilities and services accompanying shipping also underwent a great transformation. The first modern dock, the West India Dock in London, was sanctioned by Parliament in 1799 (and opened in 1802), and the Warehousing Act was passed in 1803, in what was still an age of sail; by the time of the foundation of the Port of London Authority in 1908, however, the London shipping world had completely changed. So too had other shipping centres, such as the port of Southampton, which, with the acquisition of its dock estate by the London and South Western Railway in 1892, passed into a new phase of its history as a rival to London. At that time Britain had more registered shipping tonnage than the rest of the world put together. It was still dominant in 1914.

Transatlantic crossings were the first ocean traffic to be influenced by steam: the *Sirius*, the first British ship to cover the whole journey by steam, crossed from London to New York in 1838, one day ahead of, but three and a half days more slowly than, Brunel's *Great Western*, 'our island's boast, our noble city's [Bristol] pride', which had made the journey from Bristol. A year later, Samuel Cunard secured the valuable North Atlantic mail contract and the Cunard line was born. By the time that the first steel ship, *Servia*, took to the oceans in 1881, the first ship to be fitted with electric light, the Suez Canal had been opened with pomp in 1869 (Thomas Cook was present at the opening). A less well-known date was 1887 when ships passing through the canal were equipped with electric headlights to allow night travel, cutting the journey by sixteen hours.

Speed, while exciting in itself, was also an agent of more wide-ranging cargo traffic, much of which was perishable. As crowded cargo ships, small or big, plied the oceans from the Arctic to the South Pacific, Rudyard Kipling could ask in one of his frequently recited poems:

> 'Oh, where are you going to, all you Big Steamers,
> With England's own coal up and down the salt seas?'
> 'We are going to fetch you your bread and your butter,
> Your beef, pork and mutton, eggs, apples and cheese.'

Not all the ships were going to the ports, like Melbourne, Quebec, Hong Kong or Bombay, over which the Union Jack flew. Some went to Buenos Aires, Bangkok, Baltimore and San Francisco, and to more remote harbours in what historians have identified as 'informal' empire.

There were also passenger boats with, at one end of the scale, luxury liners, complete with brightly lit salons and richly furnished cabins, and at the other, ships with much lower standards (though these too were improving) in which large numbers of emigrants travelled to lands of imperial settlement, like New Zealand or Canada, or crossed the Atlantic to find a new life in America. As many as two-thirds of the three million people who left to form a new life overseas between 1850 and 1880 went to the United States.

The emigrants' motives were as mixed as their backgrounds. Some were pushed out of England in hard times; many hoped for a better life and were attracted by opportunities not to be found in their own country. The first settlers in Australia had been convicts, but transportation was brought to an end in 1849. Meanwhile, New Zealand and South Australia were settled from the start by free men on 'principles calculated to promote the earliest and greatest prosperity'. 'Impossible to describe their energy, their ardour, their decisiveness,' wrote the French observer Taine of two young people, born into a family of twelve, who were about to leave for New Zealand in the 1850s: 'one feels a superabundance of energy and activity, an overthrow of animal spirits.' And for almost all the emigrants there was no return: Ford Madox Brown chose the right title for his famous painting 'The Last of England'.

Colonial society was very different from that at home. A fashionable Englishman in Adelaide in 1854 was appalled when a wharf hand, refusing to carry his carpet bag or to be lectured on deference to his superiors, retorted, 'You may keep your dignity and I will keep my blue shirt and we shall see who will wear the best and longest in this country.' A great imperial city like Melbourne might think of itself as a Victorian city like Birmingham or Leeds, and might celebrate Queen Victoria's Jubilee of 1887 'with an enthusiasm that was not excelled in any part of the Empire', but only thirty years earlier the colony of Victoria had been turned topsy-turvy by the great gold rush of the 1850s.

The values not of the city but of the outback came to be appreciated late in the century and were ultimately to shape a distinctive 'Australian' legend. In 1823 a young Australian at Cambridge University, who came second in the competition for the Chancellor's medal, had yearned for an 'Austral Milton', even an 'Austral Shakespeare', but seventy years later there was a very different strain in verses called 'Old Australian Ways':

> The narrow ways of English folk
> Are not for such as we:
> They bear the long-accustomed yoke
> Of staid conservancy:
> But all our roads are new and strange,
> And through our blood there runs
> The vagabonding love of change
> That drove us westward of the range
> And westward of the suns.

By the final decades of the century, however, the greatest imperial expansion came not through settlement but through conquest and rule, reaching its zenith between the 1880s and 1914 when over 4,500,000 square miles were added to the areas of the world printed red on maps. There were many different versions of the imperial mission, presented by missionaries, traders, industrialists, politicians, poets and professors, and their arguments for colonization ranged from 'carrying light and civilization to the dark places of the world' to the expansion of British trade and support for British industry (and British working men) and to the search for adventure and romance. Whatever the motives behind formal and informal empire – or the rhetoric – there was one necessary condition of imperial existence, the *Pax Britannica*, and that in turn relied on a command of the oceans. The ships of the Royal Navy were essential not only for defence, but to maintain peacetime links between Empire and 'mother country'.

If ships were ubiquitous in 1914, aeroplanes were rare. As late as 1901 H. G. Wells, prophet of 'the shape of things to come', stated that he did not think it at all probable that aeronautics would 'ever come into play as a serious modification of transport and communications', although he conceded generously that 'very probably by 1950 a success-ful aeroplane will have soared and come home safely'. In fact, friends of the early English pioneer of aeronautics, Sir George Cayley, a baronet, sixth in his family line, had founded an Aeronautical Society in 1866, nine years after his death.

The first historic breakthrough, dependent like that in the history of the automobile, on gasoline-powered engines, came across the Atlantic when Orville and Wilbur Wright made the first powered flight in December 1903, and the second, as far as England was concerned, in 1909, when Louis Blériot flew across the Channel from France to England in forty minutes. Although it was not until around 1950 that civil aviation became a major form of transport, already, while England was in command of the world's oceans, it had lost its secure island status. 'Aeroplanes actually in stock', read an advertisement in *Aero* magazine in the year Blériot crossed the Channel. 'Prices from £200 . . . FREE TUITION given with all aeroplanes and one mile guaran-teed flight on delivery.' Five years later a German aeroplane was to drop a bomb on English soil for the first time in history.

10 VICTORIANISM: PRELUDE, EXPRESSIONS, AFTERMATH

> The Victorians knew that they were peculiar; they were conscious of belonging to a *parvenu* civilisation . . . They took the brunt of an utterly unique development of human history.
>
> Humphry House, *Are the Victorians Coming Back?*, 1940

> The middle third of the nineteenth century does not, I acknowledge, appeal to me. It is probably due to the natural ingratitude which we are apt to feel towards our immediate predecessors.
>
> A. J. Balfour, *University Address*, 1905

> People don't realize that the Victorian age was simply an interruption in Britain's history.
>
> Harold Macmillan, quoted by Anthony Sampson, 1981

> Victorian values were the values when our country became great.
>
> Margaret Thatcher, in a television interview with Brian Walden, 1983

Blériot and the German bomb were post-Victorian. Before Victoria died there were some eminent Victorians, watching the world move by, who sharply questioned the triumphs both of communication and industrialization. Matthew Arnold, for example, complained of 'this strange disease of modern life with its sick hurry, its divided aims'. England was always something more than an industrial society. 'Traditional' influences, notably the survival of pre-industrial forms of social hierarchy and their accompanying values, prevailed until the last decades of Victoria's long reign (1837–1901) and often impressed themselves upon visitors more strongly than what was new.

'Palaces, halls, villas, walled parks all over England, rival the splendour of royal seats,' wrote R. W. Emerson, an American commentator who visited England in 1833 and 1847. 'Primogeniture built those sumptuous piles.' The so-called New Domesday survey of English land showed that in 1873 four-fifths of the land was held by 7,000 individuals, peers prominent amongst them. Nor was it only the great owners, bound together more than any other group by 'a common blood, a common condition, common pursuits . . . and a common prestige', who commanded deference through their titles as well as through their possessions. For the Revd John Hamilton Gray in the preface to the fourth edition of Burke's *Landed Gentry* in 1862, some peers were 'mere mushrooms when compared with a large proportion of our country gentry . . . whose families were established as a county aristocracy at a date when their lordships' ancestry did not possess an acre of land.' Walter Bagehot suggested three years later in his brilliant essay on the English constitution, that even the insolvent squire 'will get five times as much respect from the common peasantry as the newly-made rich man'. The whole of society, including, to the horror of Richard Cobden, industrialists, continued to give precedence to status that was transmitted rather than acquired.

Bagehot was at pains to insist, as many earlier social commentators had done, that Queen Victoria reigned over a society dominated by contrasts. On one side were men of ideas and men of power, who had made their way to success or inherited it; on the other side were 'ignorant' Dorset labourers, who would pelt 'agitators' rather than listen to them. For Bagehot, the 'characteristics of the lower regions' of society resembled 'the life of old times rather than the present life of the higher regions'. An American visitor to England in the same decade discovered 'queer little villages' in Wiltshire 'which looked as if the cottages were built by the immediate followers of Hengist and Horsa'. Despite the rise of 'public opinion' (and its organ, the press), there were limits to effective social communication, even in the cities. One writer in Liverpool claimed, for instance, that 'two communities dwell side by side within sound of the same bells and under the same chief magistrate . . . practically as wide apart as if they lived in separate quarters of the world.'

According to Bagehot, there were large numbers of Englishmen who believed that the queen, and not Parliament, governed the country.

The civil servants most Englishmen knew were tax collectors and inspectors of various kinds, whose activities, like those of the police (another largely Victorian invention), were often resented. In reality the civil service, which doubled in size between 1854 and 1900, was playing an increasingly important part – along with local government officials – in the task of administering the country. An uncorrupt civil service, chosen after 1870 not by patronage but by open competitive examination, has been rightly described as 'the one great political invention in Victorian England', and its role in shaping the course of legislation has been carefully analysed. Another distinctive feature of Victorian England was the low level of direct taxation. Although income tax was re-introduced in 1842 by Peel, reducing or abolishing a whole cluster of indirect taxes, it was still possible for the Liberal Prime Minister W. E. Gladstone, who hated all taxation, to contemplate getting rid of it in 1873. Meanwhile, from 1866 the Select Committee on Public Accounts, serviced by a Comptroller and Auditor-General, was supervising government spending and at the same time safeguarding institutional morality.

The adjective 'Victorian', which first became noticed in 1851, the year of the Great Exhibition, remains a more fitting label to apply to a highly distinctive age than labels like 'industrial society'. It carries with it a sense of the conflicts and compromises of the times, and all their self-consciousness and pride. Yet it is an adjective that must be used with care. There were many changes in attitudes during Victoria's long reign, and there were many differences within society at each point within it. The notion of a single, shared moral code, to which the label 'Victorianism' has been attached, becomes absurd when one places Florence Nightingale, the 'lady with the lamp', a woman of spirit with the highest sense of service, alongside the Earl of Cardigan, Crimean War commander, who fought a duel as late as 1840, was accused of adultery and spiriting away the chief witness in 1843, and once ordered his men to wear 'cherry-coloured pants', which, according to The Times, were 'as utterly unfit for war service as the garb of the female hussars in the ballet of Gustavus'. Eccentricity was always an important part of the Victorian pattern.

Victoria's sixty-three-year reign, with all its light and shade, can most usefully be divided into early, middle and late periods. It is the middle period, which was a time of economic progress, social stability and cultural diversity – punctuated by the Crimean War, which is often left out of the reckoning – that has been allowed to colour too strongly the interpretation of the whole. In fact the early years, which came to an end with the Great Exhibition, have more in common with the late Victorian years that began with a 'watershed' in the 1870s. Then, as it was brilliantly put by the young liberal John Morley, 'Those who dwell in the tower of ancient faiths look about them in constant apprehension, misgiving and wonder . . . [for] the air seems to their alarm to be full of missiles, and all is doubt, hesitation and shivering expectancy.' During the middle years there was a balance of interests; during the early and late years a divergence of interests, even a sense of rebellion.

During the 1840s the voice of prophets, notably Thomas Carlyle, could always be heard, and the language of both working-class Chartists and middle-class anti-Corn Law Leaguers was often violent and their rhetoric romantic. Landlords were 'a breadtaxing oligarchy', 'unprincipled', 'unfeeling', and 'rapacious'. At the same time, Lord Melbourne, Victoria's first Prime Minister, could call the League 'the wildest, maddest scheme that has ever entered into the imagination of man to conceive', and he had even less sympathy with its leaders than with Chartist 'fustian jackets and unshorn chins of England'. A survivor from the eighteenth century, he was not alone in contemplating the possibility of revolution. Although in 1828 the Metropolitan Police Force had been founded by Peel, Melbourne's Conservative successor, there was no adequate provincial police force to control the local scene until the 1850s, and the Army (and special constables) had to be called upon to deal with the threat of physical force which Chartism seemed to carry with it.

In carrying through the repeal of the Corn Laws in 1846 Peel refused to put his trust in the language of 'movement': he wanted to keep a balance between agriculture, which interested him personally as well as politically through his party, and industry, the source of his own wealth. He wanted also to contribute to the solution of the much debated 'Condition of England' question by reducing the price of bread.

During the middle years of the century, such a balance was achieved, although Peel himself was killed in 1850 when he was thrown off his horse in London's Constitution Hill. Many of the fires of discontent burnt out, and the contemporary emphasis was on interlocking interests and on specific and limited pieces of improvement, local as well as national, the need for which was usually forced on the attention of the public by a particular mid-Victorian scandal. There were still storms, but many of them were storms in teacups. Palmerston, 'Lord Evergreen', the leading politician of the age, was very different from Peel: in the words of Bagehot, Palmerston, Prime Minister from 1859 to 1865, was a statesman of the moment, who managed to reconcile 'self-help', the ideal which lay at the heart of mid-Victorian thought and behaviour, with the older ideal of 'the gentleman'. In a speech on foreign policy in 1850, he told the House of Commons, still elected on a limited franchise, that

> We have shown the example of a nation in which every class of society accepts with cheerfulness that lot which providence has assigned to it, while at the same time each individual of each class is constantly trying to raise himself in the social scale not by injustices and wrong, not by violence and illegality, but by persevering good conduct and by the steady and energetic exertion of the moral and intellectual faculties with which the Creator has endowed him.

Foreigners could not easily translate either 'self-help' or 'the gentleman' into their own languages, but there were many English people who were as well aware as Palmerston was of how to reconcile the two ideals in practice. Thus, the hero of Mrs Craik's much-read *John Halifax, Gentleman* (1854), the story of an orphan who made a fortune, built a house and bought a carriage (the most important Victorian status symbol), was told by his son, 'We are gentle folks now.' 'We always were, my son,' was the father's reply.

Much that is thought of as characteristically Victorian belongs to this middle period of the reign, when the aristocracy retained its social and much of its political influence and no single political party dominated the scene. Meanwhile, a new Liberal Party was in the course of formation which appealed to conscience as well as to interest and which drew on belief in human progress. The favourite mid-Victorian historian, the Whig Lord Macaulay, whose *History of England*, published in several volumes, was extremely popular with his own contemporaries, extolled not only past triumphs, notably the constitutional settlement of 1688, but also, with a touch of complacency, the current burst of economic, technical and scientific progress. Recent scientific progress, he claimed, had

> lengthened life . . . mitigated pain . . . extinguished diseases . . . increased the fertility of the soil . . . given new securities to the mariner . . . furnished new arms to the warrior . . . spanned great rivers and estuaries with bridges of form unknown to our forefathers . . . lightened up the night with the splendour of the day . . . extended the range of human vision . . . multiplied the power of human muscles . . . accelerated motion, annihilated distance . . . facilitated intercourse, correspondence, all friendly offices, all dispatch of business; and enabled man to descend the depths of the sea, to soar into the air.

At the time that Macaulay was writing, England was the richest country in the world, with a *per capita* income 50 per cent higher than that of France and almost three times that of Germany in 1860. Moreover, all sections of society seemed to be benefiting from prosperity. Prices were rising, but not sharply, and money wages were rising faster, particularly for skilled workers. (One-seventh of the workers, according to the mid-Victorian statistician Dudley Baxter, secured one-quarter of the total remuneration.) Profits were rising too, as were rents and farm incomes, a fact of equal importance in ensuring harmony. The repeal of the Corn Laws had not taken the prosperity out of the land; the mid-Victorian years, indeed, were a golden age of high-profit farming.

There was a place in these years, however, for argument, and even for doubt and pessimism. In the remarkable year 1859, the year in which Darwin's *The Origin of Species* was published, along with Fitzgerald's *The Rubaiyat of Omar Khayyam*, and Smiles's *Self Help* (which admitted that 'prodigality is more natural to man than thrift'), John Stuart Mill's *Essay on Liberty*, which attacked social conformity and pleaded for full play to be allowed to man's individuality, also appeared. The most controversial of these books was undoubtedly *The Origin of Species*, which reinforced religious doubts that already existed and which shocked not only religious fundamentalists and Evangelicals, but also leading figures within the scientific community. But it was Mill's *Essay on Liberty* that raised most questions about the pattern of contemporary society. Mill's father had been a close friend of Jeremy Bentham, whose insistence that government should seek to realize 'the greatest happiness of the greatest number' pointed towards both more responsible and more efficient government, free of corruption. Mill had been brought up as a Benthamite utilitarian, but now he was primarily concerned with the quality of society and less with individualism than with the character of individuality.

There was always scope for criticism in mid-Victorian England, both of loose thinking and of dubious practice. 'Cant', in particular, was much under attack by essayists and poets, among them Arthur Hugh Clough, a close friend of Matthew Arnold, who commented in his famous *New Decalogue*:

> Thou shalt not steal: an empty feat
> When it's so lucrative to cheat.
> Thou shalt not covet, but tradition
> Approves all forms of competition.

The critique could be broader. Following a murder trial at Aylesbury in 1857, for example, the *Saturday Review*, a sharp-edged periodical, summed up the difference between fact and fancy in the often sentimentalized countryside:

> Fornication and adultery, incest and murder, abortion and poisoning –
> all the tangled annals of the poor – this is 'Our Village' at work – this is
> Christian and happy England.

In the less sentimentalized town Emerson saw childhood 'oftenest in the state of absolute beggary' and women as 'cheap'.

Nonetheless, the critics were never in the majority. The *Saturday Review* was an edgy voice, and only one of the wide range of periodicals that, along with novels, constituted favourite mid-Victorian reading. Carlyle's prophecies were most welcomed when they were in line with existing prejudices. Emerson, who went with him on a visit to Stonehenge, choosing the company of the 'latest thinker' in the 'oldest place', was convinced that England had produced 'more great men' than any other country. The cult of greatness was always strong, turning naturally into hero worship.

Charles Dickens, the most popular member of a galaxy of great Victorian novelists, who reserved his own life from his readers, knew that there was much in mid-Victorian society that many mid-nineteenth-century readers (and most writers) believed had to be kept out of view because it was 'debasing' and not 'elevating', a favourite

Victorian adjective, applied to buildings, books and ideas. Melbourne had dismissed Dickens's *Oliver Twist* as 'all about Workhouses, and Coffin Makers, and Pickpockets': 'I don't like that low and debasing view of mankind.' And now a new generation was shocked by everything that did not fit into the accepted pattern, sharing the pontificating Mr Podsnap's prejudice: 'I don't want to know about it; I don't want to discuss it; I won't admit it.'

During the early years of the reign there had been sharp conflicts of style – above all between revived and revered Gothic, style among styles, and disparaged but not discarded classical – and argument continued between those who favoured 'old' styles and those who pressed for a 'new' style appropriate for a 'new age'. There were many would-be taste-makers in this changing society, a society which was influenced both by fashion and by some 'elevated' taste-makers who wanted to stay above it. During the eclectic mid-Victorian years, however, there were so many combinations and compromises that historians of the arts and crafts, and of design and architecture, have written of an unprecedented 'bastardization' of tastes. You could choose anything from Ancient Egyptian or Norman to Moorish-Spanish and Chinese.

There was also a plenitude of new things, more than ever before, and of new materials, like gutta-percha, brought in from Malaya in 1842, and 'silver electroplate', made by a process discovered one year before Victoria came to the throne and commercialized in 1840. Another new process was invented by William Baxter and used in his widely distributed Baxter prints. These could fill every inch of wall space. Indeed, within the mid-Victorian middle-class home – and often outside it – there was little free space. Most of the surfaces were decorated, curves were generous, nothing, least of all the table leg, was allowed to be bare, and the anecdotal pictures on the wall usually carried with them messages. There were changes in taste, however, in Victorian interiors: Baxters and Staffordshire portrait figures were out of fashion before Queen Victoria died. There was far less clutter.

The collapse of the great Victorian boom of the late 1860s and the early 1870s was one of the breaks between the middle and later Victorian years. So, too, was the collapse of high farming during the 1870s, which produced not only a marked drop in the incomes of farmers and landlords, but a change in the appearance of the countryside – far more pasture and far fewer fields of wheat, 'from corn to horn', as the saying went, with more market gardens, orchards and hopfields during the 1880s. And while foreign competition was driving some farmers to demand a return to protection, industrialists were also complaining of the threat from abroad. Nonetheless, the countryside was becoming an increasingly desirable place of retreat for businessmen, and working men were enjoying a wider range of cheap consumer goods from overseas than they had done earlier in the century.

There were other themes in the period, too; organized political parties; belated changes in school education; the multiplication of voluntary organizations; the growth of the professions in terms of numbers, organization and influence, which brought with it more expert – and more specialized – knowledge; the extension of the franchise in 1884 to village labourers; the rise of organized unskilled labour; the new demand not for limited, but for organic, reform; the impact on English politics of Irish home rule, which split Gladstone's Liberal Party in 1886 and left the Conservatives in power for the better part of two decades; local government re-organization, which led to the setting up of elected county councils in 1888; and changes in taxation, notably death duties in 1889.

'A country of respectful poor, though far less happy than where there are no poor to be respectful,' Bagehot had written, 'is nevertheless far more fitted for the best government.' But this was an axiom that fewer people now shared. Henry Mayhew had sketched the life of sections of the London poor in 1861, and poverty came under statistical survey in Charles Booth's multi-volume study of London life and labour, volume 1 of which appeared in 1889, the year of a great dock strike. There had been demonstrations of the unemployed also and rioting in Trafalgar Square.

The extension of school education was almost inevitable in such circumstances – and Morley thought it the most important national question of the day – but social and cultural anxieties persisted. George Gissing and Thomas Hardy were two novelists who expressed them. What was the difference between a 'market' and a 'public'? Was quality being debased? Were traditional values adequate? What were women's roles or women's rights? It was a woman, Elizabeth Chapman, who wrote in 1888 of a 'general revolt against authority in all departments of life which is the note of an unsettled, transitional, above all democratic age', while the prolific anatomist of his time, T. H. Escott, perceived 'old lines of demarcation' being obliterated, 'ancient landmarks of thought and faith removed . . . The idols which were revered but a little time ago have been destroyed.'

The Victorian critics of 'Victorian*ism*' were more determined and audible during the late Victorian years than they had been at the beginning. It was not only that 'self-help', 'character' and 'respectability', essential elements of Victorianism, began to be questioned, or that manifestations of these Victorian qualities in action, such as industry, abstinence and thrift, came under attack, but that the tone in which the qualities were discussed was very different from before. Thus, 'earnestness' was completely out of fashion during the early 1890s. Oscar Wilde could play with all its dubious associations in *The Importance of Being Earnest* (1895), subtitled 'a trivial comedy for serious people', and the novelist Samuel Butler could treat the Christian name Ernest more ironically still in *The Way of all Flesh*, written between 1873 and 1875, but not published until 1903. 'The virtues of the poor may be readily admitted,' Wilde and the socialist playwright George Bernard Shaw explained, 'and are much to be regretted. The best among the poor are never grateful. They are ungrateful, discontented and rebellious. They are quite right to be so.'

During the last decades of the century there was also a general 'reaction' against mid-Victorian styles when the designers of more simple 'Arts and Crafts' objects (the term 'Arts and Crafts' was coined in 1888) challenged eclecticism and when *art nouveau* appealed to a sophisticated minority. It was then also that a new generation of Victorian 'domestic' architects built homes in styles, including 'Queen Anne', into which older mid-Victorian objects just would not fit. These were bridge years in the making of the 'modern movement', although there was as much talk of *fin de siècle* as of *art nouveau* and all the other 'new' phenomena from the 'new woman' to the 'new unionism' or the 'new journalism'. It was not, however, that luxury disappeared from the world, for if the landed interest was facing increasing financial problems, a new 'plutocracy' was coming into its own. 'The great advantage and charm of the Morrisian method', wrote Walter Crane, a socialist disciple of William Morris whose influence remained strong, 'is that it lends itself to either simplicity or splendour.' You might have an oak trestle table and rush-bottomed chairs and a piece of matting or 'gold and lustre . . . jewelled light and walls hung with rich tapestry'.

The reign of Edward VII (1901–10) was to provide many further contrasts. Not only were many Victorian restraints removed, but increasing recognition of the inequalities of society produced sharper feelings of guilt and more organized forms of protest. After statisticians had probed poverty and popular newspapers had publicized their conclusions, Liberal politicians, returned to power with a huge majority in 1906, turned to social reform as an issue. The franchise question had dominated reform politics in the nineteenth century; now the time seemed ripe to make England, in the words of the new Liberal Prime Minister Campbell-Bannerman, 'less of a pleasure ground for the rich and more of a treasure house for the nation'. Yet in some respects social contrasts became more picturesque still. This was the golden age of the country weekend, of the London season, of the new business tycoon, of the Gaiety Girls (who sometimes married not tycoons but aristocrats), of the bustle and of the top hat, but, above all, of the golden sovereign. It was also an age, however, when real wages were falling and when farm labourers were worse off than many of the casual labourers in the docks. Maud Pember Reeves was the author of a much publicized book of 1913 entitled *Round About a Pound a Week*. Nearly eight million people were living on incomes of less than twenty-five shillings a week, 'underhoused, underfed and insufficiently clothed'.

It is the first age in history for which we have oral evidence, following Paul Thompson's tape-recorded interviews with 500 surviving Edwardians, but other kinds of evidence including snapshots are relevant too. It was a diplomat, however, the American ambassador, who wrote in 1913 – a year when there were many signs of protest on the part of working men and, above all, of militant women, the Suffragettes – 'the sad thing is the servile class'. Many historians have been impressed by the fierceness of social conflict in the years between Lloyd George's radical budget of 1909, which produced a constitutional crisis when it was thrown out by the Lords, and the outbreak of the First World War. Trust in the law seemed to be giving way to intransigent assertion of the will. 'They place the golden age behind them,' *The Times* wrote of many of its readers in 1909. For the ambassador, however, it was the 'abjectness' of the servile class which stood out. 'It does not occur to them that they . . . or their descendants . . . might ever become ladies and gentlemen.'

What, in retrospect, had been most remarkable through the breaks of Victoria's reign was a shared continuity of experience, finally to be broken in 1914, that defied social stratification. It was landmarked experience, too, stretching back self-consciously to the Great Exhibition, and reaching later climaxes in the two great Jubilees of 1887 and 1897, the latter, the Diamond Jubilee (a new concept), drawing in the Empire too. By that time the weekly magazine *Punch*, which since its first publication in 1841 had often caught the middle-class mood, was in no doubt that the queen herself represented continuity in a changing society and culture. No monarch after Elizabeth I had left such a powerful impression on contemporaries.

'We have come to regard the Crown as the head of our morality,' wrote Bagehot. 'We have come to believe that it is natural to have a virtuous sovereign.' But this was a new belief. During the Regency and the reign of George IV (1820–30), who left Brighton Pavilion as *his* memorial, almost the opposite had been taken for granted. Queen Caroline had been the heroine of the radical press, which like the radical poets, pointed to all George's deficiencies of character (and, at that time, appearance). His zest for the arts – and knowledge of them – meant little to his contemporaries, many of whom were shocked less by his politics than by his debauchery. There were, in fact, signs of 'Victorianism before Victoria' in his reign, like Dr Bowdler's carefully tidied 'family version' of Shakespeare, published in 1818. It was Queen Victoria herself, however, who gave her name to a new 'ism', probably uniquely among monarchs; and, despite rare signs of active republicanism during the 1870s, after she retired from public view following Albert's death, by the time of her own death in 1901 the editorial of a popular newspaper could read:

> The Queen is dead. No language can express the sense of personal loss ... Few of us, perhaps, have realized till now how large a part she had in the life of everyone of us; how the thread of her life, in binding and strengthening like a golden weft, the warp of the nation's progress, has touched and brightened the life of each and all her subjects.

The *Annual Register*, searching for precedents for such reactions, had to look as far back as Alfred.

At the core of Victorianism there had been what Gladstone, never the queen's favourite, called 'the rule of ought'. He introduced the twenty-ninth volume of his remarkable *Diary*, a key document for an understanding both of the private man and of the public figure (only recently published and superbly edited), with the two compelling lines:

> He spoke no word, he thought no thought
> Save by the steadfast rule of Ought.

For many Victorians, duty took precedence over inclination, and the moral law over the pursuit of pleasure or of power. Gladstone, who, like many of his eminent contemporaries, was a convinced Christian – before and after he became a Liberal – found the 'rule of ought' difficult to follow himself, and in trying to do so – or in pointing out to the public that his rival Disraeli did not – he neither neglected the opportunities nor avoided the perils of politics. Indeed, he became a popular politician, who bridged the transition to democracy on the platform and in print and lived long enough (1809–98) to become 'a Grand Old Man', lampooned as well as worshipped. Many of his most devoted supporters were Nonconformist chapelgoers, who, in supporting public causes, like the campaign against 'Turkish atrocities' which gripped Gladstone, demonstrated the operation of what was known at the time and since as 'the Nonconformist conscience'.

The motive of public service, local or national, was as active a force in Victorian society as the profit motive, and though it had not been absent in previous periods of history, many of its features were unmistakably Victorian. It not only guided individuals like Florence Nightingale, who set out to reform nursing, but mobilized voluntary organizations and pressure groups of every kind, such as the Royal Society for the Prevention of Cruelty to Animals, for foreigners a characteristic English institution, itself founded before Victoria came to the throne. 'In England', one of Wilde's characters was to exclaim, 'a man who can't talk morality twice a week to a large, popular, immoral audience is quite over as a serious politician.' Yet moral reform cut across the increasingly sharp dividing lines of party and could cross social and religious barriers also. The best-known of all social reformers was the Conservative seventh Earl of Shaftesbury, an Evangelical who was inspired by his religion to take up such causes as that of the factory workers battling for the Ten Hour Day and that of the chimney sweeps who were too young and weak to battle for themselves. He was also a prominent supporter of public health reform and of strict Sabbath observance. At his funeral in 1885 large numbers of the working men whom he had tried to help were in attendance.

If moral reform often united, religion often divided, and although judges insisted that Christianity was 'part and parcel of the law of the land' there were sharp divisions not only between Dissent and the Church of England but within the Church of England itself. From the 1830s onwards, Evangelicals, who did much to shape 'Victorianism', confronted high church Tractarians, some of whom, like John Henry Newman, moved 'over to Rome', to the alarm of their contemporaries. Other Tractarians considered disestablishment, a course favoured by militant dissenters. The debate on the nature of religious authority, which divided Evangelicals from Tractarians from the beginning of the reign, was extended in later years into dispute about styles of worship in the Church, plain or colourful, Protestant or Catholic. There were Protestant disturbances in Anglo-Catholic churches and savage cartoons in the press.

Yet both Evangelicals and Anglo-Catholics shared a fear of developing nineteenth-century science, which challenged most established versions of Christian orthodoxy; and it was left to a third 'Broad Church' party, neither Tractarian nor Evangelical, to seek to align itself with the liberal forces of the century. Meanwhile, religious 'agnostics' – a new term – found it possible to share Victorian moral values and rules of conduct while doubting Christian beliefs. Thus, the great non-Christian novelist, George Eliot, believed fervently that it was necessary to be good for the sake of Good, not for God. She once deeply impressed a Cambridge don by telling him 'with terrible earnestness' in the evening light of a college garden that whenever she heard talk of the three powerful Victorian words 'God, Immortality and Duty', she felt that the first was inconceivable, the second unbelievable, and the third peremptory and absolute.

The moral law spoke from inside; it was not imposed. Those Victorians who felt its demands were 'inner-directed' people, and the demands lost their absolute quality only when indifference took the place of opposition, when relativism became fashionable, and when the power of the 'unconscious', a word used by Samuel Butler, came to be appreciated. The perils of indifference, particularly in the cities and among the working classes were fully recognized both in the middle years of the century and at the end. In the new diocese of Manchester alone £1,500,000 might be spent between 1840 and 1876 to create parishes and build new churches, but as the one national religious census of the nineteenth century, that of 1851, showed, there were large numbers of people outside the influence both of Church and Chapel. Late nineteenth-century evidence, some of it collected by the statistician Charles Booth, corroborated the point.

Gospelling seemed a duty in such circumstances; nor was it only a religious activity. If Gladstone and Shaftesbury could turn liberalism and conservatism into gospels, T. H. Huxley, taking up Darwin's cause, could do the same with science. And so, also, late in the century, could socialists, who dreamed of a transformed society based not on privilege and power but on the acceptance of fundamental human principles of equality and justice. Indeed, for many years they were less inhibited than other politicians in their gospelling by reason of the fact that they were not associated with one single party. They were not forced, therefore, either to make compromises, as the Liberals were, or to depend on support from the vested interests of property, as the Conservatives did. The ethical note of socialism, its appeal to 'truth and righteousness', was strong. 'The meaningless drivel of the ordinary politician', Keir Hardie wrote in 1888, 'must now give place to the burning words of earnest men whose hearts are on fire with love of their kind.' The new society was to be characterized by solidarity (or 'brotherhood'), but within it all individuals would be able to realize their full individuality.

Even during the 'naughty 1890s', when conventional behaviour as well as mid-Victorian values were under attack, the 'rule of ought' finally held sway. In the very year when *The Importance of Being Earnest* was produced, Wilde's trial, the *cause célèbre* of the century, which centred on his homosexuality, not only destroyed him personally, but broke the spell of other rebel influences. After the trial all forms of 'decadence' and all attacks on 'respectability' were now pilloried. There was a huge gulf between the *Yellow Book*, the creation of the *avant garde*, and the new popular 'Yellow Press', as its critics called it. The weekly magazine *Punch* wrote definitively after the trial:

> Reaction's the reverse of retrograde,
> If we recede from dominant excesses,
> And beat retreat from novelists who trade
> On 'sex', from artists whose *chefs d'œuvres* are messes,
> 'Tis time indeed such minor plagues were stayed.

Then here's for cricket in this year of Grace,
Fair play all round, straight hitting and straight dealing
In letters, morals, arts, and commonplace
Reversion into type in deed and feeling
A path of true Reaction to retrace.

The sense that cricket, represented in these lines by W. G. Grace, 'the British lion', was quintessentially English was well brought out eight years later when G. K. Chesterton wrote that 'we have a much greater love of cricket than of politics' and 'C. B. Fry [another great cricketer] represents us better than Mr Chamberlain.' The phrase 'not cricket' had first been used in 1867.

If the intricate conventions of team games were linked in some sense with the 'rule of ought', the home was its shrine. 'The possession of an entire house', the author of the introduction to the 1851 census had remarked, 'is strongly desired by every Englishman, for it throws a sharp, well defined circle round his family and hearth – the shrine of his sorrows, joys and meditations.' The special place of the home, 'Home! Sweet Home!', was a continuing theme of the period. This was the first generation, G. K. Chesterton also wrote, 'that ever asked its children to worship the hearth without the altar'. The hearth featured prominently not only in cottage parlours and in the back rooms of palaces, but in brand new Gothic Victorian villas, where the middle classes lived out of view; and it was Ruskin, whose 'family life' was far odder and sadder than that of Queen Victoria, who described the family, with a note of longing, as 'the place of Peace; the shelter, not only from all injury but from all terror, doubt and division'. It was hailed as a refuge, too, from the competitiveness of business life.

What many Victorians *wanted* the home to be was in fact very different from the 'lodgings' in which many of them lived for part, at least, of their lives. 'Household happiness, gracious children, debtless competence, golden mean', sang the modern poet of the age, Alfred, Lord Tennyson, given his peerage under Gladstone, but in practice there was often a huge gap between ideal and reality, the kind of gap which was to make 'Victorianism' suspect as a code. The game of happy families was only a spectator game for some of the most eminent Victorians, and the kind of reverence that ran through Coventry Patmore's poem 'The Angel of the House', a hymn to conjugal love, was out of fashion by the end of the century. Family values within the working-class home are still largely hidden from the historian's view; there was a contrast there, however, between the 'respectable' and the 'rowdy', the latter drawn from childhood into the life of the streets.

The biggest city homes were detached villas, complete with lawns, shrubberies and, in the richest homes, conservatories, sometimes with pineapples growing in them. There were even bigger Victorian country houses, of course, some of the last such houses to be built – most of them used now for other purposes, like schools or nursing homes, or already pulled down – ornate piles, draughty and uncomfortable as well as imposing. In the towns, semi-detached houses (an invention of the nineteenth century) were commonplace, but so, too, were standard terraced houses and, in a few places, 'back-to-backs'. The smallest city and village homes were 'cruel habitations' packed into limited space, cramped as well as cluttered. Sir John Simon, a pioneer of public health, pointed out in his *Report on Sanitary Conditions of the City of London* in 1854 that 'it was no uncommon thing in a room of twelve foot square or less, to find three or five families styed together . . . in the promiscuous intimacy of cattle.' The terms 'overcrowding' and 'slum,' were new in the early nineteenth century, and there was increasing awareness of their reality towards the end of it.

Contrasts were evident at every point within the 'domestic economy'. The biggest divide was between those who employed domestic servants and those who did not; during the twenty years following the Great Exhibition the number of domestic servants increased by 60 per cent, twice the rate of increase of the population. Not all the families who did employ servants were rich by the standards of the day, but those who did not employ them were indubitably poor. The pattern varied. Great households employed elaborate hierarchies of servants, while upper- and middle-class families had their own different versions of the upstairs/downstairs divide. Lower middle-class families, dependent on one or two servants, had to make do within small space.

There were similar variations in patterns of manners, food and dress, although belief in the 'roast beef of old England', if not the ale that accompanied it, was shared across the social divides. In her successful, often reprinted and still famous *Book of Household Management* (1861) Mrs Isabella Beeton included dishes which depended not only on lavish ingredients, but also on servants for their preparation (and sometimes, given their scale, for their consumption). She was not writing for the working classes, and while there was a vaunted increase in working-class consumption of foodstuffs, particularly during the mid-Victorian and late Victorian years, the adulteration even of relatively cheap food, including bread and milk, was a serious and much publicized problem, and popular addiction to pickles and to beer has also been attributed – too easily perhaps – to decaying food and filthy water. Annual tobacco consumption, the social costs of which, unlike those of beer and of spirits, were not measured, had already risen from 14 oz to 1½ lb *per capita* between the 1830s and the late 1870s. Cigarette smoking was not common until the end of the century: it soon became ubiquitous.

It is necessary to peer through the cigar and pipe smoke into Victorian domestic life before taking Victorian sermons on the family and home, or books and novels about them, at their face value. Many of the biggest changes of the late Victorian years, leading through into the twentieth, related to demography. The hidden features of Victorian family patterns became the subject of a considerable literature for the Victorians themselves, more extensive and searching from the 1870s onwards. One particularly illuminating mid-Victorian book on sex, the first edition of which appeared in 1857, was Dr Acton's *Functions and Disorders of the Reproductive Organs in Youth, in Adult Age, and in Advanced Life, Considered in their Physiological, Social and Psychological Relations*. Acton, who has been described as the Samuel Smiles of continence, stated categorically – and he was not alone in this appraisal – that 'intellectual qualities are usually in an inverse ratio to the sexual appetites. It would almost seem as if the two were incompatible; the exercise of the one annihilating the other.' His choice of the adjective 'intellectual' was too restricted, for his prized quality of 'abstinence' was closely related to foresight, self-control and thrift, the qualities demanded not of the thinker but of the businessman. And there was a widespread opinion among Victorian – and Edwardian – middle-class observers that it was lack of foresight that most distinguished the working classes.

Leaving on one side questions of social circumstance, a moralizing attitude to sex was inevitable in an age when there was a moral colouring to all social argument. Yet as the nineteenth century went by, sexuality, even when repressed, emerged from a conspiracy of silence and became a part of social consciousness. The late Victorian revolt concerned itself with sex as well as with class (and with the relation between the two). It also seemed bound up with national destiny, so that Havelock Ellis, born in 1859, who wrote profusely about sex, could argue that it was 'not merely the instrument by which race is maintained and built up', but 'the foundation on which all dreams of the future must be erected'. Genetics became a topic of national importance.

It is not easy to relate either mid-Victorian ideals or late Victorian criticisms of these ideals to practice. While 'the woman' was apparently 'venerated' within the mid-Victorian home at least as much as the queen was in the nation as a whole, the pedestal on which she was placed was false. Women had to be 'pure': chaste before marriage and 'modest' after marriage. Their sexuality was explicitly denied, and annual pregnancies guaranteed their dependence.

> Man for the field, woman for the hearth,
> Man for the sword and for the needle she:
> Man with the head and woman with the heart,
> Man to command and woman to obey.

The father who expressed these thoroughly pre-industrial sentiments in Tennyson's 'The Princess' was a good Victorian. Yet the influence of prostitution, which was acknowledged as 'the great social evil' in the mid-Victorian years (contemporary estimates of the number of prostitutes varied widely from between 30,000 to 368,000), derived not from a different but from the same male moral code, a code that long preceded the Victorians. There were many 'secret lives', some of the most active of which often crossed class lines. While bachelors who married late might turn to a prostitute, married men with enough money might take a mistress. 'Fallen women' were the 'victims'. Rebel voices openly attacked this double standard of morality in the late nineteenth century, and a 'social purity alliance', led by Josephine Butler, was formed to campaign against the Contagious Diseases Acts. Their suspension in 1883 (three years later they were repealed) was followed by a Criminal Law Amendment Act in 1884 which set out to suppress brothels, raised the age of consent for girls to sixteen, and introduced eleven new penalties against male homosexual behaviour. There was to be further tightening-up of legislation in a Vagrancy Act of 1898 and a second Criminal Law Amendment Act in 1912.

In marriage the dominating position of the husband was buttressed, as it had been in previous centuries, by the law, and it was not until 1870 and 1882 that the Married Women's Property Acts were passed, granting women rights to property whether secured before marriage or after. (Political rights were not to come until after the Suffragette agitation had passed its peak.) The first of a chain of divorce acts, the Matrimonial Causes Act of 1857, which set up secular divorce courts, had authorized divorce on different terms for those few men and women who could afford it. A husband needed only to show evidence of his wife's adultery: a wife had to show evidence of other marital failings too, like cruelty or desertion. For social and economic reasons, as well as religious ones, the number of divorces remained low throughout the Victorian years, affecting only 0.2 per cent of all marriages at the end of the century.

There was clearly a great variety of relationships between husbands and wives. In particular, there were significant class and local differences; and there may well have been less restrictive attitudes to pleasure or enjoyment in working-class than in middle-class (if not in aristocratic) families by the end of the century. Nevertheless, artisans were marrying later, illegitimacy rates had fallen since the mid-nineteenth century, and rates of first pregnancy conceived before marriage dropped from 40 per cent to 20 per cent between the early nineteenth and early twentieth centuries.

In general, Victorian families were big. In 1851 their average size was 4.7, roughly the same as it had been in the seventeenth century, but the 1½ million couples who married during the 1860s, which the historian G. M. Young described as the best decade in English history to have been brought up in, raised the figure to 6.2. Only one out of eight families had one or two children, while one in six had ten or more, so that the counsel 'little children should be seen and not heard' was prudent rather than simply authoritarian advice.

The most obvious of the many new 'facts' that stood out in nineteenth-century England was the growth of population and its concentration in increasingly segregated districts. The decennial statistics are almost as compelling as the imposing studio-posed photographs of family groups and crowded shopping streets, another new kind of evidence for the social historian. Total population rose from 16.9 million in 1851 to 30.8 million in 1901, increasing at a faster rate than that of Germany, Italy or Russia, and at a far faster rate than that of France.

Families might have been larger still had not infant mortality remained high, although, as it was, one out of two Englishmen in 1871 was under the age of twenty-one and four out of five under forty-five. The aged Victorians with their great beards were a small minority, although these mid-Victorian years were undoubtedly peak years for the *pater familias*, years of potency and fecundity, years of pride more than of fear.

At the beginning of the century there had been national fears of over-population, and Thomas Malthus, clergyman, political economist and moralist, who believed fervently that social measures like outdoor relief for the poor or indiscriminate alms-giving would add to demographic – and human – problems, was widely quoted in early Victorian England. The tough new Poor Law of 1834 was not directly inspired by him, but many of its defenders were 'Malthusians' who wanted discipline to be enforced in workhouses, the often terrifying places which the Victorians described simply as 'institutions' and in which all types of poor were confined. By the middle of the nineteenth century, however, in defiance of Malthus, family size had reached its peak, and by the late Victorian period there were already scattered fears of under-population, which were to grow during the twentieth century.

We know little about the crucial change in late Victorian demography – a fall in the birth rate during the 1870s, the decade of Victorian uncertainty. The rate, which had been nearly stable for half a century at around 35 per 1,000, fell between 1875 and 1880 – without any obvious new display of what Malthus called 'moral restraint' – before falling more sharply still to around 24 per 1,000 in the years before 1914. By the last decade of the nineteenth century, average family size had fallen to 4.3 and by the outbreak of the First World War to 2.3. There had been a steady rise in the mean age of marriage, in the proportion of childless marriages and in the percentage of people who did not marry at all.

What kept total population up – it increased substantially between 1871 and 1911 – was a steady fall in the death rate from 1875 onwards. By the end of the century it had dropped (if patchily) from around 22 per 1,000 to 14 per 1,000, while life expectancy had risen from forty to forty-four for men and forty-two to forty-eight for women. A significant rise in the proportion of the population over sixty-five was registered in the Census of 1911. There was no Malthusian explanation for this phenomenon either, since it clearly reflected a measure of social, if not individual control, which was no more envisaged by Malthus than the great increase in economic productivity achieved in the nineteenth century. Other factors were clearly at work in the change of attitudes to family size from the 1870s onwards. Improved living standards and rising material expectations seem to be among them, and family budgets reveal some of the underlying economics.

Nutritionists as well as economists and sociologists have analysed both what the Victorians ate and how much of it. From the late 1870s onwards, cheap American corn began to arrive in the country in large quantities, along with refrigerated meat and fruit from Australia and New Zealand, and in a period when both farmers and businessmen were complaining of depression, standards of living rose higher than they had ever done. The change began each day, as Victorian writers frequently pointed out, with the food on the breakfast table – with eggs and bacon as staple fare for the middle classes – and went on through tea, high or low, to multi-course dinners or fish-and-chip suppers. The poor were eating better as well as the rich. The annual *per capita* consumption of sugar, which had increased from 18 lb to 35 lb between the queen's accession and 1860, rose to 54 lb in 1870–99 and 85 lb in 1900–10; that of tea, which along with beer had now become a national drink, went up from 1½ lb, first to 4¼ lb and then to 6 lb.

Yet the key to the explanation of change in family size is not hidden in menus or in bills, or, in the case of working-class families, in lost calculations about how much children cost (from 1876 they were compelled to go to school) and how much they could earn. More important was the growing sense that children were not just 'sent by God' and that the number of children within each family could be 'controlled' in relation to circumstances. Work and leisure patterns and considerations concerning the upbringing and care of the individual child were part of these circumstances. So, too, was religion, although it was no longer the determining guide to conduct for large numbers of people.

The term 'birth control' was coined just before the First World War, not in England but across the Atlantic. Death control had come earlier as a response, in part at least, to the terrifying statistics of differential mortality in the 1830s and 1840s. Given that people in different areas and social groups had such enormous differences in their chances of death, could not the gap between their fortunes be narrowed? The

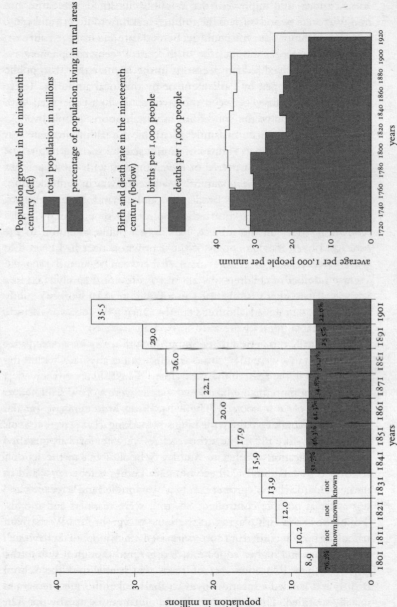

Population in the nineteenth century

Population growth in the nineteenth century (left)

☐ total population in millions

■ percentage of population living in rural areas

Birth and death rate in the nineteenth century (below)

☐ births per 1,000 people

■ deaths per 1,000 people

'sanitary idea' and improvements in public health in the early, and mid-Victorian period, such as the Public Health Acts of 1848 and 1869, had a moral dimension: you could get behind Fate and manage your own destiny. In retrospect, the quest for 'birth control' seems complementary, although it involved hidden decisions in the home rather than public decisions in the open by Parliament or by the local authority. There were links, of course, between the two, as doctors concerned with public health exposed the conditions in which poorer people lived.

Given the multiplicity of family decisions, the fall in birth rate was bound to be differential. Figures of family size by social group reveal different chronological patterns of development, with the upper and professional middle classes apparently leading the way in contraception. The trial in 1876 of Charles Bradlaugh, spokesman for the secularists, and of Annie Besant, the future theosophist, for republishing Charles Knowlton's tract on the subject, had drawn public attention to the issue, and over 200,000 copies of the Knowlton tract had been sold within five years. For couples married between 1890 and 1899 the average number of children was 2.8 in a professional family, 3.04 in a white-collar worker's family, 4.85 in a skilled manual worker's family and 5.11 in an unskilled labourer's family. During the following decade the comparable figures were 2.05, 1.95, 3.24 and 4.09.

It was during this period that compulsory schooling introduced a set of influences that were to become as significant as any from within the family. Indeed, the tasks of the new Board Schools were conceived of as social even more than educational: pupils were to be disciplined to accept their place in society. There had been little emphasis on the regulation of conduct in the wide range of working-class private schools in existence before 1870, where the teachers were not formally qualified – moral inculcation was left to Sunday Schools – but in the schools controlled by religious or other voluntary bodies before 1870, and in the new Board Schools, 'proper conduct' was instilled and 'street culture' was as far as possible controlled. So, too, were manners and morals. 'Found boys and girls playing in the same playground,' a Rotherham school log book recorded in 1890, 'witnessed much indecent behaviour'.

Secondary and higher education, reorganized though it was in the important new Education Act of 1902, which abolished the School Boards and handed education over to the local authorities, remained socially stratified. The grammar schools, given new scope by the Act, took in a limited number of local boys, some of ability demonstrated in scholarship examination, some of them as fee-payers, while the 'public schools', many of them explicitly high church or Evangelical, fed by 'preparatory schools', educated a segregated section of the community along lines designed to assure that those leaving them would be 'gentlemen'. Their tasks, too, were pre-eminently social. As a writer in the *Athenaeum* put it in 1860, they were in harmony

> with a certain rude, vague, yet quite intelligible something, which may be called the English Scheme of Life. The Great Endowed Schools are less to be considered as educational agencies, in the intellectual sense, than as social agencies.

By the end of the century the public schools, some of which had turned team sports into schools of values, even religions, had produced many Flashmans, as described in *Tom Brown's Schooldays*, Thomas Hughes's gripping novel set at Rugby School. They flourished alongside the kind of spiritual and political leaders that Dr Arnold, its great headmaster, had set out to produce, and the middle-of-the-way boys like Tom Brown himself. All three types found opportunities for themselves on the frontiers of empire as well as in the City and in the professions at home, including the Church. Wherever they went, 'good' or 'bad', they represented above all else 'the English scheme of life'.

II THE DIVIDES OF WAR

War is everywhere, and is more and more conceived as an end in itself.
The Nation, 7 October 1916

I am not getting any new flags though, only using an old one I had left
over from the last war.
Woman overheard in a bus, *Mass-Observation*, 1945

But the old world was restored and we returned
To the dreary field and workshop, and the immemorial feud
Of rich and poor: Our victory was our defeat.
Herbert Read, *To a Conscript of 1940*, 1946

Never such innocence again.
Philip Larkin, 'MCMXIV' in *The Whitsun Weddings*, 1964

When Winston Churchill, educated at Harrow, wrote that 'the story
of the human race is War', this was before the First World War, when
he was directly involved for a time in the conduct of operations and
long before the Second World War, during which he emerged as one
of the greatest twentieth-century war leaders. Yet in 1900, even though
English troops were fighting in South Africa, led by ex-public school-
boys, few people could have forecast that war and peace would be a main
theme in twentieth-century world history. Bagehot had represented the
views of many nineteenth-century Englishmen when he had argued
earlier in the century that modern society had moved from the 'fighting
age', a relic of feudalism, into the 'age of discussion'.

There was not much English experience to suggest otherwise. The
great European wars of the twentieth century, both of which became

world wars, were very different in scale and character from the 'little wars' of the nineteenth century, in some of which Churchill had been personally involved as a young man. The latter had been fought along the lines of many of the wars of the Roman Empire, by small numbers of regular soldiers against hostile forces on distant frontiers (Sikhs, Afghans, Ashanti, Zulus and Sudanese). Sometimes they were punitive expeditions to enforce law and order, sometimes they were more ambitious campaigns to annexe territory. As little theory was applied to warfare as to industry, and the armed forces themselves had undergone only very limited changes until the last decades of the century. At the close of the protracted Napoleonic Wars, the last great struggle, there had been 220,000 men in the regular Army. By 1840 that number had fallen to just over 100,000, although it climbed back to 200,000 during the last decades of the century following major War Office reforms carried out by Edward Cardwell, a staunch supporter of Gladstone, between 1868 and 1874. The purchase of Army commissions was abolished, short service enlistment was introduced, and the War Office itself was re-organized. Nevertheless, the emphasis was still placed on traditional continuities: 'Great Britain has produced a race of heroes who, in moments of danger and terror, have stood as "firm as the rocks of their native shores",' wrote 'A Voice from the Ranks' in the popular book *A Soldier's Experience* at the end of the century.

The Royal Navy remained the senior service and the guardian of the *Pax Britannica*. Tennyson described its importance for England:

> Her dauntless army scattered, and small,
> Her island – myriads fed from alien lands –
> The fleet of England is her all-in-all.

Yet, while the Royal Navy had recognized the significance of technological change, naval strategy had not been re-examined during the 1860s and 1870s in the light either of new technology or of the fact that the more densely populated country was more vulnerable than ever before to blockade. It was only in 1884, immediately following the widening of the franchise, that a supplementary naval appropriations Act was passed. This introduced a five-year plan of naval build-ups, the prelude to the Naval Defence Act of 1889 which authorized the building of eight large and two small battleships and heralded an age of naval expansion.

By then, there had been war between France and Germany in 1870. Britain had remained neutral, but between then and the end of the century there had been a significant growth both in war expenditure and in the popular appeal of militarism. In 1900 'soldiers of the Queen' were engaged in the most protracted and controversial of the colonial wars, not against 'native tribes', but against white Boers in South Africa. And this war pointed to general questions which could not be answered easily – the low physical fitness and educational standards of the recruits; the need for 'efficiency' in production; the links between war and social policy; the role of public opinion and of propaganda; and, above all, the horror rather than the glory of battle. 'Our days are spent with reading our papers ever clamouring for more action,' wrote an English friend of Alfred (later Viscount) Milner, Britain's leading representative in South Africa, in November 1899, 'our nights in dreaming of all that is and is to be . . . The war affects all, rich and poor alike. All have friends and relations in it.' A few months later, however, another knowledgeable correspondent was suggesting that the 'English public' was war-weary: 'the heroics are over'.

There was a growing sense during the Boer War that 'the Empire's destinies for good and evil' were 'in the hands of the masses of the people.' Yet crucial decisions relating to war and peace between 1902 and 1914 were taken behind the scenes, many of them inside the newly established Committee of Imperial Defence, which was described in 1909 by A. H. Asquith, the Liberal Prime Minister, as a 'useful, indeed an invaluable addition to our constitutional machinery'. The origins of the Great War, difficult to disentangle, were located in Europe, not in distant lands overseas, and the public was not aware of the dangerous implications of an evolving network of diplomatic alignments which guaranteed that if war did break out it would not be restricted war, as it had been in 1870 or 1900. It was the naval race between Britain and Germany that hit the headlines in the popular press, and it was at this time that the word 'crisis' entered popular language.

Opinions about international issues were as divided as they were about empire. The Nonconformist conscience was strong, but so were undercurrents of jingoism. And there was an increasing literature of violence, including a popular invasion and resistance literature which, looked at in retrospect, helped to prepare opinion for war. As the young philosopher Bertrand Russell put it, 'the barbaric substratum of human nature was being tapped.' There was flirtation with violence in Britain, too, between 1910 and 1914, in England as well as in Ireland, so that it has been possible to interpret the arrival of war not as a surprise, but as a consummation.

The small regular army with which Britain entered the war, backed by a large contingent of reservists brought back to the colours who constituted 60 per cent of the first Expeditionary Force, was quite inadequate; and although a 'New Army' created during the first fourteen months of war – in response to the appeals of a charismatic Secretary for War, Lord Kitchener – eventually attracted over 2,250,000 volunteers, it was still not big enough. And very soon it was losing its officers. By the end of 1914 the dead included six peers, sixteen baronets, six knights and eighty-four sons of knights. After a series of compromises, general conscription was accepted in the early summer of 1916, and by 1918, when the war ended, the Army's total strength, which had been 164,000 in August 1914, had risen to a remarkable peak of 5,363,352; indeed, there were far more men in the newly formed Royal Air Force alone (30,127 officers and 263,410 other ranks) than there had been soldiers in 1914. The men were backed with animals and internal combustion engines: the animal ration strength rose from 27,500 in 1914 to 895,770 in 1918, while petrol consumption in France alone rose during the same period from 250,000 gallons a month in 1914 to 10,500,000. 'This has been called an engineers' war', wrote the 'Temporary Lieutenant' author of *The Motor Bus in War* in 1918, 'and petrol is the key to it.' The horses, however, were still in the thick of battle.

The relentless demand for munitions as well as for men, animals and machinery forced government to intervene increasingly in the management of the economy. The taking over of the railways in 1914, to be administered 'not by government but for the government', was the first of many wartime limitations on private enterprise, and by the end of the war large new government departments, like shipping and food, had been set up, some of them almost overnight. What has been called 'a command spiral' took the place of the laws of supply and demand, leading inevitably from one government intervention to another. The result was a great increase in the number of civil servants, although power at the top, particularly after 1917, was frequently in the hands of businessmen turned politicians.

Attempts were made to control the land as well as industry, and Milner of South Africa was appointed Chairman of the Committee on Agriculture in the summer of 1915. In practice County War Agricultural Committees were not very effective, and one useful wartime change, the introduction of 'summer time' in May 1916, met with farmers' protests. By 1917, when there was only about three weeks' food supply in the country and the Women's Land Army was set up, two-thirds of the industrial workforce were subject to governmental regulations. There was also a system of food rationing, limited in scope but bureaucratic in organization. A *Punch* cartoon of 1918 with the caption *David in Rhonddaland* showed David Lloyd George, Asquith's successor as Prime Minister, arguing with Lord Rhondda, businessman turned Minister of Food. 'I'm often away from home,' says David. 'How do I get sugar?' 'You don't,' replies the 'Mad Grocer' (Rhondda). 'You fill up a form.' 'But I *have* filled up a form,' David insists. 'Then you fill up another form,' the Mad Grocer tells him.

Lloyd George had been appointed Prime Minister in 1916 after Asquith's government collapsed, and it was he more than any other politician who drew businessmen into government. It was he who had been in charge of munitions, the sinews of war, before 1916, and it was he who had been taken up by the press as the right war leader. Both he and Asquith were Liberals, although from 1915 onwards the governments they headed were Coalition governments. Liberalism, indeed, was one of the casualties of the war. 'War is not conducted according to the rules of liberty,' wrote one well-known Liberal in 1918, 'although the war has been the only means by which liberty can be preserved.' The Defence of the Realm Act (DORA) of 1914, extended in 1915 and 1916, involved a degree of government interference with individual freedoms which would have been thought intolerable before 1914. In such circumstances military conscription was a particularly difficult issue for the Liberals to have to face.

So too were wartime economic controls, bringing to an end decades of free trade and low direct taxation. In 1914 the highest rate of income tax had been 1s. 2d. in the pound, so that even the richest taxpayer was not called upon to pay more than one-seventeenth of his income to the State: by 1918 the standard rate of income tax was 5s. in the pound, and there were now six times as many taxpayers. Even then, heavy borrowing was necessary, and Liberals were not alone in expressing profound anxiety about the post-war burdens this would carry with it. 'We have started this war,' Charles Trevelyan (brother of the historian) said in a speech of 1915, 'on the assumption that our resources are so vast that we can do anything that occurs to us.' And by 1918 the national debt was four times the 1914 figure. Indeed, as late as 1932 the burden of debt was twelve times greater than it had been when war started.

It would have been no consolation to most staunch pre-1914 Liberals that one of General Haig's officers could write in 1916:

> Here at GHQ. . . nearly every one of the ramifications of civil law and life has its counterpart in the administrative departments . . . Food supply, road and rail transport, law and order, engineering, medical work, the Church, education, postal service, even agriculture, and for a population bigger than any single unit of control (except London) in England.

One prominent left-wing Liberal economist, J. A. Hobson, whose writings on imperialism had influenced the exiled Russian leader Lenin, believed after 1914 that militarism would remain an enemy in the peacetime future. It was at the centre, he claimed, of a 'vicious circle of Improperty' along with 'Imperialism, Protectionism, Legalism, Distractions and Emollients (Charity, Sport and Drink etc.), Regulative Socialism, Conservatism, State Absolutism, Authoritarianism (Church, School, Press etc.) and Bureaucracy'. Not many Englishmen, however, thought in such terms. In fact, there were soldiers and civilians who wanted more 'Distraction and Emollients' rather than less. All the great hotels and restaurants were thronged 'for feasting and dancing'. So too were night clubs. 'Every girl has her man in khaki,' a Cambridge professor of economics wrote to the editor of the *Economist*.

The craving for 'Distractions and Emollients' was an inevitable by-product of the kind of war which was waged. Many soldiers had gone to war eagerly in 1914 to the sound of cheering crowds; some were romantic about it. In Rupert Brooke's phrase: 'Now God be thanked who has matched us with this hour.' Yet the reality of war in the trenches soon dispelled all hints of romance. For years there was stalemate since neither side, hard though it tried (and with appalling losses), had sufficient force to break through. There were 6,000 miles of trenches, numbered by sections and given names like Piccadilly, Hyde Park Corner and Marble Arch by the soldiers serving in them, not only to distinguish them but to try to 'humanize' them. The confined horizons of the trenches enclosed a world of mud and barbed wire, and it seemed sinister when map references were exchanged for names. When Wyndham Lewis first heard the name Passchendaele, where there were to be 144,000 casualties in 1917, he felt from its suggestions of 'splashiness' and 'passion' that it was 'pre-ordained' that 'nonsense' would come to its full flower there. 'Evil and incarnate fiend alone can be the master of this war,' the painter Paul Nash had written in 1915. 'No glimmer of God's hand is seen anywhere.' 'Everywhere the work of God is spoiled by the hand of man,' wrote young Second Lieutenant William Ratcliffe, who was killed in 1916.

Nash's war-torn landscapes contrast sharply with his paintings of the peaceful English countryside. Only the poppies were common to both, but in Flanders fields, where they grew prolifically, 'sunset and sunrise' were 'blasphemies'. In his verses the war poet Isaac Rosenberg huddled together the men in the Flanders fields. Post-war cemetery keepers were to place crosses over their graves neatly, side by side, in rows:

> Iron are our lives
> Molten right through our youth
> A burnt space through ripe fields
> A fair mouth's broken tooth.

The slaughter was appalling, although the English lost far fewer men than the French. And while it is true that war deaths among the troops, estimated at some 850,000 soldiers, were fewer than the number of emigrants from the British Isles in the decade before the war, such a demographic statistic did not matter. Over time, it was said, people began to get used to the deaths, a terrifying form of adaptation. Yet as families were broken up and communities ravaged, a pall of grief hung over all sections of society. Asquith himself lost a brilliant son, killed in the Somme; almost one in five Oxford students were killed. Wives lost their husbands, sweethearts their fiancés; some women were never to marry. Personal relationships were irretrievably affected – not always, of course, for ill – and there were breaks in the continuity of management in nearly every local and national institution. These were the great divides of the twentieth century: one writer has compared them to the Grand Canyon.

Death, which was a matter of luck, was not the only human sacrifice to a new Moloch. Injured, gassed, shell-shocked, blinded men staggered back from the wars to a life that would never be the same again. Of the 8,000,000 men who were mobilized, some 2,000,000 were wounded, and in 1922 more than 900,000 war pensions were being paid out. In 1928 forty-eight special mental hospitals were still catering for over 60,000 victims of shell shock. The most popular poem of the First World War during the 1920s and 1930s, Laurence Binyon's 'For the Fallen', repeated annually in the shadows of the new local 'war memorials', linked memories and realities:

> They shall not grow old, as we that are left grow old:
> Age shall not weary them, nor the years condemn
> At the going down of the sun and in the morning
> We will remember them.

It was written only seven weeks after the beginning of the war, before the extent of the sacrifice was appreciated. A still more forceful reminder of the level of sacrifice are the far later lines by Henry Reed:

> When war is spoken of
> I find
> The war that was called Great
> Invades the Mind.

'Cheerful' letters from the front, duly censored, deliberately concealed the truths of the war, although some soldiers must have revealed them privately on leave in 'dear old Blighty'. The historian R. H. Tawney, then Sergeant Tawney, who took part in the assault on the Somme in July 1916, complained of the popular stereotype of 'the Tommy' as 'a merry assassin, invariably cheerful, revelling in the excitement of war, rejoicing in the opportunity of a scrap'. There were such Tommies but truth about others was revealed in public only after the war ended, in books like *Her Privates We*, whose author concealed his identity, putting only his number on the title page, 'Private 19022'. There were tough as well as tender memories.

This was lyric, not epic, war, although Haig and the generals would obviously have preferred the latter. The most they could achieve was a kind of stoical silence, while Wilfred Owen's deeply felt poems, such as the 'Anthem for Doomed Youth' – though his attitudes were not shared by all soldiers – can still speak across the divides of time and place:

> What passing bells for those who die as cattle?
> Only the monstrous anger of the guns,
> Only the stuttering rifle's rapid rattle
> Can patter out their hasty orisons.

Primitive horror was bursting through disciplined routines, and the sardonic soldiers' war-songs like 'The Bells of Hell' are very different from 'Tipperary', which was written just before the war began.

Human sacrifice was more real than technical advance during the war. Zeppelins were used by Germans and not by the British – there were around forty raids – and it was the Germans also who in 1917 began to launch aeroplane attacks on London, producing a feeling that 'the raiders have London at their mercy'. At the front, tanks (another new weapon) were used in numbers by the British only in 1917 after church bells were rung (prematurely) to celebrate their effectiveness at Cambrai. The claim of the press lord, Northcliffe, now raised to great power, that the men of the tank crews were 'dare devils' entering upon their task 'in a sporting spirit with the same cheerful enthusiasm as they would show for football' must not be forgotten. Yet one of the most memorable – and powerful – images left over from the war remains that of Siegfried Sassoon's tank rolling down the stalls of a theatre in London:

> I'd like to see a tank come down the stalls
> Lurching to rag-time tunes or Home Sweet Home
> And there'd be no more jokes in music halls
> To mock the riddled corpses round Bapaume.

Rag-time rhythms had come in before the war, along with those of the tango – a hundred years before there had been the waltz – but it needed the war itself to create a sense of black comedy.

Many civilians were anxious to share the burden of war, and voluntary organizations contributed substantially to the war effort, handing over to the soldiers 1,742,947 mufflers, 1,574,155 pairs of mittens, 6,145,673 hospital bags, 12,258,536 bandages, 16,000,000 books and 232,599,191 cigarettes. The cheap cigarettes ('fags') they supplied were as much a part of the life of the trenches as the barbed wire, and one of the main army chaplains was named 'Woodbine Willie' after a cigarette. Meanwhile, the Salvation Army, a product of the 'darkest England' of the 1880s, was as active a social agency among the troops as it had been in city slums before 1914. But the psychological gap between 'civvy street' and the 'soldiers' war' was far wider between 1914 and 1918 than it was to be during the 'people's war' from 1939 (or at least from 1940) to 1945.

Just as big a psychological gap bedevilled relations between politicians and generals. 'Politicians gave no credit to the Generals,' wrote another press peer, Lord Beaverbrook, owner of the *Daily Express* and sharpest of all writers on the political scene of that time. 'The Generals denounced the politicians. Soldiers and sailors serving in the Forces had little confidence in either. The public had no heroes.' In 1917 and 1918 there were many signs of war weariness, for it proved difficult to discern, amid what a liberal periodical called 'the stormy welter of waste and woe', any 'stream of cause and effect' pointing the war effort towards 'a determinate conclusion'. The entry of the Americans into the war in 1917 brought with it, however, new talk of war aims as well as indispensable human reinforcement; and revolution in Russia, culminating in the Bolshevik victory of October 1917, directed attention to fundamental social issues. It was in such circumstances that politicians now began to talk more and more of 'reconstruction', of changing society after the war. 'No such opportunity has ever been given to any nation before – not even by the French Revolution,' Lloyd George proclaimed. 'The nation is now in molten state . . . We cannot return to the old ways, the old abuses, the old stupidities.'

Already, however, through war experience itself – learning how to improve welfare conditions in the munitions factories for example – issues of social policy had been raised. Meanwhile, trade unionists in particular, most of them patriotic supporters of the war, had urged the need to deal sensibly with social discontent if war production were to be maximized. In 1914 their leaders had urged both employees and their own rank and file 'to make a serious attempt . . . to reach an amicable settlement before resorting to a strike or lock-out,' but as the war effort intensified, such a self-denying ordinance was difficult to maintain, at least at the shop-floor level. Shop stewards were a new force, forging links across the country, and unrest was not stilled when Lloyd George included Labour ministers in his government. One of them, George Barnes, enumerated the reasons for continuing unrest: 'the feeling that there has been inequality of sacrifice, that the government has broken solemn pledges, that the trade union officials are no longer to be relied upon, and that there is a woeful uncertainty as to the industrial future.'

The War Emergency Workers' National Committee of 1914, designed 'to protect working-class interests during the war', was by 1917 waging a 'conscription of riches' campaign, which culminated in the insertion in the new Labour Party constitution, adopted in February 1918, of the unequivocally socialist Clause 4:

> to secure for the producers by hand and brain the full fruits of their industry and the most equitable distribution thereof that may be possible upon the basis of the common ownership of the means of production and the best obtainable system of popular administration and control of each industry or service.

Arthur Henderson, the busy Secretary of the Labour Party, had left Lloyd George's cabinet in August 1917 after sharp differences on foreign policy (in particular, in relation to international labour solidarity and attitudes to post-revolutionary Russia), and the break was to have even longer-term implications than Clause 4. As A. J. P. Taylor has argued, it represented 'the real parting of the ways between Lloyd George and "the people"'. Labour gave notice to quit. And although the reconstructed Labour Party (now with individual as well as corporate members and with a firm constituency base) won only fifty-seven seats when Lloyd George was swept back to power in the General Election of 1918, its electoral position was far stronger than it had been in 1914. Indeed, within a few years it was to take the place of the Liberal Party as the second party in the State.

Labour's position was stronger in other ways also. The Representation of the People Act of 1918 guaranteed for the first time in history a genuinely democratic franchise, and an increase in trade-union membership to a peak of more than six million provided the reconstituted party with a corresponding increase of funds. Moreover, in the long run there was no disadvantage in the fact that the party leadership included men who had opposed war in 1914 and who had been counted among the much pilloried conscientious objectors when 'super-patriotism' was at its height. During the uneasy 1920s there was to be a sharp revulsion against 'super-patriotism' itself.

It was possible by then to see many of the other wartime social changes in perspective. One of them was the changing role of women, some of whom benefited from the 1918 extension of the franchise, which gave the vote to women householders and wives of householders over the age of thirty. This cautious reform opened the gates; and nine years later, when it had been demonstrated that the peacetime female electorate was not going to subvert the constitution, women secured the vote on the same terms as men. Most pre-war Suffragettes had responded at once in 1914 to the call of the 'war effort': 'this great war,' Christabel Pankhurst had written, 'is God's vengeance on the people who held women in subjection.' And by 1917 the influential journalist J. L. Garvin could write, 'Time was when I thought men alone maintained the State. Now I know that the modern State must be dependent on women and men alike.' In the same year it was Asquith, pre-war English enemy and target of the Suffragettes, who moved a parliamentary motion calling for an early bill to effect a recommendation of a recent all-party conference 'to confer some measure of woman suffrage'. The role of women had been greatly extended during the war: some had worked as nurses at the front, far more at the bench in munitions factories, and many others in offices and in occupations hitherto closed to them. Yet by 1921 they constituted exactly the 29 per cent of the workforce that they had done ten years before, and despite the vote which they now had won they were not to transform politics.

Perhaps the biggest changes in the role of women were evident in the home rather than the factory or the office, for the struggle for food could be as relentless as the struggle in the trenches. Two weeks before Christmas 1917, *The Times* reported long rows of women queuing for margarine outside multiple-shops in London, some with infants in their arms and many with children at their skirts. Bread and potatoes were never rationed, but staple prices had to be subsidized in 1917, and potatoes were often in short supply. The first commodity to be rationed was sugar in January 1918, after *Punch* had invoked a highbrow nineteenth-century ghost:

> O Matthew Arnold! You were right:
> We need more Sweetness and more Light;
> For till we break the brutal foe
> Our sugar's short, our lights are low.

Weekly *per capita* consumption of sugar fell between 1914 and 1918 from 1.49 to 0.93 lb. and of 'butchers' meat', which was rationed by coupon later in 1918, from 2.36 to 1.53 lb. yet despite the grumbles about short supplies and increase in prices – and they were not confined to the middle classes – the calorie intake almost kept up to the pre-1914 level, and Englishmen ate much better than their opponents. Indeed, some working-class English women and children were better fed than they had been before 1914 due to improved employment, canteen meals and easier access to the weekly pay packet. An official report of 1918 noted that School Medical Officers in London had observed that 'the percentage of children found in a poorly nourished condition is less than half the percentage in 1913.'

A social policy spiral directed government inexorably from one kind of intervention to another, just as the command economy did in relation to economic policy. Lord Rhondda insisted that there should be a new post-war ministry before he took up the controversial post of Minister of Food. And when in 1919 Christopher Addison, a doctor and one of Lloyd George's aides-de-camp in the 'reconstruction' campaign, introduced the bill creating the new Ministry of Health, he glanced sideways at education and drew special attention to physically unfit children in the elementary schools: 'We have them in every age and in every year, not a company or a brigade, but an army.' Addison was one of a group of Liberals who later joined the Labour Party. One of his colleagues in the 'reconstruction team', the businessman Seebohm Rowntree, pre-war analyst of poverty in York and advocate of new housing policies, remained faithful to Lloyd George.

By 1918 it was recognized that children as well as women were in need of increased attention on the part of the State as a result of both the experience and effects of war. It may well be that their wartime role and that of 'adolescents', a term not then in general use, changed even more than that of women as the number of children of fourteen or under at work quadrupled. It certainly seemed to need new definition, and so too did the word 'juvenile', which had meant 'a little wage earner' and was now redefined to mean a 'workman and citizen in training'. And when five months later in 1918 the Minister of Education, H. A. L. Fisher, best known as a historian, introduced the first major Education Act since 1902, he justified the raising of the school-leaving age to fourteen on the grounds that 'industrial pressure on the child' should cease.

Fisher, who believed in wider opportunities for 'advanced instruction' as well as primary education, pressed for continuing education after school and defended the abolition of all fees in public elementary schools for the same reasons – that talent should not be wasted. He appealed also to the 'increased feeling of social solidarity' generated by the war and argued that conscription, which had caused so much liberal concern, implied that 'the boundaries of citizenship are not determined by wealth'. J. A. Hobson, whose diagnosis of the effects of war (and conscription) was so different, was in complete agreement with this particular conclusion.

Addison also introduced the crucially important and far-reaching Housing Act of 1919, which was to influence future shapes of family life and the whole appearance of the environment (not to speak of party politics). The Act laid on local authorities the duty of surveying the housing needs of their areas and submitting plans for building houses to be subsidized from State funds. Although subsidy arrangements varied significantly during the post-war years, it was this legislation which provided the basis on which local authorities, assisted by the State, went into the business of providing council houses, often in new housing estates. Both women and children were to be given a new home environment.

There were moral issues here as well as social ones. The war had broken up families, and 'keeping the home fires burning' was never an easy task. Nor did earlier marriage – one of the effects of war – make for stability. Children's futures were being plotted by politicians at a time when they had often been left to themselves more than ever before. 'Discipline' had slackened as juvenile wages increased and religious restraints were further weakened. 'Nonconformity' in particular began to look old-fashioned: its canons of behaviour were difficult to follow, let alone enforce, in wartime conditions. Sexual *mores* were changing too. Illegitimacy rates increased and contraceptives were increasingly taken for granted: according to one witness, by 1919 'every village chemist was selling them'. The Registrar-General accounted for an upsurge in the illegitimacy rate in 1916 in terms of 'the exceptional circumstances of the year, including the freedom from home restraints of large numbers of young persons of both sexes'.

There was a flood of moral criticism both during and after the war, ranging widely (usually over *other people's* changing lifestyles) from dress (short skirts, for example) to drinking (notably by women in pubs).

Much of the criticism was class-biased and much of it was anti-urban in tone. And it did not take account of awkward facts, like a fall of illegitimacy rates in the 1920s to figures below those of 1914 or the marked decline in drunkenness (convictions had fallen to a fifth during the wartime years). Obviously, however, many surviving Victorian certainties had gone. Contemporaries themselves collected whole anthologies of social comment. 'Everything now being relative,' wrote the novelist John Galsworthy, who had once been a critic of Edwardian society, 'there is no absolute dependence to be placed on Free Trade, Marriage, Consuls, Coal or Caste.' In the equally eloquent words of a woman graduate, the war shattered 'that sense of security which brooded over Victorian homes and made men buy estates and lay [wine] cellars against their old age and for the benefit of their sons'.

Economic changes led to further disruption and anxieties. 'England is changing hands' was a stock remark of 1919, when over a million acres of land were sold. The Marquess of Lansdowne, who had favoured a negotiated peace, used to show visitors a large map of England with the parts belonging to country squires marked in green, exclaiming 'practically all those are doomed to disappear.' In the background was a short-lived post-war boom, but for the government it sometimes seemed that a revolution was in the offing. During both 1919 and 1920 there was a dramatic wave of strikes, with even the police joining in. The boom was followed by what the *Economist* in 1921 called 'one of the worst years of depression since the industrial revolution'. The peacetime temper of organized labour could be as militant as that of the troops in wartime, although the difficulties of bringing different sections of the trade-union movement together were well illustrated on 'Black Friday', 15 April 1921, when the railway and transport unions, bound in 'triple alliance' with miners, called off a joint strike a few hours before it was due to begin. The most frequent response of Lloyd George's Coalition government to pressure was not to redress injustices – indeed, it drastically disbanded wartime controls (except for those on rents) – but to temporize while its intelligence service investigated 'subversive' activities. It knew that it was backed by a majority in Parliament and by middle-class opinion, with *The Times* proclaiming, for example, that 'the domestic economic war, like the war with Germany, must be fought to a finish.'

Unlike the Great War, however, the domestic war was not fought to a finish because, in the last resort, there was not the same degree of determination on either 'side'. The fall of the Coalition government in 1922 and the return to power of the Conservatives gave the Labour Party the opening it needed; in 1924 it came to power for the first time as a minority government. But events thereafter showed that there was little pressure inside England for revolutionary change. The Labour government itself did nothing to suggest that it wished to carry through even a far-reaching radical programme. Nor did a second minority Labour government, in office from 1929 to 1931. Indeed, faced with financial crisis, Labour's Prime Minister Ramsay MacDonald, who had been a pacifist during the war, chose (without a general election) to head a 'national' government consisting predominantly of Conservatives. Clearly, the social framework of the country, by then tested by severe economic depression, had not changed as much as many of the commentators of 1919 and 1920 had suggested.

Nor should the General Strike, called on 3 May 1926 in support of the miners, a unique event in English history, be considered evidence to the contrary. The response was total, and practically no trade-union members in any occupation returned to work until the strike was called off. But the Conservative government, returned to power in 1924, was able to keep sufficient services running to maintain supplies – and order – and to avoid breakdown, largely as a result of voluntary support. And despite propaganda from both sides, there was relatively little social tension. It has been suggested by one historian that 'though each side attributed extremist policies to each other, neither meant it seriously.' Despite rank-and-file commitment, the trade-union leaders at the centre, who had been reluctant to embark on the strike, were lacking in the will-power to continue it, while the Prime Minister, Stanley Baldwin, who believed in seeking consensus, was more anxious to encourage reconciliation than to impose unconditional surrender. The General Strike was called off on 12 May with no assurances to the miners, who were left to fight alone at heavy cost.

In 1927 the government passed a new Trade Disputes Act, which sought to ensure that there would be no doubt in the future as to the illegality of a general strike, and the trade unionists were insistent that they would repeal it as soon as possible. Nevertheless, some of their most important leaders took part a year later in talks with employers about the future of industry which were arranged by Sir Alfred Mond, head of the massive Imperial Chemicals Industries Company, an example of large-scale, concentrated post-war industry. There were so many forces making for collaboration rather than for confrontation that the General Strike has been seen in retrospect not as the high-water mark of class warfare but as the moment when the class war ceased to shape the pattern of British industrial relations – until the 1970s. At the time the General Strike ended, the editor of the Labour newspaper the *Daily Herald*, first launched in 1911, detected 'a feeling of intense relief everywhere'. 'I saw just now a placard in a shop window, "Peace with Honour",' he went on, 'I hope it is.' The point was as much debated as 'peace with honour' in Europe was twelve years later after Neville Chamberlain, who succeeded Baldwin as Prime Minister in 1937, returned from Munich waving in his hand an agreement with Hitler. The novelist E. M. Forster summed up the mood of the intervening years when he wrote, 'the twenties react after the war and recede from it; the thirties are apprehensive of war and are carried towards it.'

Baldwin himself was strongly aware of the shadow of the last war, 'a war to end wars', as the shadow of a new war approached. 'Its memory still sickens us,' he explained in 1935, when he stressed the necessity to preserve 'the lives of our children and grandchildren, the familiar sites and institutions of our own land and all the boundary stones of our spiritual estate'. This was the language Baldwin always liked to use. England was neither fascist nor communist, he insisted, by reason of the history of its people. It was too late by then to pass from history to economics and to count the cost of the Great War, for already rearmament, designed not to prepare Britain for a new war but to save it from one, was about to stimulate the economy. In fact, Britain had never fully returned to 'normalcy': 40 per cent of its merchant fleet had been lost and foreign investments drastically cut, and while British manufacturing production had fallen during the war, that of the United States had increased by 22 per cent and that of Japan (a formidable rival in the post-war textiles industry) had risen by 79 per cent between 1913 and 1920. Markets abroad were lost while new competitors industrialized. In 1932, on the eve of Hitler's rise to power in Germany, 2,750,000 people in Britain, including large numbers of uninsured black-coated workers, were unemployed, and the structural problems of the economy were to persist in the 1930s.

Baldwin left it to Chamberlain to try in vain – although with the backing of a sizeable proportion of the electorate – to 'appease' Hitler while Britain 'prepared'. Yet Hitler could not be appeased, and when war did come it was to be even longer than the Great War. On this occasion there was none of the remarkable enthusiasm of 1914. Nor did the news of its beginning break upon the country by surprise; a significant proportion of the electorate opposed 'appeasement' and believed that Hitler should have been 'stopped' sooner. Conscription had already been introduced and 'air raid precautions' organized on a limited scale.

At first, however, the struggle against Hitler was perceived rather as a 'phoney' war, called by one Mass-Observation correspondent the 'rummest war I ever knew'. There was little excitement to stir a public which had been led to expect a quite different kind of struggle – experts had predicted that 600,000 people would be killed and the same number injured in the first air attacks, which would last sixty days. When the first air raid siren sounded on Sunday 3 September 1939 one woman not untypically 'clasped' her baby, 'sent aloft a prayer and waited for the worst'. Characteristically, however, that warning was a false alarm. The worst did not come, and soon, amid the 'blackout', there was a sense of anti-climax. The number of children evacuated from their homes was ten times the size of the Expeditionary Force sent to France, but the serious psychological and social problems spotlighted by the evacuation had more to do with pre-war deficiencies than wartime exigencies. Closing cinemas, now a leisure mainstay, and theatres and putting the BBC into a straitjacket did not help, although the former soon reopened (and prospered) and broadcasting rapidly became an indispensable agency both to inform and to sustain. Meanwhile, it did not help either that to foster a mood of confidence, the Ministry of Information, an unpopular wartime innovation, was making a conscious appeal to history, and that one official's suggestions for the Ministry's first poster had been a picture of

> a long bowman from the Hundred Years' War, standing with his feet outspread (to represent steadiness) and drawing his bow (to denote vigour). Behind him there would be a silhouette of England (in green): one of the man's feet might be in Devon, the other in Kent . . .

It was not until the hot summer of 1940, following a German offensive in the West, that the country experienced what Winston Churchill –

who in May 1940 had replaced Chamberlain and formed a Coalition government including Labour – proudly called its 'finest hour'. British troops – 225,585 of them – were forced to leave the European mainland and escape in an improvised fleet of small boats from Dunkirk between 26 May and 4 June, and for a time the island seemed to be in danger of invasion. 'Be ye men of valour,' Churchill commanded as there were signs of pride in standing 'alone' against Hitler. The threat of invasion ('careless talk costs lives') led to the mobilization of a 'Home Guard', which has passed into legend, but very soon air raid wardens were to be more in demand than platoons of soldiers as the German Air Force attacked the island in strength. It was fortunate that barrage-balloon Britain was supported by the Empire, by allied governments in exile and quietly, behind the scenes, by the President of the United States and large numbers of its people.

A fascinating picture of life in bombed London has been reconstructed from contemporary accounts collected by Mass Observation, which had been set up in 1937 'to supply accurate observations of everyday life and *real* public moods'. It was one of the most interesting new ventures of the 1930s, started by Tom Harrisson, who watched human beings in the same way as he watched birds; and during the war some of its scattered surveyors were drawn into public reporting. There was, in fact, no single response to the protracted German attack in either London or the provinces, where there was massive destruction in towns like Coventry and Hull, but in general 'the Blitz' brought people closer together to share their burdens.

This was the 'people's war', when J. B. Priestley's Yorkshire voice so proclaiming it on the BBC was almost as influential as Churchill's. And while both men sought consolation in English history and the countryside, Priestley demanded with equal firmness equality of sacrifice and a new and more equal deal when the war was over. 'We're not fighting to restore the past,' he exclaimed. 'We must plan and create a noble future.' Churchill's 'unknown warriors' were to be not merely allowed but encouraged to win both the war and the peace. This was the message too of the lively illustrated magazine *Picture Post*, which had been launched in 1938, although for cinema's British Movietone News it was enough that 'we live in the presence of history'.

One point was certain. The wartime experience itself remained very different from that of the First World War, particularly after the entry into it of the Soviet Union and the United States in 1941. Although, therefore, the First and Second World Wars were separated by less than twenty-one years, often described as the inter-war years, it would be completely misleading to telescope them together as if they were one. As the eloquent writer Vera Brittain wrote, 'to look upon it this way would not only be to get the two wars wrong, but to drastically simplify twenty years of lost history.'

The differences between the two wars were striking. First, there were few trenches and fewer horses. ('Horses have ration books,' a Mass Observer noted in 1942, 'I wonder when they'll issue them for cats.') Second, there were many tanks. Third, there was more science, including radar, primitive computers and atomic power. Fourth, there were many fronts, and much of the war was fought in strange places, including deserts and jungles, which contrasted sharply with the English countryside. Much of it too was fought on the 'cruel sea'. In the early and middle months of 1940 it was airmen and, above all, sailors who bore the brunt of the German attack. Literature reflected this, as did films and art: in this war Paul Nash painted not barbed-wire fences but wrecked aircraft. 'In the Spitfire,' wrote Richard Hillary, who was the 'type of a new generation' just as the Spitfire was the type of a new breed of fighter aircraft, 'we're back to war as it ought to be. Back to the individual combat, to self-reliance, total responsibility for one's fate.'

The most important difference, however, was the participation of civilians: children were encouraged to do their best 'to help to win the war' and women played an active part on many fronts. By 1944 there were almost 500,000 women in the Forces, another 200,000 in the Women's Land Army and well over 300,000 (48 per cent of the total labour force) in the civil service. Garvin's 'dependence' had become greater than even he (or the Germans) could have foreseen.

As the war proceeded, more and more people were involved in it, and the human toll of civilians in the front line was often heavy. During the four months from 7 September 1940 to 1 January 1941, for example, 13,339 people in London were killed and 17,937 severely injured, with the worst still to come – on 10–11 May 1941, 1,436 people were killed and 1,752 injured. In such circumstances courage became a necessary civilian quality. 'My landlady in Pimlico was as brave as a lion,' says a character in Charles Snow's novel *The Light and the Dark* (1947). By the end of the war 60,000 civilians and 35,000 merchant seamen had been killed, while combatant casualties, 300,000, were less than half those of the Great War. The front line ran through Hull, Bristol, Southampton, Plymouth, Coventry and, in London itself, deep below ground, in the 'good old London tube'. The sculptor Henry Moore's superb shelter drawings catch the flavour; they were given top priority printing in July 1941, when four times as many were printed as a year earlier. And occasionally phrases in the most private diaries catch the flavour too. One civilian wrote:

> When the bombing first started, people were rather nervous, and they didn't know what to do, but after a few days they soon got accustomed to this. When they came along to the shelter in the evenings, they fetched their belongings, insurance cards, the cash, the jewellery, if they had any, a flask of tea, milk for the kiddies, boiled sweets, and the Council started dancing in the parks.

Popular entertainment was increasingly necessary as material austerity had to be enforced. By May 1943, four million workers in nearly 7,000 factories were listening to 'Music While You Work' and to 'Workers' Playtime', given the blessing of Ernest Bevin, the powerful trade unionist whom Churchill chose as his able and effective Minister of Labour. The Council for the Enjoyment of Music and the Arts, known as CEMA – one of the many familiar wartime acronyms – was almost as well known as ENSA, the Entertainments National Service Association, although Bevin thought it 'too highbrow'. It had support from all classes.

When the government gave its first grant to CEMA late in 1939, a popular newspaper described the grant as 'madness' on the grounds that 'there is no such thing as culture in wartime . . . and cultural activities . . . must now be set aside.' But there were far broader cultural aspirations during the Second World War than during the First: Myra Hess's wartime piano concerts in the National Gallery, for example, were deeply appreciated by a cross-section of Londoners, and so too were Sadler's Wells Opera's performances in the provinces. Only cultural minorities were involved – the other side of the picture was the crowded Hammersmith Palais de Danse – but minorities were important in the switch from patronage and voluntary organization in the arts to increased State involvement: the post-war Arts Council was a child of CEMA.

If all this was in some sense the 'superstructure' of war, the material austerity was far more evenly shared than it had been from 1914 to 1918, and a higher proportion of the long-term burdens of war were borne by taxation rather than by borrowing. Rationing, plans for which were worked out before the war started, was tightly enforced, but it was sufficiently imaginatively handled to allow for an element of choice through a 'points system', introduced at the end of 1941 for non-basic items. Ration levels were related also to nutritional requirements, neglected or misunderstood a quarter of a century before, so that many people were better fed in nutritional terms than they had ever been before. In 1944 total protein intake was higher than it had been in 1939, and the only possible deficiency was in vitamin A. Bread and potatoes were never rationed, and a 'dig for victory' campaign allowed for a regular, if not always plentiful, supply of vegetables in many homes. Communal feeding was encouraged in canteens as well as in schools and in 'British Restaurants' (Churchill coined the term). The Ministry of Food, headed for much of the war by the former general manager of David Lewis's retail store, Lord Woolton – an avuncular politician, new to politics and later to be given charge of 'reconstruction' – was well organized, and its propaganda, though often lampooned and in retrospect dated, was not ineffective. Bread, eggs, meat and cheese were all subsidized, and the food prices index at the end of 1944 stood only 20 per cent higher than in 1939. Whatever the privations of war – from censorship to black-out – food controls, coupled with full employment (never achieved during the 1930s) and steadily rising real wages, ensured a relative improvement in the economic position of the lower third of the population.

Warfare and welfare seemed to go together. The number of school meals doubled in 1940–41, as their provision ceased to be a relief measure and became instead a social service. Likewise, more attention was paid to post-natal care, 'putting milk and orange juice into babies', while the Emergency Hospital Service was extended so that by the end of the war it provided 'a solid basis upon which a National Health Service could be built'. In 1944 future social policy was forecast when the Disabled Persons Act made it possible to force employers to take a prescribed quota of rehabilitated workers.

Soldiers, sailors and airmen were as deeply concerned as civilians for their future after the war was over. And so also were the many other people who had either volunteered for, or had been conscripted into, the war effort. 'They don't expect the millennium,' Howard Marshall, skilled pre-war broadcaster, said of the troops, 'They do expect a fair deal.' The pre-war experience of the 'bitter society', as Arthur Marwick has called it, was turning people towards the vision of a better society.

It seemed necessary, therefore, as the war went on, to follow Priestley's approach and not only talk about the future but plan for it. Churchill, preoccupied with 'winning the war', remained reluctant to do so, but it was impossible for him to ignore the immense popular interest generated by Sir William (later Lord) Beveridge's Report on Social Security, published late in 1942, which became a 'symbol of the new Britain', not least for servicemen, who read about it in one of the most discussed pamphlets of the Army Bureau of Current Affairs (ABCA). Beveridge favoured not only a comprehensive social insurance system but economic policies designed to maintain full employment, a national health service, child allowances and a 'new deal' in housing and education. By 1945 most of these matters had either been discussed (often at length) in other official reports, in a 'white paper' chase, or had become objectives of the government. Critics behind the scenes might complain of the cost, but there was little public awareness either of the economic problems of the future or of Britain's wartime economic dependence on the United States. All aspects of social policy from insurance to town planning were explored. Of around 400 memoranda submitted to the principal War Cabinet committees on 'reconstruction' between 1941 and 1945, only sixty-four dealt with Britain's economic future. The mood had been caught in 1940, when England was in greatest danger, by the historian E. H. Carr, writing in *The Times*:

> If we speak of democracy we do not mean a democracy which maintains the right to vote but forgets the right to work and the right to live. If we speak of freedom, we do not mean a rugged individualism which excludes social organization and economic planning. If we speak of equality, we do not mean a political equality nullified by social and economic privilege. If we speak of economic reconstruction, we think less of maximum production, though this too will be required, than of equitable distribution.

The corollary was a greater involvement of the State in 'planning', a much used term, although any increase in the power of the state was given less attention (outside the pages of von Hayek's book *Road to Serfdom*), than an extension of common citizenship. Churchill, the great war leader, was to lose the general election of 1945 to Labour, which secured a huge majority, because he did not seem fully prepared to make the future different from the past.

In relation to education, action which had a direct bearing on that future came in wartime itself at Churchill's instigation. Ironically, the day that had been set for the raising of the compulsory school leaving age to fifteen in 1939 had been the very day war broke out, but R. A. Butler's Education Act of 1944, the culmination of an insistent demand for educational reform and the product of much backstairs negotiation, more than compensated, it seemed, for the delay. The Act went much further in its proposals than the Education Act of 1918: its object was 'free secondary education for all'. 'War woke people up to the fact that the nation possessed a supply of ability never ordinarily used to the full.' The Act provided a framework within which educational change could continue in the classroom 'according to the age, ability and aptitude of the pupils', and it even envisaged compulsory part-time education in county colleges for all persons under eighteen not receiving other kinds of education. The society of the future was to be a better educated society than ever before, although what kind of education there should be was thought out far less carefully.

The two words 'for all' were the clue words to most wartime proposals relating to social policy. Thus, Beveridge insisted on 'universality' in his social security proposals, referring back to the 'solidarity' of the nation in wartime: 'in a matter so fundamental it is so right for all citizens to stand together without exclusions based upon differences of status, function or wealth.' Thus, proposals for housing and planning stressed the need both to build homes and to plan communities. 'Bombs', wrote the editor of the monthly journal of the Federation of British Industries in October 1940, 'have made builders of us all.' In the wartime film *Dawn Patrol* (1941) one home guard told another, 'We found out in this war how we're all neighbours, and we aren't going to forget it when it's all over.'

There was one bomb, however, that was to change the shape of the post-war years, a bomb which fell miles away from war-weary London in distant Japan on 6 August 1945. The first atom bomb to be dropped laid waste four square miles and killed over 50,000 civilians, leaving behind the terrifying threat of lingering death to the survivors. A second bomb followed on 9 August, in turn followed by the surrender of Japan. The bomb had been the product of Anglo-American science, and its implications – military, medical, moral, political – were global, not solely Japanese. It threatened the end of mankind through self-destruction.

For some writers and artists – and for some politicians – this was the 'real break' of 1945. As Jeff Nuttall put it, writing retrospectively in his book *Bomb Culture* in 1968, 'VE Night [the end of the European war] took place in one world and VJ Night [the end of the Japanese war] in another.' It was at that point that 'the generations became divided in a crucial way'. Many people from that point onwards believed that atomic bombs and hydrogen bombs – the first British hydrogen bomb was tested in 1954 – were not deterrents but threats to life itself. The Campaign for Nuclear Disarmament, founded in 1958, organized Aldermaston marches at Easter to demonstrate resistance to nuclear bombs. Against a background of 'cold war' the cause was taken up by a representative of an old generation, (Earl) Bertrand Russell, born in 1872. The cold war lasted longer than the Second World War and did not end until 1988 when the Soviet Union collapsed and 1989 when the Berlin Wall was battered down.

12 ENDS AND BEGINNINGS

One can doubt whether such a thing as happiness is possible without
steadily changing conditions involving enlarging and exhilarating
opportunities.

H. G. Wells, *A Modern Utopia*, 1905

You're hurt because everything's changed. Jimmy's hurt because everything's the same. And neither of you can face it.

Alison in John Osborne's *Look Back in Anger*, 1956

Be a force for change.

Invitation to join *The People's Summit*, May 1998

We may our ends by our beginnings know.

Sir John Denham, *Of Prudence*, 1688

During the immediate post-war years of austerity, when rationing
continued and in some cases was extended (bread, 1946–8; potatoes,
1947), the 1930s served as a reference decade. Yet the Labour Party
manifesto on which it won the general election of 1945 was called *Let
Us Face the Future*. Life would be hard, but there were hopes of a
millennium. In the 1990s a 'real' chronological millennium is around
the corner, although it is thought of, less dramatically, as the gateway
to a future which stretches indefinitely into time. The only hazard in
the way is a malignant 'millennium bug', the usual way of describing
the inability of many computer systems and other electronic devices,
public and private, to cope with the date change from 1999 to 2000.

For both journalists and historians, 'decades' are more favoured time
units than 'millennia' even as a real new millennium dawns. Endowed

with often spurious identities and labelled with memorable adjectives, like 'naughty nineties' (the 1890s) or 'swinging sixties' (the 1960s), they are less revealing units for social historians to choose than either 'trends', impersonal though these, like 'problems', may seem, or 'generations', the term that at first sight seems most natural. That was a point recognized by the BBC in 1937 when it gave the title *One Generation to Another* to a series of discussions on population which in book form was entitled *The Population Problem*. The population problem then was defined simply as declining numbers.

Before considering 'trends', which continue across generations as well as across decades, sometimes across centuries, it is useful to contrast three very different twentieth-century decades, separated from each other by generations – the 1930s, the 1960s and the 1990s. As yet the 1990s have no generally accepted adjective attached to them: the 1980s have been called turbulent. Across the century the 1930s are the last decade which we can see already in perspective, partly because not only time but also the Second World War separates us from them. We can also see the beginning of the century in perspective, stripping away surrounding rhetoric.

On 1 January 1900 one newspaper boasted (in the midst of the Boer War) that 'the Empire stretching round the globe, has one heart, one head, one language, one policy'. It was not true then, but it lost all its possible point after the Second World War when one of the main trends was the contraction of Empire. Another trend, with more obvious effects on English society, was the contraction of manufacturing industry. For Paul Theroux, writing in 1983 in his *Kingdom by the Sea*, the 'nightmare' of England's north was no longer blackened factory chimneys and smoke and slag-heaps but empty chimneys and clear air and grass growing on slag-heaps. For a London evening newspaper that had survived 'crises' in the newspaper industry itself, it seemed that 'the great Victorian engine of Britain's prosperity had finally run out of steam'.

The nearer we approach the fleeting present, the more difficult interpretation is. The 1990s are usually compared not with the 1980s or with the still controversial 1960s but with the 1890s, a decade given many labels besides 'naughty'. Both decades, separated by a century, have favoured the word 'new', although before the 1890s were out there was reaction against too much 'newness', a reaction for which compensation has now been made. On the day of the centenary of Oscar Wilde's *The Importance of Being Earnest*, 14 February 1995, a stained glass window dedicated to him was unveiled in Poet's Corner, Westminster Abbey. Sir John Gielgud read from *De Profundis*, the Irish poet Seamus Heaney gave an address, choirboys sang a traditional Irish melody, and Dame Judi Dench and Michael Denison performed 'the handbag scene' from the play.

This was almost as remarkable a 'combination' as Princess Diana's funeral service in September 1997 was to be: this incorporated the reading of a lesson by the Prime Minister; a frank address by her brother, an Earl; a song by 'pop star', Elton John; and a homily by the Archbishop of Canterbury. This was the late twentieth century on parade. More frequently, for instance, in St James's Church, Piccadilly, there were religious events in the 1990s which introduced not only representatives of Islam and Buddhism, the Crescent and the Wheel alongside the Cross, but of the ancient pagan religions of Britain.

Despite late twentieth-century drama, including tragedy, the title of this chapter, 'Ends and Beginnings', may suggest a sharper thematic contrast between the two than detailed social history warrants: there have been continuities as well as discontinuities. It is a fair title, however, for there have indeed been many ends and beginnings. The most stirring of the ends was Churchill's funeral in 1965, watched by more people on television than Queen Elizabeth's coronation in 1953: no politician more lamented the end of an empire which he did not wish to be simply called a 'Commonwealth'. Another international ending nearly a quarter of a century later – the reunification of the two post-war Germanys and the fall of the Soviet Union – was more than symbolic. It suggested to some commentators 'the end of history'.

The greatest new beginning for Britain was its entry into what came to be called the European Community, sought for in vain and with varying degrees of enthusiasm both by Harold Macmillan, Conservative prime minister from 1957 to 1963, and Harold Wilson, his Labour successor from 1964 to 1970 – always in face of opposition from inside their own parties. It was an opposition which was never to be silenced, not even when Margaret Thatcher was Prime Minister from 1979 to 1990, and which did immense damage to John Major, her chosen successor, although he won more votes at the general election of 1992 than Tony Blair was to do in 1997. The prime minister who with persistence and imagination had 'taken the country into Europe' in 1972 was Edward Heath, Wilson's immediate successor (1970–74), although his choice was subsequently required to be ratified by referendum. This was a new departure in British politics, devised by Wilson who had returned to power in 1974, a grim year of economic and political crisis. In the words of a well-known broadcaster and writer, Andrew Shonfield, in 1972 the country was now beginning 'a journey to an unknown destination'.

Metaphors like 'journey' shape historical interpretation and, like words, among them 'crisis' and more recent 'buzz words', themselves need to be charted and interpreted. One of the most overworked words of the immediate post-1945 period was 'revolution', applied not only to technology but to education, health – and sex, just as 'heritage', a way of describing what we choose to carry forward from 'past times', is overworked now. 'Revolution' speaks – or seems to speak – for itself. The 'heritage', now highly commercialized, has to be regularly 'interpreted'. Historians must interpret too, never one-dimensionally, recognizing the need both for selection and revision.

The vantage point of the new edition of this *History*, the late 1990s, is very different from that of 1983 when the first edition appeared. Then Thatcher, Britain's first woman prime minister, won the second of three general elections in the aftermath of the Falkland Islands war. In 1997 Tony Blair was elected Labour prime minister with more seats in Parliament (418:241) than Attlee had won in 1945, claiming confidently that 'a new generation ha[d] come on' that did not have 'the outdated attitudes of the past'. *The Week*, essential source for the changing present, went further and headed its article on 'Labour's Landslide' with the question 'Has this election changed things forever?' *Time* magazine got near to claiming that it had. Its cover on 27 October 1997 bore the words 'Renewed Britannia'. There were, in fact, both continuities and discontinuities, as there had been in 1945. Many economic and social policies with their origins in the Thatcher years continued to be pursued after 1997, just as many of the social, though not the economic, policies of Attlee's post-1945 Labour government had been devised by the war-time Coalition government in which Labour had taken part.

It is easier to talk of 'change', the word most frequently used both by journalists and historians, than to achieve it. Happily jargon-free, it is not a metaphor, although Macmillan's reference to 'wind' or 'winds of change' in speeches delivered to African, not British, audiences, remains memorable. 'Change' is now applied, often enthusiastically, both to individuals and to institutions – and, not least, to the constitution, including monarchy: Queen Elizabeth II is one of the people who have used it. A more vague word than 'progress', it is more ambivalent too – to accept the need for it does not necessarily imply approval – and it can be applied in so many contexts that it needs to be supported by other words. 'Transition' has gone out of fashion; 'brink', a favourite word of the 1970s and 1980s, has given way in the late 1990s to 'cusp'; 'contract' to 'bonding' – words barely heard then. Every year sees an invasion of new words.

Politicians are often foremost in dwelling on the need for change, and, for this reason, political choices, set out by political parties, however they are presented – and styles change – cannot be left out of social history. In 1964 Wilson attempted a re-definition of socialism in terms of 'scientific and technological change', and his successor Heath promised in 1970 to embark on 'a change so radical, a revolution so quiet and total' that it would 'change the course and the history of this nation'. Yet neither of them could achieve what they wished and were embroiled in situations which they could not control. In 1970 Britain, despite contracting manufacturing industry, was still an industrial rather than a post-industrial society, and Heath was forced to cope with serious strikes of militant miners in 1972 and 1974, against the background of an international oil crisis.

The year 1974 was a year of two general elections in one year, when a three-day working week had to be imposed in a state of emergency. There were restraints too that influenced 'leisure' behaviour: among them television programmes had to end at 10.30 pm to make people go to bed earlier. The Central Electricity Generating Board was alarmed that a simultaneous switching off by viewers would bring chaos to the system. A mass television audience, built up since the 1950s, was geared to broadcasting schedules. They dictated leisure.

Politicians on or off television do not always find it easy to strike the right notes. Churchill, who hated the screen, believed confidently that history was the best guide to action – 'the longer you look back, the further you can look forward'. Having led the country through the Second World War, to his great disappointment he could not lead it through the first years of peace. Nevertheless, he returned to power in 1951, after Attlee's Labour Government (still supported by a numerical majority of the population), had carried through a comprehensive and far-reaching programme of legislative change. In 1945 a majority of electors wanted full employment, a national health service, social security and at least a measure of nationalization. In 1951 Churchill confidently offered a different recipe – ladders not queues, less austerity, and more choice.

From the vantage point of the general election of 1945, the 1930s stood out as 'the Devil's decade'. It was a decade that began in slump, leading to political crisis and the formation under Ramsay MacDonald of a National Government. Still dominated by mass unemployment, the main theme of Walter Greenwood's *Love on the Dole* (1932) and the Jarrow hunger marches, it was to end (after rearmament) in the disaster of war. Class feeling was strong. From a later vantage point, the 1960s – heralded by Macmillan, who had served in Churchill's war-time government, with the words 'most of our people have never had it so good' (1957) – marked a significant break in values. A 'generation gap' for once seemed more obvious than a 'class gap'. Most traditional English institutions, including what within 'the social fabric' was now called 'the Establishment', were under attack from below as debate raged on the implications of living in a 'permissive society', the most obvious features of which could be watched on the burgeoning television screens. There had been no such debate – or exposure – in the 1930s.

Both the 1960s and 1930s have been reassessed, and both decades can now be seen in terms of longer social and cultural 'trends'. The noun 'trend' became a serious key word for economists, sociologists and historians during the 1960s, after the fashion word 'trendy' had itself become fashionable. It was not until 1970, however, that a now indispensable annual official publication, *Social Trends*, first appeared in parallel to *Economic Trends*. The word 'mega-trend' followed in 1982, but it seemed an unattractive American term, and there was little enthusiasm in England for its message of 'computerized and electronic joy to all mankind' by the year 2000.

Before the 1930s ended, a thoroughly revised *Handbook of Suggestions* for elementary school teachers, published in 1937 (there are no elementary schools now left), could already describe how 'the general standard of life' had improved and how life itself was being lived 'at a faster rate' without actually using the word 'trend'.

> The universality of motor-transport, of broadcasting, and of . . . cinemas presents new features in the common life, while better housing, the increasing use of electrical and other mechanical devices, the possibility of increased leisure and wider social contacts for all, with their increased opportunities for the enrichment of experience, make it necessary for those engaged in education to review their task afresh.

The Devil was left out of this judgement, which still stands; and subsequently economic historians have pointed to other signs of 'progress' before 1939. Thus, the index of industrial production stood 75 per cent higher in 1935–8 than it had in 1910–13, although many 'staple' industries continued to decline and the official unemployment rate never fell below 10 per cent. At its peak in 1932 it reached 22.5 per cent. For those at work real wages increased by 50 per cent during the same period, and the length of the working week decreased by 10 to 14 per cent.

The same historians have offset the development of 'new' industries (and of new industrial areas) against the doldrums of old industries (and of the grim 'depressed areas'), and have moved away from the images of closed ship-yards and derelict mills and mines, to the images of new laboratories and brightly lit shops. Employment in the electrical industry more than doubled between 1924 and 1938 – before the word 'electronics' had been invented – while that in the distributive trades went up from 1,661,000 in 1920–22 to 2,436,000 in 1937–8.

There were no 'supermarkets' then – these were new retailing institutions of the 1960s and 1970s, with far-reaching social consequences not only for small shopkeepers but for whole communities – but between 1929 and 1939, turnover in Marks and Spencer's department stores, defying depression, multiplied nearly ten-fold: both turnover and profit rose each year. This was the golden age too of the chain stores: Burton, 'the Tailor of Taste', the largest manufacturer and retailer of tailored men's wear in Britain, set the style – 'respectable', never 'casual'. (The firm was to supply over a third of the 'demob suits' issued to members of the Forces when they were demobilized after the Second World War.)

Unlike the United States, Britain was not thought of as a 'consumer society' during the 1930s, but it was on its way towards becoming 'a nation of customers'. Patterns of spending were changing too, with the employed (if not the unemployed) benefiting from low prices. Thus, weekly expenditure on food fell from 60 per cent to 35 per cent of income during the decade and on rent from 16 per cent to 9 per cent. The consumption of fruit increased by 88 per cent; twice as much was now being spent on fruit as on bread. Net imports of butter doubled, and those of meat rose by 50 per cent.

Weekly expenditure on so-called 'other items' in working-class housekeeping rose from a negligible sum in 1900 to almost 16 shillings in the mid-1930s. This was the prelude to everything that has happened since – the rise in the material standard of life. At the end of the nineteenth century, Rowntree in an influential survey of poverty in York (1901) had ignored all such items in determining where to draw his poverty line. By 1936, however, when he repeated his survey he observed that it was only in order to save himself from charges of 'sentimentality' that he had offered in his first survey 'a standard of bare subsistence rather than living'. There was little sentimentality even in 1936. Reading materials of various kinds still did not figure on the Rowntree list, except for newspapers and weeklies, although with the first Penguin paperbacks having appeared in 1935 they might well have done. Nonetheless, 'licences for dogs and wireless, food for pets, etc.', hairdressing, laundry and domestic help did appear.

Concerned about the moral as well as the material aspects of change, Rowntree, a Quaker, welcomed the continuing decline in drunkenness as a social problem – in the home and on the street – a change brought about neither by the power of the State nor by the vigour of organized teetotallers, but by changes in education and manners and the diversification of social activities, but he was horrified by the fact that in 1938 £40,000,000 was spent on football pools.

The consumption of beer had, in fact, declined dramatically, although the consumption of Guinness stout, brilliantly advertised, had risen. (Wine was still an article of consumption for the better off.) Tobacco had won, however, where alcohol had lost: from 1913 to 1938, *per capita* consumption of tobacco and cigarettes practically doubled. Smoking was a habit shared by all social classes until the early 1970s, when tobacco consumption began to fall sharply under the influence of authoritative medical advice and high taxation on tobacco products. And then – and this would have surprised cigar-smoking Churchill and pipe-smoking Priestley alike – there was a proportionate increase in the number of women smokers. There were class divisions too. The proportion of male smokers in 1997 was to be highest among unskilled and semi-skilled manual workers (44 per cent) and lowest among professionals (11 per cent). There were very few 'occasional smokers' (those smoking one cigarette or less per day), but amongst young women, 41 per cent of those who had been occasional smokers in 1984 were regular smokers seven years later. Smoking by juvenile males was higher also.

Gambling, described by the *Economist* in 1936 as Britain's second biggest industry, was not a new industry, but one which was being organized in a new commercial way. In Liverpool, the promotion of football pools became big business a generation before football itself did. Like boxing, gambling remained an upper-class as well as a working-class pursuit, although for the lower income groups it was more than diversion: for millions of people the pools opened up prospects of immense riches, as the National Lottery was to do after its introduction in 1994. When Macmillan introduced savings premium bonds in 1956 (affording small rewards to the lucky), the Archbishop of Canterbury warned him against the danger of morally contaminating the nation.

In the light of what has happened since, just as much attention has to be paid to the dynamics of the market as to welfare legislation in charting and interpreting twentieth-century social change. Yet Acts of Parliament and the pressures leading up to them can never be left out. This is particularly true of the 1960s when Parliament, from a mixture of motives, initiated a number of measures, sometimes across party lines and usually in the face of opposition, which marked a significant change in attitudes to the law; several of these drew a crucial distinction between 'the realm of private morality' and 'the realm of the law'. In 1959 a Conservative government had carried a Suicide Act which removed the penalties of the criminal law from a practice which had consistently (and almost universally) been condemned by Christians and which had hitherto been punishable by law. It was left to a Labour backbencher MP, however, Leo Abse, to introduce and carry eight years later an Act permitting homosexual acts between two consenting adult males in private.

None of this legislation would have been possible in the 1930s, when the legislation that was most relevant to the electorate was concerned not with personal liberation but with social support. At the head of Rowntree's revealing list of 'other items' in the working-class budgets of the 1930s were National Insurance contributions, first statutorily provided in 1911 on a limited scale by a Liberal government in which Churchill was a leading figure. In retrospect, these provisions were sometimes seen as the first achievements of an embryonic 'welfare state'. So, too, was the formal end in 1929 of the 1834 Poor Law, once conceived of as new, then obviously old. The Board of Guardians now passed into history. Two years later, however, MacDonald's Labour Government split over the size of cuts in National Insurance, and the new National Government which he also headed was left to cope with means tested national assistance. MacDonald's Britain was at best a 'social service state', not a 'welfare state', and until 1947 there was no National Health Service, although there were influential doctors who urged the need for one. Women suffered most.

Equal fourth on the Rowntree budgetary list came trade-union subscriptions and expenditure on 'cinemas, theatres, football matches, etc.', with holidays last. This last item would not have been there without a reduction in working hours and a more enlightened pay policy; and this was a change influenced both by the market and by legislation. During the 1920s as many as 1,500,000 wage earners were already entitled to a holiday with pay. By 1938, however, the figure was 3,000,000, and as a result of the Holidays with Pay Act, passed in that year, the figure rose to 11,000,000 in 1939.

Lifestyles, which began to be spotlighted in the late 1950s and 1960s, now figure as the subject of the last chapter of *Social Trends*, and were already being promoted during the 1930s. Holiday camps – the best known of them, Billy Butlin's super-organized camp at 'sunny Skegness', opened in 1937 – were widely advertised: their cheerful approach to their customers was as much of an attraction as their low charges. They did not appeal to all sections of the working classes, however, many of whom, not only on economic grounds, favoured 'day trips'. On the August Bank Holiday of 1937 over half a million visitors arrived in Blackpool. They continue to visit it, however much lifestyles have changed – with politicians of all parties favouring it as a conference centre. In 1996 its Pleasure Beach was to top the list of free tourist attractions: the British Museum came second.

Leisure was being increasingly commercialized during the 1930s; and while the seaside landlady, a familiar figure on comic postcards, still flourished, her traditional version of commercialism was already at odds with tempting resort and travel posters, the latter at the height of their influence as carriers of information. She was almost to disappear (although not Bed and Breakfasts) between the 1960s and the 1990s. Even Blackpool was under threat. By 1971, in an age of package tours by coach, train and, above all, air, over 4,000,000 people were taking holidays abroad, a total that tripled in the next ten years, reaching over 20,000,000 in 1991 and over 27,000,000 in 1995. Spain was the favourite destination. It offered sun, sand and sea.

Trade unionists in the 1930s – and there were then almost 5,000,000 of them – had pressed 'not very hopefully' for a forty-hour week, with few signs of militancy: French and American workers had to a large extent already secured it. Wages were the main item in English collective bargaining, and 'overtime' money remained popular. In the 1990s employees in England were still working an average of 45.8 hours a week (some of it called 'overtime') while the French were working only 40.6 hours. The history of twentieth-century trade unionism was to be a history of peaks and troughs, of both immense influence and none, with membership peaking in 1980, but it could never be left out as a factor in local or national social history. Until the 1970s structural changes in unionism were fewer than might have been expected or were thought desirable by its critics, including press and television critics, who were to gain in influence; and it was not until the Wilson government of 1966–70 that a Royal Commission under a Judge was set up to examine them.

Faced with trade-union opposition Wilson failed to find an alternative 'in place of strife'; and Heath's answer, a new Industrial Relations Act (1971), which provoked bitter and unanimous trade-union opposition, was an attempt to end a tradition in the name of economic growth in an increasingly competitive world. Hitherto, as the Labour lawyer Kahn-Freund put it, there had been 'perhaps no major country in the world' in which the law had 'played a less significant role in the shaping of [industrial] relations than in Britain'. Now there was to be registration of trade unions, legally binding agreements, codes of unfair industrial practices and a national Industrial Relations Court to hear cases and appeals. Ironically this was an Act that was seldom tested in action. Indeed, there was to be more adversarial conflict after its passing than there was before.

Miners' militancy, grounded in union history, and not yet destroyed in 1974, was driven by well-grounded fear for the future of coal, the basis of 'traditional' industrial society. It was intensified, however, by the fact that there had been a great inflationary consumer boom between 1971 and 1973, a spending spree with new pennies and old pounds. (Britain had 'gone decimal' in 1971.) The spree, which used credit cards as well as coins, was over in 1974, but it was not the last spree of the century. Industrialism in its late stages moved, as in its early stage, through booms and slumps, with new technologies leading to structural unemployment (redundancy) that made full employment impossible.

The return of a Labour government to power in 1974 did not end industrial unrest. Indeed, it was intensified in the winter of 1978–9 after Britain had been forced to accept financial assistance from the International Monetary Fund. Wilson's successor James Callaghan, who had been a member of Attlee's government, put his trust in a new 'social contract' which would provide trade-union backing for progressive legislative measures, economic and social. But this was not forthcoming at the grass roots level. In 1979, therefore, Thatcher deliberately abandoned political 'consensus', and with it not only the prices and incomes policies which her predecessors – Labour *and* Conservative – had followed since the 1960s, but any residual commitment to 'full employment', the agreed 1945 target. Financial stability was put first. The immediate cost was a further contraction of industry. The fall in output at the beginning of the 1980s exceeded that at the beginning of the 1930s, and in 1982, for the first time, there was a net loss on trade with the rest of the world in manufactured goods.

This was a watershed. Trusting the market, and uneasy about the very word 'society', Thatcher was more than willing both to privatize nationalized industries and to intervene drastically in industrial relations as an essential part of her strategy. In 1975 a Gallup opinion poll had found that Jack Jones, a leader of the Transport and General Workers' Union, one of what were then called 'the big six trade unions', was the most powerful man in the country, and Thatcher knew that 'to take on the trade unions' would win support from outside as well as from inside the Conservative Party. An Employment Act was duly passed in 1982 removing several hard-won legal immunities of the trade unions and limiting their most effective forms of industrial action.

This was followed by the defeat of the National Union of Miners in the bitter miners' strike of 1984 and 1985, the most important industrial struggle of the late twentieth century. It had implications for trade unionism as a whole as well as for the coal industry, with power shifting from manual workers involved in industry to the service trades, most of which, including advertising, hotels and tourism, now, and without any sense of irony, described themselves as industries. In 1993 there were important trade-union mergers, as there had been in industry itself. Trade-union membership, which had risen from less than 10,000,000 in 1960, to more than 11,000,000 in 1970 and nearly 13,000,000 in 1980, was to fall sharply during the 1980s, by which time less than a third of all employees were members of a trade union. Yet the main reason for this was not legislation but unemployment which reduced workers' bargaining power.

The fortunes of coal, as so often in the past, still expressed much not only about trade unionism but about society and its underlying economics. The decision to close a large number of pits 'losing money' in the 1990s, with a great loss of jobs, suggested both to miners and to those sympathetic to their cause – most of them living far away from the old pit communities – that all Britain's remaining deep coal mines would disappear by the millennial year 2000. And while privatization was imposed and there was an unprecedented increase in productivity during the 1980s, it did not save many surviving mines. Symbolically the Queen's traditional gift of coal to needy Windsor pensioners was to be dropped in 1993. While arguments about energy policy continued – gas, electricity, oil – this too was an end.

Trade unionism in its modified form did not end. It had never been possible to measure its influence in numbers alone or even in terms of the quality of its leadership, which in the 1980s and 1990s had become more professional. The local trade-union branch had enjoyed a social life of its own in the 1930s, and until constitutional changes in the Labour Party in 1995 took away the trade-union block vote, the national Party depended on trade-union funds. 'New Labour' had a very different relationship with the unions. It did not repeal the basic changes in the law (ballots; picketing) which had been passed under Conservative governments between 1979 and 1997; and there were disagreements too about the level of a 'minimum wage' (one of Rowntree's dreams) which both Party and unions were anxious to achieve. There was no actual break, however, and common interests continued to be stressed.

There were more changes in sport between the 1930s and the 1990s than there were in trade unions, many of them strongly influenced by television, most reflecting market economics. There were trends here too, and there were both class and generational implications. Distinctively working-class sports had established their place (and their organization) in local and national life before 1914; and as early as 1898 a worried middle-class observer had noted how, on a night walk around a northern industrial town, almost every fragment of overheard conversation was a 'piece of football criticism or prophecy'. By 1938 football was the great 'spectator sport' with its great heroes and even its great managers. Neither on the stands nor in the open, however, was there much intimation of hooliganism – or indeed, of the commercialization of sport as a whole. Large salaries, huge transfer payments, the use of agents, and international deals belonged to the future.

There was football rivalry, however, in the 1930s; not only between towns and cities, but between England, Scotland and Wales (as there was in rugby football which had clearly divided codes: Rugby Union and Rugby League, amateur and professional). Athletics were entirely amateur. There was still little use of the generic term 'sport', although the BBC broadcast running commentaries on football, cricket, tennis, racing and the Boat Race. The last of these, like the Twelfth of August, the beginning of the shooting season, figured on T. S. Eliot's 1947 list of 'the characteristic activities and interest of the English people' which constituted the core of their culture. Other sporting events on his list were the FA Cup Final, Wimbledon, Derby Day, the Grand National and Henley Regatta. The 'pin table' and the 'dart board' figured also, along with 'beetroot in vinegar' and the music of Elgar.

Commercialization was still strictly limited in 1947 – and had barely touched 'the heritage' – as was sponsorship, which had barely touched the arts. In particular, the monopolistic BBC was free from advertising, and those directing its affairs thought in terms of a radio audience not of a market, of public service not profit. By contrast, the cinema was commercialized – both films and 'picture palaces' – and there were the same kinds of complaints among 'the great and good' about cinema 'addiction' as there were about 'addiction' to sport, and as there were to be about addiction to television. Hollywood and its 'stars' set the tone on the screen, and it was not until after the War that films like the Ealing Comedies and the Carry On series were to stand out as supremely 'English'. The London and provincial theatre was commercial too in the 1930s, and there was no National Theatre Company until 1963.

Cultural interactions were more complex than the cultural products of this mixed system, still rarely conceived of in terms of 'popular' as opposed to 'high culture', as they were to be with the growth of 'cultural studies' in the 1960s. There was often a wide gap between the value judgements of observers and the attitudes and behaviour of the observed, as only sensitive psychologists – and there were not as many of them in the 1930s as in the 1990s – fully recognized. The cinema, for example, selling 987,000,000 tickets in 1938, provided warmth as well as glamour and glitter. There was obvious escapism, but there was also a strengthening of community provision that enhanced local life. (Multiple stores, though selling standard products, had similar impact.) A still thriving local press, different in style from the national press – 'quality' or 'popular', only partially 'tabloid' – faithfully recorded what was going on, paying thorough attention to people who were in no sense 'celebrities', offering history from below.

Football, in particular, strengthened the sense of community, thriving significantly in some of the most economically depressed areas in the country: it had deep neighbourhood roots, which still remained there (very deep) after it became big business, even global business, in the 1990s. Then Rupert Murdoch was to transform the code and to change the season of the most community based of all English sports, Rugby League, popular in the 1930s only in Yorkshire and Lancashire. He was to turn to professional soccer also.

Cricket was popular too in Yorkshire and Lancashire in the 1930s, where there were Saturday leagues and where the annual 'Roses Match' was a grimmer struggle than any Cup Final. Yet the 'culture' of cricket, with its county associations, its 'amateur' leadership and its Test Matches, contrasted sharply with that of football. It also strengthened national feeling. One of the 'sayings of the year' in 1933, year of the strident 'body-line bowling' controversy, was 'I am not one of those who believe that England is degenerate if it has lost the Test Match.'

There was only one England when the competitor was Australia, but inside the country, changing in appearance (suburbia; ribbon development; housing estates) as well as in styles of life, there were many different 'Englands' in the 1930s, well described by Priestley in his book *English Journey*, published in 1934. Drawing all the necessary contrasts, it set the England of factories against the England of cathedrals; the England of long dingy backstreets (the 'Coronation Streets' of the 1950s) against the England of semi-detached houses and well kept suburban gardens; the England of scrap-iron against the England of aluminium and bakelite.

There was still an upper-class England too, which Priestley did not describe: it is brought back to life in diaries, like those of 'Chips' Channon. London had its three-month season, shorter than it had been before the First World War, but much photographed and publicized: balls were held and débutantes were presented at Court. This was an England of diamonds and champagne. The country house had survived the Great Depression just as it had survived the so-called agricultural depression of the late nineteenth century. It was in large part to survive the Second World War also – after a lapse and with the help of the National Trust – although less self-sufficient and far more open to cross influences from outside, including paying visitors. In the 1930s the dance hall, a Mecca, was far removed from the hunt ball. In the 1990s hunt balls are known to a wider public than surviving dance halls.

The coexistence of different Englands in a small country means that interpretations of moods of the 1930s depends much on whether 'the spotlight' is turned on Skegness or Oldham, Slough or Jarrow, Birkenhead or Oxford, Aston or Ascot – or, somewhat by itself, George Orwell's Wigan. For Orwell – and he was an old Etonian – the 1930s were a personal reference decade in which he learned about 'Empire' in Burma and 'the working class' in Lancashire; and in his concise but illuminating book *The British People* (1947) he deliberately concentrated not on 'the property owning class' but on the millions. ('Blackpool is more typical than Ascot, the top hat is a moth-eaten rarity.')

For him both geographical and class differences were 'blatant'. 'The great majority' of Englishmen and women could 'be "placed" in an instant by their manners, clothes and general appearance', above all by their language. 'Whichever way you turn the curse of class difference confronts you like a wall of stone. Or rather it is not so much like a wall of stone as the plate glass of an aquarium.' (As Wyndham Lewis had put it, the English working class were 'branded on their tongues'.) And the differences affected all institutions. Public houses, most traditional of English places, were as different from each other in class 'tone' as holiday resorts (for example, Blackpool and Southport) were, and each was split in the middle between the 'lounge' and the 'public bar'.

Objectively, every available social indicator, beginning with infant mortality, pointed to profound differences between the social classes, with even more frightening gulfs between classes in property than there were in income: in 1936–8 as few as 2 per cent of people with property owned between them as much as 66 per cent of all private property, and one in a hundred adults bequeathed over half the total property passed on to the next generation. Two-thirds of the dead left less than £100 in the form of possessions.

Using the essential word 'class' without any social or political colour to it – American observers, in particular, added the colour, and thought of it as supremely English – classes had been defined in occupational terms by the Registrar-General in the 1911 Census and by his successors. Class I (wholly non-manual) was 'Professional'; Class II, 'Intermediate Income Groups', Class III, 'Skilled Occupations', and Class IV, 'Partly Skilled Occupations' were 'mixed'; Class V, 'Unskilled Occupations', was wholly manual.

Within Classes III, IV and V there were considerable differences both in income and status – differences of great importance to market researchers. The 'white collar' labour force was increasing during the 1930s, part of a longer trend: the number of 'clerks' was to more than double from 1,404,000 in 1931 to 2,994,000 in 1961, and the number of manual workers was falling. These trends were already set by 1931. The number of professional people was increasing too, and the range of professions, among them surveyors and accountants – to grow in importance during the 1970s and 1980s – was widening.

For a time the *bellatores* (the warriors) were out of view, but by the end of 1939 there were 1,128,000 in the Army and another 300,000, altogether, in the Navy and in the RAF. There were more men in the 'Services' between 1939 and 1945 (over 5,000,000) than there had been in any wars of the Middle Ages. Conscription (call-up: national service) did not end until 1960, when the size of the Army fell from 690,000 to 375,000. No substitute was provided for 'national service'. Budgetary cuts in 1991 reduced the Army to its smallest size since 1830, and a year later the end of historic regiments generated both sadness and anger.

Further changes in 1998 were described as 'fundamentally reshaping our Forces to face modern warfare', and the Territorial Army (the 'Terriers'), formed in 1908, was reduced by a third.

The Army, like the House of Commons (and the Conservative Party inside it) had already changed (although not completely) in social composition. In society as a whole, class differentials continued to vary substantially – and often surprisingly from region to region, according to levels of employment and the range of community services and amenities. They were surveyed in detail in the late 1930s by G. D. H. Cole, author of detective stories, a favourite form of fiction, and co-author with Raymond Postgate (pioneer prophet of wine), of a history of the 'Common People'. Along with R. H. Tawney and Harold Laski, Cole was one of England's leading academic socialists. Comparing the diet of a family of five earning the average industrial wage with that of a middle-class family of the same size earning £500–600 a year, he noted in 1937 how the richer family ate on average 12 per cent less bread and flour and 16 per cent less potatoes than the poorer family, but consumed nearly 36 per cent more meat, more than twice as much fish and fresh milk, 68 per cent more eggs, 36 per cent more butter and only half the quantity of margarine.

Even during periods of 'trade boom', like the rearmament boom after 1936, at least 15–20 per cent of all working-class people, however 'sensibly' they disposed of their incomes, were unable to afford a carefully calculated British Medical Association diet that would ensure 'health and working capacity'. They were living in 'primary poverty', one-third of it attributable to earnings below the minimum subsistence line, one-third of it to inadequate unemployment benefits, one-third to old age. (Pensions, first introduced in 1908 and essential to social security, did not meet minimum needs.)

Patterns of deprivation and expectation did not coincide: indeed, it has been claimed since, that it was 'not feasible' for a working-class family during the 1930s to aspire to 'anything approaching the standards of the family of the middle-class wage earner' and that, in so far as the expectations of manual workers were rising during the late 1930s, they were rising only 'in terms of limited reference groups'. Class I was so far removed from Class V, which had its own differences of status and income within, that 'from below' it inhabited a different world with lifestyles which were too exotic to provoke envy. There was also less consciousness of property differences than of differences of income, and, possibly, less envy in society than there had been twenty years before and there was to be forty years later. 'It occurred to me today as I sat stirring my third cup of tea', wrote Margaret Halsey, an American visitor to England in the late 1930s, that a 'relaxed, late-afternoon atmosphere extends over a good deal of English life'. This was the England of Barbara Pym's novels, not those of Evelyn Waugh.

Perceptions of status and well-being and expectations for the future were influenced by two long-term generational trends noted in 1945 both by Cole, then Chairman of the Fabian Society, and by Orwell. They each gave their approval to a little book by the pioneering market researcher, Mark Abrams, *The Condition of the British People, 1911–1945*, in which he pointed to two trends – towards longer life and towards greater material prosperity. 'As against thirty years ago people are larger and heavier, live longer, work shorter hours, eat more, spend more on amusements, and have household facilities which their parents would have found unimaginable.'

The words 'larger and heavier' and 'longer life' pointed to the future even more than to the past, and when *Social Trends*, now on the Internet, first appeared in 1970, it began not with the economy or with culture – or, indeed, with technology, treated by many American writers as the driving force of history – but, apparently firmly enough, with demography. The number of people aged over sixty-five has increased in every decade of the second half of the century – by more than a half between 1961 and 1996 to 9,300,000. By 1981 people aged sixty-five and over made up 17 per cent of the population, compared with 15 per cent in 1961 and 5 per cent in 1901, and for every twenty people of working age there were now thirteen who were either over retirement age or under sixteen years of age. The number of over-eighty-fives, 350,000 in 1961, was to increase to nearly 1,000,000 in 1996.

Other demographic facts were presented in *Social Trends*, including the movements of the birth rate, which rose dramatically after the Second World War to a peak in 1947, and after a decline climbed again to a smaller peak in 1966. It was not until the 1970s that it decreased sharply again before falling in 1977 to an even lower point than it had been in 1933. In 1976 the number of births in the United Kingdom was lower than the number of deaths for the only time in the century. By then less attention was being devoted to decline than to the consequences – political and social, as well as economic – of a huge increase in world population, biggest in a Third World which attracted more social concern in Britain, particularly among young people, than the Empire had done.

Demography could never be separated from economics and, increasingly, demographic trends influenced policy making, first in education – the size and composition of education budgets in schools and universities, determined by 'Bulge' (demography) and 'Trend', and later in social welfare – the likely costs of pensions, which became a major concern as the century proceeded. As early as 1949 the Royal Commission on Population had reported guardedly that it was 'impossible for policy to be "neutral" to the effects of changes in the birth rate'. A generation later it had become axiomatic that all demographic changes had policy implications, not least in relation to housing and to the balance between city and countryside.

Policies were judged by their social impact related to their cost, although it was solely their impact that Rowntree considered in 1951 after the Labour Party had been in power for six years. In a third and final survey, dealing with the immediate post-war period, he concluded that as a result of 'welfare measures' already introduced since 1936, along with full employment, which in 1951 was being taken for granted, there were now only 846 families in York in primary poverty (1.66 per cent of the total population and 2.77 per cent of the working class) as compared with 31 per cent of working-class families in the same condition at the time of a second survey in 1936. In that year in York, unemployment, the scourge of society, which had accounted for only 2.31 per cent of primary poverty at the end of the nineteenth century, now accounted for 44.5 per cent. Now in 1951 in no single such case was unemployment of an able-bodied wage earner the cause. Meanwhile, the proportion of people aged over sixty-five in the population had risen from 5 per cent to 11 per cent between 1901 and 1951, and old age had become the primary cause of poverty.

In retrospect, it was the taking for granted of full employment in the third survey and the relative stability of the price levels in the last two surveys rather than 'ageing' that most stand out. It was possible to compare budgets with relatively minor adjustments, and one item, 'travelling to work', actually stayed at the same level in the account – at one shilling in 1936 and in 1951. In the 1960s, a Labour politician,

Michael Stewart was to claim that unemployment had 'passed into history'. It had not. Indeed by 1982, under Thatcher, when it rose over the 3,000,000 mark, it had once more become a bleak fact of life. In January 1986 it touched 3,400,000 or 14 per cent of the working population. The average length of unemployment also increased.

Before 1979 there had been a broad measure of consensus on the need to keep unemployment low, even though it rose under Heath and increased further between 1974 and 1979 from 600,000 to 1,500,000. The word 'stagflation', as ugly a word as 'compunication', was coined to describe what seemed to be the curious conjunction of unemployment with inflation, a phenomenon unknown to Rowntree. The condition was, of course, uglier than the word, for it affected all sections of society, employed as well as unemployed. After 1979, control of the rate of inflation, not of the level of employment, became the major object of Thatcher's financial policy and although the rate rose from 14.5 per cent in 1979 to 22 per cent in May 1980, it thereafter declined sharply. In 1986 it was only 3 per cent.

During the mid-Thatcher years, when 'enterprise culture' was being prematurely extolled ('hippies' had given way to 'yuppies'), there was even a sense of 'boom'. Yet it affected the City of London – where the name 'Big Bang' was given to fundamental reforms in the Stock Exchange, negotiated in 1983 and carried out three years later – more than the industrial areas of the country, and in 1990 industrial unemployment rose sharply again. The City's business was international and had never been confined to the Empire, and it benefited now from European transactions. Yet there could be 'crisis' even in the City. When sections of Lloyds – the huge international insurance business with seventeenth-century origins, even older than those of the Stock Exchange – collapsed, the collapse profoundly affected the lives and fortunes not only of people working in the City, as the Big Bang had done, but of families scattered throughout the country, both urban and rural.

Within the context of disturbing long-term economic and financial change, the welfare state was not dismantled, but some of its premises were challenged. Thatcher, who distrusted and deliberately abandoned contemporary political consensus, believed in what were called 'Victorian values' – and legislative measures were carried by her government which deliberately reversed the trend of nearly forty years. The National Health Service, a service for all, introduced by Aneurin Bevan in 1947, was, she stated, 'safe in her hands', but social security policy as fashioned under the influence of Beveridge had to be radically reformed. One of the biggest changes was carried through in the Social Security Act of 1986, which was based on providing through a Social Fund various forms of 'income support' for the poorest families while ceasing to provide for the rest. A large number of benefits were cut or disappeared, among them child benefit, first introduced in the form of family allowances in 1945. Nonetheless, there were limits to the efficacy of the legislation. Because of mass unemployment, the overall social security budget, which accounted for 30 per cent of public expenditure when the Act was passed, continued to grow.

Thatcher gave her name to an *ism*, as Queen Victoria had done, and the *ism*, although it was never a system, crossed both the Channel and the Atlantic. Her forceful personality won admiration in central and eastern Europe, and, indeed, in the Soviet Union which collapsed before she did. Yet Britain's economic problems persisted through the Thatcher years whether the main stress was on monetarism or on 'privatization' of industry. The further narrowing of the manufacturing sector: inadequate investment both in private industry and in public utilities; too small a research and development base; the growing costs of maintaining an infrastructure, even if the 'family silver' − to use Macmillan's image − was sold to privatized bodies; a huge import bill, with imports reaching a record level in 1984 in spite of a fall in oil imports; overdependence on revenue from North Sea oil (too summarily treated as a 'bounty'); an ominous fall in Britain's share in world trade in services provided through the City of London. United Kingdom output rose by only 6 per cent in the years 1979−91 compared with an OECD average of 35 per cent, leaving Britain in the twentieth position out of twenty-one. Clearly, however strong political will might be − and no prime minister's will could have been stronger than Thatcher's − long-term economic trends could not be reversed.

In her last years economic recession, international in its origins, was deep and prolonged enough to survive her resignation in 1990, an event which one Conservative MP compared with an Elizabethan tragedy. She had won three elections in all, the second in 1983 in the aftermath of the Falkland Islands war which buttressed her position, and the third election five years later. Her resignation, however, like her earlier successes, was less the consequence of disagreements on domestic policy within her party than on damaging differences on European questions after she had supported, despite her aggressive style, critical moves towards Community reorganization at the European summit of 1986 which approved the Single European Act.

There was one domestic issue which had alienated large sections of public opinion. A 'community charge' – described more usually in forthright fourteenth-century language as the 'poll tax' – which changed the basis of local rating taxation, generated bitter local grass-roots opposition. In Liverpool, for example, always a problem city for her, which challenged every Thatcherite policy, non-payment of community charge reached 52 per cent. In parts of England very different from Liverpool – and in middle-class circles too – there was anger not only at the poll tax but at high mortgage rates, which at one point rose to 15.5 per cent, and anxiety about falls in property prices. There were empty houses – and empty shops. Not surprisingly, there were mass demonstrations in Trafalgar Square.

There were imprisonments too. As late as 1998 a grandmother in a wheelchair was jailed for three months for failing to pay £600 poll tax arrears. She was very quickly released. All things in social history connect. The person at its centre was divorced, but shared her council house with her husband, a former miner in the militant South Yorkshire coalfield. She was under the care of the National Health Service for two hip replacements, an operation of great importance to sufferers, but one involving long queues. She compared her brief time in prison after being taken there by bailiffs not with that of other prisoners but with that most popular member of the royal family. 'I was treated like the Queen Mother.' She chose a royal reference point very different from the limited reference points of the 1930s.

That grandmother was not a typical prisoner, but no account of the social history of the years after the 1950s can leave out crime, about which Rowntree said little and what Orwell had said lost any point. There was relatively little violence in pre-war society, but in 1951 the number of indictable criminal offences, which had risen by a half during the Second World War, reached a new peak: in 1938, only one in a hundred of the age group from fourteen to seventeen committed such an offence (one statistical measure, to be examined critically), but in 1951 the figure was one in fifty. There was little public criticism of the police at this time, and more attention was being focused on conditions in prisons, particularly for young offenders (Borstals) and on the system of probation.

There were to be big changes in crime numbers and in policies, not all of them pointing in one direction, between the 1960s and 1990s. Whatever the relationship between unemployment and crime – and Thatcher refused to bracket them together – the number of recorded offences (another statistical measure), which had been around 3,000,000 in 1981, rose during the last Thatcher years, and in 1996 reached 5,000,000, with the police reporting that less than half the crimes committed in the country were being reported. Households in housing estates and tower blocks were the main victims. The peak age of offending was eighteen for males and fifteen for females, and many offences were drug related. The press made the most of young children's crimes, some of them sensational, including murder of other children – in 1996 one boy had committed no fewer than 300 crimes before the age of fifteen. Yet it also made much of the extraordinary educational achievements of young children: one boy in 1998 passed a GCSE examination at the age of six.

How to deal with the increase in crime (and its causes) – and with the relentless pressure on prison space – divided opinion and political parties, and even the police. (In the mid-1990s Britain had the third highest proportion of prisoners in the population in the European Community.) The bitterly contested Criminal Justice and Public Order Act, which came into force in 1995, included among its provisions restriction of the right to silence, increased police powers to take action in suspicious circumstances, but measures to restrict trespassers, squatters and illegal campers. Home Office powers were already substantial without new legislation, and surveys showed that Michael Howard, last Home Secretary in the Major government, had strong public backing for his tough line on crime, a line to be largely followed by his Labour successor, Jack Straw. They showed also, however, that there was creeping mistrust of the police (82 per cent of people polled in 1995, as against 92 per cent in 1982, thought that the police were 'doing a good job') and of the system of criminal justice.

There were inevitable strains too, inside what was still a decentralized police force – both in the Metropolitan Police, which was vulnerable to corruption, and the provincial police, which was supported by 'county opinion'. When its independence of government seemed to be jeopardized in 1993 and 1994, the periodical *Police*, the 'Voice of the Service', described the Sheehy Report on policing as 'a blueprint for disaster', claiming that 'the balance sheet' had become 'the bottom line in policing'. Such complaints may be compared with the professional complaints of teachers (including university teachers), soldiers, doctors and lawyers when confronted with new systems of management.

During the 1960s it had been obvious that patterns of authority in society were changing – in schools and universities (where pupils and students asserted their claims more forcefully); in hospitals, some of them new – and large – and on the railways (where matrons and stationmasters no longer ran their little empires); in the factories (where shop stewards addressed, but did not always convince, mass meetings); and on the football ground and tennis court (where referees and umpires became suspect). And it was in this context that police authority itself looked less benevolent as police constables on the beat (the 'Dixons of Dock Green') gave way to detectives in 'Z Cars'.

The introduction of a new standard language of management (at its worst, jargon) came later, penetrating both economic and cultural institutions, while the role of business consultants, following in the wake of accountants, was enhanced before 'spin doctors' were heard of. Everyone now became a 'customer': everywhere 'admin' became 'management'. The 'cult of the amateur' was the enemy at first – and the MBA became an increasingly important qualification for businessmen – but old professional interests proved resistant to the 'logic' of 'internal markets', in health, in education (and in the BBC).

Orwell, with his interest in language, would have been critical of such change, which was encouraged by politicians: despite talk of openness, they were themselves to resort increasingly to consultants. Yet he would probably have been more deeply interested in changes in housing, another element in our poll tax prisoner's case history. For Rowntree, who had been interested in the provision of public housing before 1914, there had been great improvement by 1936. Whereas in 1900, 5.7 per cent of the working-class population of York lived in overcrowded houses and 26 per cent lived in slums, the comparable figures for 1936 were only 1.7 per cent and 11.7 per cent. But a 'housing problem' persisted in the 1930s, even if it had been largely solved for the middle classes. Although 5,000,000 new houses were built between 1911 and 1939 and 350,000 slum properties were demolished, in 1939

4,000,000 people were still living in largely 'unmodernized' nineteenth-century houses, and these were to deteriorate further during the Second World War when repairs were difficult and few new houses were built.

The problem was not merely quantitative. There was a social as well as an environmental dimension, for 'slums' had their own social identities, and new municipal housing estates often did not. Built on the edge of towns and cities or beyond their limits, they were to leave behind them 'inner city' decay which, along with deteriorating infrastructure, was to be forced to the forefront of local and national politics in the 1970s and 1980s. But that was not the immediate problem. While the estates varied in appearance and quality, in many of them little attempt was made to introduce or even to encourage community facilities, and they could be lifeless, silent and dull. Transport facilities were restricted. Bus timetables dictated daily life.

Gardening (laburnum: floribunda roses: dahlias) was the favourite outdoor occupation – some people had 'allotments' – radio (sometimes crosswords) the main indoor. There was little immediate change in class relationships after the change of place, but there was often a sense of social dislocation; and even after the end of the Second World War, when a New Towns Act of 1946 was passed (followed a year later by a new Town and Country Planning Act which laid more emphasis on community provision), underlying social concerns, beginning with density and dispersal, were not laid aside. 'Must Utopia always disappoint?' asked Harold Orlans in a study of Stevenage, one of the twenty-two new English towns, published in 1952.

As for the old towns and cities – and the metropolis – there was one major general improvement. In 1956 a Clean Air Act was passed. The least celebrated piece of post-war legislation, the Act did more to change the urban environment than any other legislative measure after 1945. Nonetheless, the problem of air pollution was not 'solved': during the 1990s it was and continues to be a serious threat to daily life in all the large cities. In a report of 1997 it was said in some cities to exceed levels harmful to health 'every five days'.

One 'solution' to the housing problems of the 1960s – huge tower blocks, rising into the sky like vertical streets – was to disappoint more than semi-detached housing-estates. Far from being lifeless, silent and dull, the blocks could be untidy, noisy and violent, and 'vandalism' became a serious complaint. It is just as difficult, however, to generalize about tower blocks as it is about the housing estates of the 1930s. They were not cheap to build. Nor did they save as much land as the authorities who provided them might have hoped. They were often very badly placed with no thought either for traffic between them or for their effects on the sky line.

A totally different 'solution' to the problem, with widespread social consequences, was the encouragement of house ownership backed by mortgages, and this affected privately rented homes as well as homes on estates or in tower blocks. In 1947, 58 per cent of housing stock was rented from private landlords: in 1973 the figure was 14 per cent. The total number of owner-occupied dwellings more than doubled between 1961 and 1996. New house building had peaked in 1968 when over half the 414,000 new dwellings were built by the private sector: in 1996 the proportion was four-fifths. The post-war low in private housing starts, however, was 99,000 in 1980. The levels of house prices and interest charges on mortgage Building Society payments became of major importance in determining private mobility. Keeping up payments was at the heart of 'family finance', now a favourite topic in the media. Likewise, council house sales were at the heart of much local finance when there were cuts in central funding or imposed ceilings on council expenditure. Local government suffered during the Thatcher years, and in the metropolis for political reasons the Greater London Council was abolished.

The housing problem, with housing associations as one of the instruments of change, took on a new shape when the extent of 'homelessness' in the 1990s was compared less with that of the 1930s or the 1960s than with that of the 1890s – attention, as then, being focused on the London scene. It was impossible to move around in London in the 1990s without seeing beggars in the daytime (buskers in the London underground stations were the most colourful) and large numbers of people, most of them young, 'sleeping rough' at night. Tracking information was necessary to identify the problem: the availability of hostel and 'special needs' housing accommodation was necessary to cope with it. The social contrasts were disturbing – and visible. There were also empty properties. In the country as a whole there were 864,000 empty homes in 1994, many, but not all, dilapidated and in urgent need of repair. In the 1960s 'squatters' in them had often had the spotlight cast on them. Now it was the turn of the homeless.

Lifestyles as well as property rights were invoked as they were to be in the 1990s, even though the styles were not necessarily or not entirely a matter of choice. For all the increase in material wealth, inequalities, measured in objective terms, grew during the 1980s and 1990s. The proportion of people with net household disposable income below the average rose from 59 per cent in 1979 to 63 per cent in 1994/5. There was talk on American lines of an 'underclass' and of a 'culture of dependence'. The number of families dependent on social security benefits increased by more than two-thirds between 1979 and 1987, and, taking a longer period, social security expenditure on sick and disabled people trebled in real terms between 1981/2 and 1996/7. About seven in ten families received some kind of social security benefit in 1995/6.

Studying similar statistics had led the Archbishop of Canterbury, Robert Runcie, to describe the country in 1984, Orwell's year of menace, simply as 'no longer a decent society', and this was not the last time that the adjective 'decent' was used in this way. More than statistics were involved. There were widely reported individual stories of dependence and distress, along with reports in the press of street mugging, football hooliganism, gang warfare, sophisticated organized crime, juvenile delinquency, drug trafficking, child crime, and child abuse. There had long been enough loneliness in the 'new society' (the title of an important new weekly periodical founded in 1962) to darken the pages of the new colour supplements of the Sunday newspapers. The first of these, that of the *Sunday Times*, appeared in February 1962, the same year as the completion of architect Basil Spence's new Coventry Cathedral. He had started work on Sussex University, the first of Britain's new universities of the 1960s, which itself figured in *Vogue*. Again, this time through contrasts, all things in social history interconnect.

Architecture, not least Spence's, was controversial then and later, and when the tower blocks were built for their Council tenants they had their aesthetic defenders, as had 'brutal' office buildings designed, like them, in blocks usually complete with 'open plan' interiors, dubbed 'contemporary'. The name of Le Corbusier was invoked. Of Centre Point in London, empty for years after its completion in 1966, the *Architectural Digest* could write that it expressed 'the confidence of professionalism, like Mary Quant and the Beatles'. These were among the great names of the 1960s, leaders of style, just as those of Gracie

Fields and George Formby were representatives of (then un-named) popular culture during the 1930s.

The popular long-running *Coronation Street* television programme recalled the pre-housing estate 1930s. London's Carnaby Street was very different. Yet *Coronation Street* has outlasted Carnaby Street, and there can still be nostalgia for the 1930s – as, of course, for the Beatles a generation later. In retrospect, much of the style sequence beginning in the 1960s seems to start with the Beatles who now belong to history. Before breaking up in 1970 they not only made records (in the beginning these belonged to the transistor age), but also established records of a different kind: the country's best selling record of all time is their 'Sergeant Pepper's Lonely Hearts Club Band', released in 1967.

Loneliness, anxiety and nostalgia, all evoked in the work of Alan Bennett, are common twentieth-century states of feeling. In Orwell's *1984* the beautiful English countryside, already being spoilt, was a source of consolation as well as of escape, although subsequently it was to become a scene of two-sided protest. The notion of 'animal rights', with antecedents in earlier English social history, was taken up by a militant minority, including 'hunt saboteurs'. Yet what described itself as another minority, the far larger 'rural minority', staged a huge 'Country Defence' demonstration in London in November 1997 within a few months of Blair's election victory. It was on such a scale that it led (if not directly) to the abandonment of a Labour backbencher's attempt by private bill to prohibit hunting.

For those who took part in such sports (and for many commentators in the press) such a 'traditional sport' was the quintessence of 'Englishness' which the poet Eliot had tried in 1947 to identify in terms of great national events. St George's Day was not one of them: the twelfth of August, was. Now in 1997 the Poet Laureate, Ted Hughes, argued that these sports kept animals alive – a very English defence of them: hunting was 'this strange system that our history has produced for us'.

People, not history, produce systems, and between the 1930s and the 1960s the countryside had already been subject to just as great a change as towns and cities (some with newly created 'conservation areas' within them, an effective idea of the Civic Trust). Planning issues often converged in the village, as they were to do in 1998 when a 'new homes' policy offered the threat of 'damage to the countryside'. Throughout its long history the countryside had owed as much to man as to nature, although nature could show its continuing force in the late twentieth century both in tree, crop and animal disease, in destructive gales, like that of 1987, and in subsequent recuperation: as the director of one Sussex Wildlife Trust observed, storms were 'an essential part of our ecology . . . showing us what Nature can do for itself'. Ends and beginnings. It was men, not nature, however, who were responsible for one of the most striking contrasts between the 1930s, when agriculture was in the doldrums, and the period after the Second World War. A so-called 'agricultural revolution' then was compared, in terms both of greater agricultural yields and of environmental change, with the neolithic breakthrough in prehistory and with the far-reaching changes in the eighteenth century. A 1947 Agricultural Act designed to save the farmer from the insecurities of pre-war farming, passed by Attlee's Labour government, laid the foundation, and long before Britain entered the Common Market it had been extended by capital grants, tax concessions and price supports.

The environmental consequences were extensive. Thousands of acres of down and heath disappeared. Barley took the place of scrub on the chalk hills of Dorset, conifers were planted, barbed wire supplanted hawthorn – 125,000 miles of hedgerow were lost after 1945, pylons stretched across the plains, corrugated iron barns and silos appeared in well-drained farmyards, and everywhere chemical fertilizers and pesticides were used. (The use of nitrogen-based fertilizers increased eight-fold between 1953 and 1976.) Nearly half of the country's woodland disappeared. Meanwhile, both animals and men had been giving way to machines for decades. In 1950 there were still 300,000 horses working on farms; in 1979 there were 3,575. In 1945 there were 563,000 regular full-time farm workers; in 1980 there were 133,000.

There was to be a subsequent reaction, beginning in 1968 with a Countryside Act, charging the Minister of Agriculture to pay attention to 'the desirability of conserving the natural beauty and amenity of the countryside', and during the 1970s a number of farmers were to develop techniques of 'organic farming', based on new versions of older farming practices. A new Wildlife and Countryside Act was passed in 1982, with more legislation and a White Paper on the Countryside to follow. While not fully satisfying 'green environmentalists', a dedicated minority group with an impact on majority politics, it seemed to point in the right direction.

The environment, first entering politics around 1970, the year of the first 'Earth Day' and of a landmark international conference on the environment in Stockholm, had become a major national concern within twenty years, and a new Department of the Environment, housed in one of the most appalling new office tower blocks in London, was expected 'to look after it'. The sculptor Henry Moore rightly claimed in 1980 that 'the special quality of the English countryside' had helped 'to shape the English character', adding that his own sculptures would have been different had not the shapes of the Yorkshire landscape existed first. Interest in 'the environment', built and natural (the distinction usually drawn), however, was broader than this. Global as well as local priorities loomed large.

The role of farmers, not a homogeneous group, was ambiguous. By 1995 only one person in fifteen was engaged in agriculture. During the 1970s and 1980s, as in the 1940s and 1950s, much of the threat to the countryside was felt to come not so much from land speculators and industrialists as from farmers, whose incomes were supported after 1973 by an agricultural price policy determined not in London (though London criticized it) but in Brussels. The 1970s and 1980s were 'good years' for farmers, yet it was the problems they faced, not the benefits accruing to them – and not all farmers shared them – that dominated the headlines in the 1990s, particularly during the 'Beef War' that followed a total ban on imports of British beef by the European Union in the spring of 1996. 'Mad cow disease', which led to the ban, had a medieval-sounding name, and the way of dealing with it – destruction of animals – seemed medieval too. Yet the origins of 'BSE' were related to twentieth-century science and to the introduction of new feeding stock mixtures; and development in turn was related to the demands of large-scale retailing at the consumer end of what was now called a 'food chain'. Meat sales fell; sale of 'organic' vegetables rose.

Such development underpinned what stands out as the biggest 'trend' in twentieth-century social history, the improvement of material standards of life, a trend that went back even before the 1930s, and which during the 1960s was expressed not only in statistics but in fashions and styles. Already in 1959 it was calculated that among the more prosperous groups in the working classes, 85 per cent of households had a television set, 44 per cent a washing machine, 16 per cent a refrigerator, and 32 per cent a car. Of a television set it was rightly said in the *Daily Mirror* as early as 1950 that if you let it through your front door, life could never be the same again, but verdicts on how it would change varied, whereas verdicts on freedom from drudgery were almost unanimous in relation to washing machines. Refrigerators were of crucial importance in relation to food and the food chain, and cars changed life in country villages and in suburban housing estates more than any other innovation, not to speak of threatening the very existence of inner towns and cities.

There was sociological investigation in the late 1950s on the impact of increased spending on 'consumer goods' on the class system: would 'the working classes' become 'middle-class'? But it did not need investigation or debate to appreciate how radically the position of women in the home was changing as it was to change later at work. The word 'emancipation' was frequently used to describe the process, which over a longer period of time was to re-pattern relationships between husbands and wives. Yet the change that had the biggest immediate impact on the thinking and feeling of the 1960s was the fact – and it was a fact – that in the late 1950s and 1960s, young people had far more disposable income than their parents or grandparents. They became eager customers.

Advertising, reaching a new peak of 1.9 per cent of consumer expenditure and 1.4 per cent of gross national product in 1960, was geared to generational as well as economic and cultural change. Indeed, advertisers, who were given new opportunities when 'independent' television was introduced (through legislation and after bitter debate) in 1955, were among the most 'creative' people. Rates of obsolescence speeded up in music more quickly than in machinery. 'Jingles' on television went with slogans off it: 'Drink a Pinta Milka Day'; 'Double Diamond Works Wonders'. There were ends, however, as well as beginnings, or what seemed 'near ends'. Thus, cinema attendances had already reached their peak in 1951, and were to touch their depth in the Orwellian year, 1984. There were to be later revivals. Cinema attendances rose in the decade leading up to 1996.

The 'Admass' materialism of the late 1950s and 1960s, Priestley's newly coined word, was only one expression of the longest and biggest of trends, for in the quarter of a century between 1971 and 1996 real disposable income almost doubled, with less stress on the 'mass' and more on the choices available. It was during these years that the luxuries of the few, including holidays abroad in the sun, really did become regular items in the budgets of the many. For example, in 1996 at least one member in a fifth of all households had a mobile phone, something beyond the power of even the few in the 1960s, and four-fifths of all households possessed a video recorder. The proportion had doubled in ten years.

How real choice was became in itself a matter of debate, although mobility came to be taken for granted, not the hard-won social mobility through education which fascinated students of society in the 1950s, but mobility as a dimension of life, thought and feeling, where less was fixed in the framework of time and space than in previous centuries. As greater wealth was expressed in consumption, every decade from the late 1950s onwards made much of fashion. Indeed, as early as the 1940s the lengthening of women's skirts – to be followed two decades later by their shortening – was felt to have symbolic as well as fashion significance. Mass Observation devoted a *Bulletin* to the subject in the autumn of 1947: it was called 'Skirt in Transition', and one 'artisan class woman, 30', quoted commented that 'if it was done correctly it would be very nice. Like olden times'.

It did not seem so to many other followers of this and other new fashions, each of which has its own specific history. For food, how to cook it as well as what to eat: for clothing, how men's, women's and children's were related: and for styles in houses, how to deal both with 'interiors' and gardens, not to speak of patios. Parallel to the continuing food boom came a wine boom, with the wine now being imported from different continents. In dress, after jeans came sneakers and trainers, a revolution in footwear that was just as notable. The number of 'joggers' grew. Athletics took a more prominent place among 'sports'. In houses colour schemes changed as much as furniture or lighting.

People could no longer be as easily 'placed' as Orwell had placed them. They also found it more difficult to identify themselves. The sense of a middle class was disappearing – with generational gaps – as much as the sense of a working class. The arts, particularly the theatre and the graphic arts, were influenced by commercialized fashion too, and there was more concern for 'design'. Long after Carnaby Street had passed out of fashion design reached Downing Street in 1997: it was held up as one of Englands' greatest assets in an age of global competition.

No consumer product reflected concern for design and fashion more than the greatest instrument of individual and social mobility – the car.

It is possible to chart changes in attitudes to almost everything else in society (beginning with the family) to changes in the content and style of car advertisements. The statistics of purchase and use of cars, and mileage of motorways, constitute the supreme example of a trend, continuing into the 1990s, if subject to cyclical movements. During the 1960s the number of licensed car owners in Britain doubled, and between the mid-1970s and mid-1990s the number rose again from nearly 11,000,000 to over 30,000,000.

The first motorway, the M1, opened in November 1959, four years before Dr Richard Beeching, Chairman of British Railways, announced a plan for extensive cuts in railway mileage. Following heavy financial losses, they signalled the closure of a quarter of the rail network, a symbolic as well as a real ending like the closure of pits. By contrast, 600 miles of motorway had been built by 1969, transforming the social geography of the country – and its appearance. New beginnings were not always popular. Minority – and sometimes majority – protests became common, often with the gentry, and even the aristocracy, joining together with the 'greens'. (The words 'gentry' and 'aristocracy' survived more easily than the word 'gentleman'.) When the last stretch of London's orbital motorway, the M25, an ill-fated road, was opened in 1986, the public was not invited to the opening ceremony for fear of cross-class protest. A car broke down on the new road at 11.16 am, within just one minute of the opening. By the 1990s, 20,000,000 cars were using the M25 each day. And it was being rebuilt.

With the freedom of the road went social controls of a new kind designed to limit accidents and to safeguard congested towns and cities, sometimes far from motorways. One-way systems became common, so did pedestrian precincts. In 1960 the first traffic wardens appeared in the streets of London, issuing 344 parking tickets on their first day. Their work rate was to rise. A year later MOT tests were introduced, and five years later the first breathalysers. One-way traffic systems were another example – out of many – of planning controls. Cars could be towed away. Safety belts were enforced. Taxation also was an instrument of policy. The demand for a tougher transport policy grew during the 1990s, with privatized rail being offered new possibilities of increasing its customer numbers. There was no satisfactory answer, however, to the problems of London's 'Tube', a major topic of public concern inside and outside the press.

Transport figures regularly in the daily routines of life, although more work is now being carried out – and will be – at home because of a different strand in the communications revolution – computerization. There was another change, however, of just as fundamental a kind, this time unprecedented, which not only has left an even bigger impact on inner cities than transport but has affected English society as a whole. Until 1948 there had been only a trickle of black and coloured immigrants into England, and it was not until the 1950s that they first became 'visible ethnic minorities'. Travel agencies, backed by advertising, actively developed the early traffic, particularly from the West Indies. Low wages and heavy unemployment there served as one spur; relative prosperity in Britain and the demand for labour in a period of labour shortage was another. In 1948, a batch of 547 immigrants, most of them young, arrived from Jamaica, 492 of them on one ship, the SS *Empire Windrush*, which landed at Tilbury Docks on 22 June; it has been described by Lesley Downer in the *Financial Times* as 'an icon of black folk history, as significant in its way as the *Mayflower* has been for European Americans'.

Before 1957 the majority of migrants were adult males, but in that year there were as many women and children for the first time, and during the next two years they were to outnumber men. There were many signs, therefore, of the desire to settle, although assimilation proved more difficult than had been expected by British advocates of an 'open door'. Most of the new immigrants looked to Britain as 'the mother country' and were aware that they had the right to enter Britain and settle, a right which had been confirmed in the British Nationality Act of 1948 but which was taken away in 1962, after the entry of immigrants had reached nearly 40,000.

Immigrants took up a variety of occupations, with men concentrating on railways and women on hospitals, and Britain came to depend upon them, not least because they were often prepared to accept jobs and terms of work which did not appeal to English-born workers. They had to face persistent discrimination, however, in employment, housing and education. The words 'racist' and 'racism' entered the language, with the *Observer* noting sadly as early as March 1965 that 'any hope that Britain might prove to be immune from colour prejudice' had disappeared – 'an ugly discovery for those who believe that all forms of racial or colour discrimination are an affront against human dignity'.

In 1958, when an estimated 210,000 people from 'coloured minorities' were living in Britain, many of them in dilapidated and overcrowded large Victorian houses originally built for middle-class families, there were serious disturbances in Nottingham and Notting Hill – not by black newcomers, but by self-styled 'nigger-hunting' youths, still vaguely known as 'teddy boys'. According to the judge who sentenced nine white youths after Notting Hill, 'it was you men who started the whole of this violence in Notting Hill. You are a minute and insignificant section of the population . . . and you have filled the whole nation with horror, indignation and disgust.' These were early manifestations of the assault on decency, but there was to be annual carnival as well as conflict at Notting Hill.

It was within a context of prejudice and conflict that the issues of racial discrimination (not at first called 'racism'), immigration control and police conduct began to be debated for the first time, although the word 'debated' is too polite in relation to much that happened. There was little general knowledge among English people of the different backgrounds from which the newcomers came or of their ways of life, even though, unlike Turkish, Spanish and Portuguese migrant workers in the German and Swiss workforce, all of them came from former colonial backgrounds with varying kinds of cultural contact with England. Unknown or forgotten social history was catching up as Caribbean immigrants were followed by immigrants from the Indian subcontinent, among them Punjabi Sikhs, Gujarati Hindus, and Muslims from Pakistan and, after the split of Pakistan in 1971, from Bangladesh. In that year the immigrant population totalled 1,200,000.

As numbers increased, so did tensions, heightened in 1968 when the then prominent Conservative politician Enoch Powell made a colourful speech describing his foreboding: 'like the Romans, I seem to see the River Tiber foaming with much blood.' Meanwhile, immigration controls had been introduced in Parliament to 'regulate the migrant flow', the first in 1962 under a Conservative government, the second, the Commonwealth Immigrants Act, in 1968 under a Labour government. The latter removed the right of entry from all British Commonwealth citizens who did not have a parent or grandparent born in Britain: would-be immigrants could apply for special vouchers, 7,500 of which would be issued annually. A further restrictive Act was passed in 1971, to be followed ten years later, when immigration had drastically slowed down, by the British Nationality Act which ended 'seven centuries of tradition' and replaced a single, unified citizenship of the United Kingdom and Colonies by three separate citizenships – British citizenship, British Dependent Territories citizenship and British Overseas citizenship.

By then political and economic circumstances in Britain had changed. By then too there were big Asian concentrations in cities like Leicester (16.5 per cent); Wolverhampton, Powell's old constituency (8.8 per cent); and Bradford (7.8 per cent); with large West Indian communities in London and the Midlands. Some immigrants had prospered through hard work, mostly in retailing, or through prowess in sport and were making a distinctive contribution to English life. Nonetheless, there was occasional rioting with a racial element, in Brixton in London (1981 and 1995) and in other places like Toxteth in Liverpool. The Scarman Report of 1981, which dealt with Brixton, sought to present a lawyer's analysis of the causes. There was more than one, Scarman concluded, leaving the relative significance of each of them as a matter of dispute: black youth unemployment; the plight of the inner city, the subject of a controversial report by the Church of England in 1986; the still more controversial role of the still decentralized police.

From the inside there were complaints from newcomers, some in sorrow, some in anger, that what were held to be 'old' English values – tolerance, courtesy, mutual respect – were in jeopardy. 'Discrimination', which took many forms, was given new meaning. In 1965 the Race Relations Act was passed, and two years later Mark Abrams wrote the introduction to a Penguin version of a detailed investigation of the subject, the first of several. A second Act was passed in 1968 which was said to have made more employers, 65 per cent of those polled, 'more conscious of the need for non-discrimination'. A term which was significantly broadened to include other kinds of discrimination, including gender discrimination. The Commission for Racial Equality was set up in 1977 and an Equal Opportunities Commission in 1975, five years after the first Equal Pay Act.

There were different impulses behind such legislation. One was the demand for equality: another was humanitarian concern. Research itself often provided a stimulus. Without the work of research charities and foundations, like Political and Economic Planning, founded in 1931 and policy-based, the course of social history would have been different. A religious impulse lay behind some of this work, in the case of a group of Rowntree trusts, Quaker in origin. The oldest of religious institutions, the Church of England – how old was a matter of dispute – played its own part, however, in characteristically English social processes that, along with the battle against discrimination, find no place in *Social Trends*.

It was Archbishop Runcie who had used the word 'decent' and had raised the nature of the relationship between material advance and spiritual values. Yet he was clearly aware of the internal problems of the Church at a time when attendance fell to lower levels than at any previous period of history, and when the Church's relationship with the State became controversial. In the late 1970s a canon of Liverpool Cathedral had described it as suffering from a 'crisis of identity', and although during the 1980s its leaders encouraged a thorough, searching examination of its role both in the inner cities and in the countryside, it could not avoid internal division.

When in 1994 the Church of England ordained its first women priests, following a decision taken by its General Synod, a new representative body founded in 1969, the opponents of change within the Church saw it as far more than a break with tradition. A number of them, including a retired Bishop of London, moved over to the Roman Catholic Church, to which under 7 per cent of the population belonged but which drew in larger Sunday attendances than the Church of England. There were echoes of older arguments during the course of this – and later – debate, some looking back to the 'primitive church', some to the Reformation, some to Victorian times. They witnessed to the fact that the Church, still 'Established', unlike the Roman Catholic Church and many other Christian sects, was open, not authoritarian, a feature resented by some of the groups inside it.

Debates on women's ordination – and later on homosexuality – were not the only religious or ecclesiastical arguments of the 1980s and 1990s. Alongside disagreements about doctrine and liturgy ('alternative services' to the Common Prayer Book, built into weekly worship in 1980), church finance was strained through mistaken investment policies. 'Ethical' investment became an issue also; church premises were often locked to keep out thieves or vandals; church leadership on moral matters was questioned: one great cathedral, Lincoln, was torn by dispute; Westminster Abbey was gripped in a Trollopian contest in 1998 between Dean and organist.

Outside the Church, charismatic bodies (present inside the Church too) gained in support, often dramatically, and Islam strengthened its influence, doubling its numbers to 1,200,000 between 1980 and 1995. Old issues of 'fundamentalism' took on new colour. Ecumenical cooperation between Christians was strengthened, particularly at the local level, but inter-faith cooperation had obvious limits. Meanwhile, 'new age' cults of various kinds – some believing in reincarnation, others claiming to be 'scientific' – received considerable attention from the press, in which astrological forecasts figured regularly. (The television programme on the National Lottery included 'Mystic Meg' as a performer.) The popularity of minority cults was frequently taken as evidence of 'spiritual crisis'.

So too was the popular response to Diana's death. Diana, the Princess of Wales, had devoted herself to many causes, identifying herself as a patron of the suffering and the handicapped, heterogeneous groups with an enhanced consciousness of common interest in post-war society (much as 'classes' had in early industrial society). When she was suddenly killed, therefore, there was a sense of popular identification with the 'People's Princess', who was seen as a victim as well as a princess. For once central London was still on the day of her funeral. Flowers and candles encircled the palaces where she had lived: she, albeit the daughter and sister of Earls, a Spencer, seemed 'one of us'.

There were many ironies in late twentieth-century social history. The recession of the 1990s was as obvious on the sea front at Hastings as it was in the middle of Rotherham. The victims of the collapse of sections of Lloyds enterprise, some of them members of the aristocracy, were often neighbours of the chairmen of business companies who were receiving such extraordinarily high salaries that they could be condemned by John Major. Under Blair, Chris Woodhead, Her Majesty's Chief Inspector of Schools, received a substantial salary increase (along with bonuses) when teachers' salaries were pegged to inflation. When Major proclaimed 'basic values', the first people to be in the unwelcome spotlight were politicians. 'Spin doctors' and lobbyists soon moved into it under Blair. The Strangeways prison riot of 1990 started in the Chapel. One element in the Camelot consortium that won the National Lottery franchise in 1994, the Cadbury business, now

Cadbury-Schweppes, had originally been built up by dedicated opponents of gambling of all kinds.

One of the clichés of contemporary speech is 'at the end of the day'. Yet despite the millennium there is no sense of an ending to this *History* in the same way as there was an end to the Second World War. Indeed, in the pursuit of the millennium during the last decade of this century those involved in the preparations for its surrounding arrangements have been concerned less with exploring the vistas of the past than with scanning the vistas of the future, helped by computers, and with building a costly and controversial Dome, conceived of (unlike the Crystal Palace in 1851) as a building, independently of what was to be put inside it.

Christians, aware of the spiritual as well as the historical significance of the millennium, have tried to deepen the message and to lengthen the time scale, but, like history itself, they have been short of sponsors. Moreover, they too can be caught up in the present. Anglicans were advised by a media group of their own, set up in 1996, to devise a new Cross-less logo bearing the innocuous words 'New Start'. The fact that since the late 1960s England has become a 'multi-faith society' has in itself complicated, without fully determining, all religious – and political – calculations.

For this and for many other reasons the social history of this century – or at least of the 'short century' since 1914, a so-called 'People's Century' – is markedly different from that of any that preceded it. The most important reason, however, is the continuing advance of what has been called the 'communications revolution', outlined in its beginnings in Chapter 9, a revolution associated in its recent stages with digitalization and with the development of interactive systems producing multimedia text, statistics, graphics, sound and moving video. After being conceived of very differently in its beginnings, the world-wide 'web' has speedily become democratic and chaotic, with 110,000,000 regular users, the numbers doubling each year, deriving its strength from below. But there is still an 'above', as there is in the press and broadcasting, now bound up in huge economic concentrations of global media power, as much without precedent as the Internet. They too are acquiring web sites and exploiting them arduously, combining news and entertainment. Technology can never be separated from economics. The strategic plans of the global organizations all have repercussions for society and culture. Already they have affected perceptions both of space and of time, of the relationship between private and public, and even of 'reality' itself.

The media, subject to even more outside criticism than most English institutions, have their own versions of history, and the term 'People's Century' was the BBC's. Preoccupied as they have been with 'today' and 'tomorrow', they have tried to lengthen the time scale also. The dinosaurs, models of which are sold as toys in shops, came first, and how their 'age' ended – it has no clear history – is as much a matter of speculation as how Neanderthal man began. Neolithic families, not too obviously, came later: discoveries relating to their lifestyles – and these can be 'simulated' – take us back to our beginnings. Time moves in great arcs as well as in circles and sequences. Reporting the findings of *2020 Vision*, a 1998 Henley Centre survey of the post-millennial future, *The Times* chose to go back in time as far as this *History* goes, close to the beginning, finding there a surprising contrast: its forward-looking headline ran '2020: Woman the Hunter, Man the Househusband'.

There were fewer surprises in the contents of the Henley Futures survey itself than in *The Times* headline. The writers of the former cannot have found it difficult to conclude that the power of computers and the influence of the Internet will lead to all manner of new social and economic developments by 2020. They have already done so. This is because they are a genuinely revolutionary new feature of 'our times'. Their significance has clearly been appreciated by a private individual, Tom Newton (the right surname), who has proposed an imaginative and highly appropriate millennial project – the pattern of a microchip should be added to the collection of England's ancient chalk-hill figures, inherited from a variety of distant ages. In a thousand years, Newton suggests, people would identify the figure as 'symbolising the very beginnings of a completely new technology. Everything that men might create in the next millennium will be attributable to one thing – the chip.' The human 'dinosaurs' will be left behind.

In this century many things besides microchips have contributed to social history, as this chapter has shown. Yet, leaving aside their effects on employment – and on perception, including the perception of 'virtual reality' – new communications have made it possible to assemble an oral and visual record (at every level) of how people have lived and thought in the People's Century, recalling their private histories as well as public history: growing up; getting older; births, marriages and deaths;

work and holidays; getting and spending; eating and drinking; homes; friends and neighbours. Memory need no longer be lost, a subject that fascinated Orwell.

School remains a powerful memory even in an age that sets store by continuing education and prides itself on the Open University, which as a pioneering new venture, took in its first students in 1970. Wider access to education, care for the future of the young, not of the old, was the major social concern of the 1960s when numbers in higher education, then a priority concern, doubled, and it remained as important through the 1970s into the 1990s as it had never been during the 1930s. When schools were at the centre of the picture there were intermittent, usually unresolved, debates about both theory and policy (including curriculum) as there were to be about social benefits and welfare in the 1990s, all of them reflecting sharp differences of values and objectives. The first comprehensive schools, challenging both traditional and meritocratic theories of education, had opened soon after Butler's Education Act of 1944, but their most rapid growth followed the Labour Party's commitment to comprehensive education after the 1964 General Election. In 1971, 34 per cent of English secondary school children were attending comprehensive schools, and by 1980 that proportion had risen to 80 per cent.

The educational and social consequences of that change were, and still are, as much a matter of debate as was its implementation. Meanwhile, the number of pupils in preparatory and public fee-paying schools, the existence of which was often condemned as divisive, increased. Their future rested not on legislation, although this was discussed (and dropped) during the mid-1960s, but on the market, to be severely tested a generation later during the 1990s when fees rose to such heights that many parents who previously would have sent their children to public schools could not afford to do so.

How to deal with the next generation was a matter for politicians as much as for parents, with repercussions not only on the family but on the community. School league tables of academic results, published in the press, were introduced by Major's government and retained by Blair's. Yet while most attention was now paid to differences in the quality of education in particular schools – and to tighter inspection – it was obvious that it was not only the quality of the education provided which separated 'achievers' from 'non-achievers' and the able from the less able (a dangerously large number of whom left school with no academic qualifications), but also other social influences bearing on 'family background' and on 'adolescence'. The latter was a term more fashionable in the 1960s than in the 1990s, when a more general term 'exclusion' was adopted as part of a changing social vocabulary and applied to more than one generation, children and adults alike.

Health became a more single-minded English preoccupation than education in the 1970s and 1980s and, inevitably therefore, the state of the National Health Service became a preoccupation too. Its founder, Bevan, had remarked once that 'when a bedpan is dropped on a hospital floor its noise should resound in the Palace of Westminster'. It did. In an ageing population expectations of health services remained high as costs, including costs of surgery, rose – making inevitable 'rationing', a word much disliked by the medical profession and, indeed, by the greatly increased number of medical administrators. Not surprisingly, structures were changed more than once, first by the National Health Reorganization Act of 1974, which set out to integrate hospital and community care. A bigger change came in 1990 when the National Health Service and Community Care Act subjected the Service to an internal market mechanism, the fashionable way of dealing with problems of management. Both organization and argument were entering a new and sharpened phase, but this was not the end of the story. The Blair government has again reorganized the structure, promising that queues for 'non-emergency' patients will (eventually) disappear.

There have been other health stories, too, including that of nurses' and doctors' pay, as active an issue as teachers' pay, and never separate from economic and social as distinct from medical history. The latter is now inseparable from the history of science as the result of the launching of a wide range of new pharmaceutical products (among them antibiotics, coagulants, anti-coagulants and contraceptives) and the introduction of innovative techniques of surgery (among them hip surgery and transplants). It was two Englishmen, Alexander Fleming and Howard Florey, who had discovered and developed the 'wonder drug', penicillin; and it was scientists working at the Cavendish Laboratory in Cambridge, one of them Francis Crick, who in 1953 discovered the structure of the DNA molecule, described as 'the secret of life'. The first heart transplant was also carried out in England, by the South African surgeon Christiaan Barnard in 1967.

There was public acclaim for radically new modes of treatment, as there was in technology for the first supersonic Concorde that took to the skies – long in preparation and far more costly than had been projected – a symbol of Anglo-French cooperation, as the Channel Tunnel was to be. Yet far less rapture was expressed than in the United States. The same was true of computerization. Although Englishmen had been among the pioneers of first-generation computers, already by the late 1950s more attention was being focused on the problematic human effects of automation than on its economic advantages, and during the 1960s and 1970s the rapid development of the microchip was achieved mainly elsewhere. The best-known robots in England in the late 1960s and early 1970s were television's Daleks from the popular science-fiction series, *Dr Who*. The kind of excitement that ran through Alvin Toffler's American study *Future Shock* was shared by only a minority in England.

As for medical care, there was as much continuing debate on in vitro fertilization as there was on abortion, running into later debate on bio-engineering and on genetic agriculture. The contraceptive pill had been introduced at a time (1962) when society, if not the Roman Catholic Church, was ready for it, and the Family Planning Act, passed five years later, allowed local authorities to provide contraceptives. Yet abortion was highly contentious (mainly on religious grounds) from the time that David Steel's controversial Abortion Act was passed in 1967 allowing abortion to be carried out under the National Health Service within twenty-eight weeks of conception if two doctors were satisfied that the operation was necessary on medical or psychological grounds. It was an Act which had vociferous defenders, but it also provoked a continuing 'pro-life' movement, a much publicized example of 'single issue' politics, if seldom completely on the more extreme American lines.

There was yet another social aspect of the health story. As more political (and media) emphasis was placed on prevention rather than on cure, millennial health targets were set, an inconceivable operation a century or half a century before. Meanwhile, a revealing detailed study of the health and lifestyle of the British population was conducted during 1984 and 1985, and was followed up for comparison in 1991 with a further study of the same sample. Of women aged between eighteen and forty-five at the time of the first survey, more reported seven years later that they were now in better health, while 64 per cent of the manual workers surveyed claimed that their health had shifted from 'fair to poor' to 'excellent to good'. These were subjective impressions not objective facts. Yet among the over-sixties more than 30 per cent of the sample were receiving drugs to combat high blood pressure. More people 'were overweight' in 1991 than in 1984 – 53 per cent of the over-thirty males and 57 per cent of the females as compared with 47 per cent and 50 per cent – prompting a reference back in time to Mark Abrams's observation in 1945 that 'as against thirty years ago people are larger and heavier'.

It also prompts a reference not to lifestyles but to styles of death. The increased provision of hospice places through charity, not all of it religious, was a sign that late twentieth-century English people were still concerned with ways of death, including those dying of Aids, the new disease of the 1980s linked in the first instance to 'gay' ways of life. Church cemeteries might now be full and city cemeteries might now be sold, while the number of cremations increased, but there was sufficient interest in funerals and in memorial services to suggest that private memory was still held dear. There have been many tragic deaths in the twentieth century to which there have been public as well as private responses, among them the death of children shot at Dunblane in March 1996, a disaster which had general consequences – a fundamental change in the law relating to the holding of guns.

Dunblane was a family tragedy, and as the oldest institution with which this *History* is concerned, the family remains the historic building block of society. 'Take care of the family and the rest will take care of itself', suggested the Roman Catholic journalist Clifford Longley in 1994. He admitted, however, that the definition of the family would have to be flexible and realistic: 'The defence of an out-of-date pattern of family life that does not connect with reality would be a lost cause.' Already the family which figures prominently, if mainly rhetorically, in many political manifestos on both sides, was a sufficiently variegated institution to need analysis as much as defence. And it was to change more. The proportion of one-parent families with dependent children nearly doubled between 1976 and 1991. In 1991 more than a quarter of households consisted of one person living alone, double the proportion of 1961. The proportion of births outside marriage more than doubled to almost one in three between 1982 and 1992.

The large families of the past had been the product of early marriages and high birth rates. During the last decades of the twentieth century the mean age of mothers for all births was to rise, as was that for the first births, reaching 27.8 years in 1992, the highest yet recorded. Families were smaller, there was less of a sense of separate spheres for husbands and wives. Women's employment, full-time as well as part-time, became common. Women were now doing jobs previously done by men. Divorce was easier too after the Divorce Reform Act of 1969, which affirmed that while the irretrievable breakdown of marriage was the only grounds on which a petition for divorce could be presented to the courts by either party in the marriage, if separation had lasted for more than five years either party was entitled to a divorce whether or not the other partner agreed. By 1974, 19 per cent of marriages ended in divorce within ten years. In 1995 there were 155,600 divorces affecting just over 160,000 children. The figure for divorces of parents with children under 16 had peaked at 95,000 two years earlier.

Divorce was an experience shared by the royal family, which at various times in the last decades of the twentieth century has had the spotlight played upon it more than any other family. To deal fully with 'the royals' (a new term), increasingly categorized as 'celebrities', requires switching from the decade, the generation and the trend to one of the oldest of all historical time units, the reign. During the course of a reign longer than that of Elizabeth I, the royal family went through as many vicissitudes as any non-royal family, seldom out of the news and during the 1990s the subject of best-selling books and television programmes. The Queen herself memorably described 1992 as an *annus horribilis*. Her *annus mirabilis* had been 1978, on the eve of Margaret Thatcher's advent to power, when the country was in economic and social difficulties: 'Liz rules – OK' was one of the many slogans chalked on the walls.

If Thatcher gave her name to an *ism* – and Blair has fully acknowledged that features of Thatcherism are 'necessary' elements for him in 'modernizing' Britain – the most that Queen Elizabeth II, a supremely constitutional monarch did for the vocabulary, was to inspire an adjective 'new Elizabethan', quickly abandoned after the glories of Coronation Year, when news of the conquest of Mount Everest arrived in London and Benjamin Britten wrote a celebratory opera *Gloriana*. If the moods and policies of the Thatcher years varied, so too, even more, did the moods of the Queen's reign as a whole. And the moods will doubtless continue to change, strongly influenced but never exclusively determined by the economic situation. There are many uncertainties, but it is plain that late Elizabethan England will be as different from early Elizabethan England as was the end period of the reign of Elizabeth I from its beginning. Meanwhile, the monarchy itself, if not the hereditary principle, remains the single main symbol of continuity.

There was no continuity – and no debt to history – in a new social classification of the Queen's subjects devised by the Economic and Social Research Council for the Office of National Statistics and published in December 1998. The 1911 classification went, but so too did all older classifications based on land, labour (manual and non-manual) and education. The Church (and the Army) virtually disappeared from the scene no more *oratores*. In a seven-class system, non-hierarchical in character – and totally non-symbolic – the emphasis was placed on 'management'. Senior police officers – and teachers – were to be placed in Class I, however, along with 'high professionals'. Class VII ('Routine Occupations') was to include car-park attendents (traffic wardens were in Class VI), refuse collectors and road sweepers (no echoes of William Morris). Computer engineers were to figure in Class III. The classification took no account of the esteem (or lack of it) which people enjoy or of income differentials. It will be used in the first Census of the Third Millennium. Is this the end of history at last – or, at least, of English history?

FURTHER READING

This highly selective guide to further reading includes major books and detailed studies at different levels of information and interpretation. The major books often include fuller bibliographies. Some of the most interesting and up-to-date reading is to be found in periodicals, although for reasons of space individual articles in them are not cited here.

I   UNWRITTEN HISTORY

I. H. Longworth, *Prehistoric Britain* (1985) provides a brief introduction. Invaluable general surveys include C. Renfrew (ed.), *British Prehistory – A New Outline* (1974) and J. V. S. Megaw and D. D. Simpson, *Introduction to British Prehistory* (1979). There are 320 excellent photographs in S. Thomas, *Pre-Roman Britain* (1965).

For the history of prehistory see K. Hudson, *A Social History of Archaeology* (1981); and P. J. Bowles, *The Invention of Progress: The Victorians and the Past* (1989), which has a good bibliography. For method and debate see, *inter alia*, the fascinating collection of articles edited by C. Renfrew, *The Explanation of Culture Change: Models in Prehistory* (1973).

For the changing face of England see W. G. Hoskins, *The Making of the English Landscape* (1955); J. G. Evans, *The Environment of Early Man in the British Isles* (1975); and I. Sissons and M. Tooley (eds), *The Environment in British Prehistory* (1982).

R. Bradley, *The Social Foundations of Prehistoric Britain* (1984) deals, amongst other topics, with the role of inference in archaeology. For the beginnings see J. B. Campbell, *The Prehistoric Settlement of Britain* (1978); J. J. Wymer, *The Palaeolithic Age* (1986); and P. J. Fowler, *The Forming of Prehistoric Britain* (1983). For later stages see D. D. A. Simpson (ed.), *Economy and Settlement in Neolithic and Early Bronze Age Britain and Europe* (1971) and B. W. Cunliffe, *Iron Age Communities in Great Britain* (2nd edn, 1978).

For Stonehenge and other places to visit see R. J. C. Atkinson, *Stonehenge* (1979 edn); J. Fowles and B. Brukoff, *The Enigma of Stonehenge* (1980); and, adding to the mysteries, G. S. Hawkins and J. B. White, *Stonehenge Decoded* (1966); *The Penguin Guide to Prehistoric England and Wales* (1981); G. E. Daniel, *Megaliths in History* (1972); and for arguments about megaliths C. Renfrew, *Before Civilisation* (1972).

For art see I. Finlay, *Celtic Art* (1973); and P. Jacobsthal and E. M. Jope, *Early Celtic Art in Britain* (1977).

For religion see A. Ross, *Pagan Celtic Britain* (1967) and T. Kendrick's classic study *The Druids: A Study in Celtic Prehistory* (1927).

2   INVASION, RESISTANCE, SETTLEMENT AND CONQUEST

It is interesting to compare the two major Oxford histories of Roman Britain, R. G. Collingwood and J. N. L. Myres, *Roman Britain and the English Settlements* (1934) and P. Salway, *Roman Britain* (1981), for changes in perspectives as well as in scholarship. Salway has supplemented his study with an excellent illustrated history (1993). See also S. Frere's impressive *Britannia: A History of Roman Britain* (2nd edn, 1978). For aspects of social history see A. R. Birley, *The People of Roman Britain* (1979); A. L. F. Rivet, *Town and Country in Roman Britain* (1958); J. Wacher, *The Towns of Roman Britain* (1975); B. W. Cunliffe, *Fishbourne, A Roman Palace and its Garden* (1971); D. J. Breeze and B. Dobson, *Hadrian's Wall* (1978 edn); and P. Marsden, *Roman London* (1980).

The most comprehensive study of culture is J. Munby and M. Henig (eds), *Roman Art and Life in Britain* (1977). Religion is explored in W. Radwell (ed.), *Temples, Churches and Religion: Recent Research in Roman Britain* (1980) and in C. Thomas, *Christianity in Roman Britain to A.D. 500* (1981). L. Alcock's *Arthur's Britain* (1933) provides a fascinating epilogue and prelude and should be compared with J. Morris, *The Age of Arthur* (1973) and P. Hunter Blair, *The World of Bede* (1990). D. Whitelock's *The Beginnings of English Society* (1952) is a sensible introduction to social history. P. H. Sawyer (ed.), *Medieval Settlement* (1976) examines a subject of increasing interest to social historians, not only medieval historians.

There are several good introductions to Anglo-Saxon history, the most recent of them being J. Campbell (ed.), *The Anglo Saxons* (1982), beautifully illustrated with a full bibliography. See also P. A. Sawyer, *From Roman Britain to Norman England* (1978); H. R. Loyn, *Anglo-Saxon England and the Norman Conquest* (1962); D. M. Wilson, *The Anglo-Saxons* (3rd edn, 1981) and N. J. Higham, *The Death of Anglo-Saxon England* (1997). See also D. Whitelock (ed.), *English Historical Documents* (2nd edn, 1981).

For the Vikings see P. H. Sawyer, *The Age of the Vikings* (1971 edn) and *Kings and Vikings: Scandinavia and Europe, 700–1100* (1982); J. Graham-Campbell, *The Viking World* (1980); and R. T. Farrell (ed.), *Viking Civilisation* (1982).

For Christianity see H. Mayr-Harting, *The Coming of Christianity to Anglo-Saxon England* (1972); M. W. Barley and R. P. C. Hanson (eds), *Christianity in Britain, 300–700* (1968); M. Deanesly, *The Pre-Conquest Church in England* (2nd edn, 1962); and J. Godfrey, *The Church in Anglo-Saxon England* (1962).

For art and architecture see T. D. Hendrick, *Anglo-Saxon Art to 900* (1938) and *Late Saxon and Viking Art* (1949); D. Talbot Rice, *English Art, 871–1100* (1952); C. R. Dodwell, *Anglo-Saxon Art* (1982); J. Beckhouse, *The Lindisfarne Gospels* (1981); R. L. S. Bruce-Mitford's *The Sutton Hoo Burial, A Handbook* (3rd edn, 1979); C. Fox, *Offa's Dyke* (1955); and B. Hope-Taylor, *Yeavering* (1977).

For 1066 see F. Barlow, *William I and the Norman Conquest* (1965); and R. A. Brown, *The Normans and the Norman Conquest* (1969). Barlow's *The Feudal Kingdom of England 1042–1216* (1972 edn) is a comprehensive survey, looking backwards as well as forwards. See also A. Williams, *The English and the Norman Conquest* (1995).

3   DEPENDENCE, EXPANSION AND CULTURE

The best general introduction is J. Hatcher and E. Miller, *Medieval England: Rural Society and Economic Change, 1083–1348* (1978). It can be supplemented by other studies, among them E. Miller, *Medieval England, Towns, Commerce and Crafts* (1995); M. Jones and M. Vale (eds), *England and her Neighbours* (1989); J. L. Bolton, *The Medieval English Economy, 1150–1500* (1980); and P. R. Hyams, *Kings, Lords and Peasants in Medieval England* (1980).

An indispensable book on the geography behind this and later chapters is H. C. Darby (ed.), *A New Historical Geography of England* (1973). See also L. Cantor, *The English Medieval Landscape* (1982). For quite different approaches see M. R. Vaughan, *Matthew Paris* (1979 edn); T. Clancy, *From Memory to Written Record: England 1066–1300* (1979); R. W. Southern, *The Making of the Middle Ages* (1953); and G. Duby, *The Chivalrous Society* (1977).

Much of the detailed research on which general studies are based is local. See, for example, E. King, *Peterborough Abbey, 1086–1310* (1973), which precisely covers the years described in this chapter; Z. Razi, *Life, Marriage and Death in a Medieval Parish: Economy, Society and Demography in Halesowen, 1270–1400* (1980); and J. Raftis, *Tenure and Mobility: Studies in the Social History of the Medieval English Village* (1964).

Older studies often deal vividly with the experience of daily life. See in particular H. S. Bennett, *Life on the English Manor* (1956); W. G. Hoskins, *The Midland Peasant* (1955); C. S. Orwin, *The Open Fields* (1954 edn); and G. C. Homans, *English Villages of the Thirteenth Century* (1940). Peasants are dealt with generally in T. Shanin (ed.), *Peasants and Peasant Societies* (1971), a book which brings out indirectly the distinctiveness of much English experience; and R. H. Hilton, *The English Peasantry in the Later Middle Ages* (1974). A. MacFarlane, *The Origins of English Individualism* (1978) is a stimulating and controversial study.

On towns see S. Reynolds, *History of English Medieval Towns* (1977); R. Holt and G. Rosser (eds), *The Medieval Town: A Reader in Urban History, 1200–1540* (1990); M. W. Beresford, *New Towns of the Middle Ages* (1967); and S. Thrupp, *The Merchant Class of Medieval London* (1948).

F. Pollock and F. W. Maitland, *History of English Law Before the Time of Edward I* (1968 edn) is a basic work. See also J. C. Holt, *Magna Carta* (1965); and A. Harding, *The Law Courts of Medieval England* (1973). An important recent work is P. Brand, *The Origins of the English Legal Profession* (1992). See also H. M. Jewell, *English Local Administration in the Middle Ages* (1972).

Castles and other medieval buildings are dealt with in F. Wilkinson, *The Castles of England* (1973); C. Platt, *Medieval England: A Social History and Archaeology from the Conquest to A.D. 1600* (1978); and A. Clifton-Taylor, *The Cathedrals of England* (1967). Monasteries are studied at length in massive volumes by D. M. Knowles, *The Monastic Orders in England, 943–1216* (1940) and *The Religious Orders in England* (3 vols, 1947–59). For the Jews see J. Parkes, *The Jew in the Medieval Community* (1938) and H. G. Richardson, *English Jewry under the Angevin Kings* (1960). See also K. Thomas, *Religion and the Decline of Magic* (1971), a seminal work.

For this and the next chapter see J. Thornton, *The Habit of Authority* (1974); E. Prestage (ed.), *Chivalry* (1928); and R. Barber, *The Knight and Chivalry* (1970). For studies of pasts and presents compare Henry Adam's classic essay *Mont St Michel and Chartres* (1980 edn); and A. Chandler, *A Dream of Order: The Medieval Ideal in Nineteenth Century Literature* (1971). For this and later chapters see also R. Burchfield, *The English Language* (1985).

There is scope for far more work on themes identified by D. M. Stenton in her *The English Woman in History* (1957) and for new themes identified by more recent writers on women's history. See, however, D. Baker (ed.), *Medieval Women* (1978) for a series of profiles.

4   ORDER AND CONFLICT

The best general introduction is M. H. Keen, *England in the Later Middle Ages* (1973). See also his *English Society in the Late Middle Ages, 1348–1500* (1990). Both have bibliographies. Barbara Tuchman, *A Distant Mirror* (1978) presents a different kind of brilliant panoramic interpretation. See also S. L. Waugh, *England in the Reign of Edward III* (1991); J. Hatcher, *Plague, Population and the English Economy, 1348–1530* (1977); and B. R. Dobson (ed.), *The Peasants' Revolt of 1381* (1983).

For the wars with France see C. T. Allmand (ed.), *The Hundred Years War* (1988); and J. Barnie, *War in Medieval Society: Social Values and the Hundred Years War* (1974). See also J. R. Lander, *Government and Community, England, 1450–1509* (1980). R. W. Kaeuper, *War, Justice and Public Order: England and France in the Later Middle Ages*, (1988). J. Huizinga, *The Waning of the Middle Ages* (1924) is a European classic.

K. B. McFarlane's *The Nobility of Later Medieval England* (1973) opened up basic themes. See also J. M. W. Bean, *The Decline of English Feudalism* (1968); G. A. Holmes, *The Estates of the Higher Nobility* (1957); and for aspects of economic history A. R. Bridbury, *Economic Growth, England in the Later Middle Ages* (1921); C. Dyer, *Standards of Living in the Later Middle Ages* (1989); and P. D. A. Harvey (ed.), *The Peasant Land Market in Medieval England* (1984). On finance see H. J. Hewitt, *The Organization of the War under Edward III* (1966); and G. L. Harris, *King, Parliament and Public Finance in Medieval England to 1369* (1975).

There is much of interest in M. W. Beresford and J. G. Hurst, *Deserted Medieval Villages* (1971), like all Beresford's work, an invitation to research through exploration. See also C. Platt, *The English Medieval Town* (1976); R. H. Britnell, *Growth and Decline in Colchester, 1300–1525* (1986); and C. Plythian Adams, *The Desolation of a City: Coventry and the Urban Crisis of the Later Middle Ages* (1979).

For wool see T. H. Lloyd, *The English Wool Trade in the Middle Ages* (1977); and for trade E. Carus Wilson and D. Coleman, *England's Export Trade, 1275–1547* (1963).

For religion see W. A. Pantin, *The English Church in the Fourteenth Century* (1955); P. Heath, *The English Parish Clergy on the Eve of the Reformation* (1969); D. J. Hall, *English Medieval Pilgrimage* (1966); and J. Hughes, *Pastors and Visionaries* (1988). B. Harvey, *Living and Dying in England, 1100–1560* (1993) deals with many aspects of 'the monastic experience'.

For education see N. I. Orme, *English Schools in the Middle Ages* (1973) and Hoeppner Moran, *The Growth of English Schooling* (1985).

Printing is dealt with in its general European context in Eisenstein, *The Printing Press as an Agent of Change* (2 vols, 1979). See also the older study by H. S. Bennett, *Books and Readers, 1475–1557* (1969 edn) and G. D. Painter, *William Caxton* (1976). See also J. Coleman, *English Literature in History* (1981).

The role of women is considered in broad context in M. Elergant and M. Kowaleski, *Women and Power in the Middle Ages* (1988); B. A. Hanawalt, *Women and Work in Pre-industrial Europe* (1986) and *The Ties that Bound* (1986).

M. H. Keen, *The Outlaws of Medieval Legend* (1961) should be studied within the context of R. H Hilton (ed.), *Peasants, Knights and Heretics: Studies in Medieval English Social History* (1976); J. G. Bellamy, *Crime and Public Order in*

England in the Later Middle Ages (1979); and A. McCall's colourful *The Medieval Underworld* (1979). See also J. C. Holt, *Robin Hood* (1982); and J. J. Jusserand, *English Wayfaring Life in the Middle Ages* (1989).

5 PROBLEMS, OPPORTUNITIES AND ACHIEVEMENTS

D. M. Palliser, *The Age of Elizabeth: England under the Later Tudors, 1547–1603* (1938) is a thorough and well-documented general introduction to the social and economic history of the later period. For other surveys and analyses see D. C. Coleman, *The Economy of England, 1450–1570* (1977); P. Ramsey, *Tudor Economic Problems* (1963); and J. Youings, *Sixteenth-Century England* (1984).

It is impossible to separate out distinctly social, even economic, history from political and administrative history. For this reason, G. R. Elton's *England Under the Tudors* (2nd edn, 1974) and A. L. Rowse's *The England of Elizabeth* (1950), important books by two very different historians, are indispensable reading. See also L. Stone, *The Crisis of the Aristocracy* (1965); P. Williams, *The Tudor Regime* (1979); J. L. Hurstfield, *Freedom, Government and Corruption in Elizabethan England* (1973); and W. T. MacCaffrey, *The Shaping of the Elizabethan Regime* (1968). Compare C. Haigh (ed.), *The Reign of Elizabeth* (1984); K. Wrightson, *English Society, 1580–1680* (1982); P. Laslett, *The World We Have Lost* (2nd edn, 1971); and R. O'Day, *Economy and Community: Economic and Social History of Pre-Industrial England, 1500–1700* (1975).

For agrarian England, see J. Thirsk (ed.), *The Agrarian History of England and Wales*, Vol. IV (1967); and for industry D. C. Coleman, *Industry in Tudor and Stuart England* (1975). J. U. Nef, *The Rise of the British Coal Indusry* (2 vols, 1932) introduced the idea of an early industrial revolution. The economy as a whole is examined in J. D. Chambers, *Population, Economy and Society in Pre-Industrial England* (1972); and N. B. Harte *et al.*, (eds), *Trade, Government and Economy in Pre-Industrial England* (1976).

Town life is dealt with in P. Clark and P. Slack, *Crisis and Order in English Towns, 1500–1750* (1972) and *English Towns in Transition, 1500–1700* (1976); and P. Clark (ed.), *County Towns in Pre-Industrial England* (1981). Local studies include P. Clark, *English Provincial Society from the Reformation to the Revolution, Religion, Politics and Society in Kent, 1500–1640* (1977); M. E. James, *Family Lineage and Civil Society: A Study of Society, Politics and Mentality in the Durham Region, 1540–1640* (1974); D. Palliser, *Tudor York* (1979); and M. Spufford, *Contrasting Communities* (1974).

For riches and poverty and charity and poor relief see J. Pound, *Poverty and Vagrancy in Tudor England* (1971); A. L. Beier, *The Problem of the Poor in Tudor and Early Stuart England* (1983); and W. K. Jordan, *Philanthropy in England 1480–1660* (1959).

For education see J. Simon, *Education and Society in Tudor England* (1967); and R. O'Day, *Education and Society in Britain, 1500–1800* (1982). For this and the next chapter D. Cressy, *Literature and the Social Order: Reading and Writing in Tudor and Stuart England* (1980) is stimulating. See also L. Stone (ed.), *The University in Society*, Vol. I (1974).

The religious changes associated with the Reformation are dealt with clearly in A. G. Dickens, *The English Reformation* (1964); R. O'Day and F. Heal (eds), *Church and Society in England, Henry VIII to James I* (1977) and *Princes and Paupers in the English Church, 1500–1800* (1981). See also J. Youings, *The Dissolution of the Monasteries* (1971). For Puritanism see P. Collinson, *The Elizabethan Puritan Movement* (2nd edn, 1982) and *Godly People* (1983); and J. Phillips, *The Reformation of Images: The Destruction of Art in England, 1535–1660* (1973). P. McGrath, *Papists and Puritans under Elizabeth I* (1967) brings two sides together. R. O'Day, *The Debate on the English Reformation* (1986) deals admirably with the historiography.

For aspects of culture see P. Burke, *Popular Culture in Early Modern Europe* (1978); C. Phythian-Adams, *Local History and Folklore: A New Framework* (1975); V. L. Neuberg, *Popular Literature: A History and Guide* (1977); and B. Capp, *Astrology and the Popular Press* (1979).

For law and administration see J. S. Cockburn (ed.), *Crime in England* (1977); A. Fletcher, *Tudor Rebellions* (1973); A. Fletcher and J. Stevenson (eds), *Order and Disorder in Early Modern England* (1985); J. H. Gleason, *The Justices of Peace in England, 1558–1640* (1969); L. Boynton, *The Elizabethan Militia, 1558–1638* (1967); and G. R. Elton, *Policy and Police* (1972). For finance see F. C. Dietz, *English Public Finance, 1558–1642* (1932); and R. B. Outhwaite, *Inflation in Tudor and Early Stuart England* (1969). J. Burnett, *A History of The Cost of Living* (1969) is useful for this and for other chapters.

For the demographic frame see E. A. Wrigley and R. S. Schofield, *The Population History of England, 1541–1871* (1981), an indispensable study; C. Webster (ed.), *Health, Medicine and Mortality in the Sixteenth Century* (1979); and L. A. Clarkson, *Death, Disease and Famine in Pre-Industrial England* (1975). Family studies include L. Stone, *The Family, Sex and Marriage in England, 1500–1800* (1977); M. Anderson, *Approaches to the History of the Western Family* (1980); and R. B. Outhwaite (ed.), *Marriage and Society: Studies in the Social History of Marriage* (1981).

For housing see M. W. Barley, *The English Farmhouse and Cottage* (1961); N. Pevsner, *The Planning of the English Country House* (1961); and M. Girouard, *Robert Smythson and the Architecture of the Elizabethan Era* (1966).

6   REVOLUTION, RESTORATION AND SETTLEMENT

The most widely read books on the century are by Christopher Hill. They include *Puritanism and Revolution* (1958); *Society and Puritanism in Pre-Revolutionary England* (1964); *From Reformation to Industrial Revolution* (1967); and most recently, *The English Bible and the Seventeenth Century Revolution* (1993). See also, however, C. Russell (ed.), *The Origins of the English Civil War* (1975) which follows a quite different approach, outlined also in his essays, *Unrevolutionary England, 1603–1642* (1990). See also G. Aylmer and J. Morrill (eds), *Land, Men and Beliefs* (1984).

L. Stone (ed.), *Social Change and Revolution in England, 1540–1640* (1965) is a guide to a protracted if outdated controversy about the gentry. See also J. G. A. Pocock (ed.), *Three British Revolutions, 1641, 1688 and 1776*; and R. Ashton, *The English Civil War, 1603–1649* (1978). For later seventeenth-century history see J. R. Jones, *County and Court, 1658–1714* (1978); J. Miller, *Popery and Politics in England, 1660–1688* (1973); and J. H. Plumb, *The Growth of Political Stability, 1675–1725* (1967).

For the economy see D. C. Coleman, *Industry in Tudor and Stuart England* (1975); Charles Wilson, *England's Apprenticeship, 1603–1763* (1965); J. Thirsk and J. P. Cooper (eds), *Seventeenth-Century Economic Documents* (1972); and J. Thirsk, *Economic Policy and Projects: The Development of a Consumer Society* (1978).

There are several interesting local studies in addition to those cited in the booklist for the last chapter. As examples see J. T. Cliffe, *The Yorkshire Gentry from the Reformation to the Civil War* (1969); B. G. Blackwood, *The Lancastrian Gentry and The Great Rebellion* (1978); A. Fletcher, *A County Community in Peace and War: Sussex 1600–1660* (1975); and J. S. Morrill, *Cheshire 1630–1660: County Government and Society under the 'English Revolution'* (1974). *The History of Myddle* by Richard Gough is a unique contemporary study of a village, explored by D. G. Hey in *An English Rural Community, Myddle under the Tudors and Stuarts* (1974).

For finance and taxation see M. Roberts, *The Military Revolution* (1956); W. R. Ward, *The English Land Tax in the Eighteenth Century* (1953); R. P. Cust, *The Forced Loan* (1987); and above all, for the later period, C. D. Chandaman, *The English Public Revenue, 1660–1702* (1975).

On religion, society and politics see, *inter alia*, P. Lake, *Anglicans and Puritans* (1988); R. O'Day and F. Heal (eds), *Continuity and Change, Personnel and Administration of the Church of England* (1976); A. S. Woodhouse (ed.), *Puritanism and Liberty: Being the Army Debates* (1950 edn); G. R. Cragg, *The Church and the Age of Reason, 1648–1789* (1960); W. C. Braithwaite, *The Beginnings of Quakerism* (1982); and W. K. Jordan, *The Development of Religious Toleration in*

England (4 vols, 1936–40). See also U. S. Henriques, *The Return of the Jews to England* (1905).

For the family see R. Houlbrooke, *The English Family, 1450–1700* (1984); and for the role of women, A. Clark, *The Working Life of Women in the Seventeenth Century* (1919); G. E. and K. R. Fussell, *The English Countryman: A Farmhouse Social History* (1953); and B. Thompson, *Women in Stuart England and America: A Comparative Study* (1974). The most recent general study is by Antonia Fraser, *The Weaker Vessel* (1984). On children see L. de Mause (ed.), *History of Childhood* (1974) and I. Pinchbeck and M. Hewitt, *Children in English Society* (Vol. I, 1969).

For the alehouse see P. Clark, *The English Ale House, 1200–1830* (1983) and for the coffee house A. Ellis, *The Penny Universities: A History of the Coffee House* (1956). For other aspects of changing culture see G. V. P. Akrigg, *Jacobean Pageant or the Court of King James I* (1962); B. Little, *Sir Christopher Wren* (1975); M. Ede, *Arts and Society in England under William and Mary* (1977); J. Summerson, *Architecture in Britain, 1530–1830* (6th edn, 1977); B. A. Reay (ed.), *Popular Culture in Seventeenth Century England* (1985); M. Spufford, *Small Books and Pleasant Histories* (1981); and D. Brailsford, *Sport and Society: Elizabeth to Anne* (1969).

For crime and 'rebellion' see P. Slack (ed.), *Rebellion, Popular Protest and Social Order in Early Modern England* (1984); and J. S. Brewer and J. Styles, *An Ungovernable People: the English and their Law in the Seventeenth and Eighteenth Centuries* (1980). See also W. R. Prest, *The Inns of Court* (1972).

For science and technology see A. R. Hall, *The Revolution in Science, 1500–1800* (2nd edn, 1973); G. N. Clark, *Science and Social Welfare in the Age of Newton* (1949); A. G. Smith, *Science and Society in the Sixteenth and Seventeenth Centuries* (1972); R. Briggs, *The Scientific Revolution of the Seventeenth Century* (1965); C. Webster, *The Great Instauration: Science, Medicine and Reform, 1626–1660* (1975); and M. Hunter, *Science and Society in Restoration England* (1988). See also H. Hartley (ed.). *The Royal Society, Its Origins and Founders* (1960).

7   THE QUEST FOR WEALTH, POWER AND PLEASURE

Roy Porter's *English Society in the Eighteenth Century* (1982) is the best of the volumes in the useful Pelican Social History of Britain: it reflects recent research and has a valuable bibliography. D. Marshall, *English People in the Eighteenth Century* (1956) and *Eighteenth-Century England* (1962) are older well-informed books. So also is M. D. George, *England in Transition* (1953). By far the best recent survey is by P. Langford, *A Polite and Commercial People: England 1727–1787* (1989). See also his *Public Life and the Propertied Englishman, 1689–1798* (1991). T. S. Ashton's *An Economic History of England: The Eighteenth Century*

(1955) is still useful, but see also C. Clay, *Economic Expansion and Social Change in England, 1500–1700* (2 vols, 1984). For contemporary comment see A. Briggs, *How They Lived, 1700–1815* (1969).

For wealth derived from abroad see K. R. Andrews, *Elizabethan Privateering* (1964); and R. Davis, *English Overseas Trade, 1500–1700* (1973). For the eighteenth century see R. S. Dunn, *Sugar and Slaves* (1973); R. Pares, *War and Trade in the West Indies* (1936) and *A West Indian Fortune* (1968); D. Boorstin, *The Americans: The Colonial Experience* (1973); and S. Jones, *Two Centuries of Overseas Trading* (1986).

For slavery and the anti-slavery movement see J. Walvin (ed.), *Slavery and British Society, 1776–1848* (1982), which places in perspective old and new controversies. For the general picture see D. K. Fieldhouse, *The Colonial Empires* (1965) and A. Calder, *Revolutionary Empire* (1981).

For landed wealth see G. E. Mingay, *English Landed Society in the Eighteenth Century* (1963) and *The Gentry* (1976); M. Girouard, *Life in the English Country House* (1979); R. A. C. Parker, *Coke of Norfolk* (1975); and, most lively and provocative, L. Stone and J. C. Fawtier Stone, *An Open Elite?; England 1540–1880* (1984); and C. Payne, *Toil and Plenty, Images of the Agricultural Landscape, 1780–1890* (1993).

For early industrialists see among other studies F. Crouzet, *The First Industrialists* (1985); G. Unwin, A. Hulme and G. Taylor, *Samuel Oldknow and the Arkwrights* (1924); and R. S. Fitton and A. P. Wadsworth, *The Strutts and the Arkwrights* (1958). On 'middling men' see P. Earle, *The Making of the English Middle Class: Business, Society and Family Life in London, 1660–1730* (1989); and for this and later chapters M. J. Reader, *Professional Men* (1966) and W. Prest (ed.), *The Professions in Early Modern England* (1989). On 'common people' see J. L. and B. Hammond, *The Town Labourer* (1917), *The Village Labourer, 1760–1832* (1919) and *The Skilled Labourer* (1919), still readable books; and J. F. C. Harrison, *The Common People* (1984). J. J. Hecht, *The Domestic Servant Class in Eighteenth-Century England* (1956) deals with an important and numerous group. See also D. Marshall, *The English Domestic Servant in History* (1969).

For the poor see D. Marshall, *The English Poor in the Eighteenth Century* (1926) and G. Taylor, *The Problem of Poverty, 1660–1834* (1969). For the Poor Law see J. R. Poynter, *Society and Pauperism* (1969); and M. E. Rose, *The English Poor Law, 1760–1830* (1971); D. Owen, *English Philanthropy, 1660–1960* (1965) is relevant for this and later chapters. See also F. N. L. Poynter, *The Evolution of Medical Practice in Britain* (1961).

On towns and cities see C. W. Chawklin, *The Provincial Towns of Georgian England* (1974); M. D. George, *London Life in the Eighteenth Century* (1925); G. Rudé, *Hanoverian London* (1971); and P. J. Corfield, *The Impact of English Towns, 1700–1800* (1981). For the relations of town and country see R. Williams, *The*

Country and the City (1973); and for the provinces D. Read, *The English Provinces, 1700–1900* (1964); and E. Hughes, *North Country Life in the Eighteenth Century* (2 vols, 1952, 1965) deal with particular areas. The industrial setting is considered in J. Rule, *The Experience of Labour in Eighteenth-Century Industry* (1981).

For urban violence see J. Stevenson, *Popular Disturbances in England, 1700–1870* (1979); and G. Rudé, *The Crowd in History* (1964) and *Paris and London in the Eighteenth Century* (1952). Law is dealt with monumentally and magisterially in L. Radzinowicz's *A History of English Criminal Law* (1948). For recent interpretations of aspects of the law as seen 'from below', turn to E. P. Thompson, *Whigs and Hunters* (1975), and along with D. Hay *et al.*, *Albion's Fatal Tree* (1975). W. K. Manchester, *Legal History, 1750–1950* (1970) is useful for this and later chapters.

On religioin see N. Sykes, *Church and State in the Eighteenth Century* (1934); W. R. Ward, *Religion and Society in England, 1790–1850* (1972); S. Andrews, *Methodism and Society* (1970); M. R. Watts, *The Dissenters* (1978); C. G. Bolan *et al.*, *The English Presbyterians* (1968); J. Bossy, *The English Catholic Community* (1975); and R. Vann, *The Social Development of English Quakerism, 1655–1750* (1969).

There are general surveys of education, covering this and other periods – B. Simon, *Studies in the History of Education*, Vol. I (1960); J. Lawson and H. Silver, *A Social History of Education in England* (1973); and R. O'Day, *Education and Society in Britain, 1500–1800* (1982). See also M. G. Jones, *The Charity School Movement* (1938).

On the origins of the 'consumer society' see J. H. Plumb, *The Commercialisation of Leisure in Eighteenth-Century England* (1973) and N. McKendrick *et al.*, *The Birth of a Consumer Society* (1982). On leisure within that society see R. Malcolmson, *Popular Recreations in English Society 1700–1850* (1975) and R. Cunningham, *Leisure in the Industrial Revolution* (1980).

For finance see J. H. Clapham, *History of the Bank of England* (2 vols, 1946); J. Carswell, *The South Sea Bubble* (1960); P. G. M. Dickson, *The Financial Revolution in England 1688–1756* (1967); and L. S. Pressnell, *Country Banking in the Industrial Revolution* (1956).

For the place of women in eighteenth-century society see B. Kanner (ed.), *The Women of England* (1980); L. Charles and L. Duffin (eds), *Women's Work in Pre-Industrial England* (1985); and C. A. Davidson, *A Woman's Work is Never Done: A History of Housework in the British Isles, 1650–1950* (1983). Sexuality is discussed in P. G. Boucé, *Sexuality in Eighteenth-Century England* (1982) and immorality in M. J. Quinlan, *Victorian Prelude* (1941). See also P. Fryer, *Mrs. Grundy* (1963).

For cultural history see I. Watt, *The Rise of the Novel* (1957); D. Monaghan, *Jane Austen in a Social Context* (1981); M. Butler, *Jane Austen and the War of Ideas*

(1975); J. Gross, *The Rise and Fall of the Man of Letters* (1969), which covers later chapters also; P. Rogers, *Grub Street, Studies in a Sub-culture* (1972); M. Whinney and O. Millar, *A History of English Art* (1957); L. Lipkin, *The Ordering of the Arts in Eighteenth Century England* (1970); B. Sprague Allen, *Tides of Taste, 1619–1800* (1945); M. Foss, *The Age of Patronage: The Arts of Society 1660–1750* (1972); T. Fawcett, *The Rise of English Provincial Art* (1974); D. Stroud, *Capability Brown* (1975); B. Denvir, *The Eighteenth Century, Art, Design and Society, 1689–1789* (1983); and J. M. Black, *The English Press in the Eighteenth Century* (1987).

For the lead into the nineteenth century see F. M. L. Thompson (ed.), *The Cambridge Social History of Britain*, 2 vols. (1990); A. Briggs, *The Age of Improvement*; J. Roach, *Social Reform in England, 1780–1870* (1978); A. Goodwin, *The Friends of Liberty* (1979); and M. Butler, *Peacock Displayed* (1979).

8   THE EXPERIENCE OF INDUSTRIALIZATION

The two volumes edited by R. Floud and D. McCloskey, *The Economic History of Britain since 1700* (1981) introduce recent research with a useful quantitative approach. See also, however, P. Mathias, *The First Industrial Nation* (1970) and the older brief study by T. S. Ashton, *The Industrial Revolution, 1760–1830* (1948). They should be compared with D. S. Landes, *The Unbound Prometheus: Technological Changes and Industrial Development in Western Europe from 1750 to the Present* (1969). S. G. Checkland's *The Rise of Industrial Society in England, 1815–1885* (1964) does not supersede older studies like W. H. Bowden, *Industrial Society in England Toward the End of the Eighteenth Century* (1925) and G. D. H. Cole, *A Short History of the Working Class Movement* (1937). See also A. Briggs, *Iron Bridge to Crystal Palace. Impact and Images of the Industrial Revolution* (1979).

For later phases in industrial history see E. J. Hobsbawm, *Industry and Empire* (1968); S. B. Saul, *The Myth of the Great Depression* (1972 edn); A. L. Levine, *Industrial Retardation in Britain, 1880–1914* (1967); K. Middlemas, *Politics in Industrial Society: The Experience of the British System Since 1911* (1979); and M. J. Wiener, *English Culture and the Decline of the Industrial Spirit* (1981).

For the statistics B. R. Mitchell and P. Deane's *Abstract of British Historical Statistics* (1962) is indispensable. See also P. Deane and W. A. Cole, *British Economic Growth, 1688–1955* (1967) and R. C. P. Matthew, C. H. Feinstein and J. C. Odling Smee, *British Economic Growth, 1855–1973* (1982). For fluctuations in the economy and their role in social history see W. W. Rostow, *The British Economy of the Nineteenth Century* (1948).

For the effects of industrialization on standards of life, including the quality of life, the best brief introduction is A. J. Taylor (ed.), *The Standard of Living in Britain in the Industrial Revolution* (1975). This may be followed through with B. Inglis, *Poverty and the Industrial Revolution* (1971); G. Himmelfarb, *The Idea of Poverty* (1984); and J. Burnett, *Plenty and Want: A Social History of Diet from 1875 to the Present Day* (1966). Burnett's useful studies, *inter alia*, introduce the reader to the Phelps Brown/Hopkins cost of living index first set out in *Economica* (1955).

For industrialization and social class, E. P. Thompson's immensely influential *The Making of the English Working Class* (1963) should be compared with H. J. Perkin, *Origins of Modern English Society, 1780–1880* (1969). See also P. Hollis (ed.), *Class and Conflict in Nineteenth-Century England, 1815–1850* (1973); and G. Stedman Jones, *Languages of Class* (1983). For the impact of industry on the imagination see F. D. Klingender, *Art and the Industrial Revolution* (1947); A. Briggs, *The Power of Steam* (1982); J. Warburg, (ed.), *The Industrial Muse* (1958); and the book by M. Vicinus with the same title (1958). K. Hudson's *Industrial Archaeology* (1962) remains the best introduction to this popular subject.

Technology is covered in Vols IV and V of the Oxford History of Technology (1958). See also from a long list of relevant books N. Rosenberg, *Perspectives on Technology* (1976); A. E. Musson and E. Robinson, *Science and Technology in the Industrial Revolution* (1969); W. H. G. Armytage, *A Social History of Engineering* (1961); L. T. C. Rolt, *Victorian Engineering* (1970); and H. I. Sharlin, *The Making of the Electrical Age* (1963).

On other aspects of labour history see K. D. Brown, *The English Labour Movement 1700–1951* (1982) which has a useful bibliography covering an extensive literature; R. Price, *Masters, Union and Men* (1980); P. Joyce, *Work, Society and Politics* (1982); A. Briggs (ed.), *Chartist Studies* (1959); D. Jones, *Chartism and the Chartists* (1975); and D. Thompson, *The Chartists* (1984).

For agriculture and the countryside in an age of transformation see P. Horn, *The Rural World, 1780–1850* (1980); G. E. Mingay, *The Agricultural Revolution* (1966); E. Hobsbawm and G. Rudé, *Captain Swing* (1973); and J. P. Dunbabin (ed.), *Rural Discontent in Nineteenth Century Britain* (1974).

Other studies include T. C. Barker (ed.), *The Long March of Everyman, 1815–1960* (1978), based on an outstanding BBC radio series; S. Pollard, *The Genesis of Modern Management* (1948); I. Pinchbeck, *Women Workers and the Industrial Revolution, 1750–1850* (1969); and M. Hewitt, *Wives and Mothers in Victorian Industry* (1958).

9 WEBS OF COMMUNICATION

For early communications history see J. Crofts, *Packhorse, Waggon and Post* (1967); T. S. Willan, *River Navigation in England, 1600–1750* (1938), *The Inland Trade* (1970) and *The English Coasting Trade, 1600–1750*. Later communications history is covered in P. S. Bagwell, *The Transport Revolution from 1770* (1974).

On roads see W. Albert, *The Turnpike System in England 1663–1840* (1972);

E. Pawson, *Transport and the Economy: The Turnpike Roads of Britain* (1977); D. Hey, *Packmen, Carriers and Packhorse Roads* (1980); J. Copeland, *Roads and Their Traffic, 1750–1850* (1968).

On canals see C. Hadfield, *British Canals* (1968 edn) and *The Canal Age* (1968); L. T. C. Rolt, *The Inland Waterways of England* (1950); and A. Burton, *The Canal Builders* (1972). J. Simmons, *The Railways of Britain* (1965) provides a good general account of the importance of railways to the economy and to society. See also his general study *The Victorian Railway* (1991); M. Robbins, *The Railway Age* (1965); and T. Colman, *Railway Navvies* (1968). For a railway town see W. H. Chaloner, *The Social and Economic Development of Crewe, 1780–1923* (1950) and for the general effects of railways on cities J. R. Kellett's illuminating *The Impact of Railways on Victorian Cities* (1969). On shipping see A. McGowan, *The Century Before Steam* (1980) and R. Hope, *A New History of British Shipping* (1990).

For bicycles see L. H. Adams, *Cycles and Cycling* (1965); J. Woodford, *The Story of the Bicycle* (1970) and H. O. Duncan, *The World on Wheels* (1927); and for the motor car see H. Perkin, *The Age of the Automobile* (1976) and W. Plowden, *The Motor Car and Politics in Britain, 1890–1970* (1971). For metropolitan transport see T. C. Barker and M. Robbins, *A History of London Transport* (2 vols, 1963, 1974). For the aeroplane see C. H. Gibbs Smith, *Aviation, An Historical Study from its Origins to the End of World War II* (1970) and D. Edgerton, *England and the Aeroplane* (1991).

On the telegraph see J. Kieve, *The Electric Telegraph* (1973) and on the telephone F. G. C. Baldwin, *The History of the Telephone in the United Kingdom* (1925) and I. de Sola Poole (ed.), *The Social Impact of the Telephone* (1977) For the wireless and broadcasting see A. Briggs, *The BBC, The First Fifty Years* (1985), which includes a full bibliography. For the Post Office see H. Robinson, *Britain's Post Office: A History of Development from the Beginnings to the Present Day* (1953) and M. J. Daunton, *Royal Mail, the Post Office Since 1840* (1985).

For newspapers see G. A. Cranfield, *The Development of the Provincial Newspaper, 1700–1760* (1962); A. J. Lee, *The Origins of the Popular Press, 1855–1914* (1976); S. Koss, *The Rise and Fall of the Popular Press in Britain* (2 vols, 1981, 1984); L. Brown, *Victorian News and Newspapers* (1985); and R. Pound and B. Harmsworth, *Northcliffe* (1959). See also L. James, *Print and the People* (1976). For the news agencies see D. Read, *The Power of News: The History of Reuters* (1992). See also R. K. Webb, *The British Working Class Reader, 1780–1848* (1955); R. D. Altick, *The English Common Reader* (1963); R. Williams, *The Long Revolution* (1961); and J. Willsberger, *The History of Photography* (1977).

10   VICTORIANISM: PRELUDE, EXPRESSIONS, AFTERMATH

The classic account of the period, still stimulating, is presented in G. M. Young's *Victorian England, Portrait of an Age* (1957 edn), which can be read with profit at different levels. See also J. F. C. Harrison, *The Early Victorians, 1832–1851* (1971); G. Best, *Mid-Victorian Britain, 1851–1875* (1971); my own trilogy *Victorian People* (1954), *Victorian Cities* (1963), and *Victorian Things* (1988); G. Kitson Clark, *The Making of Victorian England* (1962); F. M. L. Thompson, *The Rise of Respectable Society* (1989); F. Bédarida, *A Social History of England, 1851–1975* (1979 edn) and the three volumes of the Cambridge Social History of Britain (ed. F. M. L. Thompson, 1990).

E. D. H. Johnson (ed.), *The World of the Victorians* (1964) is a useful anthology of contemporary poetry and prose. See also W. E. Houghton, *The Victorian Frame of Mind* (1957). There is a good anthology edited by P. Keating, *The Victorian Prophets: A Reader from Carlyle to Wells* (1981). Biographies with an obvious social content include S. E. Finer, *The Life and Times of Sir Edwin Chadwick* (1952); E. Hodder, *The Life and Work of the Seventh Earl of Shaftesbury* (3 vols, 1886); J. Morley, *The Life of William Ewart Gladstone* (2 vols, 1908); R. Blake, *Disraeli* (1966); K. Robbins, *John Bright* (1979); P. T. Marsh, *Joseph Chamberlain* (1994); Elizabeth Longford, *Victoria RI* (1964); and R. Rhodes James, *Albert, Prince Consort* (1983).

For selected aspects of politics see C. R. Fay, *The Corn Laws and Social England* (1932); N. Gash, *Politics in the Age of Peel* (1977 edn); W. L. Burn, *The Age of Equipoise* (1964); H. J. Hanham, *Elections and Party Management* (1978 edn); J. Vincent, *The Formation of the British Liberal Party* (1976); J. Butt and I. E. Clarke (eds), *The Victorians and Social Protest* (1973); J. P. Parry, *Democracy and Religion* (1986); M. Richter, *The Politics of Conscience* (1964); and H. Pelling, *Popular Politics and Society in Late Victorian Britain* (1968).

For government and society see K. B. Smellie, *A Hundred Years of British Government* (1951 edn); P. Stansky (ed.), *The Victorian Revolution: Government and Society in Victoria's Britain* (1973); and V. Cromwell, *Revolution or Evolution: British Government in the Nineteenth Century* (1977). On the civil service see E. W. Cohen, *The Growth of the British Civil Service, 1780–1938* (1965). On the press see P. Hollis, *The Pauper Press* (1970); and on the first twenty years of *Punch*, A. Briggs and S. Briggs, *Cap and Bell* (1972), with copious illustrations.

For the country see the two-volume work edited by G. E. Mingay, *The Victorian Countryside* (1981); F. M. L. Thompson, *English Landed Society in the Nineteenth Century* (1963); D. Spring, *The English Landed Estate in the Nineteenth Century* (1963); M. Girouard, *The Victorian Country House* (1978); P. Horn, *The Rural World, 1780–1850: Social Change in the English Countryside* (1980); R. Samuel (ed.), *Village Life and Labour* (1975); G. E. and K. R. Fussell, *The English*

Countryman, 1500–1900 (1955); M. K. Ashby, *Joseph Ashby of Tysoe* (1961 edn); and N. Philip, *Victorian Village Life* (1993). For the imaginative responses to nature see U. C, Knoepflmacher and G. B. Tennyson, *Nature and the Victorian Imagination* (1977).

For towns and cities see A. Briggs, *Victorian Cities* (1968 edn); H. J. Dyos and M. Wolff (eds), *The Victorian City* (2 vols, 1973); P. J. Walker, *Town, City and Nation, 1850–1914* (1983); J. Walvin, *English Urban Life 1776–1851* (1984); D. Fraser, *Urban Politics in Victorian England* (1976); E. P. Hennock, *Fit and Proper Persons* (1973); R. Dennis, *English Industrial Cities of the Nineteenth Century* (1984), an admirable study by a geographer; J. Garrard, *Leadership and Power in Victorian Industrial Towns* (1983); D. Cannadine, *Lords and Landlords: The Aristocracy and the Towns* (1980); G. Stedman Jones, *Outcast London* (1971 edn); and R. Scola, *Feeding the Victorian City* (1992).

On poverty see, in addition to books cited in the list for the next chapter, J. H. Treble, *Urban Poverty in Britain, 1830–1914* (1979); M. Tebbutt, *Making Ends Meet: Pawnbroking and Working-Class Credit* (1985); G. R. Boyer, *An Economic History of the English Poor Law, 1750–1850* (1990); N. Longmate, *The Workhouse* (1974); and M. E. Rose (ed.), *The Poor and the City: The English Poor Law in its Urban Context, 1834–1914* (1985). C. L. Mowat, *The Charity Organization Society, 1869–1913* (1961) explores basic attitudes and actions. It should be read in conjunction with A. F. Young and E. T. Ashton, *British Social Work in the Nineteenth Century* (1956) and K. Woodroofe, *From Charity to Social Work* (1962). For business see B. C. Hunt, *The Development of the Business Corporation 1800–1867* (1969 edn); W. D. Rubinstein, *Men of Property* (1981); and G. R. Searle, *Entrepreneurial Politics in Mid-Victorian Britain* (1993).

For labour history see E. H. Hunt, *British Labour History, 1815–1914* (1981); J. Benson, *The Working Class in Britain, 1850–1939* (1989); K. Brown (ed.), *Essays in Anti-Labour History* (1974); K. Brown (with I. A. Clarkson), *The English Labour Movement* (1982); E. Hoplins, *A Social History of the English Working Classes* (1979); and K. Burgess, *The Challenge of Labour; Shaping British Society, 1850–1930* (1988).

J. K. Walton deals with *The English Seaside Resort 1750–1914* (1985), as does J. Walvin in *Beside the Seaside* (1971). See also Walvin's *Leisure and Society, 1830–1950* (1978); P. Bailey, *Leisure and Class in Victorian England* (1978); J. A. R. Pimlott, *The English's Holiday* (1947); J. Lowerson and J. Myerscough, *Time to Spare in Victorian England* (1977); J. Lowerson, *Sport and the English Middle Class, 1870–1914* (1993); S. Inglis, *The Football League and the Men who Made It* (1988); T. Mason, *Association Football and English Society, 1815–1914* (1980); A. Ross, *The Turf* (1982); and M. Clapson, *A Bit of a Flutter, Popular Gambling and English Society, c. 1823–1961* (1992).

For housing and 'the home' see A. S. Wohl, *The Eternal Slum: Housing and*

Social Policy in Victorian London (1979) and *The Victorian Family* (1978); E. Gauldie, *Cruel Habitations* (1974); and J. Burnett, *A Social History of Housing, 1815–1970* (1978).

On religion see R. Currie, A. D. Gilbert and H. Horsley, *Churches and Churchgoers: Patterns of Church Attendance in the British Isles since 1700* (1977); W. O. Chadwick, *The Victorian Church*, (2 vols, 1966, 1970); K. Inglis, *Churches and the Working Classes in Victorian England* (1963); B. Hilton, *The Age of Atonement* (1988); P. T. Phillips (ed.), *The View from the Pulpit: Victorian Ministers and Society* (1978); T. W. Lacqueur, *Religion and Respectability: Sunday Schools and Working Class Culture* (1975); J. Cox, *The English Church in a Secular Society* (1963); I. Sellers, *Nineteenth Century Nonconformity* (1977); D. W. Bebbington, *The Nonconformist Conscience* (1982); C. Binfield, *So Down to Prayers: Studies in English Nonconformity* (1977); and R. V. Holt, *The Victorian Contribution to Social Progress in England* (1952). V. D. Lipman's *Social History of the Jews in England, 1850–1950* (1954) should be read in conjunction with L. P. Garner, *The Jewish Immigrant in England, 1870–1914* (1960); C. Holmes, *Anti-Semitism in British Society, 1876–1939* (1979); and D. Feldman, *Englishmen and Jews, 1840–1914* (1994).

For publishing see J. J. Barnes, *Free Trade in Books* (1964); J. Sutherland, *Victorian Novelists and Publishers* (1976); and N. Cross, *The Common Writer: Life in Nineteenth-Century Grub Street* (1985). On education see A. Digby and P. Searby, *Children, School and Schooling in Nineteenth Century England* (1981); E. C. Mack, *Public Schools and British Opinion since 1860* (1941); J. F. C. Harrison, *Learning and Living, 1790–1860: A Study in the History of the English Adult Education Movement, 1760–1960* (1961); M. Sturt, *The Education of the People* (1967); R. de S. Honey, *Tom Brown's Universe* (1977); J. Pinchbeck and M. Hall, *Children in English Society*, Vol II (1973); W. J. G. Armytage, *Civic Universities* (1954); W. R. Ward, *Victorian Oxford* (1965); and R. Rotblatt, *The Revolution of the Dons* (1968).

On crime and punishment see I. J. Tobias, *Crime and Industrial Society in the Nineteenth Century* (1972); D. Philips, *Crime and Authority in Victorian England* (1977); C. Emsley, *Crime and Society in England, 1750–1900* (1897); and V. Bailey (ed.), *Policing and Punishment in Nineteenth Century Britain* (1981).

On morality – fact and myth – see S. Marcus, *The Other Victorians* (1966); R. Pearsall, *Public Purity, Private Shame* (1976); R. Walkowitz, *Prostitution and Victorian Society* (1980); P. McHugh, *Prostitution and Victorian Social Reform* (1980); and A. McLaren, *Birth Control in Nineteenth Century England* (1978).

The pioneering study by J. A. Banks, *Prosperity and Parenthood* (1954) may be studied within the context of N. L. Tranter's *Population and Society* (1973); and J. Weeks, *Sex, Politics and Society* (1981).

On the links between late-Victorian and Edwardian England see J. Harris,

Private Lives, Public Spirit, A Social History of Britain 1870–1914 (1993); J. Nowell Smith (ed.), *Edwardian England* (1964); D. Read, *Edwardian England* (1972); and S. L. Hynes, *The Edwardian Turn of Mind* (1968). E. H. Phelps Brown's excellent *The Growth of British Industrial Relations* (1959) is far more wide-ranging than its title suggests. G. R. Searle, *The Quest for National Efficiency, 1899–1914* (1971) is illuminating. Paul Thompson's *The Edwardians* (1973) is a revealing study based on oral history, while Henry Pelling's *Social Geography of British Elections 1885–1910* (1967) charts the political map. G. Dangerfield, *The Strange Death of Liberal England* (1935) is a brilliant narrative account, open to criticism for its interpretation. 'Plutocracy', a favourite theme is discussed in J. Camplin, *The Rise of the Plutocrats* (1978), while poverty, an equally favourite Edwardian theme, is examined in S. Meacham, *A Life Apart: The English Working Class, 1890–1914* (1977).

For the role of women see J. Lewis, *Women in England, 1870–1950* (1984) and *The Politics of Motherhood* (1980); E. Roberts, *Women's Work* (1988); S. Rowbotham, *Women, Resistance and Revolution* (1972); M. Vicinus (ed.), *Suffer and Be Still* (1972), R. Fulford, *Votes for Women* (1959); B. Harrison, *Separate Spheres* (1978); and D. Gittins, *Fair Sex: Family Size and Structure, 1900–1939* (1982).

For the Victorian and Edwardian Empire see C. J. Bartlett (ed.), *Britain Pre-eminent* (1969); C. A. G. Bodelson, *Studies in Mid-Victorian Imperialism* (1960); R. Robinson, J. Gallagher and A. Denny, *Africa and the Victorians* (1961); A. P. Thornton, *The Imperial Idea and its Enemies* (1959); J. E. Flint and G. Williams (eds), *Perspectives of Empire* (1970); E. J. Hobsbawm, *Industry and Empire* (1970); and J. M. Mackenzie, *Imperialism and Popular Culture* (1986). Much has recently been written from the periphery including R. Hughes, *The Fatal Shore* (1989), a brilliant Australian study. From the centre J. Morris, *Pax Britannica* (1968) is a highly readable account.

II THE DIVIDES OF WAR

For J. R. Green, Victorian social historian, there was too much military history. In recent years, however, the gap between the work of military historians and social historians has appreciably narrowed. See J. Keegan, *A History of Warfare* (1993) which provides a necessary, often missing, perspective.

For links between the nineteenth and the twentieth centuries see A. Briggs (ed.), *The Nineteenth Century* (1970); B. Bond, *Victorian Military Campaigns* (1967), which deals with 'little wars'; O. Anderson, *A Liberal State at War* (1967), which deals with the Crimean War; and T. Pakenham, *The Boer War* (1979). I. F. Clarke's *Voices Prophesying War, 1763–1984* (1966) is a stimulating study of war and the imagination.

For the twentieth century see A. J. P. Taylor, *English History, 1914–1945* (1965); A. Marwick, *Britain in a Century of Total War* (1968); and the stimulating study by A. D. Harvey, *Collision of the Empires: Britain in the Three World Wars, 1783–1945* (1992) which looks back to the war against Napoleon. The literature on the two World Wars is immense. Good introductions are A. J. P. Taylor, *The First World War* (1963) and B. Collier, *A Short History of the Second World War* (1967). See also P. Addison, *The Road to 1945* (1975).

The social history of the First World War is explored in A. Marwick, *The Deluge* (1965), which has a full bibliography. See also J. Terraine, *Impacts of War, 1914 and 1918* (1970) and J. Winter, *The Great War and the British People* (1986).

For the changing role of women in war see A. Marwick, *Women at War, 1914–1918* (1977); and G. Braybon and P. Summerfield, *Out of the Cage: Women's Experience in Two World Wars* (1987).

For the inter-war years see C. L. Mowat, *Britain Between the Wars* (1955), an excellent survey; R. Graves and A. Hodge, *The Long Week End* (1940); J. Stevenson, *British Society, 1914–1945* (1984); J. Stevenson and C. Cook, *The Slump* (1979); R. Skidelsky, *Politicians and the Slump* (1970); and N. K. Buxton and D. H. Aldcroft (eds), *British Industry Between the Wars* (1979). There are many books on the General Strike, including P. Renshaw, *The General Strike* (1975); M. Morris, *The General Strike* (1976); and S. Skelley (ed.), *The General Strike, 1926* (1976). See also R. Charles, *The Development of Industrial Relations in Britain, 1911–1939* (1973); K. G. T. C. Knowles, *Strikes* (1952); and E. Wigham, Strikes and the Government 1893–1974 (1976).

The social history of the Second World War is well covered in A. Calder, *The People's War, 1939–45* (1974). See also T. Harrison, *Living Through the Blitz* (1976); N. Longmate, *How We Lived Then* (1971); and a huge anthology edited by D. Flower and J. Reeves, *The War, 1939–1945* (1960). I. McLaine, *Ministry of Morale* (1979) deals with propaganda, explicit and implicit. S. Briggs, *Smiling Through* (1975), with excellent illustrations, should be supplemented by A. Marwick's *The Home Front* (1976). For a different side of the coin see F. Smillies, *Crime in War Time* (1982).

The Oxford Institute of Statistics, *Studies in War Economy* (1946) is a revealing contemporary book. So too is Mass-Observation, *People in Production* (1942). See also J. M. Winter (ed.), *War and Economic Development* (1975). P. H. J. Gosden, *Education in the Second World War* (1976) is one of a number of retrospective official histories. Two of the early volumes are particularly valuable – R. J. Hammond, *Food*, Vol. I (1951) and W. H. B. Court, *Coal* (1951).

C. Barnett's *The Audit of War* (1980) provides important link reading between this chapter and chapter 12. See also A. S. Milward, *The Economic Effects of Two World Wars on Britain* (1977); M. M. Gowing, *Britain and Atomic Energy* (1964);

R. M. Titmus, *Birth, Poverty and Wealth* (1943) and *Problems of Social Policy* (1951); and J. Harris, *William Beveridge* (1977).

12   ENDS AND BEGINNINGS

Newspapers and periodicals, along with radio and television programmes, provide the most important source for recent social history, but they should be read critically. *New Society* through articles and reviews dealt directly with many of the themes of this chapter from 1962, when it was founded, to June 1988 when it merged with the *New Statesman*. It was a sign of the times when *The Oldie* was launched in 1992. *Social Trends*, an indispensable official publication, has appeared since 1970 and *British Social Attitudes* since 1983.

There is a substantial pamphlet literature expressing widely different ideas and policies, the latter also covered in depth official reports. Compare the pamphlets of the Child Poverty Action Group, founded in 1965, and those of the Institute of Economic Affairs which published over 300 pamphlets between 1964 and 1970.

For the family see M. Young and P. Wilmot, *Family and Kinship in East London* (1957) and *The Symmetrical Family* (1973); P. Townsend, *The Family Life of Old People* (1957); R. Fletcher, *The Family and Marriage* (1962); F. Musgrave, *The Family, Education and Society* (1966); C. Rosser and C. G. Harris, *The Family and Social Change* (1965); P. Lomas, *The Predicament of the Family* (1967); M. Wynn, *Family Policy* (1972); and R. and R. N. Rapoport, *Fathers, Mothers and Others* (1977).

A. H. Halsey, *Trends in British Society Since 1900* (1972) is essential reading along with his own interpretation of them in *Change in British Society* (1981 edn). See also M. Abrams, *The Condition of the British People, 1911–1945* (1945); and J. Ryder and H. Silver, *Modern English Society* (1977 edn). Other interpretations of society at particular times include J. B. Priestley, *English Journey* (1934); G. Orwell, *The English People* (1942); E. Watkins, *The Cautious Revolution* (1951); F. Zweig, *The British Worker* (1952), one of a number of Zweig's interesting studies of changing society; G. Gorer, *Exploring British Character* (1960); T. Harrisson, *Britain Revisited* (1961); G. Carstairs, *This Island Now* (1963); J. Nuttall, *Bomb Culture* (1968); C. Booker, *The Neophiliacs* (1969); B. Levin, *The Pendulum Years* (1970); M. Warner, *The Crack in the Teacup* (1979); T. Nairn, *The Break-up of Britain* (1981); R. Dahrendorf, *On Britain* (1982); C. Barr (ed.), *All Our Yesterdays* (1986); R. Critchfield, *An American Looks at Britain* (1990); and C. Dellheim, *The Disenchanted Isle* (1995).

Key books (or plays) of their times were A. Greenwood, *Love on the Dole* (1934); F. von Hayek, *The Road to Serfdom* (1945); B. Wootton, *Freedom Under*

Planning (1945); K. Amis, *Lucky Jim* (1954); J. Osborn, *Look Back in Anger* (1956); R. Hoggart, *The Uses of Literacy* (1957); Colin MacInnes, *City of Spades* (1957); H. Himmelweit, *Television and the Child* (1958); H. Thomas, *The Establishment* (1959); M. Young, *The Meritocracy* (1958); D. Gabor, *Inventing the Future* (1964); J. Aitken, *The Young Meteors* (1967); P. Drucker, *The Age of Discontinuity* (1968); E. F. Schumacher, *Small is Beautiful* (1973); and R. Hughes, *The Shock of the New* (1980).

For films and pop music see British Universities Film Council, *Researcher's Guide to British Film and Television collections* (1997 edn); I. Whitcombe, *After the Ball: Pop Music from Rag to Rock* (1973); D. Hamilton, *The Music Game* (1980); and I. Chambers, *Urban Rhythms: Pop Music and Popular Culture* (1985).

There have been many surveys, based on statistical information, some repeated, and it is interesting to compare B. S. Rowntree's *Poverty, A Study of Town Life* (1901), with his *Poverty and Progress, A Second Social Survey of York* (1941) and his last study, with G. R. Lavers, *Poverty and the Welfare State* (1951). Before Rowntree, Charles Booth's massive seventeen-volume *Life and Labour of the People in London* (1889–1903) turned the spotlight on the metropolis. See for an invaluable analysis R. O Day and D. England, *Dr Charles Booth's Inquiry* (1993) and for a less ambitious follow-up H. Llewellyn Smith (ed.), *New Survey of London Life and Labour* (1931). Other surveys include A. M. Carr-Saunders and D. Caradog Jones, *A Survey of the Social Structure of England and Wales* (1927, rev. edn, 1937); G. D. H. Cole, *The Post-War Condition of Britain* (1956), which should be compared with his earlier book, written with his wife Margaret, *The Condition of Britain* (1937); A. M. Carr-Saunders, D. Caradog Jones and C. A. Moser, *A Survey of Social Conditions in England and Wales* (1958); D. C. March, *The Changing Structure of England and Wales* (1965); and G. Heald and R. J. Whybrow, *The Gallup Survey of Britain* (1986). See also M. Abrams, *Social Surveys and Social Action* (1951).

On immigration and ethnic issues see R. Glass, *The Newcomers* (1960); S. Patterson, *Immigration and Race Relations, 1960–1967* (1969); N. Deakin, *Colour, Citizenship and British Society* (1980); P. Fryer, *Staying Places, the History of Black People in Britain* (1984); C. Holland, *'Race' in Britain* (1984); L. Henry and P. D. Rich (eds), *Race, Government and Politics in Britain* (1986); and R. Skellington and P. Morris, *Race in Britain Today* (1992).

For health see J. Boyd Orr, *Food, Health and Income* (1934); Political and Economic Planning, *Britain's Health* (1939); S. Loff, *Social Medicine* (1953); P. Vaughan, *Doctors's Commons* (1959); C. Webster, *The Health Services Since the War*, 2 vols, (1988, 1996); A. Cartwright, *Patients and their Doctors* (1967); H. Jones, *Health and Society in Twentieth Century Britain* (1994); and G. Rivett, *From Cradle to Grave: Fifty Years of the NHS* (1998).

For housing see R. Roberts, *The Classic Slum* (1971); M. J. Daunton (ed.), *Councillors and Tenants: Local Authority Housing in English Cities, 1919–1939* (1984); R. Donnison and C. Ungerson, *Housing Policy* (1982); and P. Dunleavy, *The Politics of Mass Housing* (1981).

For towns, cities and the countryside see R. E. Pahl, *Patterns of Urban Life* (1970); W. D. C. Wright and D. H. Steward (eds), *The Exploding City* (1982); A. A. Jackson, *Semi-Detached London* (1973); V. Bonham Carter, *The English Village* (1952); W. W. Williams, *The Sociology of an English Village* (1957); A. Edwards, *The Design of Suburbia* (1981); R. Blyth, *Akenfield* (1969), a classic study of a village; M. Stacey, *Trend and Change: A Study of Banbury* (1960), a town which can be compared across the centuries; R. Body, *Agriculture, the Triumph and the Shame* (1983) and (with M. Shoard), *The Theft of the Countryside* (1980); and B. Ilbury, *Agricultural Change in Great Britain* (1992).

A textbook covering part of the period, A. Marwick, *British Society Since 1945* (1996 edn) follows on from C. L. Mowat's *Britain Between the Wars* (1945). For other books on the inter-war years see those listed in Chapter 11. For post-1945 history see also P. Calvocoressi, *The British Experience, 1945–1975* (1978); J. Bartlett, *A History of Post-War Britain, 1945–1974* (1977) and A. Sked and C. Cook, *Post-War Britain, A Political History* (1984). An important linking book is P. Addison, *The Road to 1945* (1975). See also V. Ogilvie, *Our Times* (1953); E. Royle, *Modern Britain, a Social History, 1750–1985* (1987); and for post-1945 Britain, H. Hopkins, *The New Look, A Social History of the Forties and Fifties in Britain* (1963), with a useful bibliography, including biographies, along with his *The Numbers Game* (1973); M. Sisson and P. French (eds), *The Age of Austerity, 1941–1951* (1963); J. Montgomery, *The Fifties* (1965); V. Bogdanor and R. Skidelsky (eds), *The Age of Affluence* (1970); A. Sampson, *Anatomy of Britain* (1962), followed by his *New Anatomy of Britain* (1971) and *The Essential Anatomy of Britain* (1972); B. Masters, *The Swinging Sixties* (1989); N. Shrapnel, *The Seventies* (1980); N. Annan, *Our Age* (1991); P. Riddell, *The Thatcher Decade* (1990); and A. Briggs and D. Snowman (eds), *Fins de Siècle* (1996), 'The Final Chapter'.

For the economics of production and the market see P. Deane and W. A. Cole, *British Economic Growth, 1688–1959* (2nd edn, 1967); H. Phelps Brown and S. V. Hopkins, *A Perspective of Wages and Prices* (1981); N. K. Buxton and D. H. Aldcroft (eds), *British Industry Between the Wars* (1979); D. Worswick and P. Ady (eds), *The British Economy, 1945–50* (1952); S. Pollard, *The Development of the British Economy, 1914–1967* (1973); H. A. Clegg and T. E. Chester, *The Future of Nationalisation* (1953); P. Berger, *The Capitalist Revolution* (1986); J. G. R. Dow, *The Management of the British Economy, 1946–1960* (1968); D. Coutes and J. Hillard, *The Economic Decline of Modern Britain* (1986); A. Pettigrew, *The Awakening Giant: Continuity and Change in Imperial Chemical Industries* (1985);

B. Fine, *The Coal Question* (1990); W. Eltis, *Britain's Economic Problems* (1976); and O. Letwin, *Privatising the World* (1988).

For trade unions and industrial relations see J. Lovell, *British Trade Unions, 1875–1933* (1977); M. Harrison, *Trade Unions and the Labour Party Since 1945* (1960); J. McIlroy, *Trade Unions in Britain Today* (1988); G. S. Brain (ed.), *Industrial Relations in Britain* (1983); P. Fosh, *Industrial Relations and the Law in the 1980s* (1985); M. Adeney and J. Lloyd, *The Miners' Strike, 1984–5* (1986); and B. Pimlott and C. Cooke, *Trade Unions in British Politics: The First 250 Years* (2nd edn, 1991).

For technology see L. Bagrit, *The Age of Automation* (1964); A. Toffler, *Future Shock* (1970); T. Forester (ed.), *The Microelectronics Revolution* (1980); J. Beniger, *The Control Revolution* (1986); J. Howkins, *New Technologies, New Policies* (1982); and the Institute for Information Studies, *Crossroads on the Information Highway* (1995) and *The Internet as Paradigm* (1997).

For consumption and distribution see J. Benson, *The Rise of Consumer Society in Britain, 1880–1980* (1994); J. B. Jeffrys, *Retail Trading in Britain, 1850–1950* (1954); A. Briggs, *Friends of the People* (1956); G. Rees, *St Michael, A History of Marks and Spencer* (1973); Hulton Press, *Patterns of British Life* (1950); M. Abrams, *The Teenage Consumer* (1959); G. Cross, *Time and Money, the Making of Consumer Culture* (1993); and D. Miller, *Acknowledging Consumption: A Review of New Studies* (1995).

For finance and the City see M. Reid, *All Change in the City: the Revolution in Britain's Financial Sector* (1988) and C. Courtney and P. Thompson, *City Lives* (1966).

For politics before 1979 see S. H. Beer, *Modern British Politics* (1965); R. T. McKenzie, *British Political Parties* (1963 edn); D. Butler and D. Stokes, *Political Change in Britain: The Evolution of Electoral Choice* (1975 edn); R. Rose (ed.), *Studies in British Politics* (1966); H. Pelling, *A Short History of the Labour Party* (1961); K. Middlemas, *Power, Competition and the State*, 3 vols. (1986–91); and J. Ramsden, *The Winds of Change: Macmillan to Heath* (1996).

See also for aspects of later change J. Blondel, *Voters, Parties and Leaders* (1981); C. Leys, *Politics in Britain – From Labourism to Thatcherism* (1989), and for Thatcher and Thatcherism, M. Thatcher, *The Downing Street Years* (1993), an insider political account. Cf. A longer personal record, from an opposite angle, B. Castle, *Fighting All the Way* (1993). See also among works which sometimes now date H. Young and A. Sloman, *The Thatcher Phenomenon* (1986); R. Skidelsky (ed.), *Thatcherism* (1988); D. Kavanagh, *Thatcherism and British Politics: The End of Consensus?* (1987); and A. Gamble, *The Free Economy and the Strong State* (1988).

For social policy see T. H. Marshall, *Social Policy* (1965); R. Pinker, *Social Policy and Social Theory* (1971); J. Parker, *Social Policy and Citizenship* (1975); D.

Fraser, *The Evolution of the British Welfare State* (1973); B. B. Gilbert, *The Evolution of National Insurance in Britain* (1966); and P. Thane, *The Foundations of the Welfare State* (1982).

For education see G. P. N. Lowndes, *The British Education System* (1955); R. Pedley, *Comprehensive Education* (1956); H. Silver (ed.), *Equal Opportunity in Education* (1973); A. H. Halsey, *Educational Priority* Vol. I (1972); W. Perry, *The Open University* (1976); R. Flude and A. Parrott, *Education and the Challenge of Change* (1979); and E. Choat (ed.), *Traders and Television* (1987).

In relation to 'law and order' annual crime statistics are published (as are educational statistics). See also Policy Studies Insitute, *Police and People in London* (1983); N. F. McLintock and N. H. Avison, *Crime in England* (1983); L. Radzinowicz and J. King, *The Guilt of Crime* (1977); C. Moore, *Community versus Crime* (1981); and B. Whittaker, *The Police in Society* (1977).

For social mobility through education and other routes see the essential study by D. V. Glass, *Social Mobility in Britain* (1954); A. F. Heath, *Social Mobility* (1981); and J. H. Goldthorpe, *Social Mobility and Class Structure in Modern Britain* (1980). For class see T. H. Marshall, *Citizenship and Social Class* (1950); D. Wedderburn, *Poverty, Inequality and Class Structure* (1974); F. Field, *Unequal Britain* (1974); I. Reid, *Social Class Differences in Britain* (1989 edn); and A. Marwick, *Class in the Twentieth Century* (1986).

For social and cultural change, largely before 1939, including the role of the media, see H. Howkins and J. Lowerson, *Trends in Leisure, 1919–1939* (1979); J. Minihan, *The Nationalisation of Culture* (1977); J. Richards, *The Age of the Dream Palace* (1984); A. Briggs, *The Birth of Broadcasting* (1961) and *The Golden Age of Wireless* (1965); S. Briggs, *Those Radio Times* (1981); and J. A. R. Pimlott, *The Englishman's Holiday, A Social History* (1947).

For studies that link pre- and post-war years see S. Rowntree and G. R. Lavers, *English Life and Leisure* (1951), M. C. H. Smith, *Paper Voices: the Popular Press and Social Change, 1913–1965* (1975); J. Walvin, *The People's Game, A Social History of English Football* (1971) and *Beside the Seaside, a Social History of the Popular Seaside Holiday* (1978); R. Holt, *Sport and the British* (1992); B. Hillier, *The Style of the Century, 1900–1980* (1983); and A. Barton, *Gossip, 1920–1970* (1978).

For the period after 1945 see C. Seymour Ure, *The British Press and Broadcasting Since 1945* (1991); A. Briggs, *Sound and Vision* (1979) and *Competition* (1995); J. Seaton and B. Pimlott (eds), *The Media in British Politics* (1987); J. Tunstall, *Advertising Man* (1964); B. Henry (ed.), *British Television Advertising: The First Thirty Years* (1986); D. J. Taylor, *After the War: The Novel and England since 1945* (1993); J. Mulgan, *Networks and the New Economics of Communication* (1991); C. Davies, *Permissive Britain: Social Change in the 60s and 70s* (1975); G. Melly, *Revolt into Style, the Pop Arts in Britain* (1970, 1989); K. Leech, *Youthquake:*

the Growth of a Counter Culture through Two Decades (1975); and S. Connor, *Postmodernist Culture* (1989).

For 'Englishness' see P. Dodd and R. Colls (eds), *Englishness* (1987); J. Lucas, *England and Englishness* (1991); R. Porter, *Myths of the English* (1992). Compare P. Wright, *On Living in an Old Country* (1985) and an Australian interpretation by D. Horne, *The Great Museum: The Re-presentation of History* (1984).

For the monarchy see J. Cannon and R. A. Griffiths, *The Oxford Illustrated History of the British Monarchy* (1988); R. Lacey, *Majesty* (1977); E. Longford, *Royal Throne* (1993); A. Holden, *The Tarnished Crown* (1993); A. Rowbottom, *Happy and Glorious: The Symbolic End of the Monarchy* (1989); A. N. Wilson, *The Rise and Fall of the House of Windsor* (1993); J. Dimbleby, *The Prince of Wales: A Biography* (1994); A. Morton, *Diana: Her True Story* (1998); T. Harrison, *Diana, Icon and Sacrifice* (1998); and F. Bridger, *The Diana Phenomenon* (1998).

For religion see B. Wilson, *Religion in a Secular Society* (1964); *Faith in the City: A Call for Action by Church and Nation* (1985); *How the Church of England Works* (1985); Y. M. Graham, *The Church Hesitant* (1993); and D. Jenkins, *God, Politics and the Future* (1988).

INDEX

Abortion Act (1967) 346
  see also contraception
    and abortion
Abrams, Mark 321, 339,
    347
Abse, Leo 311
Act of Supremacy (1559)
    139
Act of Uniformity (1662)
    162–3
Act of Union (1707) 172–3
Acton, William 270
Acts of Settlement 161, 170
Adam, James and Robert
    200
Adam of Usk 96
Adams, Henry 67
Adams, William 175
Addison, Christopher 290,
    291
Addison, Joseph 201
adulterine castles 57
advertising 310, 313, 315,
    334, 336, 337
Aelfric, Abbot of Eynsham
    (Aelfric
    Grammaticus)
    49–50
Aethelbert of Kent 42, 51
Africa 175, 179, 181, 182,
    185, 186, 220, 307
Agincourt, Battle of (1415)
    96
Agricola 31
Agricultural Act (1947) 332

agricultural crises 83–4, 85,
    331–2, 333
agricultural practices 10,
    16–17, 61–2, 75–6,
    84, 160, 191, 192,
    332
  see also ploughs and
    ploughing
agricultural productivity
    10–11, 74–5, 76,
    161, 332
agriculture and farming 7,
    8, 36, 37, 41, 59,
    70, 101, 191–4,
    260–61, 332
Aids/HIV 347
air raids 252, 286, 295, 296
air travel 234, 249, 252, 346
airships 252, 286
Aitken, 'Max' *see*
    Beaverbrook
Alaric, the Goth 38
St Alban 276, 67
Albert, Prince 210, 264
Alcuin of York 43–4
alehouses *see* public houses
Alfred, King of Wessex 44,
    46, 47, 49, 264
Alleyn, Edward 141
alphabet and writing 37,
    40
America (to 1883) 175,
    178–9, 180, 181,
    183, 186, 188–9
  Spanish possessions 181

Virginia 176, 178, 179
  see also Canada
    United States (1883 on)
American Stamp Act
    (1765) 188
American War of
    Independence
    (1775–83) 172,
    188–9
Angevin Empire 57
Anglo-Saxon language 43,
    55
animal rights 331
  see also hunting and
    hawking
Anne, Queen 172
anthropology 5
Antonine Wall 31
apprentices 81, 102, 114,
    130
Aquae Sulis *see* Bath
Aquinas, Thomas 64
Arab world 63, 64, 66
archaeology 3–4, 5–6, 7, 8,
    11, 13, 16–17, 18,
    26–7, 30, 36–7, 41
  see also geology
archbishops and bishops 42,
    43, 47, 51, 52, 55,
    61, 66, 68–9, 87,
    88, 92, 94, 95, 109,
    153–4, 305, 311,
    330, 340
  see also religion and
    worship